SIMPLIFIED

REEF KEEPING

**The first
easy-to-understand guide
to building, maintaining, and enjoying
a successful reef tank**

Fourth Edition

Robert M. Metelsky

Requests for permission or other information should be mailed to:
Robert M. Metelsky, Box 954 Farmington Connecticut, USA

http://www.simplifiedreefkeeping.com   robert@simplifiedreefkeeping.com

Concept Design: Robert M. Metelsky
Copy Editor: Steve Morris
Copy Editor Second Edition: Elizabeth Flores
Illustrations: Kelly Marchetti and Kieran Coleman

ISBN 0-9652843-0-1
Library of Congress Catalog Card No. 96-94458
First Edition 9/1/1996
Revised Edition 8/11/1998
Second Edition 12/12/1999
Third Edition 9/9/2000
Fourth Edition 1/5/2002
Printed in the United States of America

SATISFACTION GUARANTEE

Complete customer satisfaction is the goal of both the author and "Shoreline Resources." If, within 14 days of receiving this book, the purchaser decides that it does not fulfill his or her needs or expectations, or desires to return this publication for any other reason, the purchaser may return this book, postage paid, in its original condition, for a complete refund, less the original handling charge.

This publication is believed to provide accurate and authoritative information about the subject matter covered. The material in this book has been developed through the use of ideas and information obtained from various sources, personal interviews, and—most importantly—applied practical experience. The information contained in this publication is believed to be reliable, but it cannot be guaranteed insofar as it is applied to any particular situation.

The author specifically disclaims any liability, loss, or risk, personal or otherwise, incurred as a consequence directly or indirectly from the use and application of any of the information contained in this publication.

To the
Master Reef Keeper,
whose Grace
has made it possible to produce this book.

Contents

8   Setting Up a Reef Tank   65

9   Maintenance   *83*

10   Supplies   *117*

11   Power Outage   *131*

12   Fabricating Components   *135*

Acknowledgments

Special thanks to:
- Steve Morris
- Bob Crelin
- Kelly Marchetti
- Greg Licnk
- Brian Flynn
- Kieran Coleman
- "Jack" at Reef Life, Inc., Ft. Lauderdale, Florida: (800) 903-3474
- American Granby, Inc. (plumbing supplies), New York: (800) 776-2266

Also, my deepest thanks and appreciation for the following peoples support.
Albert Theil
Al Biasky
Barry Hatton (Puget Sound Aquarium Society
Brian Griffen (Reefers)
Daniel Lipton
DC Potts
Don Dewy (F.A.M.A)
Gary V. Deutschmann Sr. R.A.I.A.R (Reef and Invert Aquarium Resource)
John Moore (Chesapeake Marine Aquaria Society)
Luis Mercado (Planet Reef)
Michael Blair
Nathan Cope
New York Aquarium Society
Norwalk Aquarium Society
Quinn C. Horn
Sanjay Mani
Thomas Heo
Tom Miller (Marine Fish Monthly)
William Horst
Winston Scoenfeld

Most of all to my readers, who have made this project worthwhile.

Foreword

The worldwide explosion in popularity of reef aquaria has spawned a number of worthwhile books and a small handful of excellent ones. This one belongs in that handful. When newcomers to the hobby ask, "What should my first purchase be?" I always suggest a good book, adding that this will not only educate you in the hobby, it will also save you time, work, and money.

Many of those entering the hobby are somewhat overwhelmed by the myriad of products and equipment currently on the market—many touted as the "magic" needed for success. With all the hype appearing in advertisements, it is good to have a sensible reference to work with. *Simplified Reef Keeping* informs with sensibility, and helps the hobbyist work through the hype and understand all the basics, thus saving the purchase of unnecessary or esoteric equipment.

The experienced hobbyist will benefit by learning maintenance techniques and cost-cutting procedures, as well as insightful information about the aquarium's inhabitants. Many practical money-saving tips will benefit the hobbyist on a budget.

What more can one ask of a book, except perhaps a comparatively low price— which the author has also given us.

Jack Freiberg
Reef Life Inc.

Chapter 1

About This Book

THE AUTHOR AND THE HOBBY

This book is about my experience with keeping a reef tank. It will also explain how to build most of the components yourself. *I do not claim to have all the answers to all the situations encountered*, but I will convey useful, practical ideas to save you money, and to simplify and enhance your ownership of a reef and your pride in the challenging effort to keep some of the most delicate creatures on earth.

This book avoids the complicated theories, complex methods, and vague summations that so plague this hobby. In fact, it takes just the opposite approach. One does not need a degree in marine biology or a Ph.D. in science to become a successful reef keeper. Although such education would certainly not hurt, the fact is that hobbyists are just that—*hobbyists*, who want to participate in this area. But many, like myself, have been intimidated by the implied complexity.

Let me tell you, there are certain things you must do to have a thriving reef tank. I don't believe we have to know exactly *why* things work; most of us just want to know *what* works, and describing that will be the goal of this text. As an example, are most of us interested where the air we breathe comes from? How it interacts with our bodies to sustain our life? If we can possibly come up with a substitute? No. Most of us are not interested in contemplating such ideas. In this hobby, most of us want to know what works and what does not. I leave the science for scientists.

I have been an enthusiast in keeping aquariums of all types for many years. When I became interested in reef systems, I found most of the information to be extremely complex, confusing, and contradictory. Fortunately, that did not stop me. I read all I could find, and talked to some "experts"—only to be misled and further confused, with my wallet drained. Again, that did not stop me. With extreme passion and fierce determination to succeed, I made all the common mistakes; *but I found out what worked and what did not*, what to buy and what can be done without, what is necessary and what is not. And yes, I did overcome the confusion. My tanks and the inhabitants speak for themselves.

Like most beginners, when I started out I made all the common mistakes. I have experienced most of the good and not so good equipment and have bought and sold countless tanks and components. As my knowledge grew so did my enthusiasm and reef aquariums became my passion.

Simplified Reef Keeping came about after seemingly endless trial and error, and an unbelievable amount of money spent. I then realized exactly what it took to have a thriving reef tank and felt compelled to write a clear concise book about the subject.

1

I wrote this book with my fellow hobbyist in mind, something that I would like to read and find useful. With text and examples that are easy to follow attempting to remove all mysterious complexity previously associated with the hobby of reef aquariums. To my knowledge there is no other book like it and I truly hope you enjoy reading it!

While studying this book please keep in mind that I do not consider my opinions and methods in this text as the *only* way to approach a reef aquarium, nor do I ever claim to have *all* the answers, or lastly consider myself an "expert". I do however claim to be a successful reefkeeper and an advanced over the edge experienced hobbyist, someone who has accumulated substantial, practical information.

I will be the first to admit that there are many others who have a wider range of knowledge than I. The main difference is… I took it upon myself and my own resources to write, produce and publish this much needed, informative book. The text has been put it together in a complete, easy to understand format, something I feel that has up until now, has been missing in this hobby. My readers have confirmed this personal belief.

I am writing to share my personal experience with you, so you won't have to be misled, confused or conned about this subject. My suggestions will save you more than enough money to offset your investment in this book. I will explain where and how to buy materials, supplies, and livestock at the most affordable prices; what to look out for; what to steer clear of. You can avoid the pitfalls I ran into, and learn from the mistakes I made when I was starting out. You can have a beautiful reef tank. There is no big mystery. I want to pass this on to you!

I can be always reached online by sending an email to robert@simplifiedreefkeeping.com Mail from my readers is usually answered the same day it was received.
Simplified Reef Keeping's website is http://www. simplifiedreefkeeping.com
The site has developed into a huge resource that has grown to 100 megabytes in size with over 1000 files.

The Best to you… my readers!

Chapter 2

Benefits of This Book

FROM INFORMATION TO EXPERIENCE

Quite obviously, man had nothing to do with creating the vast, complex ocean waters that cover much of the earth. Although modern man has made technological advances which provide him with an abundance of information, his knowledge is limited.

For the hobbyist, taking on the challenge of recreating a coral reef is admirable in every respect, and this responsibility should not be underestimated. Before committing to such an undertaking, one should be well informed with clear, concise knowledge of this subject.

Knowledge, as defined by *Webster's New American Dictionary,* is "Understanding gained by actual experience." *Webster's New World Dictionary* defines it as "The fact or state of knowing," or "What is known; learning."

Unfortunately, lack of knowledge, and an unwillingness to share knowledge clearly, are problems that pervade this hobby.

Another problem the hobby faces is greed: financial benefit gained by keeping novice hobbyists confused about methods, beliefs, and recommendations that seem to change constantly. If you have been in this hobby for any length of time, I am sure you can agree with me.

There is no doubt that knowledge has to come from experience. When an inexperienced person wants to learn something he knows little about, he will most likely seek out information. Because this hobby is relatively new, the conditions for exploitation abound (including keeping knowledge and experience hidden from, and mysterious to, the novice aquarist). This leads to many expensive and unnecessary purchases, and often to the death of fragile and rare living creatures.

This should not happen! Knowledge and experience must be shared clearly and concisely with those who seek it, if this hobby is to be morally responsible—not available only for the people "who have paid their dues." For by the time a hobbyist has paid his dues, he already has his own firsthand experience of the subject.

Those who have "learned the hard way" have invaluable experience and knowledge. They have considered all the ambiguity about what to do and what not to do, and have cast much of it aside as wordy speculation. Once a certain level of experience is achieved, a new level of "successful" reef keepers emerges. It is up to the

Finding people who are knowledgeable about reef keeping

hobbyist with actual experience to share clearly and concisely with others who are interested. These knowledgeable individuals are usually willing to convey what they have learned, but the problem for the novice is where to find them.

I have found some of them through aquarium societies. These societies often have "true enthusiasts" as well as all levels of aquarists. For a virtually insignificant cost in relation to other costs in this hobby, you can join one or more of these clubs. This will be a wise investment. You will find people with experience, who will be willing to tell you frankly what works for them and what they have found to be necessary.

Another source is through some magazines that feature lists of hobbyists who are interested in communicating with others. This type of mini-network can be very informative, with hobbyists comparing notes about what works and methods that they have used, as well as cost and value comparisons of merchandise and materials. Exchanging information through the mail may be a little slow, but the communication is aquarist-to-aquarist, with no one pursuing financial gain at the expense of someone else.

Do not pass over a chance conversation with others while in pet and supply stores. Strike up a conversation on your interests, and you may find someone with some good ideas and tips to pass on. Or, in turn, you may share some experience you have acquired. You may meet some great people who are interested in networking with you.

Then there is the Internet. There you can find hobbyists from a wide range of backgrounds who are eager to share their experience with others.

And, of course, there are the "real experts." They can be found in the national magazines, where you can regularly find their editorial columns and articles pertaining to our subject; their books are also available. Some of them are interested in marine biology and coral reefs, and have spent a lot of time researching reefs and the ocean environment. These educated experts provide extremely valuable information for the hobbyist.

Let's face it, not everyone has the knowledge and expertise that comes from dedicating one's life to a particular subject. Nor can many of us dive on a reef, or get financial backing to research this subject. Without this group of dedicated individuals, we would not be where we are today in the hobby. I am personally grateful for their works. Some of my favorites are Albert Thiel, Bob Goemans, Edward Prasek, Sam Gamble, Jim Oliveros, Jack Fong, Martin Moe, and Julian Sprung. Most of these experts have columns in national magazines, where they address questions on all levels, from novice to expert.

To summarize, information is power. It is the power over the life and death of the creatures we keep, and also the power for us not to go broke or reach our wits' end from attempting to keep a reef in our homes. It is up to us to seek out clear, concise information from knowledgeable, experienced sources, apply this information, get our hands-on experience, and share what we learn with others who are interested in this hobby. Sometimes the information changes, so it is up to us to be aware of current ideas and new information in the field.

When you apply the knowledge of others in your reef keeping endeavors, you will definitely acquire your own experience. This experience is most valuable. As you read and talk with others about the hobby, you will know from keeping your own tank successfully (1) what is really important, and (2) what methods you have found to work best. Once you have this experience, you will observe those who do not have the knowledge and experience making a big deal out of simple matters.

Some people seem to like getting bogged down in information and ideas suggesting mysterious complexity. As I stated from the beginning of this reading, the coral reef is extremely complex.

> *The needs of **some** creatures are uniquely met in their native habitats, and cannot be met in an enclosed system of any size*

However, there are many discussions of what is not known, such as the needs of extremely delicate species that are difficult to keep alive. *These discussions can intimidate the hobbyist, leading him to believe that all species have the same needs.* This is not true. This is what can make the novice spend excessive and unnecessary money on products that imply they will provide a higher level of natural conditions in the reef. This is the "carrot in front of the horse" scenario, leading one to believe the equipment he has is not good enough, and that if he uses this new method or product he will be able to keep a more delicate array of specimens.

If you really want to keep creatures that don't do well in captivity, you will probably be forced to play this guessing game. Personally, I believe all creatures of the reef are beautiful and interesting. *However, some of them are less demanding and will do well in captivity for extended periods of time.* For my interests, and in the interest of the wild reef, I prefer to keep those creatures that lend themselves to being kept. A list of desirable livestock I have found to be hardy and long-lived are listed in Chapter 13.

I do not see any point in keeping creatures in captivity that will not do well. To me, this is an exercise in futility. One wrong move or slight variance, and you risk losing the fragile livestock. This is not fair to the livestock, and it has a psychological and monetary cost to you, the reef keeper. Let's face it. We are desiring to keep creatures from the vast ocean, some of which have needs unique to their particular area that cannot be met in an enclosed system (regardless of its size). We all should remember this, no matter how much we know or how fanatical we get.

NOTES:

Chapter 3

Before You Begin

Chapter goal:
to discuss the items you will need for a successful reef, and provide an
idea of their cost

INITIAL COST

Reef keeping is very expensive! Be forewarned and prepared. It is not for anyone with shallow pockets or on a tight budget. *This is the high end, the ultimate challenge in keeping living things alive in water in an enclosed space. Everything to do with it is expensive!* In this book I will describe the ways and means I have found to save money in this hobby. Money is a definite and serious factor here.

The first mistake many people make is to start out with the wrong size tank. They base their decision on the assumption that if they start small they can cut costs. To a certain extent this is true. If you really want a small tank, that is fine. However, I do not recommend starting with a small tank as an experiment to see how it goes before getting what you really want. A small tank requires all the same apparatus as a large tank. The setup will be the same but smaller. It will cost a little less, *but when you change to the larger size you really want,* the components of the smaller system will be of little use. Therefore I suggest giving careful thought from the beginning to the size of your tank, as this decision will dictate all the other decisions you will have to make.

> *A common mistake: starting out with the wrong size tank*

The second mistake is to try to cut corners with the components needed for a reef. Many times the novice will decide, "I'll do without this," or "I don't need that." For those of you who do not have the experience needed to actually *know what and what not to use on the reef*: please do not cast aside the recommendations of experienced reef keepers. You will find that if it is really not needed it will not be on the following list.

> *The second mistake: trying to cut corners without actually knowing what is needed*

It may worthwhile to note that depending on your experience level it would be advised to begin your tank with the hardier fish and more importantly – hardy corals. Generally speaking, LPS (Long Polyp Stony) corals require less light and much considered hardier and easier to keep. My advise is to begin with easier to keep, lower light requiring corals, then as your experience grows so will you level of confidence with reef husbandry. You can then decide if you wish to pursue the more advanced creatures. If you take these suggestions your chances of success will be greatly enhanced and overall it will cost you less money and provide a higher level of overall satisfaction.

Let's get an idea of the cost of items for a 55-gallon set up.

It's highly advised that you read the entire book before making any purchases.

WHAT YOU WILL NEED FOR A 55 GALLON REEF AQUARIUM

	ITEM	RETAILC OST
1.	Deionizer or reverse osmosis water purifier	$ 270
2.	Resin for above, to replace every 6 months: 1 gal.	60
3.	Bulbs: 48" actinic blue & actinic white, 4 @ $25	100
4.	30" protein skimmer (Venturi)	300
5.	Pressure pump for skimmer, 500 to 600 GPH	90
6.	Carbon prefilters for tap water: 1 @ $60, 1 @ $25	85
7.	Cartridges for above: 2 @ $12, 1 @ $5	29
8.	Sump box (for prefilter)	150
9.	Material, 6 packages floss prefilter	50
10.	Main pump 500 to 600 GPH	90
11.	Tank: 55 gallons	70
12.	Tank stand	75
13.	Light canopy to house four 48" bulbs (with VHO ballast)	300
14.	Salt mix: 1 for setup for 55 gallon tank	18
15.	Salt mix for water changes	18
16.	Phosphate test kit	20
17.	Test kit for ammonia, pH, nitrite, nitrate	45
18.	Test kit for K.H. $12, calcium $12	24
19.	Specific gravity meter	12
20.	Misc. (books, power strips, Kalkwasser, trace elements, etc.)	100
	TOTAL:	$1,906

> *All the items here are recommended for a successful reef tank*

$1,906 divided by 55 gallons = $34.65 per gallon! I should have told you to sit down before you read this. Its worth noting that survey results indicate an average CPG (cost per gallon) to be an average of $35 per gallon. As I said, this is very expensive. Do you want to go on? O.K. Let's look at what goes into the tank.

First let's look at the livestock that goes into the tank set up with all live rock.

SAMPLE COST OF LIVESTOCK FOR A 55 GALLON REEF AQUARIUM

	ITEM	RETAIL COST
1.	Mat for live rock frame (eggcrate)	$ 15
2.	Sand aragonite: 1 10-lb. bag	10
3.	Live rock: 1.5 lbs. per gallon, x 55 gallons = 83 lbs. @ $10	830
4.	Turbo or Astrae snails (herbivores): 10 @ $5	50
5.	Coral banded shrimp: 1	15
6.	Cleaner shrimp: 4 @ $15	60
7.	Serpent starfish (scavengers): 2 @ $12	24
8.	• Algae eating hermit crabs 24 @ $1	24
9.	• Hardy corals: 4 @ $45	180
10.	Tridachna clam: 1 or equivalent livestock	50
11.	Yellow tang, small: 1	35
12.	Hippo tang, small: 1 (Note: not a herbivore)	35
13.	Sailfin tang, small: 1	35
14.	• Basslet: 1	35
15.	• Goby: (your choice of type): 1 or equivalent livestock	35
16.	• Misc. invertebrate (your choice): 1	35

> *To keep costs down you may use less livestock on items marked with •*

TOTAL $1,468

> *$—Money saver—$*
> *Buy live rock, and some livestock, wholesale*

$1,468 divided by 55 gallons =	$26.69	per gallon for livestock.
+ $1,906 divided by 55 gallons =	34.65	per gallon for setup.
3,374 divided by 55 gallons =	61.34	per gallon complete!

These prices are retail and approximate, although I am sure they are pretty close to what you could expect to pay. At least they are what I paid when I started. One of the reasons for the high cost is that the livestock is from the wild, and must be collected and shipped. Don't be discouraged yet. Remember I said I will show you how to save money, and I will. Read on.

As you can see, this reef hobby is going to be expensive. I wanted to get you familiar with the cost of various items before you start, so you

> *It is important to get an idea of the cost of items so you can plan further*

will know what you will be in for. *All the component items for the tank are mandatory to have a successful reef.*

There are a couple of items I left out, such as a wave maker or surge buckets, timers for the lights, electronic pH testers, a generator in the event of a power outage, etc. I omitted these from the startup figure because they are not absolutely essential at the very beginning. They are important, beneficial components, but they can be added to the system later on if you prefer.

Throughout this book you will find suggestions on getting the most for your money and setting things up. For now I want to stay focused on what to do before you begin.

The most important thing to do is to plan. The reason this chapter is so important is that

> *Planning will help you avoid doing things in reverse! (This is a common mistake)*

so many people would like to get into this hobby, but they don't plan before they purchase. They walk into a pet store, see some nice live rock and coral and invertebrate, and they want to start a tank with that. After their purchase, they find their light is not strong enough, their water isn't pure enough, and they don't have test kits or the right size protein skimmer. Their tank has not been properly conditioned, so the livestock they bought dies. At this point, they are shocked at what it will cost to get the proper items, and many just give up. Some others try to go on with half of the items they really need, still with bad results. Do not take this approach!

Summary – Understanding what's involved:
- **Can you afford a reef tank?**
- **Get an idea of a tank size**
- **Write a plan**
- **List actual costs of items in your area**

PLANNING

Some ideas to consider and questions to answer:

- **The location of your tank**
- **The size of your tank**
- **The cost**
- **The time involved**

---

1. What size tank? Its location, preferably near a sink (for water supply and drain). Will the floor carry the weight of the tank? Preferably away from direct sunlight. How much floor space will all the equipment take? Is there enough power supply to run all the equipment? Will there be enough room to service behind the tank? (See Chapter 12, on large tank location.)

2. Your budget. Can you afford it? List and plan (very important). You may not be able to have everything up and running right away. But if you are patient and plan ahead, buying what you need as you can afford it, you will end up with the largest, most pleasing setup you can have. Put a lot of effort into the functioning of the system first, before adding live creatures to it. Plan for the ease of water changes and waste water drainage, the location of your tap water purification system, a large protein skimmer, and high-power lights with the proper bulbs. Once you have these in place (proceeding to each item as you can afford it), you won't have to worry about jeopardizing the livestock you will buy. This is definitely the best approach. The next pages will give a recommended sequence for purchases.

3. Your time. Remember: only bad things happen fast in this hobby, usually due to lack of

> *In this hobby only bad things happen fast, due to lack of time spent on planning*

time spent. Patience is invaluable. Keeping a reef will take a considerable amount of time, especially if you fabricate the components yourself. However, the rewards are exceptional! You will get tremendous satisfaction from knowing that you built components that are practical to maintain, and far exceed factory-built standards. But all this takes time—a lot of time. Are you willing to do water changes every two to three weeks? Are you ready to change your prefilter every week? Make limewater as needed for evaporation? Remove algae as needed? These are all responsibilities you have to take into consideration. (See Chapter 9, "Maintenance.")

Here is a recommended sequence for procuring and setting up the components of your reef system. Refer to corresponding chapters for expanded information.

SEQUENCE FOR SETTING UP A REEF AQUARIUM

1. Tank, stand, and location. (Chapter 4.)
2. Tap water source near the tank, for purification. Reverse osmosis or deionizer with carbon prefilters. (Chapter 6.)
3. Sump: connect the "supply" and "return" hoses to the tank. Drill the tank? Overflows, drill the spraybar. (Chapter 7.)
4. Waste water drain system: into a drain or outside hose?
5. Protein skimmer: locate and connect to tank and sump. (Chapter 7.)
6. Pumps: main and skimmer. (Chapter 7.)

> *Nothing will take the place of a good plan*

7. Make-up water container powerhead, for mixing. (Chapter 9.)
8. Determine whether you will use a live sand filter or set the rock up on eggcrate. Cut up and lay out eggcrate. (Chapter 8.)
9. Make all water connections to tank and fill up with regular tap water (with no salt), to make sure of proper operation. Run until you are satisfied with water level, absence of leaks, etc. Then drain. (Chapter 8.)
10. Lighting canopy. Enclosure, reflectors, ballast's and bulbs, power supply and timers. (Chapter 5.)

When you have all the above components in place, you are ready to proceed with the next step, which is setting up and cycling.

CYCLE THE TANK WITH LIVE ROCK ONLY

This is the sequence of events for the planning stage. I recommend that you completely read through the rest of this book before adding livestock.

1. Purchase all (or if your budget is low at the time, get at least 1/2) of the live rock you will use, and proceed to step 2. When ready, get the second 1/2 of the rock.

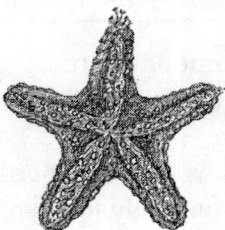

2. When all the live rock is in the tank, test for ammonia and nitrite. You need to get a zero reading, which could take 2 to 6 weeks, depending on the amount of die-off on the rock. Do not proceed to step 3 until steps 1 and 2 are complete.

3. Begin to add inverts (clams, shrimp, starfish, crabs, and snails). Add a few at a time, checking ammonia and nitrite. After all inverts are added, and the test results for ammonia and nitrite are zero, proceed to add your corals, a few at a time. Continue to test for ammonia and nitrite until all your corals are added. When the readings are at zero (this will usually take about 2 weeks, possibly longer), proceed to add the fish in the same manner as above, until all the fish have been added.

4. When the test results for ammonia and nitrite read zero, and you begin to test and record nitrate, your tank is completely cycled. When you cycle this way, the live rock does most of the conditioning. *This is the way to start your system.* It is definitely the safest procedure, because it is hard to know how much die-off the live rock has on it. This way you won't endanger the valuable, delicate specimens you will add later. *Remember*, only bad things happen fast. You will need to exercise patience, resisting the impulse to do things in reverse. *Remember:* live rock first, inverts second, corals third, and fish last. You are now up and running. This will take about 2 to 6 weeks, possibly longer.

SUMMARY

As you might have noted, I have spent a lot of time explaining what to do before you begin. I feel this is the most important chapter in the book. I have seen many beginners fail in this hobby because they did not fully understand what they were getting into. I have explained the significant costs, and most of the main components that go into the setup, so you can plan ahead. *With a good plan, you will succeed.* I suggest that you go with the largest tank you desire, can afford, and have room for. The following pages will provide an expanded look at what I have described.

> *Cycling the tank with live rock is the simplest, most trouble-free way to start a reef tank.*

Planning

- Plan and use the recommended sequence of procedures
- Avoid doing things in reverse order
- Review your plan
- Decide where to buy your supplies
- Decide what you will buy first

Common Mistakes

- Starting with the wrong size tank
- Assuming you can cut corners
- Underestimating the cost
- Doing things in reverse order

NOTES:_____
_____
_____
_____
_____
_____
_____
_____
_____
_____
_____
_____
_____
_____
_____
_____
_____
_____
_____
_____
_____
_____
_____
_____
_____
_____

ESTIMATED COST OF THE REEF AQUARIUM							
ITEM - FROM	TANK	STAND	PUMPS	TWP	SKIMMER	LIVESTOCK	MISC

NOTE: For your convenience all charts appear on the CDROM
Also see "Tips & Techniques" for more ideas on planning your reef aquarium.

Chapter 4

Types of Tanks

Chapter goal:
To guide the reader to the most functional, stable, and desirable size of tank

Your selection of a container for the reef environment is as important as all the other decisions you make. The tank will not only house imported specimens from faraway oceans; it will also be illuminated with expensive high-tech lighting apparatus, and it will contain triple-filtered, deionized or reverse-osmosis processed water that is probably more pure than the water you consume.

> *Your choice of tank can have long-term effects, either positive or negative*

Yes, the tank will become your pride and joy—your statement of how successful you are as a reef keeper. It will constantly be on display for your visitors to admire and envy. People will exclaim, "Oh wow!" and "It's beautiful!" and "What kind of creature is that?" You will be answering many, many questions once your reef is set up.

The tank must be designed for the environment you are trying to create: a well-lit, uncramped display of a natural-appearing coral reef. The choice of a tank can make or break this desirable goal.

MINI REEFS

These are small tanks, usually 10 to 20 gallons. They are sometimes suggested because they are significantly less expensive to set up and maintain, so they are more affordable to more people. If you really want a 10-gallon reef tank, a mini reef may be for you. The first paragraph in Chapter 3, "Before You Begin," describes some pitfalls of starting out small. There are other disadvantages as well:

> **Drawbacks of Mini Reefs**
>
> - **A smaller tank is less stable than a larger one. It is substantially more affected by temperature, biological load of livestock, accumulated waste, water changes, and adding trace elements (i.e., Kalkwasser, iodine, and strontium).**
> - **A 10-gallon reef tank is biologically fragile.**
> - **A 10-gallon reef will cost between $400 and $600, which is $40-60 per gallon.**
> - **In mini reefs, water changes and make-up are usually done with distilled water purchased from a store in gallon containers. Over a period of time this can be expensive, costing $1-2 per gallon for pure water.**

COMMON TANK SIZES

> *A large tank is an impressive display*

There are many different types of tanks. Size is usually the main factor when selecting a tank. The most common sizes are 10, 20, 30, 55 and 125 gallons. Of course, there are also in-between sizes, long or tall styles, and special show styles—hexagon, round, etc.

You will find that lighting fixtures, covers, hoods and stands are made for "common" sizes. For example, light fixtures are basically sold in 2, 4, 6 and 8-foot lengths. With any tank slightly larger than the bulb, you will need a space filler for the cover.

TALL TANKS

> *Stay away from "tall" tanks*

For a reef setup, I would definitely stay away from any type of tall or hexagonal style. These will force you to stack some rock on top of other rock, resulting in light being dispensed over less of the rock surface than in a "long" type of tank. This will also make cleaning the rock and crevices much more difficult, which can lead to problems with hidden waste buildup. Tall tanks also provide a *lower surface* area to volume ratio for gas exchange.

ODD-SIZED OR SECOND-HAND TANKS

I have talked to a few beginner reef keeping candidates who said, "Well, I have this odd tank someone gave me," or "I have an extra tank out in the garage that I was going to use for my reef." After asking them a few questions about the proposed tank, I pointed out that it would be a near disaster if they used "what they had." Don't get me wrong. If you have the proper style tank on hand, by all means use it. This section may help you make your decision.

BOTTOM AREA

> *Having a tank with large bottom area makes better use of vital lighting dispersion, needed by most reef organisms*

One of the main factors to consider when selecting a tank is the bottom or floor area. The reef structure (live rock) will rest on this, and the corals will rest on the rock. Bottom area is important because it will affect: (1) your cleaning access to all areas of the live rock, and (2) dispersal of light onto the rock.

The area of the tank "floor" or "bottom" is calculated in square inches: the length of the bottom, multiplied by its width. For example, let's take a 55-gallon tank, whose bottom is 48" long by 12" wide. Multiplying 48 x 12, we find that the tank has 576 square inches of bottom or floor space. This will be the foundation of your reef; you want to have as much bottom space as possible.

> *The two most common tank sizes are 55 gallons and 125 gallons*

Let's look at the ratio of floor space to gallon volume, in several different tanks. For each tank, we will calculate how much bottom space there is for each gallon of water in the tank. We multiply the length of the bottom by its width, and divide that figure by the number of gallons in the tank.

(If you don't know the gallon volume of a tank, you can calculate it from the tank's dimensions.)

Tank volume (gallons)	Bottom length (inches)	Bottom width (inches)	Bottom area (square inches)	Ratio of Bottom Area to Tank Volume
55	48	12	576	10.47
89, tall (36" high)	24	24	576	6.47
125	72	18	1,296	10.37
239, self-made	96	24	2,304	9.64

When you are evaluating different tank sizes and shapes, do the math to check their ratios of floor space to volume. A ratio of about 10, or slightly more, seems standard in commonly available, desirable tanks. Notice in the above table that the tall tank (89 gallons) has the same bottom area as the common 55-gallon tank, but has a much smaller ratio of bottom area to tank volume. As discussed earlier, this is one of the drawbacks of "tall" tank designs.

The two most common sizes that work well are 55 and 125 gallons. A 55 is the most

> *55 gallons is the smallest reef tank size the author recommends*

commonly available, and in my opinion you should not start with anything smaller. Its floor size, as we saw above, is 48" by 12", giving you 576 square inches. It does not cost a lot of money (about $65, which comes to $1.18 per gallon), and it will do well for a reef system.

A 125-gallon tank produces a much better display, because it has a lot more floor space.

> *A larger tank is more stable than a smaller one*

Its floor dimensions, 72" by 18", yield 1,296 square inches of area (more than twice the bottom area of a 55-gallon tank). This size tank is also readily available, and the cost per gallon is very reasonable (about $250, or $2.00 per gallon). I don't think you will be disappointed if you select a 125. It is a great choice.

LARGER TANKS (OVER 125 GALLONS)

Tanks that are larger than 125 gallons command a premium price! If you can afford it, by all means go for it, keeping this in mind: you want one with a lot of floor space—one that is long and wide, not high! Check the ratio of bottom area to gallon volume, aiming for something around 10 or higher, as in the table above. Also calculate the cost per gallon, as I do throughout this book. This will give you an idea of what you are getting for your money.

Remember, it is easier and less expensive to get accessories for standard size tanks (55 or 125 gallons). This applies to items like hoods, light bulbs, stands, and so on. Tanks taller than 24" can be a problem, as this is the deepest you can reach in with your arm!

I have found that tanks larger than a 125 are very expensive, as are the accessories that go with them. The strong desire to have a larger

> *Divide the cost of the tank by the size in gallons, to get the cost per gallon*

tank prompted me to learn how to make my own. I have done this with fine results, and I recommend that you do the same if you want a large tank.

SELF-MADE TANKS

There are many advantages to building your own tank:

1. The cost per gallon is less than a large factory-built tank.
2. You can make just about any size.
3. They can be easily drilled and customized to fit your filtering design.
4. You can have a large tank. 200 to 300 gallon sizes are common.
5. They can be customized to fit the decor of your home.
6. They are not as fragile as all-glass aquariums.
7. Custom-made tanks lend themselves to other custom-made items—lighting, stands, filter enclosures, etc.
8. You get tremendous satisfaction from building your own setup.

The disadvantages are:

> *Self-made components can far exceed factory-available standards*

1. You will need some woodworking skills and tools (or you should know someone who has them).
2. You will need a place to do the work.
3. You will have to spend a considerable amount of time working on the project.
4. The self-made setup will still cost a considerable amount of money, even though it will be less expensive than a comparable store-bought setup.
5. A self-made tank can only be viewed from the front (the sides and back are epoxy-coated wood).
6. If this is your first reef tank, there will be a lot of work to do, and you may get overwhelmed by starting from scratch (making your own tank)
7. Making your own tank or any component is a lot of work.

At any level, this hobby is expensive and demands a lot of work! And yes, a smaller tank will be less money and work, but it will also be a smaller display of some of the most beautiful and interesting creatures on earth. The choice is yours, and you will want to make the right choice—a commitment you can fulfill.

> **Remember:**
>
> **If it were easy,**
> **everyone who wanted a beautiful reef tank**
> **would have one.**

As you can see, there are advantages and disadvantages to making your own tank. I have made several tanks and sump boxes in my time, and when I expand there will be no doubt in my mind that I should go with self-produced components. Once I crossed the line into self-made products, there was no going back to any other way.

I make tanks from 3/4" marine grade plywood, sealed

> *Chapter 18 provides you with details about constructing your own tank*

with 5 coats of high-quality marine grade epoxy, tinted black. The plywood costs about $70 per 4' x 8' sheet; you will use 2 sheets to build a 200 or 239 gallon tank. The top-of-the-line epoxy costs about $65 a gallon; you will use 1 gallon.

Here is a general idea of the materials needed for making a 239-gallon tank, and what they will cost:

Materials needed (239-gallon tank):

Marine grade plywood, 3/4"	Two pieces, 4' x 8', each $70	$140
High quality epoxy	One gallon	65
Plate glass, 1/2"	One piece, 2' x 8'	180
Oak picture frame	Three pieces, 1" x 4" x 96", each $8	24
Silicone sealant	Four tubes, each $6	24
Miscellaneous fasteners, adhesive, finish		50
	TOTAL:	$483

Rounding that total off to $500, we get a cost of $2.09 per gallon ($500 divided by 239 gallons).

Of course, this does not include your labor. My estimate would be two men, working together for approximately 10 hours, to build this tank. If you do not have the skills, it may take longer. Compare this cost to a factory-made 240-gallon tank. See what it works out to be, and whether you are willing to go this route.

SUMMARY

- Is a mini reef for you?
- The most common tank sizes are 55 and 125 gallons.
- Large floor area provides best lighting for all the livestock.
- To have good floor area, you should get a ratio of about 10 when you multiply the length and width of the tank's floor, and then divide by the gallon capacity of the tank.
- I described the cost and labor involved in making your own tank, larger than 125 gallons.
- Determine the cost per gallon of any tank you are considering.

NOTES:

Chapter 5

Lighting

Chapter goal:
To describe the need for proper bulbs designed specifically for reef tanks;
also to discuss correct wattage and duration of lighting

In a reef tank, the lighting does much more than just providing illumination for our viewing convenience. Many people, when admiring a certain creature, will ask, "What does it eat?" The usual reply is, "It gets most of its nourishment from the lighting." They then look at me in amazement and repeat, "The lighting?" "Yes," I explain, "many creatures of the reef are photosynthetic, meaning that lighting is one of their most vital requirements."

The subject of lighting a reef aquarium is probably the most hotly debated topics within this hobby. Buzzwords like "PAR" (Photosynththetically Active Radiation), microEinsteins (mE) which is the measuring unit of PAR, has kept the scientists talking - and some hobbyist's eagerly trying to parrot what they've heard. I'm assuming the reader of this particular book is a beginner who at this point would be better served by concentrating on the big picture of planning their reef tank set up - concentrating on the initial and long term costs, rather then getting bogged down in such esoteric measurements.

As I maintain throughout out this book, if you're particularly interested in pursuing information pertaining to the advanced principles of lighting I would applaud your efforts. However if you are a beginner, I would like to make very clear this un necessary. In this hobby there are a small handful of reputable lighting manufacturers. These companies produce extremely high quality reef lighting and it's usually as simple as determining what requirements your livestock will have and then choose a setup for your needs. In other words the company does the work for you. You purchase your lighting and move on.

COMMON EXAMPLES OF mE REGARDING REEF LIGHTING
110 WATT VHO approximately 1000mE – Natural sunlight is approximately 2000mE

When I began in this hobby, I pursued information on lighting for my reef. Soon I was dealing with the complex terminology used to measure and describe the various aspects of illumination. In response, I tried to find a substitute for the expensive reef-type bulbs. (In the trade they are called "lamps." Most of us use the term "bulbs," so I will use that term in an effort to simplify matters.) I investigated all the technical information, desperately trying to find a common, locally-available alternative to the premium bulbs.

The long and short of the story is that the reef needs a specific type and quality of light. I could go on about color temperature, which is the whiteness of the bulb, or the CRI ("Color Rendering Index"), which is how natural objects appear (to you) while illuminated. The higher the CRI, the better the color rendering properties (see Glossary). Kelvin is a temperature scale, "lux" and "lumens" are for intensity. I have experimented with most

commonly available lamps, trying to find the correct combination of lighting parameters recommended for a reef tank; I have always gotten poor results from these experiments. Although Normal output Tri-phosphor bulbs may be used to supplement metal halide or for extremely low light requirements. Look for:
Tri-phosphor with a CRI of 80 and a color temperature of 75000K

To simplify the subject: buy the correct bulbs for your reef. There are many companies specifically dedicated to providing you with the correct bulbs. There really are no other common, inexpensive light bulbs that provide the proper lighting spectrum requirements for the reef.

The enclosed reef should have between 3 and 5 watts per gallon, and the lighting should stay on for approximately than 9 hours a day. A survey of 100 reef aquarists showed these averages.

LIGHTING SURVEY RESULTS OF 100 REEFKEEPERS – AVERAGES

5.2 Watts per gallon	16 Metal halide	16 VHO
10.5 Hours per day	36 Metal halide & fluorescent	12 Power compact & fluorescent
98% Use timers		21 Power compact

I am using 6 bulbs on 3 timers so that the lighting in my tank varies over the day. The cycle starts the day at about 3 watts per gallon, gradually increases to the maximum of 5 watts, and then diminishes back to 3 at the end of the day. This is a humble attempt to mimic the rising and setting sun.

If you use fluorescent bulbs, you will need special ballast's to achieve the proper wattage. Using 4 watts as an average for comparing, the 72" bulbs would be appropriate for a 125-gallon tank, and the 48" for a 55-gallon.

As you can see, what type of ballast's you employ makes a substantial difference. The above figures were calculated using 4 watts as an average, for comparative purposes. You will want to make your own calculations so they will be in the 3 to 5 watt-per-gallon range. Not only are the types of ballast's different, but the bulbs are different also. Because of the various amperages, the bulbs for the different ballast's are not interchangeable.

Wattage Calculation for Your Tank:

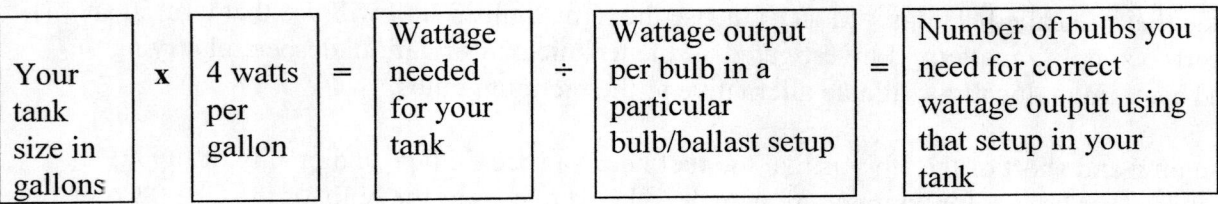

Your tank size in gallons	x	4 watts per gallon	=	Wattage needed for your tank	÷	Wattage output per bulb in a particular bulb/ballast setup	=	Number of bulbs you need for correct wattage output using that setup in your tank

Keep in mind when planning the system that one ballast will usually operate two bulbs. Older style tar ballast's are heavy, and generate a considerable amount of heat. By keeping the number of ballast's to a minimum, you ensure that your lighting system will generate the least amount of heat possible. It will also be lighter. Aim to get your desired wattage with the minimum number of ballast's. This will usually require 3 high-output ballast's.

For a 55-gallon tank, you will need between 165 and 275 watts. Remember the minimum is 3 watts per gallon, and the higher end is 5 watts per gallon. At 3 watts per gallon: 3 x 55 = 165. At 5 watts per gallon: 5 x 55 = 275.

One H.O. ballast can run two 60-watt bulbs, for a total of 120 watts. Two H.O. ballast's, powering four 60-watt bulbs, would provide 240 watts. Three H.O. ballast's, powering six 60-watt bulbs, would provide 360 watts.

As already discussed, the maximum wattage for a 55-gallon tank is 275 watts. The two-ballast setup, producing 240 watts, would be 35 watts under maximum, and very acceptable. The three-ballast setup, producing 360 watts, would be 85 watts too much. This is not recommended, but may be used if you plan to keep livestock that require more intense lighting.

For an average reef tank, 3 to 5 watts per gallon is the recommended lighting parameter. In fact, when I designed and built the canopy for my 55-gallon tank, I installed three H.O. ballast's; that gave me a system that produced 360 watts of lighting. I found that this amount of light was unnecessary for the creatures I was keeping. (I had 2 pink tip anemones, a carpet anemone, 60 pounds of live rock, 30 pounds of live sand, 3 clown fish, 3 cleaner shrimp, and miscellaneous hermit crabs, starfish and snails.) I disconnected one of the H.O. ballast's. The creatures are doing fine, and the electricity bill is slightly lower.

Lighting for my 200-gallon tank is done with two H.O. ballast's powering four 85-watt actinic white bulbs (= 340 watts), and one V.H.O. ballast powering two 160-watt actinic blue bulbs (= 320 watts). This gives a total of 660 watts. Divided by 200 gallons, that yields 3.3 watts per gallon. This is on the low end of the wattage range, although the lighting system provides adequate life-sustaining properties for my livestock.
If I were to upgrade my system, I would remove one H.O. ballast and replace it with a V.H.O. This would add 150 watts to the system, increasing the total wattage to 810 watts. Divided by 200 gallons, this would upgrade the wattage of my lighting system to 4.05 watts per gallon.

TAR BALLASTS Vs ELECTRONIC

Tar ballast's are not sold specifically for reef lighting. You will only find these if you plan to purchase from a local electrical supply house. Tar ballast's are not really the best choice for powering your lighting. They run very hot, are heavy and difficult to conceal, although they do work. A much better choice is the electronic ballast. Electronic ballast's are very light, easy to conceal and they actually run cool. Their only drawbacks are that they are somewhat delicate and expensive. An excellent recommendation for electronic ballast's is the Ice cap brand.

AMOUNT OF ELECTRICITY USED

High intensity lighting is very expensive to operate over an extended period of time! Some reef keepers think that if some is good, more must be better; but this is not true. *Also, when it comes to lighting, we should think about the extended period of time the lighting will be in operation.* It will be on for 9 hours a day, 365 days a year, for a total of 3,285 hours a year!

Multiply that by your wattage, and you can see the amount of electricity you will be consuming over the period of a year. In my case, this is 660 watts x 3,285 hours: 2,168,100 watt-hours per year! That is the equivalent of turning on 21,681 100-watt light bulbs for an hour!

And that is from illuminating my tank at the low end of the wattage scale (3.3 watts per gallon)!

We have to be careful as to what creatures we select for our reef. Be aware if you choose livestock that requires more intense lighting. You will have to provide the electricity to keep it alive over an extended period of time. Also, even if you select only one or two creatures that have a high light requirement, the whole tank will be receiving the high-power illumination!

USING TIMERS

Inexpensive plug-in timers are very convenient and useful. They take away a lot of the guesswork as to when to turn the lighting system on and off. The reef should be lit 9 hours a day, and of course we would like to be around when it is lit. My schedule is such that I am not home during the day, so the lights come on at 2:00 P.M. and go off at 11:00 P.M. When I come home around 6:00 P.M., the lights have been on for 4 hours, and the tank is "coming alive" (the corals are extended, etc.).This is one of the benefits of operating a reef tank. You can choose when some things happen.

Using one timer for each set of bulbs, you can have the lights come on gradually. For example, one set could come on at 2:00 P.M., the next set at 4:00 P.M., and the last set at 6:00 P.M. The reverse would be one set going off at 9:00 P.M., the next at 10:00 P.M., and the last at 11:00 P.M. This approach is more natural and less shocking to the livestock than turning all the lighting on or off at one time.

If this system is employed over a period of time, the creatures expect the lights to come on at a regular time. Many photosynthetic creatures have an internal clock that expects the vital illumination at a specific time, and the most foolproof way to do this is with timers.

Another benefit of timers is that you never have to touch the lights. The timers do the work for you. This is very convenient. If you go to bed early, or are not home for a day or so, the timers will still be working, turning the lights on and off on schedule. They are an inexpensive, valuable tool for your lighting system, and can be purchased at many stores for about $7 each. It's worth noting that approximately 98% of the reef keepers surveyed use timers.

MEASUREMENT OF LIGHT WAVES

The wavelength (which determines its color) is measured in nanometers. Most light companies provide charts showing peaks and valleys with numbers vertically and horizontally. Across the bottom are numbers ranging from approximately 310 to 760. They represent the colors put out by the bulb. The colors and nanometers are as follows:

Color	Wavelength (nanometers)
Violet	410
Blue	470
Green	520
Yellow	570
Orange	620
Red	710

The vertical numbers on these charts show the relative power output of each color. This can clarify where the bulb peaks within the color range, and at a glance you can see what color the bulb is really putting out.

As you can see, "white" is not listed. Beneficial white for reef purposes is a combination of several colors, mainly blue and a color halfway between green and yellow. It contains very little red, since red is thought to induce micro-algae growth. When the color "white" is referred to, it means the proper balance of colors to achieve the life-sustaining needs of enclosed reef creatures, while still appearing white to our eye.

Most fluorescent reef bulbs will be white or blue. The white is not just any white; it is what is called "life spectrum white." The naked eye cannot tell the difference, but your photosynthetic livestock can! Do not waste your time as I have done in the past, trying to substitute ordinary high-intensity lighting available at electrical supply houses for the premium lighting made specifically for enclosed reef tanks. "Grow lights" or other commonly available lights will also not work.

If you insist on trying this alternate approach, and your reef doesn't seem to be thriving, try the recommended bulbs, and I'm sure that will convince you that they are necessary.

The blue bulbs are essential for providing the proper balance of spectrum in the enclosed reef. Basically, a combination of blue and white light is most desirable. Most common bulbs emit light from the red and yellow parts of the spectrum, and these kinds of light are thought to encourage micro-algae. The white and blue areas in the spectrum provide the least lighting that is beneficial to undesirable algae.

OVERVIEW OF LIGHTING

Using Increased / Higher Watts per gallon

Benefits
- You can keep higher light species such as SPS

However
- Algae will grow faster.
- Substantial increase in electricity use. Consider this over an extended period of time.
- Higher Calcium demand.
- Increased heating of the tank.
- Overall higher cost to operate.
- Increased evaporation.

HEAT BUILDUP

High intensity fluorescent light bulbs will put out a considerable amount of heat. This should be dissipated from the canopy box by a fan that is wired into the main light timer line, so when the first light comes on with the timer, the fan is also activated and begins to circulate air through the canopy box. The fan should be at one end of the box, blowing air from the room into the box and over the bulbs. The other end should have an outlet hole so the heat buildup can be expelled. This will keep the temperature lower in the light box, and the tank from becoming over-heated by the light canopy. Even with one or two fans in the box cooling the bulbs, heat will still be transferred to the water, increasing the temperature of the reef. Cooling fans can be purchased at Radio Shack in most sizes appropriate for this purpose. They cost about $15 each.

Light Canopy & Remote Ballast Board

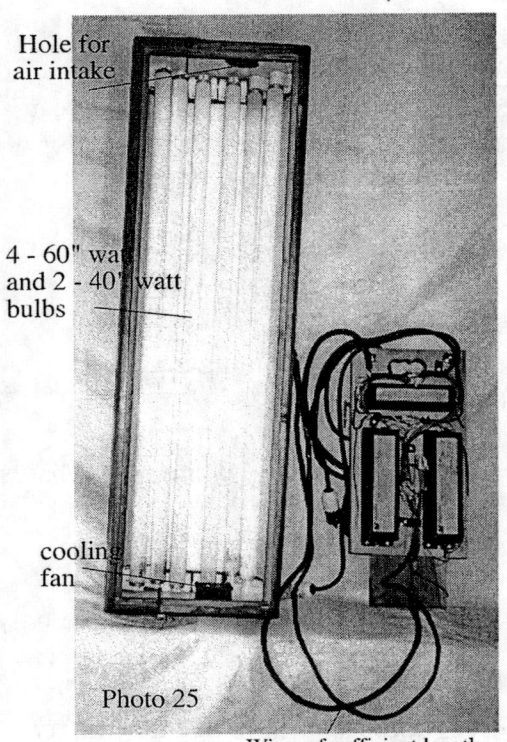

Hole for air intake

4 - 60" watt and 2 - 40" watt bulbs

cooling fan

Photo 25

Wires of sufficient length to "remote" ballasts

The heat transfer from your lighting will have a substantial effect on the temperature of the tank. Depending on the ambient temperature you may of may not need a heater for the tank.

If a heater is used it may be best to locate it in the sump where it will have a more uniform affect on the tank rather than overheating certain areas of the aquarium.

REMOTING THE BALLAST

Remote Ballast Board

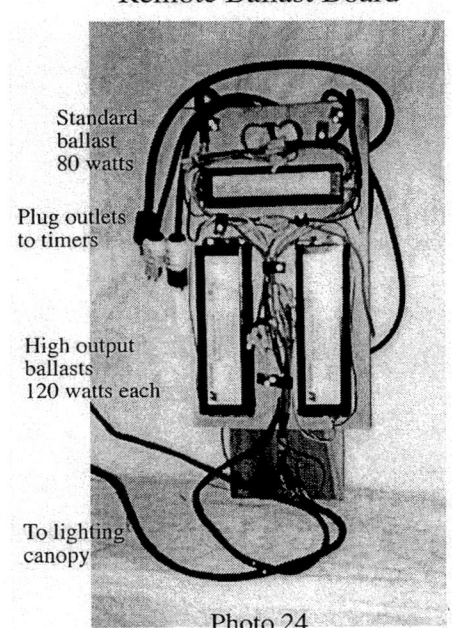

Standard ballast 80 watts

Plug outlets to timers

High output ballasts 120 watts each

To lighting canopy

Photo 24

Example of a remote tar ballast

High intensity ballast's put out a tremendous amount of heat and must not be enclosed in the canopy box. They should be wired to a "remote" board. This simply means you fasten the ballast to a piece of plywood with a handle cut into it, or attached to it. The ballast's are heavy, and this handle will make moving it much more convenient. Once you have the ballast fastened to the board, you connect the light fixture to the ballast with lengths of separate wires that are approximately 8 to 10 feet long. This will allow you to place the ballast board out of harm's way and into an area that is not enclosed, also away from any material that would be affected by the heat being generated.

The ballast's I have been talking about can be purchased from an electrical supply house. They are either "high output" (H.O.) or "very high output" (V.H.O.) There is a more modern "electronic" ballast on the market today, which is not as heavy, and do not put out as much heat as the conventional ballast. This newer ballast may be worth looking into if you are going to fabricate your own light canopy. Although these electrical ballast's are remoted in the same manner, keep in mind that they generate high voltage. This is not something you want hanging over the tank!

METAL HALIDE LIGHTING

Metal halide lighting is quite different from fluorescent lighting. The bulb is more like a common incandescent bulb, clear, and screw-type. These bulbs are extremely high-power and generate considerable heat!

Personally, I prefer the fluorescent type of lighting. It is my belief that fluorescent lighting disperses the light more evenly. The halide bulb is very powerful but smaller, and therefore illuminates an individual area more intensely. The older styles used individual bulbs with a high wattage, usually 500 watts or more, in a "pendant." The bulb was screwed into the socket and covered by a shroud, directing the light to the designated area. These pendants were large and unsightly, and usually had to be hung from the ceiling.

Because of the high wattage, power, and heat that is generated, it was very important to have the bulb a certain distance away from the top of the tank. People who used this older type of system realized it was an expensive and inefficient means of lighting. The more modern application is to have less powerful halide bulbs, usually 175 to 250 watts, enclosed in a well-ventilated canopy. Halide lamps that are enclosed in a canopy are best to be positioned perpendicular with the front of the tank. Because of the small oval design of metal halide bulbs having them perpendicular allows for better dispersion of the light. Its also important to note if you are planning to use halide lighting a good reflector is very important. Make sure the reflector is included in your metal halide package.

Visualize the difference: you can place small, high-wattage halide bulbs in one or two areas of the canopy box, adding up to the desired total wattage for the tank; or you can have long fluorescent bulbs that span the length of the tank and distribute the light evenly. This has been one of my reasons for preferring fluorescent over metal halide. The other reason is that the halide bulbs generate heat in a more localized area, and therefore could cause an uneven dispersal of the heat from the bulb into the tank.

Some new light systems incorporate both metal halide and fluorescent light. I am sure you can find just about any combination of lighting imaginable. Another drawback with halide lighting is that it does not provide the deep, long-wave spectrum of blue light that is available from fluorescent bulbs. This is one of the reasons for having a combination of fluorescent and halide bulbs in the newer light canopies. Although halide manufacturers are moving toward producing a 10,000K and 20,000K. (K=kelvins)

When these bulbs become available fluorescent lighting may be un necessary although it worth noting that actinic blue fluorescent lighting adds a very nice eye appeal of the tank rather than making the tank look overly "bright". A mix of Metal halide and actinic blue is probably the best bet for a high light reef tank while VHO fluorescent running on Ice cap ballast's would be my preference for the beginner tank of a tank with lower light species.

Metal halide bulbs are expensive, ranging from $60 to $70 each. They are factory-rated to last for about 4,000 hours. This 4,000-hour life span of the bulb, divided by 9 hours a day, means the bulb will last about 444 days, or about 15 months. The factory rating for fluorescent bulbs is higher than that of halide. We reef keepers who are familiar with photosynthetic livestock cut this figure in half to get the actual duration of the bulb's life-sustaining properties. Our reef creatures are not familiar with factory ratings.

Most experienced reef keepers change the bulbs for their tanks every 6 months, no matter what the factory rating. Any time over 6 months, and the light-loving creatures will suffer from not having the illumination they need in order to thrive. When you install new bulbs, you will see a noticeable difference in the photosynthetic livestock. Everything that is light-dependent will "come alive." The benefits of proper lighting are amazing. We humans cannot tell the difference, but the reef livestock most definitely can!

You will have to select your lighting system based on the information you have and the creatures you choose to keep. It is recommended that you illuminate your tank with from 3 (minimum) to 5 (maximum) watts per gallon, for 9 hours a day. One-third of the wattage should be in the proper white spectrum, and the remaining two-thirds should be in the deep blue spectrum.

There are many quality lighting manufacturers dedicated to reef lighting who would be more than happy to provide you with the essential components. Also see Chapters 10 and 12 of this book for more information on lighting components.

Chapter 6

Water Quality

Chapter goal:
To address the most common mistakes of water usage, while directing the
reader to the necessary method of using deionized or reverse osmosis
water purification.

Nothing will insure your success as much as the quality of your water! One of the most important elements of an enclosed reef system is the water. With human beings, clean fresh air is necessary for good health; in a reef tank, the water is the vital component.

Do not make the mistake of assuming your tap water is suitable. Most likely it is not. Many a novice reef aquarist has paid dearly for overlooking the composition of plain tap water. Let's look at three approaches.

> *The water you use will have the greatest effect on the success or failure of your reef tank*

USING PLAIN TAP WATER

The first approach is to try to use your tap water, just as it comes out of the faucet. This seems like the easiest way, but it has the most potential problems. If you insist on using your tap water, I would strongly suggest that you have it tested in a laboratory. You will find such laboratories listed in the Yellow Pages. The tests cost about $10 each. You want the lab to test for phosphate and silicate (algae producers), nitrate, lead, and copper. So you need five tests @ $10, which is $50. Depending on where you live your local water company may be able to provide testing for you, however. Even if the readings are low, you cannot be absolutely sure the water won't cause problems at some point. Although you may get extremely lucky and be able to use your tap water however the composition of tapwater may change over time particularly city water, which by the way may be chlorinated. Using non-purified tap water may also lead to contaminants build up in the tank.

If you take this approach, there will be only one way to know whether it is satisfactory: once you have the tank set up and you have

> *Average tap water will usually induce micro-algae*

done the initial cycling process, if you don't have a persistent algae problem and your livestock seems to be thriving, then you may assume the water is okay. I would not recommend this approach, as you may risk stressing or even killing the delicate and valuable specimens you have purchased. This may seem like the easiest and cheapest way to go, but I have found out that it is not.

USING OCEAN WATER

The second and most ideal approach would be to get your water from the actual ocean! I don't mean Long Island Sound or bays and inlets, but the open ocean—if you live by the ocean. This method would be great, *but it is not practical, and you will still need pure fresh water to add for your make-up water (to compensate for evaporation).*

> Water from the ocean would be ideal, but it is not practical for most reef keepers

I have considered this approach for time, effort and myself involved in getting ocean water frequently, and the inconvenience of storing it, is just not worth the advantages. My tank is 200 gallons, and I do a 35-gallon water change twice a month. That requires 70 gallons a month, or 840 gallons a year. Add 200 gallons for the initial startup , making a total of 1,040 gallons. That is a lot of water to handle!

If your tank is smaller, and you live by the ocean, calculate the amount you will need, and consider whether you are willing to go this route. Also, do not forget about your make-up water. If you use non-purified tap water, you can be sure you will be adding undesirable elements to the ocean water you worked so hard to get. These elements in the tap water may cause serious algae problems or other complications.

Some people say, "No way would I use random water from the ocean—what about parasites and possible contamination?" There has been much said about the many benefits of natural saltwater, and how to handle it. Since I do not use this method, I will not go into the details, as I feel it is not a practical way to maintain my aquarium. However, I do feel it is worth mentioning.

USING PURIFIED TAP WATER

The third and best approach is to use purified tap water. I have found this has been the most convenient, least expensive method to get top-quality water when and where you need it. This is a primary requirement of the reef.

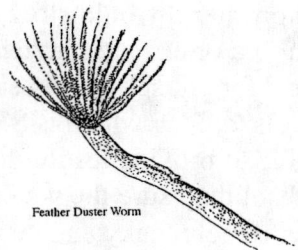

Feather Duster Worm

What You Will Need

- 1 carbon prefilter, single stage (plumbing supply house)
- 1 carbon filter, dual stage
- 1 reverse osmosis or deionizer (see Chapter 10 for comparison)

Keep in mind that you cannot afford to cut corners in this area of your system. As stated from the beginning, nothing will ensure your success as much as the quality of your water.

THE AUTHOR'S WATER SYSTEM

Let me describe my system. First, it is necessary to have a cold water supply from your home, preferably near by the tank. In my setup, the tank is about 8 feet from a sink. I purchased a 3-way tap to tie into the cold water pipe, connected a piece of 1/2" plastic water pipe, and ran that next to the tank with a plastic garden hose type spigot. (See Photo 3, "Under-sink Connections.")

Water Purification System

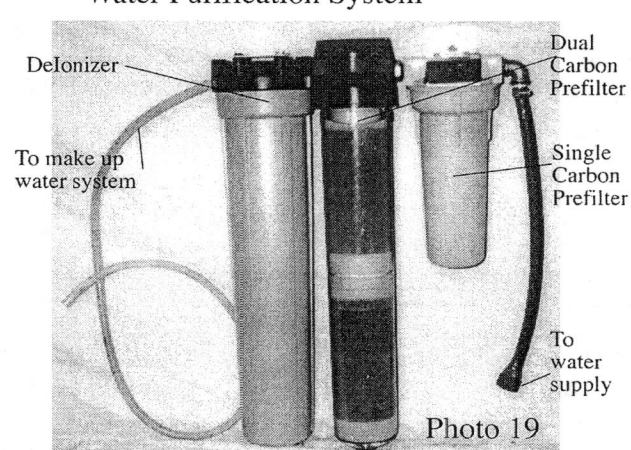

Delonizer

To make up water system

Dual Carbon Prefilter

Single Carbon Prefilter

To water supply

Photo 19

Now I have a water supply right at the tank, with a shutoff, which is ideal. This is extremely helpful when you do water changes

> *Having a water supply at the tank is convenient and practical*

and when adding the make-up water, which will be done frequently. I prefer not to have to wrestle with messy and inconvenient buckets and containers full of water.

To the male spigot I connect a length of garden hose, approximately 36", with a female end to it. This is connected in series to a single-stage carbon prefilter, then to a dual-stage carbon filter, and finally to a deionizer, which has a 36" length of vinyl tubing for the outlet. The result is pure triple-carbon-filtered, deionized water. My make-up water system is located on the side of the tank, where I mix the water for bimonthly water changes and the make-up water for evaporation. (See Chapter 10 for a comparison of deionization and reverse osmosis.)

The whole idea is that the more conveniently you set up the most important part of the system (the water source), the easier it will

> *This shows a cold water connection to the RO/DI unit as well as a drain hose connected to the wastepipe from the skimmer drain.*

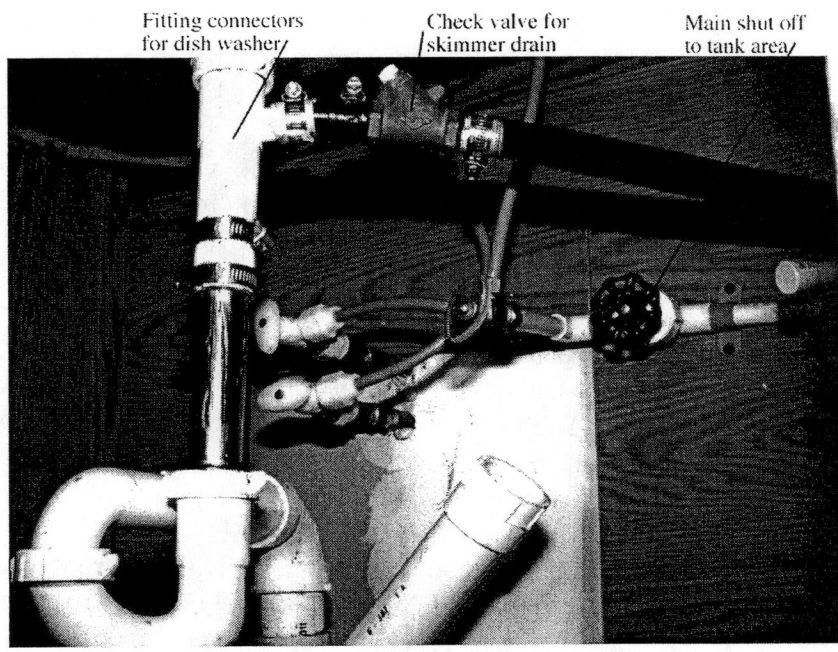

Fitting connectors for dish washer

Check valve for skimmer drain

Main shut off to tank area

Photo 3   Undersink Connections

be to use and maintain.

SYNTHETIC SALTWATER

Once you have the purified tap water in place, as previously described, and the tank is situated as described in Chapter 12 under "Tank Location," you can fill the tank and convert the water into saltwater, which is done with the highest quality synthetic salt mix you can find.

> *Select the highest quality salt mix, and stick with it*

Some people will say, "Salt is salt. It doesn't matter which brand you use." I do not agree with them. In my opinion it is best to start with and continue to use one specific brand. That way, if a problem arises, and you have been using a specific salt with good results, you can most likely rule out the salt as the cause of the new problem. Also, some manufacturers use different ratios of trace elements to salt, which will make the mixed saltwater a different composition than your reef has been accustomed to. Also, some brands of salt mix may contain nitrate or phosphate. Based on my experience, if the mix does not say "Nitrate and phosphate free," I assume that they are present in the mix.

I myself use Coralife Salt Mix, with very good results. (See Suppliers Reference Section.) Here are my reasons for using this brand:

1. It claims not to contain nitrate or phosphate.

2. It claims to contain all the necessary trace elements.
3. My reef likes it, and does extremely well with it.
4. It is sold in 80-pound boxes that make 300 gallons of saltwater. It is economical and convenient to purchase a large amount to have on hand, so you don't ever have to put off doing water changes. It comes in a heavy-duty box with a resealable tie, so moisture doesn't make the salt lumpy and hard to dissolve.
5. It dissolves perfectly in purified tap water.
6. I know other successful reef keepers use it with good results.

It's worth noting here that the preferred salt of the majority of reef keepers is Instant Ocean Approximately 80% use Instant Ocean followed by Coral Life.

> *One dry measuring cup of salt dissolved in 3 gallons of purified water yields the desired salinity of 1.021-1.024*

Once you have chosen your brand of salt, the next question will be: what is the ratio of mix to use to achieve the proper salinity? I have researched the topic of salinity, and again, this can become a bit confusing. Some will tell you that temperature is a vital factor to consider, and give you intimidating charts with temperatures from 20 degrees to 120 degrees, showing how much salt should be added to achieve the desired salinity throughout that temperature range. The fact is, most of us keep our reefs at 73 to 85 degrees, depending on the time of year and allowing for minor fluctuations. So we're really talking about a temperature change of 12 degrees, slowly over a period of time.

In fact, the salinity in the ocean also fluctuates with different influences. A lower temperature gives a higher salinity, and a higher temperature gives a lower salinity, with the same amount of salt in the water. This subject could become very complex, with all its terminology. ("Temperature-calibrated hydrometers" may be fine for the folks who have been using them, but they can be confusing in a discussion.) The most convenient measuring device I use to determine salt content is a "specific gravity meter." This is a small plastic device with a floating needle. It is filled with water, and the needle designates the salt content. These plastic floating needle hydrometers are considered imprecise although once the tank has been running for they are handy to have. Actually I would recommend to have a glass floating hydrometer which is more accurate and compare the readings. Both hydrometers should be rinsed well with freshwater to remove salt residue.

In an effort to simplify matters, here is my approach. "Specific gravity" (S.G.) is a measure of water density; the more salt there is in the water, the denser it is. Ideally you want an S.G. of 1.021 to 1.024. To achieve this, my finding on a regular basis is: 1 dry measuring cup of salt mix dissolved in 3 gallons of purified tap water produces saltwater with an S.G. of 1.024 at an average temperature of 75 degrees. I have found this to be the most practical method for measuring and mixing saltwater easily and accurately, and I highly recommend it.

To sum up about salinity: shoot for a S.G. that stays between 1.021 and 1.024, allowing for the slight temperature differences that we always encounter. I would also recommend that you get into the habit of checking the salinity of the tank just before you add new water, and then check the new water. If they are both in the above range, you are okay. If not, adjust the new water to match the tank (unless you are trying to reduce or raise the salinity of the tank).

MIXING SALTWATER

What you will need:

- **A specific gravity meter (cost: about $12)**
- **Purified tap water**
- **High-quality salt mix**
- **A clean plastic container to hold 12-15% of the tank's volume**
- **A powerhead pump**
- **A 3'-6' section of flexible hose**

When you mix the salt with the water, it will take some time for the salt to dissolve. Usually I mix it for about 8 to 12 hours, to be sure that it is completely dissolved. The best mixing method is using a powerhead with a hose attached to it, so the water will be thoroughly pumped around the mixing vessel. Also, with the hose attached to the powerhead, when the mixing is done the water can be pumped into the tank or the sump after you have done a water change.

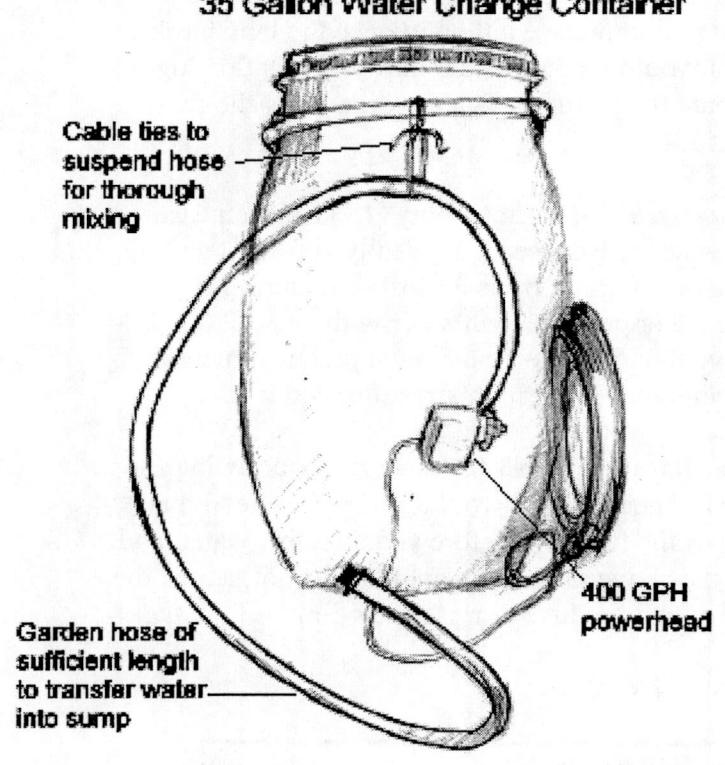

35 Gallon Water Change Container

Cable ties to suspend hose for thorough mixing

Garden hose of sufficient length to transfer water into sump

400 GPH powerhead

I use a 35-gallon plastic drum with a 400 GPH powerhead and a 7-foot length of garden hose. The drum, powerhead and hose are used only for this purpose, and the pump and hose are kept

in the drum with the lid on when they are not in use. Again, this system works great. These 35-gallon plastic drums are heavy-duty and have locking lids. You may substitute a new, clean garbage can if you need a large container.

WATER TESTING

In this hobby, there is much discussion about water testing. Some people suggest it is extremely important to be precisely informed of the condition of the water, on a regular basis. This is usually done with test kits consisting of reagents and color comparison charts. A reagent is a substance used to detect, measure, or react with another substance. In this case, the other substance is the water in your reef. The test kits range in price from about $50 to over $200 for a laboratory grade. One of the main problems with most commonly available test kits is that it is very difficult to get an accurate reading with the color comparison chart. If the kit has a paper chart, the color on the paper fades; if it is a plastic color-graduated chip, the color can also fade, and it is still difficult to get a true reading. What you will get is a fairly accurate reading depending on the type of kit you are using.

After going through many different test kits, I have found that in my opinion the best kit for the money is the "Fastest," by Instant Ocean. It costs about $45 in stores—approximately $1 per test. This kit has plastic chips that are graduated. They are best viewed with a white piece of paper behind the container under natural light. When not in use the chips are to be kept in the box out of direct sunlight or indirect light. The "Master Kit" has tests for pH, ammonia, nitrite, and nitrate. They also have a kit called "Reef Master," which has tests for low nitrate, phosphate, and calcium. I would highly recommend these two kits. If you are interested in more accurate test kits Hach, LaMotte and Salifert produce extremely accurate results although they are much more difficult to use and cost substantially more that the aforementioned test kits.

Electronic meters are another type of measuring device. The ones I have used cost about $100. They are really neat and will give you a reading constantly or with the flip of a switch.

Unfortunately, they do have their problems. First, they are 9-volt battery powered, so you either have to buy an adapter kit (about $18 in stores), or get rechargeable batteries and a battery charger. The main problem is that the electrode lasts only about 3 months, and the cost of replacing it is about $65. Yes, cleaners are available, but I have found that the constant exposure to saltwater is tough on the electrode. They do work extremely well, but they need constant cleaning (about once a week), along with a recalibration. Eventually they will give you inaccurate readings, which is when the electrode needs replacing. Also, to my knowledge, they are only available for testing pH, oxygen, oxygen-redox potential, and conductivity. So they won't do much for ammonia, nitrite, nitrate, calcium, or phosphate. They are nice to have and they work well, but they need constant maintenance and periodic replacement.

> *Over-reacting to test results from cycling can in fact inhibit the cycling process*

The big problem with testing your water is that most beginners are told to test constantly and record the results, or test and adjust. *That is the problem, testing and adjusting.* When you adjust or react to the test results, you throw off the balance that the water is naturally trying to achieve. And stability is critical to the inhabitants!

Let's look at a typical cycling example.

You add the live rock and you begin to test for ammonia. Let's say you add the rock on Monday. On Wednesday, you test for ammonia, and you get a reading of 2. On Thursday you get a 3, Friday a 4, Saturday a 5, and by Sunday it is 8. By now you are becoming concerned. You might have been told that high ammonia readings are not good for the rock, and that you should do a water change. So you do the change, and the levels of ammonia go down for a few hours, only to go higher than they were before. You are concerned and are patiently waiting for the reading to come down, so you test daily. By now you are probably running out of reagent, so you take a trip to the store, and by now this ammonia cycle has cost you about $15 to $20.

> *High ammonia readings are normal when you are cycling a new tank, and they will balance out naturally*

The fact is when you put in the rock, there is a significant amount of die-off on and in the rock. You can test as much as you want, and that will not speed up the natural process. In fact, by reacting to the test results (water changes or chemical additives to reduce the ammonia), you are delaying the normal cycle. In this situation of a new tank, you are encountering what is called N.T.S. ("new tank syndrome"); depending on the rock, N.T.S. can last from 2 weeks to 2 months.

My suggestion is to test for ammonia as *infrequently* as your patience will allow! This is why it is so important to cycle your tank in the manner described on page 38 before you add any other livestock. There is very little if anything you can do to control this process. You just have to let it happen. Keep in mind that the rock most likely came from a stable environment, and now is in a new sterile environment which will cause additional die-off. Fortunately, your rock is far from doomed. You just have to accept that a certain amount of die-off will occur, and is all part of the natural process of conditioning a new tank. I hope you can see that daily testing of the water is not necessary.

I recommend that you test and record the results in your log book every 4 to 5 days, and when you begin to see the readings on their way down, it is safe to say that they will continue in that direction. Keep in mind: probably the most important ammonia test you do will be the *last* one, when it reads zero.

> *Ammonia and nitrite are a natural occurrence in a new tank, and a sure sign that the cycling process is under way*

Next you will test for nitrite. Nitrite will be a welcome indication that the ammonia is definitely being processed by naturally appearing nitrosomonas bacteria, and a sure sign that the natural cycling process is well on its way. Nitrite tests a lot like ammonia: you don't have to overdo it. After it is first detected in a small amount, it will gradually increase, recording at higher and higher levels. There is little you can do about this, except observe the cycling process. Nitrite processes much faster than ammonia, usually in about half the time or even less. You can plan the testing accordingly.

> *The duration of the cycling process depends on how fast the nitrifying bacteria multiply to catch up to the waste being produced in the tank*

Ammonia and nitrite are produced by living and dying organisms. When you set up a new tank you start with the purified tap water and salt mix, and then add the live rock. But there is one important element missing in sufficient numbers, and that is nitrosomonas bacteria! These wonderful bacteria thrive on ammonia, and will only multiply to a number that balances with the amount of food that is available to them (namely ammonia).

One of the big misconceptions is that the live rock is loaded with nitrosomonas bacteria. Yes, they are present in the rock, but only enough for what that rock was producing in its stable environment. When the rock is moved from its stable, balanced environment, taken out of the water, bagged, boxed and transported, taken out into the air again, and finally put into your tank, a certain amount of die-off of many organisms takes place. The balanced bacteria become not so balanced, which is why you will get ammonia readings.

So when you start up a tank, or add a *large* bio-load (livestock) to an existing tank, you throw the environment out of balance and create a situation that is stressful to any living organisms, because they are not accustomed to the added waste products. This will occur any time you add a significant bio-load, although once the system is established (with plenty of nitrosomonas and nitrobacter), the cycles will then become mini-cycles.

In a brand-new tank, nitrosomonas are missing. Once the nitrosomonas bacteria begin converting ammonia to nitrite, nitrobacter appear to convert nitrite to nitrate. This process of "cycling" continues, converting ammonia to nitrite and nitrite to nitrate, until you won't get any measurable ammonia or nitrite readings with your test kits. At that point you will begin to get nitrate readings. The tank has then "cycled."

Points to remember:

- You cannot have a nitrate reading without nitrite being present.
- You cannot have a nitrite reading without ammonia being present.
- A zero ammonia reading indicates that nitrosomonas bacteria have completely processed the ammonia to nitrite.
- A zero nitrite reading indicates that nitrobacter have completely processed all nitrite to the less toxic nitrate.
- When ammonia and nitrite cannot be detected by test kits, the nitrifying bacteria have multiplied to balance with the level of waste in the tank. The tank has then been "cycled."

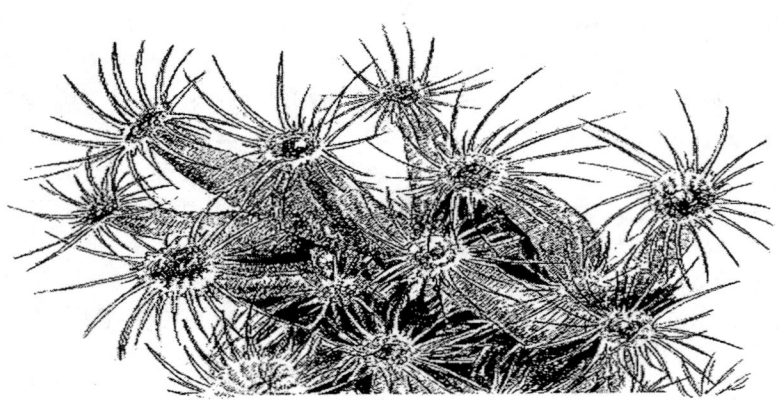

NITRIFICATION PROCESS

- Livestock produce ammonia (very toxic).

- Nitrosomonas bacteria thrive on ammonia and produce nitrite (toxic).

- Nitrobacter bacteria thrive on nitrite and produce nitrate (least toxic).

- This is called the "nitrification process."

- Both nitrosomonas and nitrobacter are aerobic bacteria, meaning they need substantial amounts of oxygen to survive and process the waste they encounter.

- Nitrate is the last measurable waste product we encounter.

DENITRIFICATION PROCESS

- Nitrate is converted to nitrogen gas by anaerobic bacteria.

- "Anaerobic" means living/active/occurring in the *absence* of free oxygen.

- Nitrate being converted to nitrogen gas by anaerobic bacteria is called "denitrification."

So, we have the nitrification and the denitrification process. Nitrification needs oxygen; denitrification needs the *absence* of oxygen. Fortunately, both of these conditions can exist side by side in our reef tank.

TANK CYCLING
(NITRIFICATION *AND* DENITRIFICATION)

Once all the rock is in the tank, the cycling of the water will begin. In approximately three days, there should be a measurable amount of ammonia. Test and record the ammonia at this time. Continue to test and record it at three to four-day intervals. The reading will rise and rise, until one day it will drop off and be zero. At that time, begin to test for nitrite.

The nitrite cycle is very similar to the ammonia cycle, so use the same procedure as described for ammonia. Do not become alarmed with the test results!
This is the cycling process, and the tank will balance out! As long as you do not have any fish, inverts or coral in the tank, you have nothing to worry about. Be patient, let nature take its course, and the tank will cycle.

When the nitrite test reads zero, you should begin to test for nitrate. You will get only very faint nitrate readings, because the tank is now balanced and has virtually no bio-load (waste products from fish, invertebrates, etc.).

When the bacteria "catch up" (multiply to process the waste in the tank), you will get zero readings of ammonia and nitrite

The tank has now had its first and largest cycle. When you add more livestock, this will increase the waste load, and the bacteria will have to multiply and catch up with the increased load. You will get mini-cycles of ammonia and nitrite when you add livestock. These small cycles will be insignificant as long as you don't add too many creatures at once. Begin by adding inverts, two to three at a time, until they are all in. Do the same with the corals (possibly slower because of the cost). Test for ammonia and nitrite a few days after each addition. If the test results are zero, proceed to add creatures as described until all inverts and corals are added. Give them a week or so to acclimate. Test for ammonia and nitrite. When they register zero, and the inverts and corals appear to be well adjusted, you are ready to add fish in the same manner as described.

The nitrogen gas can be observed as bubbles on the rock and glass. This gas is released into the air and dissipated into the atmosphere. Apparently, millions of tons of nitrogen gas is released in a similar way by all living things on earth yearly. This is nature's way of processing its natural waste.

In our reef, we need to create favorable conditions for these natural water purification processes, aerobic and anaerobic, to happen.

For aerobic processes, we want oxygen-saturated water. This will be achieved by large protein skimmers, high flow rates from our water pumps, and a lot of turbulence in our sumps, produced by our overflow pipes and drip plates. Also, we need a surface on which the bacteria can colonize. This has normally been done in fish-only tanks with spherical plastic or other media. In a reef we have something even better: live rock. The live rock is ideal for the aerobic bacteria because of its porous nature, but also because of its proximity to the waste products.

For anaerobic conditions, the live rock also is ideal. Because of its porous rock-like quality, the outer layer of rock harbors aerobic bacteria.
On this outer layer oxygen-rich water passes over the surface, while ammonia and nitrite are right there to be used up by the bacteria. These aerobic bacteria produce nitrate. The nitrate then accumulates in the water surrounding the rock.

Anaerobic conditions occur *inside* the rock, or in other areas where the oxygen has gotten used up by the aerobic bacteria that colonize the outer layers of the rock. There is minimal oxygen in the core of the rock; denitrification takes place there.

Anaerobic conditions can also be encouraged in denitrifying sand filters (see Chapter 8), and in separate denitrifying columns (see Chapter 12).

It is my opinion that lack of conditions for denitrification causes the high nitrate readings that seem to plague many reef keepers. Denitrification can be readily created in the enclosed reef, and this is the goal of the "natural system."

TYPES AND FREQUENCY OF WATER TESTING
ONCE THE TANK HAS CYCLED

pH:

Every 1-2 weeks at first; monthly once the tank is established. Record each pH reading at approximately the same time of day. Absolute lowest is 8; 8.2 - 8.4 is most desirable. pH is kept in this range by adding calcium hydroxide at regular water changes and when compensating for evaporation. A quality salt mix will yield a pH of 8.2 on a regular basis.

Calcium:

Every 1-2 weeks at first; monthly once the tank is established. Record each calcium reading at approximately the same time of day. Lowest acceptable level is 350; 400 - 450 is average. Above 450 is high; although desirable, this level may be difficult to maintain. Calcium level is kept stable by adding calcium hydroxide, and by regular water changes. It can be "boosted" with a more concentrated "turbo" calcium, but this must be done extremely carefully, closely following the directions that come with the product. Make adjustments slowly over a 24- to 48-hour period with calcium hydroxide. *Once the calcium level is established, fluctuation should be minimal as calcium hydroxide is added regularly with make-up water. If the reading is constantly low, try increasing the amount of calcium hydroxide mixed with the make-up water or increase your evaporation with fans over the sump. Increased evaporation will demand more frequent additions of Kalkwasser.*

Salinity:

Test before and after each water change. Range should be between 1.021 and 1.024. Record at approximately the same temperature each time, with known amount of water; be sure the tank is not "shy" of water from evaporation. Use specific gravity meter. Make adjustments slowly over a 24- to 48-hour period. Once the salinity is established, adjustments should be minimal.

Nitrate:

Test monthly, between water changes. Record each nitrate reading at approximately the same time of day. 10 PPM is average, with a standard range test kit. Readings below 10 are desirable and indicate proper denitrification. Readings above 10 denote insufficient denitrification, possible lack of photosynthetic livestock, and increasingly diminished water quality. Nitrate is kept 10 or under by proper amounts of live rock, photosynthetic livestock, proper lighting, and regular water changes.

Oxygen:

I do not test for oxygen content, because I know that the water in my reef is kept oxygen-saturated by a combination of large protein skimmers and the flow and turbulence in the sump.

Phosphate:

Phosphate is considered to encourage the growth of micro-algae. Phosphate tests are primarily done to test a substance (typically water or carbon) *before* it goes into the reef. Perform the test with phosphate-free water, and drop in a few grains of the questionable material. The test should indicate whether phosphate is present. Test and record phosphate results when the tank is first set up, and monthly after that. Phosphate levels will usually climb slowly at first, indicating the accumulation of nutrient waste products. React to the test results *slowly*, so as to maintain balance in the tank. The correct action is to increase the volume of your water changes slightly (by 5-7%), and continue to monitor phosphate levels regularly. In my opinion increasing the volume of water changes reduces not only phosphate, but also all other undesirable nutrients in your tank. (There are also resins that remove phosphate, but it is easy to become dependent on artificial, chemical means to correct natural conditions.)

dKH:

This term refers to the "degree of carbonate hardness" in the water. Levels should be recorded between 7 and 12 with the test kit. The level can be increased artificially with "buffers" that raise the carbonate hardness or alkalinity of the water. However, recommended levels of KH should be easily maintained with (1) regular additions of calcium via Kalkwasser, and (2) water changes using purified tap water and a high-quality salt mix.

Some aquarists, in an attempt to create better-than-ideal conditions, will constantly try to raise carbonate hardness with all kinds of products, including sodium bicarbonate. Some will think that by adding inexpensive baking soda they will improve conditions related to KH. This approach, however, is not an adequate substitute for the regular maintenance procedures of water changes and adding Kalkwasser to raise the pH and maintain an alkaline solution. With a high pH (8.2 to 8.4), the solution is alkaline. If the pH drops (becomes more acidic) due to accumulated waste in the system, the alkalinity also drops. The carbonate hardness is considered to act as a buffer stabilizer against pH drops.

One should test and record KH monthly. Observe the readings on a long-term basis, while performing regular water changes and additions of Kalkwasser. If you must increase the KH level to get readings between 7 and 12, use a commercially available buffer made for this purpose. Add the product slowly, and follow the manufacturer's directions carefully.

Other tests: I have not found it necessary to perform tests other than those listed above.

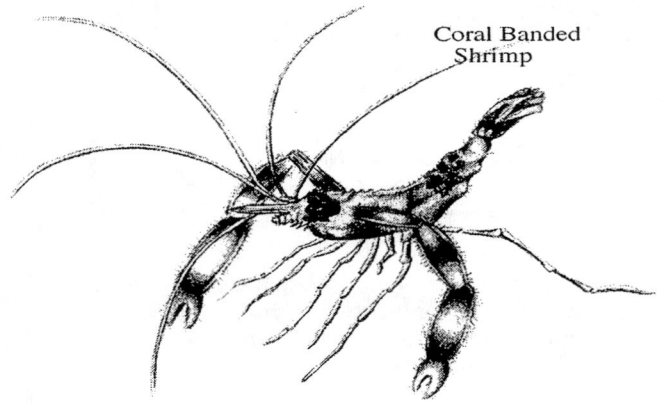

Coral Banded
Shrimp

THE NITRIFICATION / DENITRIFICATION PROCESS

Stage One
Add: Purified tap water
High-grade salt mix

Produce: "Sterile environment"

Stage Two
Add: All or most of
Liverock

Produce: "Ammonia & Die off

The Nitrification Cycling Process

****
Tank is lacking
Nitrosomona
Bacteria
RESULT: High
Ammonia reading

Stage Three
Add: Nitrosomona population
naturally appear

Produce: Nitrite

****
Tank is lacking
Nitro Bacter
Bacteria
RESULT: High
Nitrite reading

Stage Four
Add: Naturally occurring Nitrosomona
& Nitro Bacter Bacteria

Produce: Nitrate

****
Tank is in full
Nitrification cycle
but lacking sufficient
anaerobic bacteria
RESULT: Measureab
Nitrate

Stage Five
Add: Conditions for
Anaerobic Bacteria

Produce: Nitrogen Gas

****
Tank balances
denitrification occurs

RESULT: Low
Nitrate reading

The Denitrification Process

Stage Six

Natural water purification

Tank is completely balanced

****
Tank balances
denitrification occurs

RESULT: Low
Nitrate reading

Chapter 7

Filtration Concepts

Chapter goal:
To explain the methods, components, and design for modern filtration of
an enclosed reef system

Most novice hobbyists who are not familiar with reef keeping will probably be unfamiliar with the concepts of modern filtration in an enclosed reef system. I agree that there is quite a wide array of filters on the market today, and it is easy to become confused as to which filter will do the job.

A filter for a reef tank is completely different from a filter for any other type of enclosed aquatic environment. It involves a unique concept that applies only to a reef. What makes a reef different from other types of tanks? It is the live rock that makes it unique! The live rock is the main element, the base, the framework. It is what you see. It is what the micro- and macro-organisms live on. It is what the corals, clams, sponges, tunicates, mussels, and other livestock attach themselves to. It is what makes a reef a reef. It is a beautiful piece of nature, *and it is also the main element of the filtration system!*

Modern reef filtration consists of:

- **1.5 to 1.75 lbs. of live rock per gallon**
- **Surface skimming (water taken from the *surface* of the tank)**
- **Large protein skimmer**
- **Drip plate with removable prefilter changed weekly**
- **Sump box for controlling and directing water flow**
- **Bimonthly water changes**

I will discuss:

- **The most current concept of filtering with a prefilter and a protein skimmer only**
- **Surface skimming**
- **Sump box with a built-in removable prefilter**
- **Calculating water volume for a sump and the desired water flow rate for a reef tank**
- **The external filtering system**
- **The prefilter: placement, function, and required service**
- **Old and new filtering concepts**
- **Nitrate buildup**
- **Denitrification**

THE CONCEPT

It has been proven by many aquarists that protein skimming (surface skimming), combined with a prefilter and the proper amount of live rock, will perform optimum filtration for the reef, resulting in nitrification, denitrification, and waste removal.

This chapter will talk about old and new filtration concepts, nitrate buildup, and the most current concept of filtering with a prefilter and protein skimmers only, which will include a sump box with a removable prefilter built in. I will describe how to calculate the water volume for a sump, as well as the water flow rate desired in a reef tank. I feel it's necessary to discuss the whole picture of the external filtering system when first describing the prefilter—its placement, its function, and the service it needs.

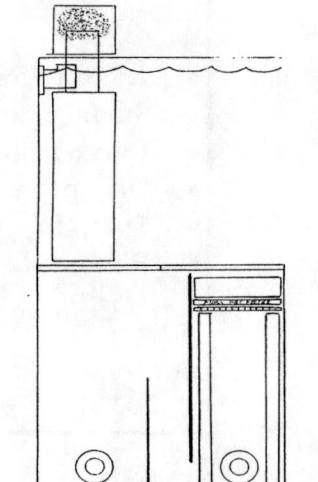

The prefilter is part of the external filtering system, and besides the protein skimmer is the only mechanical filtering device needed for a modern reef system. This may seem like a new concept in filtering, and in some ways it is.

Sump Box Protein Skimmer Tank Relation Diagram. 6

SURFACE SKIMMING

In most older aquariums water was drawn out of the tank either from the bottom or from approximately halfway up the tank. All advanced reef keepers agree that this is incorrect. The fact is that nitrogen gas, along with other elements, rises to the *surface* of the water. This can be observed by the existence of a "scum line" at the water level of the tank. It is at this surface waterline that you must draw the water to feed the skimmer. This ensures proper gas exchange between oxygen from the atmosphere and the nutrient-rich water that rises to the surface.

This concept of surface skimming will employ either overflow pipes or a dam-type wall over which surface water flows out of the tank. For filling the tank by using the main pump, my personal preference is to have a spraybar at the bottom rear of the tank. I believe this results in a more consistent water flow and exchange throughout the tank.

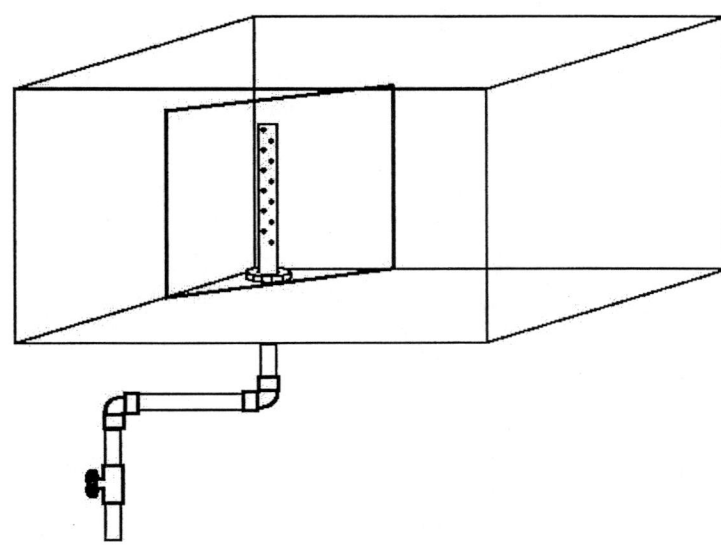

In order to have a true modern reef tank, surface skimming of the water is essential; all water flow out of the tank *must* be from the *surface*. (See Diagram 9.) This water then enters the protein skimmer, where the bulk waste products get removed. Then the water passes through the prefilter.

THE PREFILTER AND WATER FLOW

The prefilter can be positioned in many locations: in the sump, in a "skimmer box," or in any other area through which all the water in the system will have to pass.

My thinking is, I don't want anything restricting the flow of water coming out of the tank, as is the case with a skimmer box. If you have a high flow rate and restrict the water in the overflow by having the prefilter there, the tank could overflow the skimmer box or the tank itself. In spite of the prefilter's name,
I have always had poor results using it *before* the skimmer. With high flow rates supplying a large skimmer, the risk of depriving the skimmer or sump box of water is not worth taking. I found it very practical to position the prefilter *after* the skimmer, on the "clean" side of the sump box.

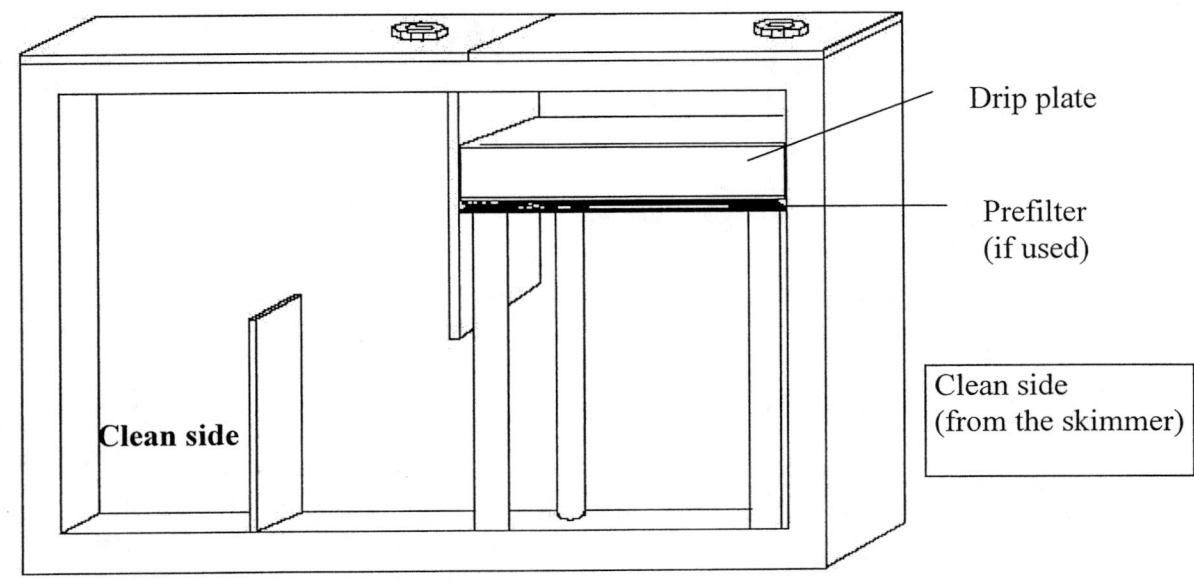

Drip plate

Prefilter
(if used)

Clean side
(from the skimmer)

Dirty side –
from the tank to
the skimmers
pump

Clean side

Prefilter area of sump box

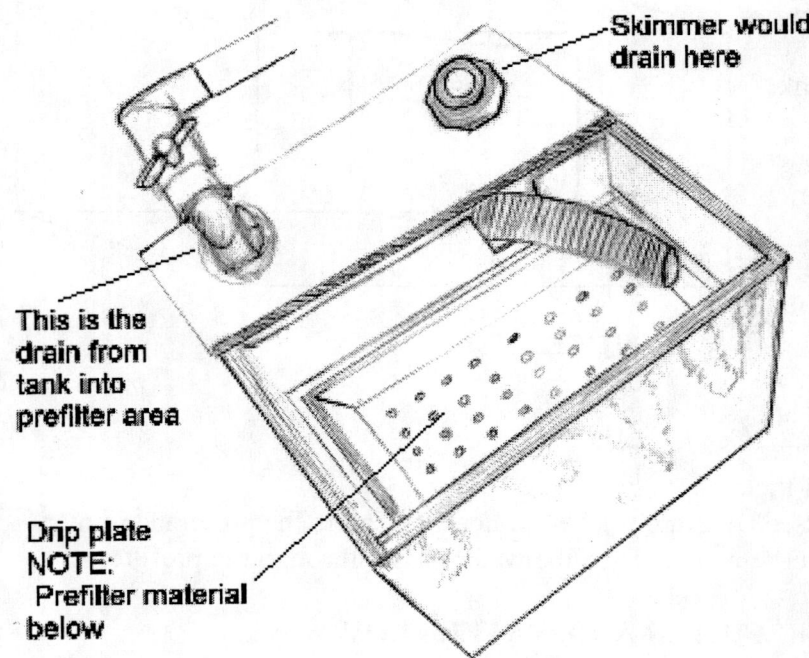

Skimmer would drain here

This is the drain from tank into prefilter area

Drip plate NOTE: Prefilter material below

I never cared for skimmer boxes with prefilter foam blocks. They are convenient (they are easily adapted to stock tanks without having to drill through for the overflow, but they seem too small and ineffective for my taste. They are also bulky, and have to depend on a "self-starting siphon." I believe in having a high flow rate of water in my reef, turning all the water over in the tank at least six times an hour. This is accomplished with a 1200 GPH main pump for a 200-gallon tank. This does not include the 1200 GPH pump used to operate the skimmer.

All these pumps have to be fed with a constantly available supply of water.

THE SUMP BOX

A sump box is the best way I can

- supply the skimmers with a consistent volume of water,
- incorporate a prefilter,
- have a "working amount of water" (the amount it takes to "work" the tank, pumping water into the tank to a desired level, so that water will flow out, and
- have the needed buffer, in case the electricity goes out and the tank drains down to the lowest point of the overflow(s).
- have an area to hold the heaters
- an area to add supplements
- an area to drip Kalkwasser

In my case, the sump box contains approximately 50 gallons. About 1/2 of that is working water, and the other 1/2 is for the overflow water, if and when the power goes out.

CALCULATING THE SIZE OF THE SUMP BOX

This figure had to be calculated before I knew what size sump I would need to do the job. I started by calculating the gallons per inch of height in the tank. I have a 200-gallon tank that is 24 inches high; 200/24 = 8.3 gallons for each inch of height. The lowest point of my overflow pipes is approximately 3 inches from the absolute top of the tank. So, at 8.3 gallons per inch, those 3 inches hold 25 gallons of water (3 inches x 8.3 gallons per inch = 24.9 gallons). This figure is from the absolute top of the tank, so it is generous.

I took this number and doubled it (since including the working water, this would be 50 gallons). I am aware that this may seem very "ballpark," but I would prefer to err on the side of having enough space in the event of an unexpected situation. This works very well, and it seems to be the perfect size when I perform a "simulated" power outage by pulling the plug. (I find that I can have anywhere from 5 to 15 gallons of empty space, depending on evaporation.)

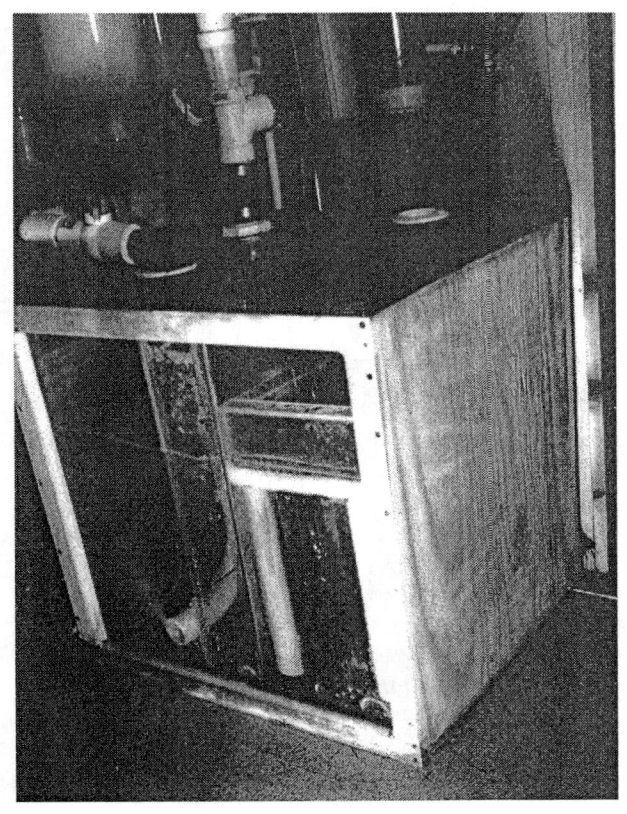

DESIGN AND FUNCTION OF THE SUMP BOX

It is desirable to have two separate areas in the sump (see Diagram 6). They are separated with a piece of Plexiglas that is high enough to keep the water separated while the sump is in operation, but not *totally* separate, so the sump can fill up completely in case of a power outage. We will refer to one side as "dirty" (water from the tank), and the other as "clean" (water from the skimmer and the prefilter).

One side is water coming from the tank, going to the skimmer. The other side is water coming from the skimmer through the prefilter, going to the main pump and back into the tank. Gravity drains water from the tank, into one side of the sump. The skimmer

> *You need an area where the water can be controlled and directed. This is done with a sump box.*

pump (on this "dirty" side) pumps this water into the skimmer. The water then drains by gravity into the prefilter ("clean") side of the sump box, collects there, and gets pumped back into the tank by the main pump.

LOCATION AND HEIGHT REQUIREMENTS FOR THE PROTEIN SKIMMER

It is very important to have enough room (height) for the skimmer's operation (draining into the sump). *This can be a problem if you have a setup with the sump under the tank.* This will almost guarantee an insufficient amount of room for the skimmer. A better location for the sump and skimmer is on the side of the tank. If you must have the sump under the tank, the skimmer will have to go on the side of the tank, and will have to be supported so it will be in the correct position. This will ensure proper drainage by gravity. *It is of equal importance for the skimmer to be very easily cleaned, disconnected, serviced, and reconnected.*

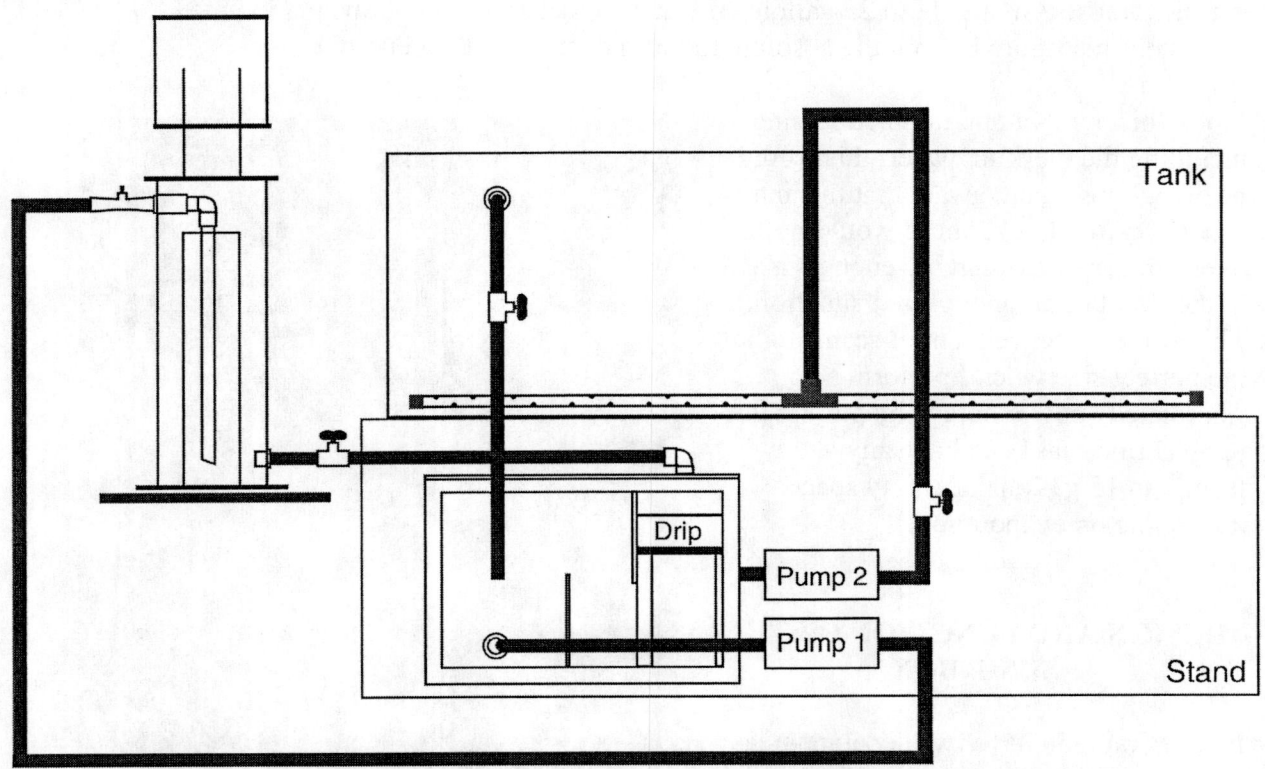

Note: Location of skimmer. Failure to have the skimmer in this location may result in improper operation. Plumbing connections are for illustration only.

The skimmer and prefilter are the only external mechanical filtering devices, and have to be cleaned regularly. If you pay close attention to the accessibility of these items when planning their location, maintenance will be much easier and therefore more frequent. This will enable you to keep a higher quality of water on a regular basis, without having to rely on unnatural methods that may affect the stability of the water.

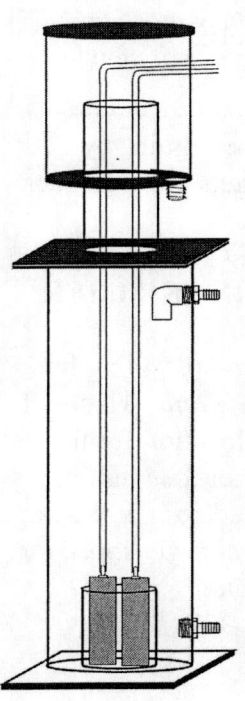

Chapter 12 contains a description of how to make your own sump, prefilter, and protein skimmer. Read and study the design and concepts. By doing this, you will have ideas that you can use or modify for your own setup. These concepts are most current, and are what should be used for best results in a reef setup.

THE PROTEIN SKIMMER

The heart of the modern reef external filter system is the protein skimmer. Make sure it is large enough to do the job. You cannot have too much skimming! Buy or make the largest one you can afford. Keep in mind: the larger your skimmer, the larger the skimmers pump will have to be. It should, however, be no larger than the main pump of the system.

> *The protein skimmer is the workhorse of your filtration system. Buy the best!*

A protein skimmer is a clear plastic cylinder, usually 4-6" in diameter and 24-38" tall. Water is directed into the column by a water pump. Inside the column fine air bubbles are introduced and mixed with the water. This is usually done with wooden air blocks placed at the bottom inside the column, and fed with a strong air pump. This type of skimmer is called "counter-current" or "air-driven," meaning that the water is pumped in at the top of the cylinder, and is directed downward at approximately a 45° angle. This makes the water swirl in the plastic column, while the fine air bubbles from the wooden air blocks rise to the top.

The bubbles drag water with them, rise to the top, and burst. Because there are dissolved proteins and wastes in the water, these too cling to the extremely small air bubbles, which rise and burst in the upper neck of the plastic column. A foam builds up in the upper neck of the plastic column, and overflows into a collection cup to be removed. This is also known as "foam fractioning," and has been used in water treatment facilities.

See Chapter 12 on the design of a protein skimmer.

Diagram 40

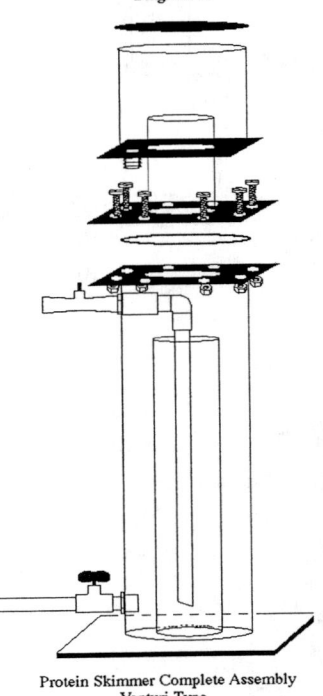

Protein Skimmer Complete Assembly
Venturi Type

A Venturi type of skimmer uses a Venturi air valve that is in line with the water being pumped into the skimmer. A Venturi eliminates the need for air pumps and blocks. It runs with a higher flow rate than counter-current systems, and therefore will need a stronger pump: one that is designed to operate under pressure, a "pressure pump." This type of pump is designed to force water through the Venturi valve (see pump description). The Venturi is considered to be more efficient and overall less expensive to operate than air-driven counter-current skimmers.

The tower type: There has been a revolutionary new design of skimmer on the market, which is neither Venturi nor counter-current. This new design is called a "downdraft" known by the model name E.T.S., for "Environmental Tower Scrubber." Water is pumped through a tall, narrow "tower" (approximately 2" wide), filled with plastic media balls. The water is under considerable pressure, and it gets forced down the small neck through the plastic media, with air pulled in from the top of the skimmer creating fine air bubbles. Proteins and waste products cling to the fine air bubbles accumulating in a collection neck, rise, and overflow. *This new dimension of skimming is extremely efficient and well worth considering, as* the *skimmer for your reef.*

All skimmers operate on water being pumped in at the top and draining out by gravity at the bottom. The bottom of the skimmer should be above the top of the sump, thereby using gravity to full advantage. Most should have control valves in line before and after the skimmer to insure proper water control and fine tuning of the skimmer.

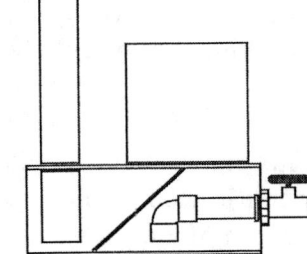

SKIMMER PUMPS

Here are some ideas on pumps.

1. Main pump, flow type: You want to have a turnover of water at least six times the volume of the tank per hour with the main pump. For example, in a 55-gallon tank the

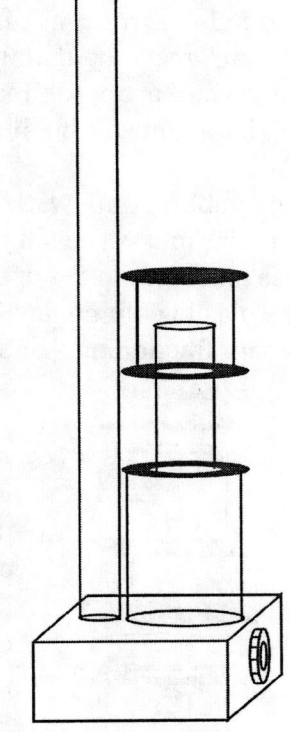

turnover should be 55 x 6 = 330 GPH. This would require a main pump in the range of 330 GPH. Also, remember to take the vertical pumping action (head) into account when selecting the main pump. As a general rule, I would also add 20% to the figure as compensation for the head pressure. In this case, 20% of 330 = 66. Adding that to the original 330, we get 396, or about 400 GPH. By adding this 20%, I am assured of the pump's capability. The main pump should be a flow pump, meaning it is designed to flow the water instead of having to force the water through something like a pressure pump. Also, I am not fond of submersible pumps, unless they are absolutely necessary in a particular situation. So, for a 55-gallon tank, we would use a 400 GPH main pump.

2. Skimmer pump: For a Venturi skimmer, you will want a pressure pump. This is needed to force the water through the Venturi valve. For a counter-current skimmer, you will want a flow pump, because pressure is not necessary in this design. You will have to be very careful when selecting a pump for a factory-built skimmer. Closely follow the manufacturer's recommendation of pump size! Skimmers are designed in such a way that the drain fitting is a certain size, and will only drain the water out so fast. I have found that valves are always needed on both sides of the skimmer. This gives you the advantage of being able to fine tune the skimmer, which is definitely necessary. If you make your own skimmer, the drain fitting can be larger than would be found on a factory-built skimmer. By having a large drain fitting controlled by a valve, you can increase the amount of water for the skimmer to process. Of course, this doesn't mean you can have a small skimmer with a large drain hole and expect to remove waste properly. However, having a sizable drain fitting will give you more control over the rates of drainage and water flow.

In this example of a 400 GPH main pump for a 55-gallon tank, the skimmer pump should be 400 GPH or slightly less. Let's keep in mind that if the main pump is 400 GPH, the water coming out of the tank will flow at 400 GPH. This water will drain by gravity into the chamber on the "dirty" side of the sump, providing water to the skimmer at 400 GPH. The skimmer pump will take this water and push it through the skimmer. It will then drain from the skimmer through the prefilter and accumulate for the main pump to return it to the tank. The separating panel in the sump is designed in such a way that any imbalance that may occur in water flow rates will be compensated for by water overflowing the separating panel. This may sometimes allow some water to pass by without being filtered (due to too much water in the system, or a power outage). The separating panel will extend upward from the bottom of the sump, usually 2/3 of the height of the sump. This will allow for adequate separation of the water, while still allowing full capacity of the sump in the event of a power outage.

THE PREFILTER

The prefilter is incorporated on the "clean" side of the sump box (Diagram 6). First, we need a drip plate to disperse the water evenly onto the prefilter material. The drip plate can be easily custom-made with Plexiglas to fit your sump box (see Chapter 12 on fabricating a drip plate; also see Photo 31).

My setup for the prefilter ("clean") side of the sump is as follows:

- I have four pieces of 1-1/2" PVC pipe placed vertically in the "clean" side of the sump.
- On top of these "support" pipes, there is a horizontal piece of eggcrate approximately the same size as the drip plate.
- The prefilter material rests on top of the eggcrate, and the drip plate rests on top of the prefilter material. See Diagram 6.

> *The sump box will need two sides: one "dirty" (from the tank), and the other "clean" (from the skimmer and prefilter)*

My sump has a removable top cover that is in two halves. It is only necessary to remove the prefilter side often, so the other side supports the skimmer. There is a bulkhead fitting through the center of the cover of the sump box above the prefilter. The skimmer drain is connected to this fitting, which hits the center of the drip plate. Water then goes through the drip plate, through the prefilter material, and "drips" into the bottom ("clean" side) of the sump box. Here there are two bulkhead fittings: one goes to the main pump and the other goes to an emergency drain hose with a shut-off valve (this is the lowest point of the system, and if necessary it could be completely drained through this hose).

From the drain on the skimmer, there is a control valve connected to a flexible clear hose that simply "slips into" the bulkhead fitting for the prefilter, on top of the sump box. This "slipping in" action allows for easy re-routing of the flexible hose from the skimmer when you remove the top of the sump box to access and change the prefilter.

The setup for the "dirty side" of the sump is as follows.

- There is a bulkhead fitting through the top cover.
- A plumbing connection is made from the tank's overflow.
- There is a large, 1-1/2", plastic gate valve to control the flow and to shut off the water completely when needed (water change or sump disconnect).
- On the inside of the cover, there is a section of flexible hose connected from the inside of the bulkhead fitting, going to the bottom of the sump.
- Here the water will collect and feed the skimmer pump.
- The flexible hose is needed to direct the water away from the inlet to the skimmer pump.
- There can be quite a bit of water turbulence draining from the tank in this area, and by directing the water away from the inlet, you do not run the risk of air getting sucked into the skimmer pump, causing erratic flow rates.

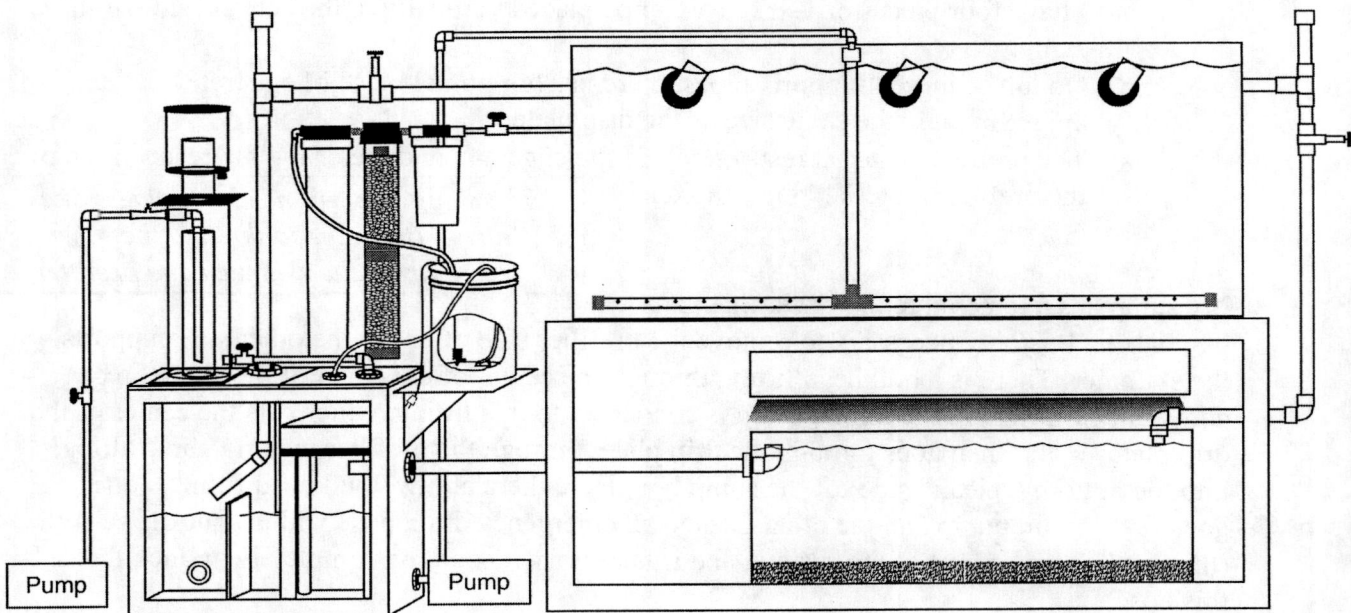

Note: *The setup below shows a refugia connected in line.*

I feel strongly about using a sump box. This is a very important area of the enclosed reef system. The main reasons for its importance is:

- It is external. You can make attachments to it for water from the tank.
- There can be a drain for the entire system (since this is the lowest point of the system).
- It is a convenient place to observe evaporation level and add make-up water when needed.
- It is also a convenient place to add salt to raise the salinity.
- You can have a prefilter, which can be changed easily and often.
- You can mount your skimmers on the top of the sump box to ensure that gravity will work in your favor.
- You will have a ready and constant supply of water coming from the reef to feed your skimmers.
- You can have valves to regulate the water flow.
- This is a great area for a considerable amount of turbulence, which will add oxygen to the water.

You can do all these things without disturbing the livestock!

NOT DISTURBING THE REEF

I believe it is important not to disrupt the livestock unnecessarily, and to be able to control the system totally, without having to make adjustments in or on top of the tank, or having to put your hands in the water except very occasionally. I am also of the belief that once you place the rock, coral, and livestock in the tank, it is best to leave it alone. Do not move items around unnecessarily to try to get the "look" that is just right. They should be positioned at the beginning, and then left alone except for minor adjustments. After you have left things alone for several months, you will see the reason for this suggestion. The coraline algae will have spread, corals and clams will have attached themselves to the rock, smaller corals will appear, and basically the enclosed reef will have balanced itself out and will begin thriving in its new location—that is, your living room.

WATER TURBULENCE IN THE SUMP

There should be a lot of water turbulence going on in the sump, caused by the high flow rate draining out of the tank and the trickling effect from the drip plate. This in my opinion is highly desirable, although it can be a bit noisy. When I think of the ocean, the pounding surf, the powerful tidal currents, and the lunar gravitational pull, I am reminded that the water is constantly fast-moving, turbulent, and relentlessly pounding. This is the action of the sea; so I am pleased to provide as much turbulence as possible, although the turbulence in my sump is minimal compared to that in nature. This turbulence can really only take place in the sump box. I believe the sound of water flowing is a necessary price to pay for having a healthy reef in our homes.

TYPES OF OVERFLOWS

I prefer a tank that is drilled through the top back of the tank. Wood tanks are easy to drill yourself with a common "hole saw" of the correct diameter for the bulkhead fittings (keep this in mind when calculating the cost compared to a glass tank). Glass will cost about $15 per hole to drill, and is best left to a professional glass company (they have the correct drill bits and the experience). I also prefer at least three holes (two for overflow and one for return) on the top back, as opposed to one on the bottom with a wall (dam type overflow, see Diagram 9). I somehow never felt comfortable with a hole through the bottom of the tank: I have visions of coming home to see a waterless tank with all the livestock high and dry. People use the dam type all the time, but I personally never felt totally confident with a fitting through the bottom of the tank.

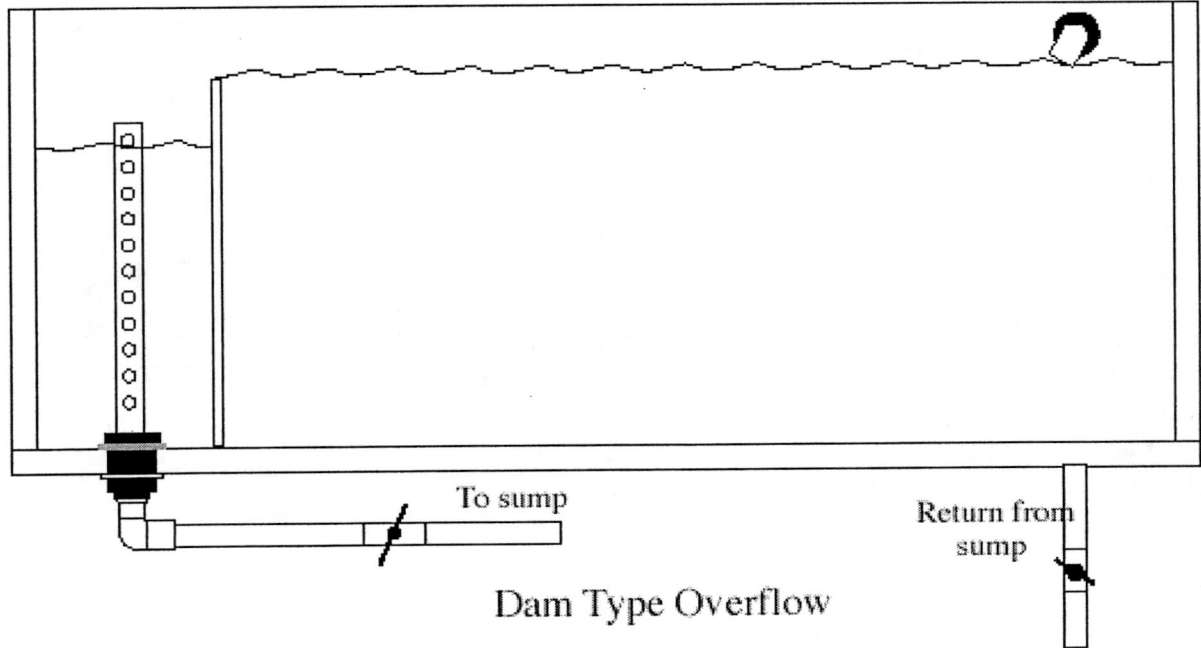

To sump

Return from sump

Dam Type Overflow

CONTROLLING THE WATER FLOW

I would have the overflows drilled through the upper rear right, left, and centered. A bulkhead fitting installed a 90° PVC or gray schedule 80 plumbing fitting for the actual overflow water from the tank. Connected outside of the tank with either hard PVC or clear, flexible, vinyl tubing attached to a shutoff valve before going into the sump box.

This will allow you to control the flow of water from the tank into the sump. It will also let you shut off the water from the tank when performing water changes (This will allow you to fill the tank to the top and shut off the water, keeping the tank completely filled when doing a water change, and will result in less live rock being exposed to air). You could also shut off the water, disconnect the plumbing attachments, and take the sump outside to clean it thoroughly.

As you can see from the author's sump box photo, there are two sides or chambers in the sump box. For simplicity, I call one side "clean" and the other "dirty." This refers to the water coming through the box. The "dirty" water comes from the tank and goes to the "dirty" side of the sump. On this side, there is a bulkhead fitting with tubing and a shut-off, feeding the pump for the protein skimmer. The "dirty" water goes directly to the skimmer. The water coming out of the skimmer goes to the "clean" side and onto a drip plate for even dispersion onto the prefilter.

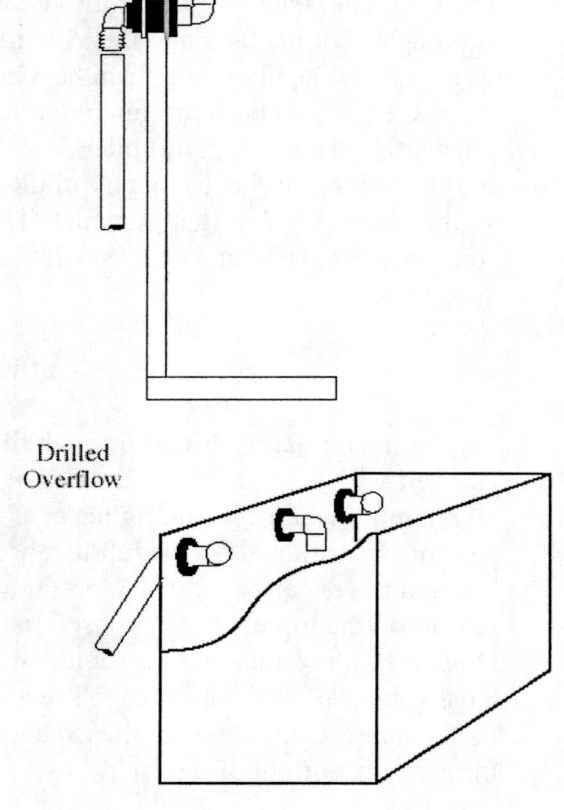

Drilled Overflow

Close up of a thru wall bulkhead

MATERIAL TO USE FOR PREFILTER; CLEANING THE PREFILTER

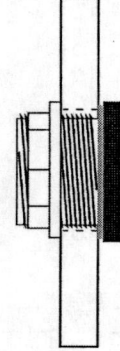

The most convenient prefilter material is Marineland #100 filter pads. This is affordable, and can be cut to fit most any size that you would need. The prefilter material must be cleaned or changed every week. You can clean it by rinsing it out thoroughly in the sink until it looks as it did when you put it in. You can do this several times before the material will become "out of shape." Or, if you are a real fanatic and don't want to bother with this rinsing action, you can just throw it away and replace it with a new piece (which you just so happen to have in your stock supplies).

Remember, you will be doing this every week, and even though prefilter material is inexpensive, it can add up, like everything else. It would be more practical to rinse the pads (clean them with running water), up to four times. Figure on replacing the pad material once a month.

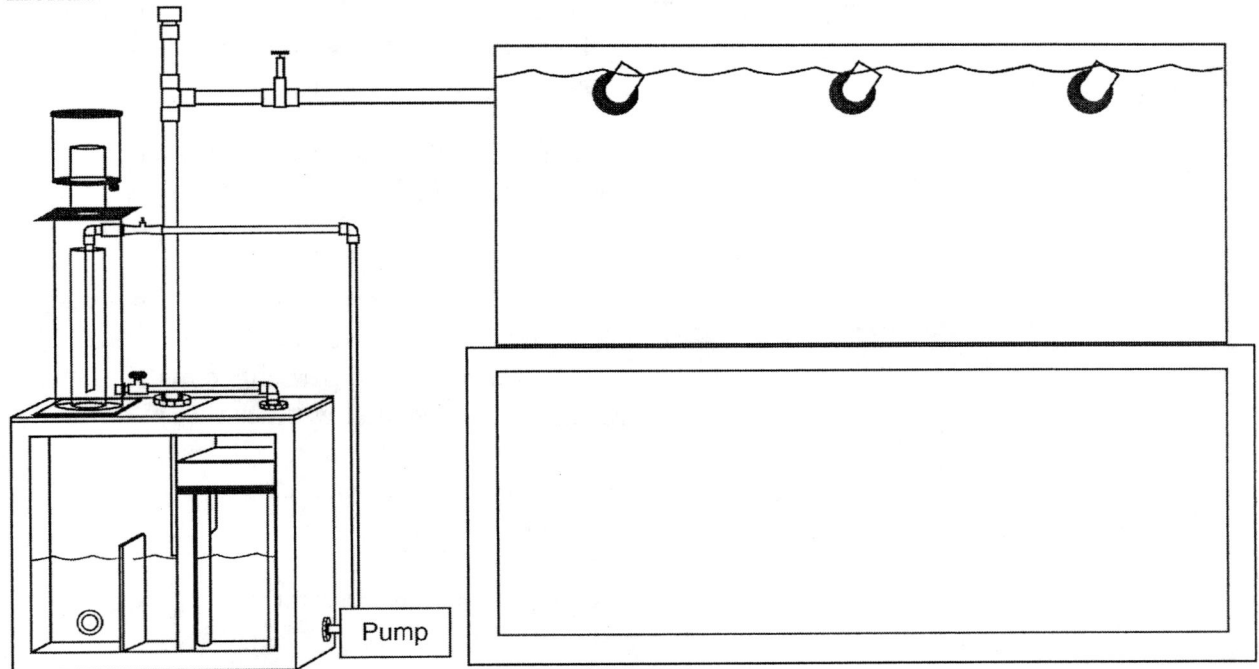

An important reminder: When you remove the prefilter pad, have a clean plastic bowl handy to catch the dripping water. If you don't, you will "wring" the pad in the sump, dislodging all the particles you have been "trapping." This will defeat the purpose. So, have a clean plastic bowl nearby to catch the dripping water and particles. Take this to the sink, and dispose of the water there.

NOT ALLOWING THE PREFILTER TO GO BIOLOGICAL

By cleaning and changing the prefilter material weekly, you prevent the pad from going "biological" (harboring aerobic bacteria). With this method, the prefilter removes particulate matter from the water and is cleaned on a regular basis.

The goal is to keep all the biological activity restricted to the live rock. The inhabitants of the tank produce waste on and around the live rock. The nitrifying and denitrifying bacteria are encouraged to colonize on the rock. They break the waste products down right there on the rock, and what remains is waste sediment, which will be removed with water changes.

The prefilter pad provides an especially attractive, oxygen-rich environment for aerobic bacteria. If the prefilter were allowed to go biological, bacteria would colonize on the filter pad as well as on the live rock in the tank. Over time, the entire tank would adjust to having two colonies of aerobic bacteria at work: one on the rock, the other in the prefilter. Then when the prefilter pad was cleaned (finally), killing all the bacteria in the filter, the tank would suddenly have fewer bacteria than it had become used to. The result would be an imbalance from which the tank would need time to recover, through a mini-cycle of ammonia and nitrite.

THE COMMON DENOMINATOR: REMOVING

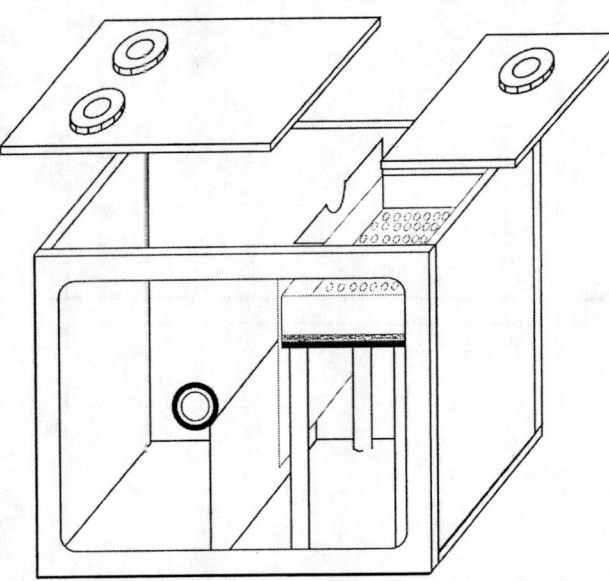

Summary of modern filtration

The debris, sediment, and waste products that accumulate on the rock and the bottom of the tank will be removed with regular water changes.

You probably have noticed that the common denominator in all these concepts is *removing*.

- The protein skimmer forms a foam waste from the water, and the foam is *removed*.
- The prefilter traps particulate matter, is regularly cleaned, and waste is *removed*.
- The sediment that accumulates on the rock is *removed* by water changes.

So we have a constant removing process going on at all times in our enclosed reef.

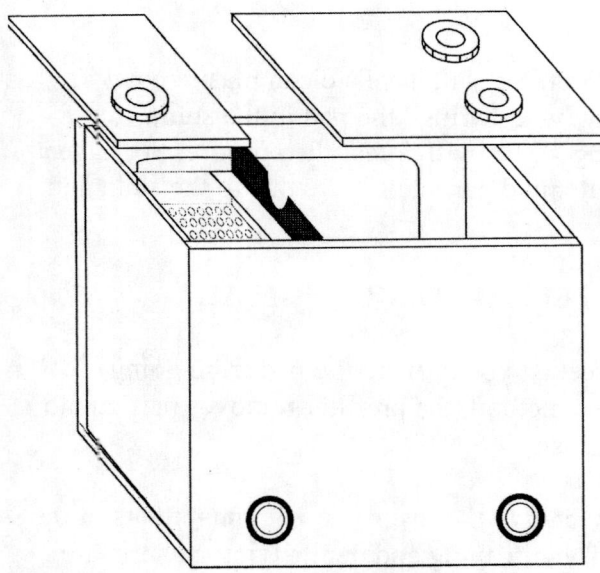

We want to isolate the sediment, leaving no room for areas that would trap waste for any period of time—one week for the prefilter, two weeks for water changes. We keep the water flowing with absolutely minimal restriction.

Water changes should ideally be done every two weeks. Some people do them every three weeks, while others go as long as a month. I would strongly recommend the two-week cycle. Although this is more work, the immediate as well as long-term benefits justify this schedule. We have valuable and delicate specimens that require optimum water quality.

WHY A TRICKLE FILTER IS NO LONGER USED

The standard method of "purifying" the water for most aquariums has been to use a filter that is separate from the tank. This device, with which I'm sure you are familiar, is a container holding material that (1) traps particles from the water, and (2) has a sufficient surface area for nitrifying bacteria to colonize. This has usually been an enclosed type or "canister" filter.

A more advanced design was the "trickle filter." This is an open style, relatively large, Plexiglas box containing a drip plate, prefilter, and spherical-type plastic medium. The drip plate would evenly disperse the water onto the prefilter material to trap particles. This in turn would trickle through the plastic medium, where the nitrifying bacteria would colonize and purify by nitrification. With all this "trickling" taking place, oxygen will get pulled into the water, ensuring that the aerobic bacteria remain aerobic.

The trickle filter is an excellent filtering system for fish-only tanks, where you need a large external area for the bacteria to colonize. Also, the open design of the trickle filter allows easy access to the prefilter material. These filters have been used on reef tanks, but most reef hobbyists realize that the bacteria will colonize any porous substrate (the live rock), and that oxygen is provided by protein skimming. The primary concern of reef keepers using trickle filters is that particles and debris get trapped and accumulate in the plastic medium. This accumulated, nutrient-rich debris then provides a food source for micro-algae.

A trickle filter on a reef system would inhibit bacteria from colonizing on the live rock, by maintaining a high flow rate of water through the media and providing oxygen to that immediate area. This would encourage the bacteria to colonize on the plastic media instead of on the rock.

> *Plastic media can trap waste, causing high nutrient levels—a food source for micro-algae*

If the plastic media were ever cleaned, the bacteria would die, sending the reef into an ammonia/nitrite cycle. This may cause death of the more fragile species of the reef, and at worst could cause a domino effect that would involve all but the hardiest specimens.

If the plastic media were never cleaned, the accumulated waste products in the plastic media would at some point guarantee a severe micro-algae outbreak that could not be controlled.

> *Eliminating external media encourages bacteria to colonize the live rock*

REMOVING THE PLASTIC MEDIA

Faced with these two outcomes of employing plastic media, and realizing that live rock is an optimum substrate for aerobic and anaerobic bacteria, many advanced reef hobbyists simply did away with the plastic media. Those who had trickle filters with plastic media in operation would remove small amounts at a time (approximately 10% at every prefilter change once a week), ensuring that an ammonia/nitrite cycle would not occur, and thereby naturally relocating the bacteria to the live rock.

When I started in the hobby, it was recommended to have a trickle filter as described above. As time went on, even though I had live rock and sand and purified tap water, algae eventually became a problem. When I described this phenomenon to a friend, he shared his knowledge of plastic media and recommended the gradual removal of the plastic media. Slowly, the algae problem diminished in my tank. I will admit I was skeptical at first, but he was correct. This has become standard practice with almost all advanced reef keepers.

USING A TRICKLE FILTER AS A SUMP BOX

In perspective, the recommended filtration is still basically a trickle filter, without the media. We can use the box for a sump (to hold and control the water), and the drip plate and prefilter to provide their benefits. *The concept is to change the prefilter once a week, to keep it from going "biological" (which could possibly lead to a small cycle), and to confine and remove the nutrient particles.*

If you are currently using a trickle filter, you may be able to use it as a sump. It would have to be large enough to accommodate all the water needed for this type of method. Also, plumbing inlets and outlets may have to be added for feeds and drains to and from the protein skimmers, and possibly a main drain for the system. Previous diagrams illustrate the concept of a sump box with a prefilter and the location of the skimmers in relation to the sump box, as well as the relation of the sump box to the tank.

LOCATION OF THE SUMP BOX

It is my opinion that the sump box should be located below the tank, at least halfway down on the tank. There is no limit for how low the box can be. Just keep in mind that the higher you have to pump the water up to the tank, the less effective the pump will be. This is known as "head pressure." Pumps are rated at 3 feet of head or 6 feet of head, and so on. This means the pump is rated to pump up to that height. Of course, if you have less restriction (less vertical pressure, pumping upward), the flow rate will be enhanced.

| *Always use gravity to your full advantage!* | The idea of having the sump at about midway on the tank's water level will ensure that

gravity will drain water from the tank into the sump. In this range, the pump will be more effective (not being lower than it has to be). Also, the placement of the sump will dictate the proper placement of the skimmer. Almost all skimmers operate with water being pumped in, and water being drained out. Draining of water is done with gravity, meaning the skimmer has to be higher than the area you are draining into. This would be above the sump.

NITRATE BUILDUP WHEN USING A TRICKLE FILTER

Nitrate buildup is another drawback of using a trickle filter. Until recently, nearly all tanks used a relatively large "trickle filter." This filter, as you probably know, was filled with a substantial amount of inert media to encourage beneficial bacterial growth. The water was directed to flow onto a drip plate through a prefilter floss medium and over small plastic balls, cubes, or rolled floss material that would become colonized with aerobic bacteria.

These bacteria would perform the nitrification process by converting ammonia to nitrite and nitrite to nitrate. The idea was that by having a large external area on which the bacteria could form, one could increase the capacity of the tank and still do a good job of filtering the water. This to some extent is true, but the end product of this type of system is nitrate buildup.

Nitrate in significant amounts can be tolerated by most fish, especially when it accumulates slowly (as it does in a trickle filter system). However, in a reef environment we have other specimens in addition to fish, such as invertebrates, coral, and delicate microorganisms that *are not* tolerant of nitrate. For this reason, it is the recommended goal to keep nitrate at the lowest possible level in a reef tank.

The nitrate is usually managed by performing regular water changes. This process of doing water changes will remove some nitrate, while diluting the remainder. It will still leave some measurable nitrate. Although the nitrate reading will be much less immediately after each water change, there will be a slow and steady rise of nitrate levels over time. The nitrate will keep accumulating, requiring more frequent water changes or requiring that a larger percentage of the water be changed at a time, in order to reduce the increasing levels of nitrate.

This can go on for some time. After a while, the situation will become unmanageable. It will require the aquarist to take relatively drastic measures—basically, taking the tank down to some degree and reacclimating the fish in new water. This is stressful on the fish and the aquarist.

Summary:
The Drawbacks of Using a
Conventional Trickle Filter on a Reef Tank

- **Media will trap waste nutrients for micro-algae, leading to diminished water quality.**
- **The bacteria will colonize both the media and the live rock instead of only the rock (which is considered a more natural system).**
- **At some point the media will be cleaned, eliminating a considerable population of bacteria and causing an ammonia/nitrite cycle.**
- **Denitrification will not occur on plastic media.**

MANAGING NITRATE IN A REEF SYSTEM

Very fortunately, one of the benefits of reef keeping is that nitrification and denitrification can take place simultaneously in the reef tank. This is done in the live rock or living sand filter, or in a separate denitrification filter.

The most current technique being used is the absence of external filter medium, such as the plastic balls and other material normally used in a trickle filter. It is believed by most advanced marine reef aquarists that this external filtering media is not only unnecessary, but in fact is an area that can cause problems by trapping waste products, and providing a food source for micro-algae, leading to diminished water quality.

For denitrification to occur, you need:

- 1.5 - 1.75 pounds per gallon of live rock, or thick sand substrate
- Photosynthetic livestock
- Proper lighting (3 - 5 watts per gallon, 9 hours a day)
- Correct water flow (the volume of the tank, 6 times an hour)

FILTRATION: NECESSARY COMPONENTS

The following is an overview of the components for a modern reef filter.

1. Live rock, 1.5 to no more than 1.75 pounds per gallon.
2. Large protein skimmer capable of turning over water in the tank 6 times per hour.

3. Easily removable drip plate and prefilter material to clean or change once a week.
4. Large main pump capable of turning over water in the tank 6 times an hour.
5. Large sump box providing considerable turbulence, and capable of holding all the overflow of water from the tank, including the "working water."
6. Denitrification areas (see Chapters 6 and 8).
7. Proper lighting (see Chapter 5).
8. Photosynthetic livestock.

FILTRATION: UNNECESSARY COMPONENTS

The following are the components I would *not* use on a reef tank:

1. Canister filters. (They are inefficient, difficult to regulate, and difficult to service regularly; they also trap and hold waste.)
2. Plastic media. (They trap waste.)
3. Hang-on-the-back prefilter boxes. (They provide insufficient water flow and rely on a self-starting siphon; the foam block accumulates unseen waste inside.)
4. Hang-on-the-back protein skimmer. (It will provide insufficient performance unless the tank is smaller than 55 gallons.)
5. Live rock exceeding 1.75 pounds per gallon. (This can cause serious problems from too much "stacking," with the result that crevices will contain unseen waste and will be inaccessible for cleaning, and light will not get to some areas of the rock.)
6. Foam block material. (This accumulates unseen nutrient waste inside.)
7. Incorrect light bulbs. (See Chapter 5 on lighting.)
8. Incorrect substrate sand material. (Use only material commercially available for reef systems, or "live sand" from a retailer or wholesaler. Local "beach sand" or "home improvement" sand can introduce contaminants including "silica," which would encourage algae growth.)
9. Hang-on-the-back filters. (Unless the tank is "miniature," these devices are insufficient and will cause more harm than good.)
10. Small protein skimmer. (Have the proper size or a size larger than needed. *Double the factory rating*. For example, a skimmer rated for a 100-gallon tank would perform well on a 55-gallon tank).
11. Ultraviolet sterilizer . (These are definitely not needed on a reef: they are unnatural, and they would kill desirable organisms and bacteria.)
12. Medications. (Use the "natural" approach; see Chapter 9.)
13. Ozone, CO_2. (These are unnecessary, costly, unpredictable, and risky.)
14. Submersible pumps. (Use only if absolutely necessary. They are inconvenient to maintain, they can clog, and they may provide restricted water flow.)
15. Protein skimmers that do not come apart for complete cleaning.

Components of a counter current skimmer

As you can see, it is not only important what to use; it is just as important what *not* to use. Some items are unnecessary, some will cause problems by trapping waste, and others will just be insufficient to perform properly. Be careful to buy the best product for the job. Your reef and the livestock depend on what you will use for the constant filtering and removing of waste, to provide the highest quality of water naturally.

DENITRIFICATION

Denitrification is the last step of natural water purification by bacteria. This is where nitrate is converted to nitrogen gas. This is a completely natural occurrence in the wild, and it is happening all over the world as you read this. The earth and its living organisms produce millions of tons of nitrogen gas every year. Without denitrification (the conversion of nitrate into nitrogen gas, which is then released into the atmosphere), waste products would accumulate at an alarming rate, endangering all life forms. Of course, nature would not let this happen. One of its solutions to removing accumulated natural waste is anaerobic denitrifying bacteria.

As I am a hobbyist, not a scientist, I will not try to give you the exact chemical breakdown of the denitrification process, nor do I personally feel it is necessary or helpful to understand endosymbiotic bacteria and the processing of nucleic acids to nucleotide ions, then to molecules, etc. In this hobby we are lucky to find a salt mix without nitrate or phosphate, or hermetically sealed retail products, or a listing of *exactly* what is contained in the products we are buying; most of us don't need to be on the lookout for nitrogenous organic molecules. If you feel it is necessary to understand the exact biochemistry of this or any other naturally occurring process in reef keeping, I am sure there are plenty of marine chemistry books available on the subject, and I would applaud your pursuit of this information.

I can only try to explain how I personally have succeeded with denitrification in my reef tanks and what practical knowledge I have found to be helpful. *One of my beliefs is that we can only have what we can get; namely, live rock and livestock from the wild. About live rock:*

- It contains complete, naturally occurring biological activity that proceeds and processes, whether we are concerned with its chemical makeup or not.
- It is not missing any chemical additives that I am aware of, which could be added with certainty to enhance its natural biological activity.
- These biological processes happen naturally all around us at all times, without our concern for the exact chemicals involved, or their interactions.
- Buy quality live rock in the recommended amounts, set it up, cycle, and then leave it alone.
- ***The live rock is, by itself, biologically complete and extremely complex!***

Bacteria that are "anaerobic" thrive in the absence of oxygen. To have a truly successful reef tank, you must have conditions for denitrification to occur. This will take place primarily inside the live rock. This substrate, being porous and coming from an actual reef, is the perfect material for the nitrification and denitrification process to take place.

Nitrification is performed by "aerobic" bacteria (needing oxygen), called "nitrosomonas" and "nitrobacter." These bacteria process ammonia to nitrite, and nitrite to nitrate. Visualize the live rock in the tank, and the waste occurring in close proximity to the rock. The nitrification process occurs right in the tank environment (the live rock).

> *Nitrogen gas can be observed as small bubbles forming on the live rock and glass*

Here, also in the same area of the tank, nitrate is being produced by the nitrification process. Nitrate accumulates in the water, the rock is in the water, and because the aerobic bacteria have consumed most of the oxygen on the outer area of the rock, this leaves the core of the rock void of oxygen, and creates conditions for denitrification.

To have denitrification take place, you need:

> *This type of denitrification takes place inside the live rock*

1. Areas with lack of oxygen
2. A surface for the bacteria to colonize
3. A food source (nitrate)
4. An open area for the nitrogen gas to be released into the atmosphere (the top of the tank).

The nitrification process is:

- Ammonia to nitrite
- Nitrite to nitrate

Then denitrification:

- Nitrate to nitrogen gas

The nitrogen gas is then released into the atmosphere, and reduced nitrate levels are recorded in the enclosed reef system.

SPECIFIC AMOUNT OF LIVE ROCK TO USE

It is very important to have the correct amount of live rock. (The survey shows an average of 1.25 lbs. per gallon) Some people have gotten carried away with the idea that if some is good, more must be better. This is not true! As with all concepts of reef keeping, balance is very important here. If you don't have enough live rock, natural internal filtration will be ineffective, because the bacterial colony on the rock will be inadequate to perform the task. Or, if you have too much live rock, you will have dead spots on it. These are areas of live rock that are covered with other rock, blocking some surfaces from light and water circulation. These dead spots are likely to trap waste, sediment, uneaten food, and many other products you would otherwise remove regularly. When waste products accumulate in these areas, they will be a sure food source for micro-algae, which will thrive, causing diminished water quality.

This is referred to as "stacking" the rock, and it should be avoided at all costs.

The correct amount of live rock to have in a reef tank is between a minimum of 1 pound per gallon and a maximum of 1.75 pounds per gallon. Somewhere in the middle, like 1.35 pounds per gallon, would be ideal. Do not exceed 1.75, unless you want to turn some quality live rock into base rock, which would take at least a year to recover and resemble what it was before other rock was stacked on top of it.

I have met many people who have jammed as much live rock into their tanks as would physically fit, in an effort to create a natural system. The only result they got was a natural disaster. Two-thirds of the rock died. The water had so much nutrients in it that it could not be reused. They had to start all over again, rinsing all the rock, buying another tank to use the excess rock, or trying to sell the rock back to the store (as base rock). They learned that when it comes to amounts of live rock, more is definitely not better. Again, do not exceed 1.75 pounds per gallon.

> *Using excessive live rock will create*
> *substantial problems !*

Many of these people had no idea that they were using too much rock. Their retailers suggested to them that it was necessary to have as much rock as would fit into the tank, in an effort to have natural nitrification and denitrification taking place. As you can see, this is incorrect. The problem manifested itself with uncontrollable micro-algae. Everyone consulted was unaware that the problem was excessive amounts of live rock. Everything else seemed normal—test readings, etc. Unfortunately, there are no test kits for high nutrient levels that accumulate and persist despite water changes, adequate skimming, prefilter changes, etc. The fact was that the stacked rock was trapping waste and sediment. This was going on unseen, and the water became extremely rich with nutrients, providing a food source for micro-algae.

My approach has been to use eggcrate to provide support for the rock, giving the appearance of a solid arrangement of live rock (see Diagrams 3 and 4 in the next chapter). With this method, you be able to use less rock with a more dramatic effect. Also, you will find that because of the way the rock sits on the eggcrate, most of the debris falls to the unrestricted bottom area of the tank. Then if you locate the spraybar at the bottom rear of the tank, where it will pump water toward the front of the tank, most of the waste will get pushed to the bottom front of the tank, where you will be able to see it and remove it when you perform water changes.

MAINTENANCE SCHEDULE

DATE	pH	AMMONIA	NITRITE	NITRATE	KH	CALCIUM	SALINITY	ACTIONS / COMMENTS

Chapter 8

Setting Up a Reef Tank

Chapter goal:
To direct the reader to the most efficient method of arranging live rock in
the tank; also to discuss using live sand

SETTING UP THE REEF

The reef will primarily consist of live rock. When considering placement of the rock without "stacking" (covering other rock), my personal choice has been to use black eggcrate material, along with a spraybar at the bottom rear of the tank, which pushes to the front of the tank any sediment that falls off the rock.

I have always been concerned with waste sediment accumulating in areas of the tank that are not accessible (the bottom, and particularly the rear bottom). These are usually dead spots that have little or no water circulation. For this reason, I personally feel it important to have a powerful pump connected to a spraybar with holes strategically located on it, so there are virtually no dead spots. This way, debris gets pushed to the front of the tank, where it can be seen and removed.

DRAWBACK OF USING EGGCRATE

Some people feel the eggcrate gives an unnatural effect. I would respond that they have not really tried it. It gives a wonderful display of the rock, and you can cut holes through it to give the appearance of caves. The fish swim through these holes, giving the appearance of a natural reef. It is also easily cut, and can be fastened with common cable ties.

One major drawback of all eggcrate is that if you have an all-glass tank, you will see the back of the eggcrate from outside the tank. The only remedy for this is to attach a covering to the glass, blocking off the view of the eggcrate. I feel this is a small price to pay for the enormous benefits gained from using this system of setting up live rock.

Blocking the back and part of the sides actually has one benefit: you will not get lighting from outside the tank that could possibly encourage micro-algae.

> *Black eggcrate is an ideal framework for live rock*

COST AND LOCATING EGGCRATE

One other important suggestion is to use *black* eggcrate. This is not really a common item in most home improvement centers. White is

> *The only critics of black eggcrate are those who have not used it*

usually the common color, and this would be unsightly in the reef. You will have to scout around the Yellow Pages to find a plastic supplier who will have black eggcrate. This is not as uncommon an item as you would think, and when you find a good supplier you will be amazed at the selection of material available. Expect to pay a little more for black than white. A 2' x 4' section of regular duty black will run about $9. This is a small price to pay for an item that will make a great framework for your live rock.

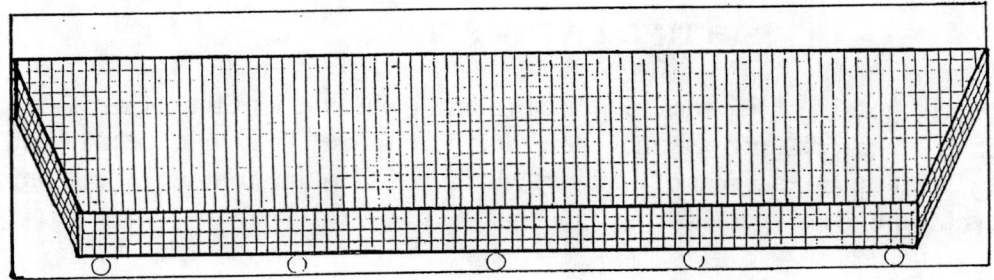

Diagram 3

When the eggcrate has been set up in the reef environment for some time, you will observe all kinds of life forms attaching themselves to this material, including pink purple coraline algae. It will become part of the reef (see Diagram 3; also see Chapter 10 for a more detailed explanation of using all-eggcrate).

> *Using eggcrate with a spraybar pushes waste to the front of the tank to be removed*

SUBSTRATE MATERIAL

One other item of concern in using this method is the substrate. Although it would be ideal not to have any bottom material restricting the sediment from being pushed to the front of the tank, I feel that some sand gives a more natural look and provides a better environment for the creatures that would normally forage on sand. Therefore I have chosen to have some bottom material. It is minimal, a 1/2" layer at most, mainly in the front and sides of the tank. It gets vacuumed and re dispersed when I do a water change. Because I have a spraybar constantly pushing sediment to the front, it is natural for the sand to shift in that direction between water changes.

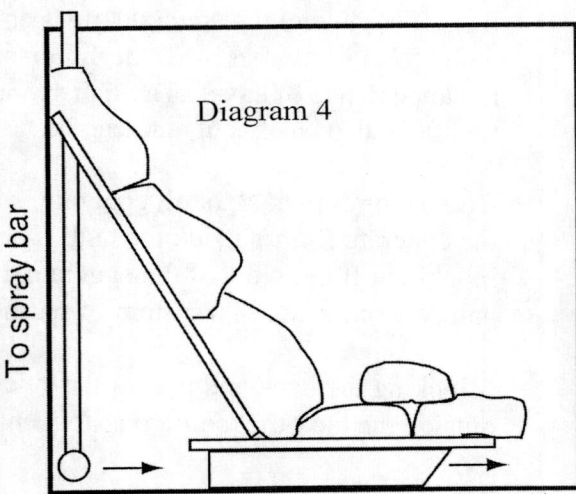

Diagram 4

To spray bar

I have used both approaches. When I began, I was very adamant about not using any bottom material at all. I wanted to see the waste, so it could be removed. As time passed, I began seriously to consider adding some sand material to enhance the look of the reef, while also providing a beneficial, natural material for my bottom-dwelling creatures.

> *Although sand substrate will restrict the flow of sediment, the benefits of using a 1/4"-1/3" layer outweigh the drawbacks*

The sand itself can also provide a small amount of denitrification, although there will only be a very thin layer of it, approximately 1/4" to 1/2" (mainly to cover the bottom). Some denitrification will take place in the sand, because it is very porous. Just as with live rock, oxygen will get used up on the outer layer of the grains of sand; then the inner core can harbor denitrifying bacteria and be in close proximity to waste products. The benefits of having some substrate (in my opinion) outweigh the drawbacks, namely that it will be a little harder to trap and restrict waste. Keep in mind that this thin layer of sand should be moved around and cleaned regularly. This will eliminate dead spots where sediment will accumulate.

LIVE SAND ALL-SAND SUBSTRATE

So far I have discussed a thin layer of covering substrate and its benefits regarding an all-eggcrate setup. Let's consider a reef tank with a live sand filter. First of all, I have both setups, and I will try to give you the picture of my results, both for and against. If you have seen both setups, you may have realized they are two distinctly different-looking tanks! For a description of live sand, see "Fabricating a Live Sand Filter,"

> *Using live sand or all live rock will result in two distinctly different-looking tanks*

AMOUNT AND SIZE OF LIVE ROCK NEEDED

The live sand tank looks more "natural," with a thick layer of sand bottom material (1-1/2" to 3", depending on the tank size). It looks more like the ocean floor that we are all familiar with, although with a live sand filter (because of its design and requirements), you will use less live rock (about 1 pound per gallon). Also, the pieces of live rock should be very thin, long, or wide. This is because you will have to move the rock from time to time, in order to clean the sand under and behind it. By having pieces that are very thin, long, or wide, you will make this job much easier. This is a necessary approach in my view, when using an all-sand bottom.

THE DISADVANTAGES OF ALL-SAND BOTTOM: WASTE ACCUMULATION

As you can see, one drawback is that the live rock will have to be moved around in order properly to clean areas where waste will accumulate, and to aerate the top layer of sand

> *If you use an all-sand bottom, the live rock will have to be moved when cleaning, in order to be thorough*

under and at the edges of the rock. Also, by moving the rock, you may damage the life forms that are growing or beginning to grow on the rock. In addition, corals or anemones may have to be temporarily relocated, and sand grains may accidentally get dropped into them. This can be disruptive to these delicate creatures, and extra care should be used when cleaning the sand around them.

These are primary concerns if you plan to have an all-sand bottom. You may not be able to have as many corals or anemones as you would like,

> *Waste will accumulate in corners and hidden areas*

or as many as your tank could hold, unless you are willing to assume the risk that will come from having to move them around from time to time when you clean the sand.

I am sure there are many reef keepers who will not move the rock around to clean the sand in difficult-to-reach areas. They would scoff at a suggestion that they should move the rock and possibly disturb the delicate invertebrates. I would ask, how do they plan to remove the sediment waste that is sure to accumulate in certain difficult-to-reach, sometimes unseen areas? The idea of using a powerhead pump to blow out the waste from behind the rock, sending a flurry of sediment through the water, is in my opinion unthinkable.

> *Moving the live rock will disturb the livestock in the tank*

Remember, we are trying to remove the waste sediment, not simply dislodge it and spread it around in the tank, to settle in other areas. One other approach others may have is to clean carefully around the invertebrates, and where the rock contacts the sand. My reply would be, you can be careful a few times; however, on regular intervals (water changes every two weeks), this would not be practical. Here, as always, we want to think of maintenance on a long-term basis. It should be thorough, convenient, practical, and easy to perform. The easier it is to do, the more enthusiastically it will be done. And we don't want to lose any sleep over unseen and hard-to-reach waste accumulating, feeding micro-algae, and leading to diminished water quality—because of the design of our reef.

A SUMMARY

How our reef is designed and set up is something we have control over, and is an important decision as to the long-term maintenance of water quality, which will have an effect on all the living creatures in the enclosed system.

IDEAS ON LIVE SAND FILTERS

The advantages of having an all-sand bottom are:

1. You will use less live rock. This will save a little money. In a 55-gallon tank, using .75 pounds per gallon less, you save 55 x .75 = 41.25 pounds, x $10 a pound retail = $412.50.
2. You will have less room on the live rock, and thereby use fewer corals—approximately 3 fewer in a 55-gallon tank (3 x $50 retail = $150).
3. Sediment and waste can be more completely removed by having large pieces of rock and being able to move them and thoroughly clean under and behind them.
4. Since the tank contains less livestock, the value of the tank is less and the monetary loss is less in the event of some type of accident or disaster.
5. An all-sand bottom or live-sand filter will provide adequate nitrification and denitrification. This will also compensate for less live rock.

The disadvantages are:

1. You will still need all the necessary components to provide the vital requirements of a reef tank, such as water purification, lighting, sump box, protein skimmer, timers for the lights, and an alternate power source (generator) in the event of a power outage.
2. You will still have to perform water changes on a regular basis to clean and remove waste/sediment. Although denitrification will occur, you will still have some

measurable amount of nitrate that should be reduced/diluted with regular water changes.

3. You will have a nice reef tank with less cost and potential risk. However, it will not be as dramatic a display as it would be if you use all live rock on eggcrate.

4. It will take approximately 80 pounds of sand to provide adequate thickness (about 2-1/2") for a live sand filter in a 55-gallon tank. This comes out to 1.45 pounds per gallon, almost twice the .75 pounds per gallon of live rock you have eliminated.

The sand, although it will cost considerably less than live rock, is still expensive. I will discuss using a 50/50 mixture of live sand and a less expensive material. Taking that approach, the expenses would be as follows:

- A 55-gallon tank will use approximately 40 pounds of live sand, retail $5 a pound = $200.
- You will also need 40 pounds of commercially available dried reef sand/material, @ $1 a pound = $40.
- Approximate total cost for the 50/50 mixture: $240.

  - By using sand you saved $412.50 on live rock, and
  - $150 on corals.
  - That is a savings of $562.50.

- Overall savings by using (50/50) sand instead of all live rock: $562.50 - 240.00 = $322.50.

THE MISCONCEPTION ABOUT LIVE SAND FILTERS

One main misconception on live sand filters is that you will not have to do water changes, or that you can do them less often. My opinion and

> *A live sand filter will not eliminate or reduce water changes*

belief is that this is not true! Denitrification will occur in a live sand filter as described. It will also occur to the same degree, if not more, using an all live rock setup with the proper amounts of rock (1.5 to 1.75 pounds per gallon).

I am not aware of absolutely complete denitrification in any enclosed system. Also, by performing water changes with a high-quality salt mix, you will be adding essential trace elements on a regular basis. This will take the guesswork out of adding separate trace elements (see "Biweekly 2: Add Trace Elements,"). It may be possible to simulate this in a unique laboratory setting, or in nature, but for reef keeping in the home by average hobbyists, water changes are a must, for the reasons given throughout this book.

DISTINCTLY DIFFERENT-LOOKING TANKS

So, as you can see, there are really limited benefits (in cost, water purification, and

> *Would you like to look at live rock or sand?*

maintenance) to choosing sand over an all live rock setup. The main difference is in the appearance of the two displays. Also, an all-sand bottom without a spraybar will require the different maintenance approach described above, involving larger pieces of rock; this will also affect the display.

It really comes down to what look you would like. Would you prefer to look at sand or at live rock? The live rock will cost more, but it will provide a framework to which corals, clams, etc. will attach themselves, resulting in a very three-dimensional display of a coral reef.

THE FUNCTION AND LAYOUT OF EGGCRATE

The way I have achieved this is with a framework for the display of the live rock, which is simple, and which gives a dramatic effect. The system I have found to work best is done with eggcrate material. The eggcrate material is suspended off the bottom with sections of PVC plastic pipe laid perpendicular to the spraybar, which is at the bottom rear of the tank. This allows any debris and sediment to fall through the eggcrate material to the bottom; then the spraybar pushes it to the front of the tank. This system works extremely well for bringing sediment to the front, where it can be seen and removed. It is also a fantastic method of positioning the live rock. Using this approach, you do not have to use a lot of unnecessary base rock (which is costly) or other bulky materials to form a framework for the expensive premium live rock.

One may think this would have a flat wall effect. I can say from firsthand experience that the live

> *A dramatic 3-dimensional effect can be achieved with eggcrate and live rock*

rock can be arranged with different-sized pieces, some sticking out much further than others to provide a dramatic three-dimensional effect! Holes can easily be cut through the eggcrate material, giving the impression of deep caves. The fish love to swim through these cave holes, and there is the illusion that fish sometimes seem to come out of nowhere. This can be very interesting.

Diagram 11 - Cave cut out of Eggcrate

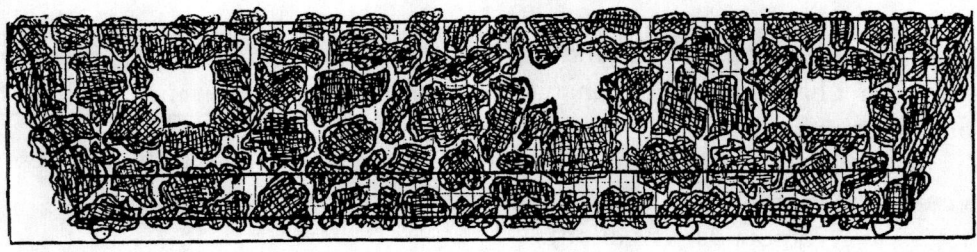

Looking at photo 3 and diagram 4 will show you the basic setup. The bottom piece of eggcrate rests on the PVC support pieces that are approximately 3-1/2 to 4 inches away from the front of the tank. This is where the waste will end up, and you want to be able to get a small, 1-inch gravel cleaning siphon in there to remove the waste sediment. This is also the area where a thin layer of sand (1/2") can be placed to cover the bottom.

Keep in mind that you want the live rock to "overhang" the front edge of the eggcrate. This way the front edge of the eggcrate is covered, keeping the reef as natural-looking as possible, while still allowing room to clean the bottom around the front of the eggcrate. When you   first place the bottom section, it will seem too small, but the rock will overhang quite a bit (about 1 to 2 inches), and when the rock is done it will be larger than the eggcrate. This will look natural and pleasing when you are done.

> *You will cover 99% of the eggcrate with live rock*

> *The live rock will "overhang" the eggcrate, creating a natural look*

The bottom piece is approximately 4 inches away from the back; it only has to extend to where the back piece will rest on it for support. The same is true for the sides. You do not want to have any unnecessary material. Use only what is needed. The eggcrate pieces consist of the bottom, the back, and the two sides. As mentioned previously, it may be more visually pleasing to cover the back and sides with a tank-backing material, or just with some plain flat cardboard, preferably painted black. This will cover the eggcrate so it will not be easily seen from outside the tank. Also, it would be convenient to have the backing easily removable, so that from time to time you can inspect behind the rock.

Eggcrate for Tanks 55 Gallons and Smaller:

Smaller tanks (55 gallons or less) will not have enough room front to back to justify using the side pieces of eggcrate material, so you may want to eliminate those pieces if you have a smaller tank.

The above image shows eggcrate in the center of the tank. This approach can be used if the tank is to be viewed from both sides. Photo from Earl Carpenter. Photo 3

ANCHORING THE MATERIAL

The main element of this eggcrate method is its anchoring system. At the very bottom rear of the tank, you will need some "anchors"—two or three, depending on the size of the tank. They are 1-inch PVC pipe, cut to approximately 1-1/4 inches long, and filled with Marine Tex or high quality epoxy into which a cable tie is placed. Once the Marine Tex is set up with the cable tie imbedded in it, you can fasten the bottom piece of eggcrate to it with another cable tie. This will keep the whole setup from sliding to the front of the tank when you arrange the live rock. I also have my spraybar attached to these "anchors," so there is no chance of it moving out of line.

If you have an all-glass tank, you will first have to "rough up" and clean the glass thoroughly for a good bond. Your local hardware store will have something convenient, like sandpaper, to "rough up" the glass.

POSITIONING AND FASTENING THE SPRAYBAR

I would first position the spraybar all the way against the back wall of the tank. Then place the "anchors" in front of the spraybar, leaving about 1/2 inch space in between for a "buffer." Mark out the placement of the anchors, and rough up and clean the area. Position the PVC anchor pieces with the cable ties in them. When all is in place, mix and pour in the epoxy. Allow a minimum of 48 hours before filling the tank with water, to allow the anchors to bond and cure completely. When they are dry, position the spraybar exactly where you want it and attach it tightly to the anchors with cable ties. Then proceed to attach the bottom piece of eggcrate.

The spraybar can easily be made from plastic water supply pipe, corresponding to the size of tubing from your pump. Common pipe sizes are 1/2", 1", 1-1/4", and 1-1/2". For a smaller pump use 1/2" pipe. For a larger pump use 1". The spraybar is basically 3 lengths of pipe with end caps, connected by a T fitting in the center. Drill holes in even increments with a 1/4" drill bit. Also drill some holes (spread farther apart) facing toward the back of the tank, so that dead spots will be minimal.

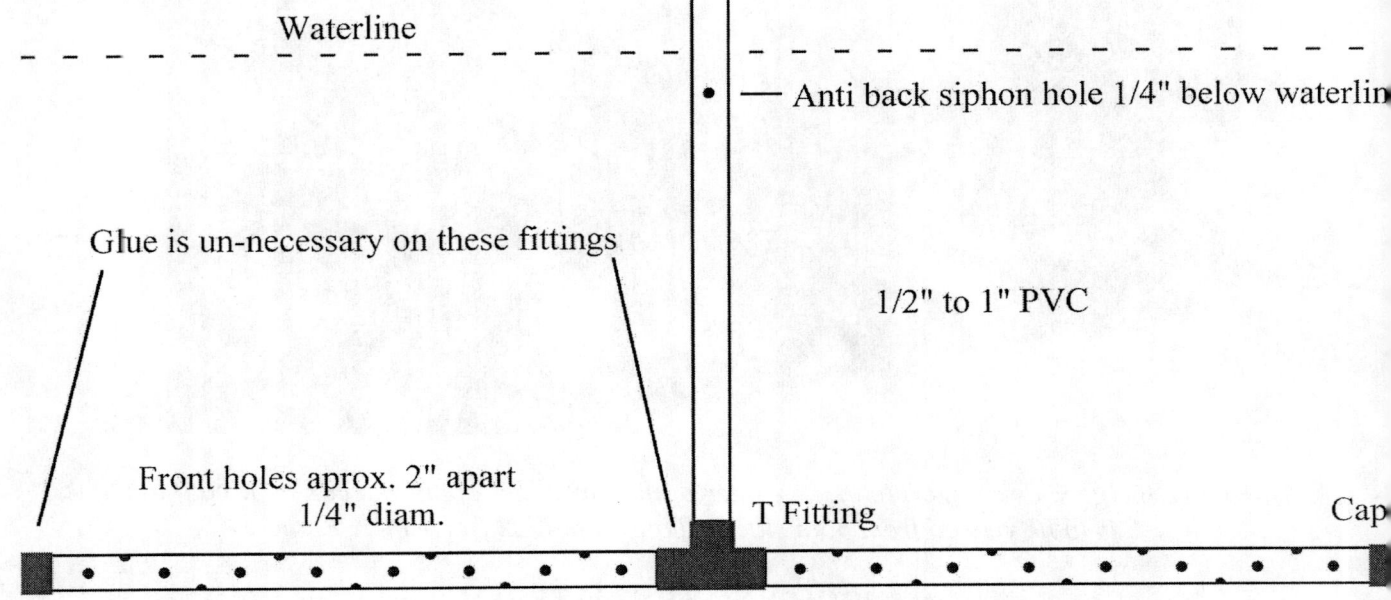

Waterline

Anti back siphon hole 1/4" below waterline

Glue is un-necessary on these fittings

1/2" to 1" PVC

Front holes aprox. 2" apart
1/4" diam.

T Fitting

Cap

POSITIONING AND FASTENING THE EGGCRATE

- The eggcrate pieces should be dry fitted with no sharp edges.
- A pair of heavy scissors or snips will cut the material.
- The sides of the bottom eggcrate piece should be

3 to 4 inches away from the front of the tank, to allow for overhanging the rock and for access of at least 2-1/2" for cleaning with a small gravel-cleaning siphon;

4 to 5 inches away from the back and sides, so there is no unnecessary material behind the back "wall."

- The cable from the anchors to the bottom piece of eggcrate may have to be doubled up to extend 4 to 5 inches from the anchor to the eggcrate.
- Attach the horizontal PVC supports at approximately 10-inch intervals with cable ties under the bottom section.
- Place the sharp cut off section of the cable tie down under the eggcrate surface.

- The front of the 1-1/2" PVC support pieces should be cut back at a 45 degree angle from top to bottom, so when you view them from the front of the tank, they will be less noticeable.
- Position and attach the bottom section of eggcrate to the anchors with cable ties.
- Set the back piece of eggcrate on the bottom section that is approximately 4 to 5 inches away from the back of the tank. The top of this back piece should be approximately 1-1/2 to 2 inches below the water line.
- Measure and dry fit the back piece of eggcrate. It should line up evenly with the back edge of the bottom section.
- Remove any sharp edges, and attach the back to the bottom piece with black cable ties.
- You will notice that the spraybar is preventing the eggcrate from resting against the back of the tank. Notch out the material so the top of the eggcrate will rest against the back of the tank.
- Make sure to remove any cut pieces of plastic! These can be a real nuisance when doing water changes!

Fitting the sidepieces can be tricky. You'll want to end up with a piece that looks like a slanted rectangle.

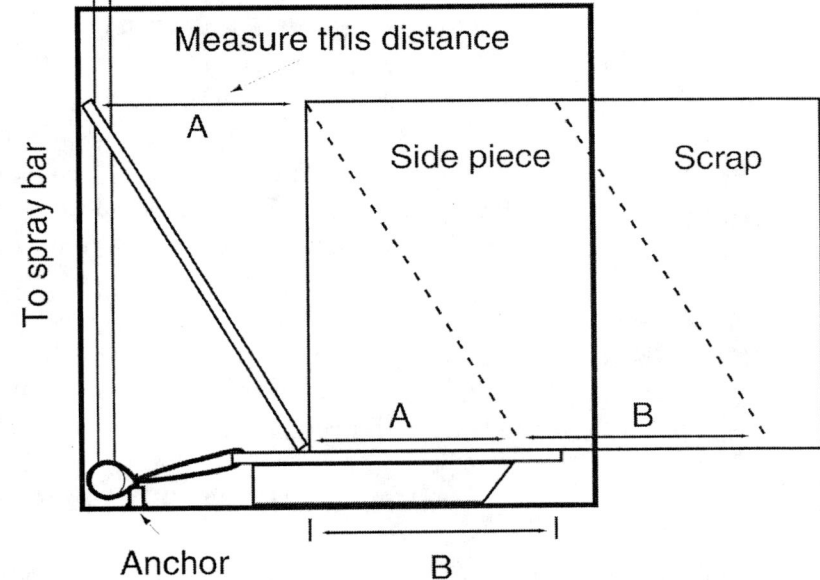

- First, measure and cut a piece of material that is the same width and height (a square). Standing on edge this piece should come to 1-1/2" below the water line.
- Set the piece where it goes on the bottom section.
- Measure the space between the top rear corner of this square side piece, and the top edge of the back piece of eggcrate.
- Make a mark at the bottom edge of the sidepiece, this same distance from the rear edge.
- Draw a line connecting this mark to the top rear corner of the sidepiece. You have marked off a triangle, which you will remove from the sidepiece.
- Take the piece to an area where any cut-off chips can be discarded.
- Cut the piece along the line you just drew, using a pair of heavy scissors or snips.
- Set it back in place, and measure, mark, and cut the piece to fit.
- I have found that the best way to mark the material is with a narrow piece of masking tape. Lay it on the side that you want to leave as a guide, and cut it, using the tape as a guide for the line you would like to cut.

Cutting eggcrate on an angle is difficult. You may find it easier to get an approximate angle by using the grids, and by cutting, say, one over and two up. This will give you an angle that will be adequate for this purpose and won't leave any unpredictable sharp edges that can easily break off.

> *Remove all plastic chips, or as many as possible, before adding water to the tank. The chips can be a nuisance when doing water changes*

The sidepiece should rest on the back piece, and is cable tied to it. This will give it extra support. Once the sidepiece has been fitted into the back corner, you can easily cut the front edge parallel to the back edge. The shape (slanted rectangle) should now be apparent. When you are satisfied with the sidepiece, take it to the other side, and dry fit it. If it fits well, use it as a template to cut the other side. Small adjustments may be necessary, such as trimming here and there, or pulling pieces together with cable ties.

PUTTING IT ALL TOGETHER

- Set the sidepiece on the bottom, and fasten it securely with two cable ties.
- Starting from the bottom and working up, fasten the sidepiece to the back with three or four cable ties.
- Cut off the excess from the cable ties, and move them into a position whereby the sharp edge that you cut will be against or under the eggcrate material, away from the upper flat surface of the eggcrate.
- Remove any scrap pieces from the cutting.

You now have an all-eggcrate system ready to go. Double-check for scrap plastic, and remove it now. This will be the last time you will be able to access this area for a while, and the scrap plastic can be a real problem when you do a water change. It can also get caught in the water pump.

Check the stability of the eggcrate structure. Add ties where needed, especially in the corners. Also at this time you may want to cut out "caves" in the eggcrate. These should be slightly more than halfway up the back, and irregular. Carefully remove plastic chips after any cutting activity.

MIXING THE SALTWATER IN THE TANK

You can fill the tank with purified water and then mix the saltwater right in the tank. Millions of small bubbles will appear on the eggcrate material. They will disappear when the water warms up and gets pumped around. When the water temperature is approximately 74 - 75 degrees, add the calculated amount of salt (1 dry measuring cup of salt mix dissolved in 3 gallons of water yields a specific gravity of approximately 1.024). Start by adding slightly less salt than you think you will need; check the specific gravity after a few hours, and add more salt as needed. It is always easier to add salt than to dilute water that has too much salt in it. Run the tank for several days, making sure everything is okay before adding the live rock. If the temperature, salt content, sump, prefilter, and skimmers are all operating properly, the tank is ready for the live rock (see Chapter 3).

PLACEMENT OF LIVE ROCK ON EGGCRATE

Start by placing rock on the front edge of the bottom piece of eggcrate. This way you can overhang the pieces for a natural look, and their placement won't be dictated by other pieces of rock. Pay particular attention to concealing the edge of the eggcrate. Use slightly irregular pieces. They should be nice, medium-quality rock, but *not the best* pieces.

After covering the front edge of the eggcrate, use base rock to fill in the remaining space on the bottom, and up to about four inches on the sides and back. Allow plenty of space between the pieces of base rock, so that waste sediment can fall through. Also, keep an eye on the pieces, so that no large crevices in the rock are facing upward, which would allow waste to accumulate in them. The amount of rock placed so far should be slightly less than 1/3 of the total rock estimated for the tank.

The second placement of live rock will be the first row along the sides and back of the eggcrate. Start from the left front corner. Select a fairly large, nice-looking piece of live rock, and place it to overhang the front side edge of the eggcrate. This will provide further support for the piece above it. Select and place mostly large pieces of rock of moderate quality, from left to right, one row across. At the left rear corner, use a flat piece that will span the corner, rounding off the straightedge surface of the eggcrate. When you get about halfway across the back with the first row, begin on the right side, repeating the process above and working your way to the back center. This way, you can overhang the starter piece just the way you want it, and make adjustments along the back wall, where they will be less noticeable.

Continue with the second row in the same manner, but use smaller, better-quality pieces. Always start from the front outer edge with the

> *The high points with "caves" in between give a dramatic 3-dimensional effect*

overhang, and span the inside corner. Make sure the pieces are secure, resting on and locking into each other naturally. This may take some time and patience. The assistance of another person, selecting and positioning the rock with you, will be helpful.

Start the rock at the cave cutouts, overhanging the eggcrate, giving a natural appearance for the cave, and work back to another full piece of rock, where adjustments can be made. Occasionally set in a larger, irregular piece of rock to offset the flatness of the eggcrate. Work your way up the surface of the eggcrate as described above, using smaller pieces toward the top. Save the smallest pieces for filling in the differences and making the rock even with the top edge of the eggcrate. The side and back wall are now covered, and you should have used almost 3/4 of the rock.

The third and final placement will involve the largest, premium-quality pieces. These will be set on the base rock bottom area, centered, pointing upward, giving the impression of dramatic irregularities or high points. These high points should be to the right and left of the cave cutouts, leaving the caves visible. A 55-gallon tank may have one high point in the center or slightly offset, with 2 cave cutouts (one on each side), while a 125-gallon may have two or three high points with caves in between.

Setting the premium pieces in this manner will give a dramatic three-dimensional look to the display of live rock. Some reminders at this time, while your hands are in the tank:

- Now is the time to make any adjustments in appearance and structural integrity: be sure the live rock rests and locks together naturally.
- Get everything just right now, while you're at this early stage.
- It will be important not to disturb the livestock that you'll put in later.
- Remember that the live rock will be in this arrangement for about a year. At that time, you will have to disassemble the reef, wash the rock, thoroughly clean the bottom of the tank, and set everything up again.

**Amounts and quality of live rock for a
55-gallon setup:
55 gallons x 1.5 = 82.5 lbs.**

- **12 lbs. base rock for bottom, fist size**
- **40 lbs. premium quality for back and sides, large flat**
- **20 lbs. encrusted octocoral, large long, for high points**
- **11 lbs. ricordia mushroom rock, for accents**

FABRICATING A LIVE SAND FILTER

A live sand filter can be an alternate source for nitrification and denitrification in a tank where you may not have, or want, the recommended 1.5 to 1.75 pounds per gallon of live rock. As I have previously discussed, I would not recommend having both a live sand filter and the full amount of live rock. A live sand filter is an ideal medium for nitrification and denitrification, but in my opinion requires more maintenance than live rock on eggcrate. The nitrification takes place on the upper layers of the sand in the presence of oxygen-rich water, while denitrification occurs in the lower layers of sand where there is little if any oxygen.

> *Do not exceed
> 1.75 pounds per gallon
> combined live rock and sand;
> 1.5 is ideal*

The question may be, "What is a live sand filter?" A live sand filter is a medium where nitrification and denitrification can occur to purify the water biologically, in contrast to most conventional filters where the water has to pass over or through a medium in which bacteria colonize. Using the old approach can lead to a buildup of waste products that become nutrients for micro-algae, resulting in diminished water quality. With a live sand filter, no water is forced through the medium (the sand). It is simply in the water, passive and inert. This provides an area for nitrifying and denitrifying bacteria to colonize. With no water flow through the sand, waste is less likely to be trapped there (although the upper layers have to be cleaned to remove accumulated sediment). This kind of passive filter will have sediment on it, but the water is not constantly forced through it; this feature makes this system unique.

What is "live sand?" It is sand that (1) was taken from a coral reef, and (2) has many micro- and macro-organisms living in it. These organisms are present naturally. They help balance the reef tank by providing a natural food source for the inhabitants of the enclosed reef, and by providing and encouraging bacterial water purification (nitrification and denitrification).

Do I need all live sand? No. You may use all live sand (and if money is no problem, that is fine), but live sand is expensive. It is not as costly as live rock, but it can still add up. I have used a half-and-half mixture: one-half actual live sand and the other half a material called "aragonite," by CaribSea. This material is designed specifically for reef tanks and live sand filters. It has all the desirable qualities without the hefty price (aragonite costs about $1 a pound). When you use this 50/50 mixture, the live sand will colonize the aragonite material, so that eventually the mixture will become all live sand.

One factor to consider: the amount of die-off on live sand is unpredictable. If you use all live sand, it will take some time to cycle. It is a biologically dense material containing millions of bacteria and other organisms, and it is rich in both living and dead life forms. As stated in the section on power outages, oxygen is needed to keep most organisms alive. Shipping and handling of this sand material can take its toll on the organisms living in it.

Another thought: when purchasing the sand, you can't really tell its quality by looking at it, as you can with live rock.

USING SYNTHETIC REEF SUBSTRATE

You may also use only aragonite, although this substance, used alone, will take considerably longer to become "live." It will eventually become colonized with organisms and beneficial bacteria from the live rock. When adding any aragonite material directly from the bag, you will need to allow a few days for the water to clear up. It will get very cloudy from the fine particles that are present in the material.

> *Do not introduce*
> *any substrate material*
> *not intended for reef use*

The best way I have found to wash this material is to put about 4 inches of it in a clean 5-gallon bucket and fill the bucket with water, swirling the mixture around with the hose as it fills the bucket. When the bucket is full, swirl it around, and dump out the cloudy water. Repeat this process until the water runs clean. Pour off the water and place the rinsed aragonite aside in another clean bucket, and proceed to wash the next 4" batch of aragonite. Continue until all the aragonite has been thoroughly rinsed in this way.

If your tap water is extremely bad (has phosphate and/or nitrate readings), it may be better not to use this washing technique. In that case I would just place the aragonite in the tank, and let it settle in for at least a week, or until the water clears. Then you can add the live rock and cycle the tank.

SUBSTRATE ALTERNATIVES?

Can I use any sand for the job? No. You should use only live sand or aragonite material. Regular beach sand, play sand, or home improvement type sand will most likely have silicate in it, which will be sure to cause problems with algae, which will be next to impossible to remove. Ordinary sand may also have "who knows what" in it, so don't use it. Use only material recommended for reef tanks.

How much sand will I need? For a recommended thickness of approximately 1-3/4 to 2 inches, you will use 1.45 pounds of sand per gallon. For a 55-gallon tank, this is 80 pounds. It may interest you to know that this works out to the same per-gallon amount as is recommended for live rock. It seems that 1.45 or 1.5 pounds of live rock or sand per gallon is the maximum amount to put in the tank.

AN IDEA FOR THE LIVE SAND FILTER

The most complete description I have found of a live sand filter was by Bob Goemans. It was published in the *Fresh Water Marine Aquarium Magazine* in the August 1995 issue. The article recommends using short "lift tubes" to hold a section of eggcrate approximately 1/2 inch above the bottom of the tank. A layer of fiberglass window screen is cut and laid on top of the eggcrate to support the sand. A 1-inch layer of sand is added on top of the fiberglass screen, which holds the sand intact. Then a top layer of sand, 1-1/2 to 2 inches, is added.

Materials needed to construct a live sand filter for a 55-gallon tank:

- Section of eggcrate 3/8" smaller than the bottom of the tank. This is to allow placement and to minimize forcing.
- A piece of fiberglass screen, twice the size of the eggcrate plus 2" on all sides. This screen will hold the sand in place.
- 1/2" PVC spacers or lift pieces, to raise the eggcrate off the bottom of the tank and create a "plenum," or dead water area.
- Cable ties to fasten the PVC to the eggcrate. This will prevent the spacer lift pieces from moving around too much.

HOW I HAVE MADE A LIVE SAND FILTER

For the "lift tubes," I laid two sections of 1/2" PVC water pipe, parallel to the length of the tank. Then, I cut a section of eggcrate to the size of the tank bottom minus 3/8 inch, so it is snug but not too tight. Using cable ties, I fastened the lift tubes to the underside of the eggcrate, so they wouldn't move around while I was installing the structure.

> *Fiberglass screen can be bought at most home improvement centers*

I then cut the fiberglass screen, making it 1-1/2" longer than the tank bottom, and 2" longer than *twice* the width of the tank bottom. The extra inches will allow for a fold of screen to lie up against the inside of the tank glass along the front and sides, to prevent sand from trickling into the empty area under the sand filter. If you cut the screen to the dimensions I described, these folds will be 3/4" longer at each side when the screen is centered (half of the 1-1/2" extra), and 1/2" along the front. This will "roll up" onto the glass, keeping the sand intact on top of the eggcrate.

> *Lay out and dry fit the parts of the sand filter*

After you lay in the first inch of sand, wrap and fold the screen up the 1-inch thickness of sand and over the top of the 1-inch layer. The top layer of the screen will also have the folds resting against the inside of the tank glass, front and sides. Sandwiching the lower sand layer with the screen protects the sand from being disturbed by digging creatures. When you add the top layer of sand, you cover the screen, and the top layer gives digging creatures something to work with. (This top layer will have to be cleaned regularly with a gravel vacuum, to remove sediment.)

Underneath the sand filter is an empty area of water, where the lift tubes are located. Denitrification can occur in this area, but the process will be more active if the area is kept dark.

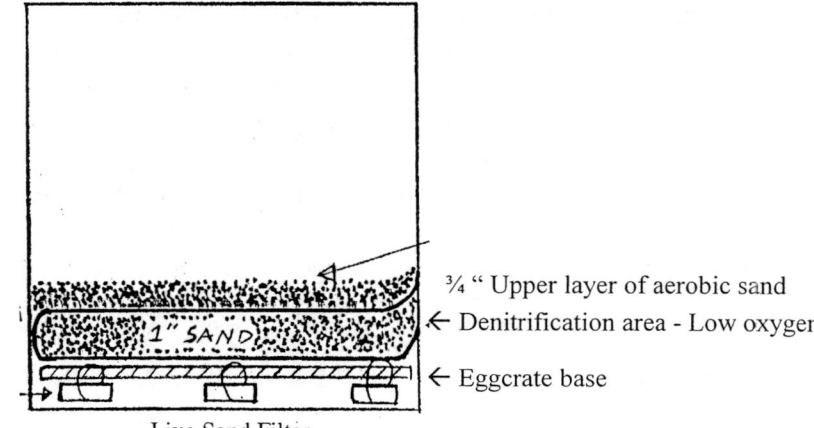

Fiberglass window screen →

1 ½" PVC tie wrapped to eggcrate

¾ " Upper layer of aerobic sand

← Denitrification area - Low oxygen

← Eggcrate base

Live Sand Filter

Therefore, once you have your sand filter set up the way you want it, apply opaque material to the outside of the tank glass so as to cover and darken the section of the tank underneath the sand filter.

The sand in the filter will stay "alive" and beneficial for about one year. Apparently, it gets "used up" after a while and should be replaced. After a year, gradual replacement of the sand is recommended, one small area at a time: approximately 1/5 of the sand every two months. This replacing action does not seem practical, but it is necessary. For this reason and many others, as I have discussed, I personally would not use the live sand or all-sand filter substrate method on future tanks. However, I do have a 55-gallon tank with a sand filter in use.

RECOMMENDED CYCLING OF LIVE SAND

If you use the live sand method, you will be well advised not to have the lights on for the first 5 to 7 days. This is the time for the sand to release its die-off and begin cycling. Since the sand has a flat, reflective, light-colored surface, there could be an outbreak of micro-algae if the lighting is left on during the initial cycling process. The probability of an algae outbreak happening is considerably lessened if the lighting remains off during the first week (longer if possible), while the tank goes through the ammonia/nitrite cycle.

Here is the sequence for cycling with a live sand filter:

- Install the live sand system.
- Run it in for a week or longer with the lighting off, allowing the dust to settle and the nitrification process to begin in the tank.
- In 7 to 10 days, check for ammonia and then nitrite.
- When they read zero and everything looks good, and you begin to get a nitrate reading, the tank is initially cycled.
- Introduce and cycle the live rock as recommended.
- Once the live rock has completed the ammonia and nitrite cycle and you begin to get faint nitrate readings, you can introduce invertebrates and fish as described previously (Chapter 3).

PICKING UP THE LIVE ROCK

Before you leave home to pick up the live rock, lay out one or two drop cloths on the floor in front of the tank. Have two clean, 5-gallon buckets ready: one with a hose to siphon water from the tank into the bucket, and another to dispose of water and debris. Also, have a pair of scissors and a sharp knife handy to cut open the boxes or bags. If you have to go to the airport, chances are you will be receiving a fairly large amount of rock. For example, 83 pounds of rock for a 55-gallon tank might come in three 30-pound boxes. Call the airport to confirm the arrival of the rock. Try to have everything ready in advance, so you won't waste time when you get home with the packages, fumbling around to find what you need to unpack, wash, and place the rock in the tank.

UNDESIRABLE CREATURES TO LOOK OUT FOR

- Bristle worms
- Mantis shrimp
- Isopods
- Rock crabs
- Anything that smells bad

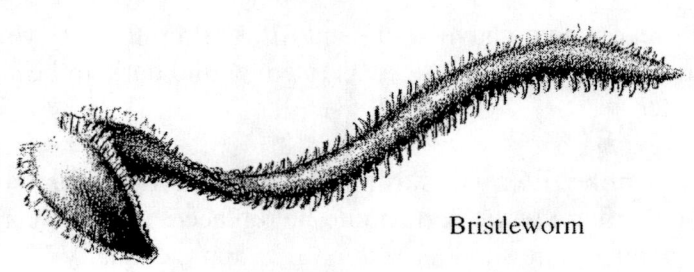

Bristleworm

Get the rock home as soon as you can. Cut open all the boxes, and see what you have. Usually, shipped live rock comes with damp newspaper to keep it moist. Discard the newspaper, and look over the rock to identify and separate the different grades and sizes. Fill the 5-gallon bucket 3/4 full of water from the tank, and select the first piece of rock to go in. Take the piece in your hand, and vigorously dunk it in the bucket several times. This will wash off a lot of the ammonia and die-off from the surface of the rock, as well as any small bits of newspaper. Place the piece in the tank, and repeat the process.

> *Keep a cautious eye out for, and remove, suspicious creatures before they go into the tank*

At the bottom of the box that the rock came in, sometimes you will find bristle worms. These look like a fat sandworm: they are long, plump, fleshy, and pink, with fuzzy legs. If you find one, discard it. If you place it in the tank, it will be very difficult to remove later. These worms are very common, and they live in live rock. They can feed on some of the nicer life-forms on the rock, and are of no good use in the enclosed system.

Mantis Shrimp

You might find a mantis shrimp on the bottom of the shipping box. This is a small, thin, light green, shrimp-like creature with a long claw. Don't hesitate to dispose of this little monster. You won't miss him at all, I assure you! The mantis shrimp is probably the least desirable of all reef creatures, and it will be very difficult to get rid of once it is in the tank. With luck, there will be no mantis shrimp in your rock.

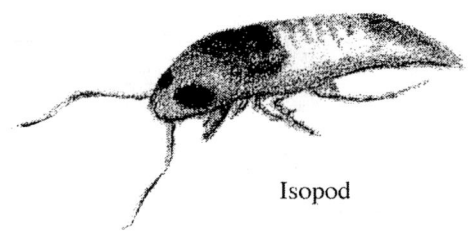

Isopod

You may also find an Isopod. This is a larva-like creature about the size of a small bean. Isopods range from clear to white; they are somewhat rounded, and have a black ring around each eye. They are carnivorous parasites that attach themselves to fish, resulting in injury or death. If you see one on a fish, net the fish and remove it briefly from water. This will usually dislodge the parasite. If it doesn't, you may have to remove the Isopod from the fish with tweezers. Like mantis shrimps and bristle worms, Isopods are undesirable, and should be removed if found.

There might also be some small, dark-colored rock crabs present. They are almost black, and have an oval shape similar to a common blue crab. These crabs, when placed in water, are extremely fast moving, and virtually impossible to catch by hand or net. They can also be destructive, and should not be allowed in the tank.

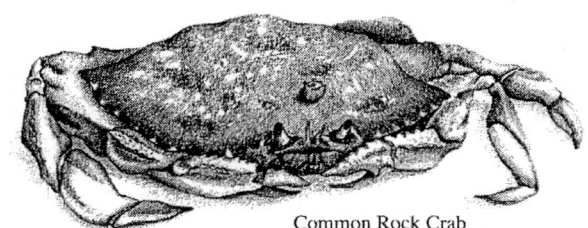

Common Rock Crab

Closely look over what has dislodged from the rock during shipping. As a general rule, creatures that fall out of the rock and end up on the bottom of the shipping box are going to be undesirable.

Of course, you may want to consult other books that list the exact habits of questionable creatures that can come with live rock. I can assure you that bristle worms, mantis shrimp, Isopods, and black rock crabs are the most common. They are all unwelcome creatures in a reef tank, and they are very difficult to trap or remove once they are in the tank. So, if you are lucky enough to find them on the bottom of the shipping box, 99% of your job is already done.

Arrowhead Crab

> *It can be unbelievably difficult to remove pests once the tank is set up*

The arrowhead crab is considered a predator of bristleworms.

NOTES:_____

Chapter 9

Maintenance

Chapter goal:
To inform the reef keeper about proven methods and practical ideas
concerning all aspects of maintaining the reef tank

RECORD KEEPING

Proper care and timely maintenance are essential for the health and well being of the enclosed reef system. Below is a list of items that should be attended to regularly. They are all important; their sequence in the list is based only on how often they need to be done.

> *A notebook will provide a long-term reference on all aspects of your reef*

It is a good idea to keep a notebook in which you record what you did and when you did it. Do not rely on your memory! Once some time has passed, your memory can fail as to when the reef was set up, when the rock was added, how long the tank took to cycle, when the inverts were added, how many of them there were, when the fish were added, how many of them went in, what kinds they were, what the results of your water tests have been, and so on.

You can also keep track of the money you spend. This will clarify the monetary value of your tank.

Unless you are an analytical type, keeping a notebook and writing down all the things you initially do to the reef will seem like a waste of time. However, as time goes on (as it has a way of doing), you will begin to see the importance and benefits of keeping the notebook. If you do this from the start, there will be a minimum of guesswork regarding water changes, water quality, how long the reef has been set up, and the monetary value of the reef.

Here is a list of maintenance procedures, followed by an expanded explanation of each one.

Daily:
1. Check general appearance of reef.
2. Adjust protein skimmer.
3. Adjust water level (compensating for evaporation).
4. Feed livestock.

As needed:
1. Remove unwanted algae (on glass and overflow pipes).
2. Clean protein skimmer; change airstones; adjust Venturi valve.

Weekly:
1. Change prefilter pads.

Biweekly (alternately):
1. Change water.
2. Add trace elements.

Monthly:
1. Test water.
2. Clean the tank cover.
3. Wipe the light bulbs.

Every 3 months:
1. Clean the cooling fan(s).
2. Inspect and clean the water pumps.

Every 6 months:
1. Take down and completely clean the sump.
2. Take down and service the pump.
3. Replace light bulbs.

Once a year: (depending if the tank displays problems)
1. Completely take down, clean, and rebuild the reef.

DAILY: 1. CHECK GENERAL APPEARANCE OF REEF

As obvious as this may sound, you want to get familiar with the habits of your livestock. The inhabitants of your reef can tell you more about the condition and quality of the water in your tank than you can learn from test kit results. Get to know their behavior, feeding habits, territorial arrangements, and so on. By doing this, after a while you will get to know them, and they will get to know you. They will be assured that someone is looking after them and providing for their needs. I believe this benefits both the keeper and the kept. Not only will you get the satisfaction from observing them (which is really why most of us get into this hobby in the first place), but also from a practical point of view, you will be able to tell if something is going wrong.

By daily observation, you will also be able to nip problems in the bud while they are still small. Note any missing livestock: some may die in the tank (and will have to be removed), while others may get into the plumbing (if the overflow holes are too large). This is unfortunate for the creature that dies, but from a larger perspective it can endanger all the remaining inhabitants of the tank by jamming the pump and slowing down the movement of water to which the reef is accustomed.

Become aware of potential problems

Note any waste buildup on the rock (this can be from the small worms and other organisms living in the rock). This may point out the homes of bristle worms. Look for gray mushy piles of waste with a hole nearby. If you see this, you may want to set a bristle worm trap in that area. These mushy piles should not be brushed off. Wait until you do a water change, and remove them by vacuuming.

This idea of keeping an eye on the tank may seem obvious, but it is an important maintenance function, one that should not be overlooked.

DAILY: 2. ADJUST PROTEIN SKIMMER

When you first set up the skimmer(s), it might tend to act erratically, in which case you should adjust the height of the water in the chamber. If you have a large skimmer, you will also have a strong pump; you can't afford to have it functioning erratically. Usually this is only a concern for the first week or so after you set up the skimmer. You may also have to adjust the skimmer if you change air blocks or add another air pump.

> *If a sink is nearby, it is a good idea to have the skimmer drain connected to a permanent waste drain*

Skimmer adjustments are made with two shut-off valves. One controls the rate of water being pumped into the skimmer, the other controls the rate of water draining out. If the pump is the proper size, the inlet valve is rarely adjusted; frequent changes in the water flow through this valve would unnecessarily strain the pump. Therefore the primary control valve for the skimmer is the drain valve. (However, both valves are necessary for "fine-tuning" the skimmer.)

In any case, the skimmer should be checked frequently. By observing it, you will notice how much waste is being removed (as evidenced by dark brown scum on the neck and sides of the skimmer). For proper skimmer operation, you should remove the scum from the inner neck by wiping it out with a paper towel. This will keep the inside surface smooth, resulting in a better-operating skimmer.

Also, you will hear talk of "efficient" skimming. This means that the skimmer is adjusted so that the accumulating foam has a relatively stiff consistency. If the bubbles are too close to the top of the neck, they will burst there (at the top), and you will not get the desired thick foam that accumulates until it reaches the top and overflows into the collection cup.

Occasionally you may get a surge from the pump. If the skimmer is adjusted too high, and not connected to a drain, a pump surge will cause the collection cup to overflow onto the floor. I have my skimmer drain hooked up directly to a plumbing drain (see Photo 3 in Chapter 6), so I don't have to worry about emptying out any waste-collection devices. If you don't plan to have such a system, the collection device is another item to keep your eye on, as it will have a tendency to overflow as well, especially if the foam is not of the desired thickness.

> *When the tank is first set up*

When the tank is first set up, a considerable amount of foam (waste) will be removed. Initially this is from die-off on the rock. The first couple of months are the most crucial from a monitoring standpoint. As time goes on and things balance out, the skimmer will be more predictable. This is good: when the skimmer is properly adjusted to produce a thick foam regularly, this indicates that the waste is being removed and the skimmer is operating correctly. The protein skimmer is the most important external filtering device of the enclosed reef, and will need sufficient monitoring for it to function properly, especially when it is first set up.

DAILY: 3. ADJUST WATER LEVEL (EVAPORATION)

Because the tank is exposed to air, and strong pumps are circulating the water throughout the filtering system (overflow pipes, drip plate, prefilter, and protein skimmer), you will get a significant amount of evaporation. In fact, the better your skimmer and the stronger your water pump (both desirable features), the more evaporation you will get. You will need to replace the evaporated water regularly. An important reminder for the new hobbyist is that the *water* evaporates, not the salt. Do *not* add salt mix with the make-up water. The result will be a higher salinity than is desirable.

Adding make-up water provides a good opportunity to replenish much-needed calcium, which gets depleted rapidly in an enclosed reef system. This vital element is used by virtually all living creatures. Some of it also gets removed by protein skimming. In my opinion the best calcium additive is "Kalkwasser," which is calcium hydroxide. It is added on a regular basis by mixing it with the purified water being added to compensate for evaporation. These regular additions of calcium hydroxide also keep the pH elevated to the desired 8.2 to 8.4 level.

The water you use to replace what has evaporated will be called "make-up water." It is extremely important to use purified tap water mixed with calcium hydroxide (a.k.a. Kalkwasser, a.k.a. limewater) for the make-up water! *Do not*, I repeat, *do not*, use regular tap water or anything else for make-up water! This is asking for trouble.

As I have stated from the beginning, nothing will ensure your success more than the quality of your water. Once you have made the investment of a water purifying system and have started the reef with purified tap water, the reef will be accustomed to that quality of water. It would be extremely foolish to try to cut corners here. This is the last place to skimp. In fact, it would be inviting disaster by possibly introducing impurities (metals, silicates, phosphates, etc.) that are harmful and troublesome (hard to remove) into the pristine environment that we have tried so hard to create.

The mixing vessel—method and location:

> *For optimum performance the bucket must be above the sump box*

This is a simple matter, actually. Let's agree to use purified tap water and Kalkwasser. I would recommend having an inexpensive, clean, 5-gallon bucket, to be used exclusively for this purpose, and placed *above or slightly higher than the sump and near the water purification system. This location is important for the ease of its operation and convenience of use. Do not underestimate this location.* For proper mixing you will also need a moderate-sized powerhead, to be used only for this purpose.

Dosing with the drip method:

You will need approximately 6 to 8 feet of airline tubing, and a weight (see Diagram 5). The weight will hold one end of the airline tubing inside the bucket, just off the bottom. A non-toxic, non-metal weight is hard to find, so once again we improvise and make one! This is done with a small, flat, harmless-looking stone: it should contain no small shiny specks, which might be metals. I use bluestone, a.k.a. flagstone or slate. A piece about 1-1/4" x 1-1/4" x 3/4" does the job nicely. To this I attach a cable tie, using Marine Tex. The stone is porous, so use a small amount (1/2 teaspoon) of mixed Marine Tex, swiped on the rock. Embed a cable tie in the wet Marine Tex, let it sit for a day or so to cure, and you have a nice weight to hold the tubing at the bottom of the bucket. While you are at it, make a few of them. You will probably use them in the future (see Marine Tex).

> *Sediment will accumulate below the weight*

Now we have the make-up water bucket *above the sump box*, near the water supply, with a powerhead in the bottom of the bucket, and a 6- to 8-foot section of airline tubing attached to a small weight that rests on the bottom of the bucket, keeping the tubing about 3/4" off the bottom.

> *Test run the system with plain tap water*

At the end of the airline tubing feeding the make-up water into the sump box, you will need a clamping device to control the flow of make-up water into the reef. This has to be relatively slow, because the make-up water, once mixed with Kalkwasser, will have an extremely high pH (approximately 12 or more). Dispensing this water into the reef too rapidly can cause pH shock, which can be fatal in a small system.

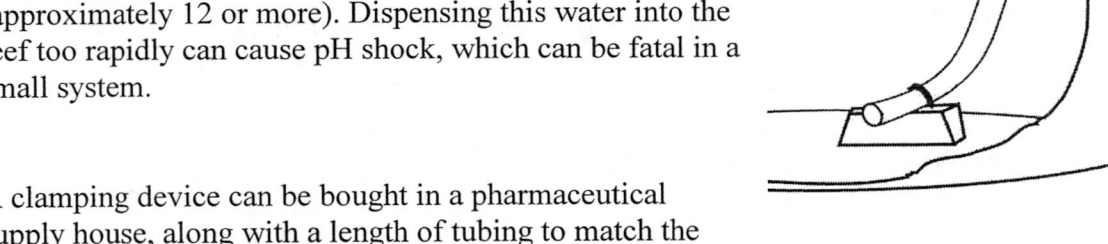

A clamping device can be bought in a pharmaceutical supply house, along with a length of tubing to match the clamp (their tubing is slightly smaller than airline). This kind

Airline weight Diagram. 5

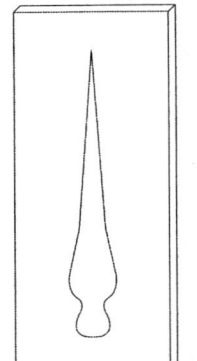

of clamp is inexpensive, and provides good control of the water flow. You can also improvise with a metal forceps type of clamp; just be sure the control of water draining through the tubing into the sump is uniform, and can be "fine-tuned" to your discretion. Another alternative is to make your own clamp as shown here. This can be easily cut with an exact o knife from a piece of 1/8" plastic and works quite well.

> *Do not introduce*
> *undissolved calcium hydroxide*
> *sediment into the tank;*
> *add only the fully-mixed*
> *cloudy solution that remains*
> *above the sediment*

I would recommend practicing the water make-up procedure described below, using regular water, to get familiar with the dosing/control method before actually mixing (and possibly fumbling with) the calcium hydroxide. You should be confident with the operation. For your test run, do everything *except* adding the regular unfiltered tap water to the tank. Drain it into another 5-gallon bucket and discard it.

Mixing the Kalkwasser:

Fill the bucket with purified tap water. Raise the clamp end of the fill tubing above the top of the bucket to prevent water from siphoning out at this time. Have a cable tie system to hold this end higher than the bucket while the water is being mixed.

Fill a 5-gallon bucket with purified water. Place the powerhead in the bucket and plug it in. Then add 3 to 4 heaping teaspoons of "Kalkwasser," and let it mix for at least 8 hours. Then unplug the powerhead, and let the mixture sit for 8 hours. *Do not move or disturb the bucket.* You want to let any undissolved calcium hydroxide settle to the bottom of the bucket. *Do not introduce this sediment into the tank!* The stone will keep the tube 3/4" off the bottom, so the sediment will accumulate below the end of the tube.

Once the mixture has settled, take the clamp end of the tubing, lift it up, and slowly submerse it into the bucket. This will fill the tube with water. When it is filled (a couple of seconds), crimp the tubing, then lower the clamp end into the sump. Release the crimp. Because the bucket is above the sump, a siphon will begin. Adjust the clamp so the flow is dripping slowly but steadily.

The method I have described is for making a 5-gallon batch of make-up water. This is a convenient amount to make, and can be used for just about any size tank. In tanks that are 55 gallons or smaller, the evaporation will be less, so you can make up half of the 5-gallon amount while still using the 5-gallon bucket mixing/method.

When to add make-up water:

Watch the water in the sump! This is where you will see the change in water level. Once you have established the "working water level" in the sump, mark it on the side of the sump box, with magic marker. This will give a quick visual reference as to the height of water that is normally in the system. As evaporation occurs, watch this mark. When the level goes down by 3 to 5 gallons, or gets close to the top of the outlet for the pump, you need to add make-up water. *Mix the water no more than one day before you add it to the tank; it starts to lose effectiveness right after it has been mixed.* It will have the highest concentration of available calcium just after the sediment settles out of the solution.

> *Add the Kalkwasser within a day after you mix it; it gradually loses effectiveness after it is mixed*

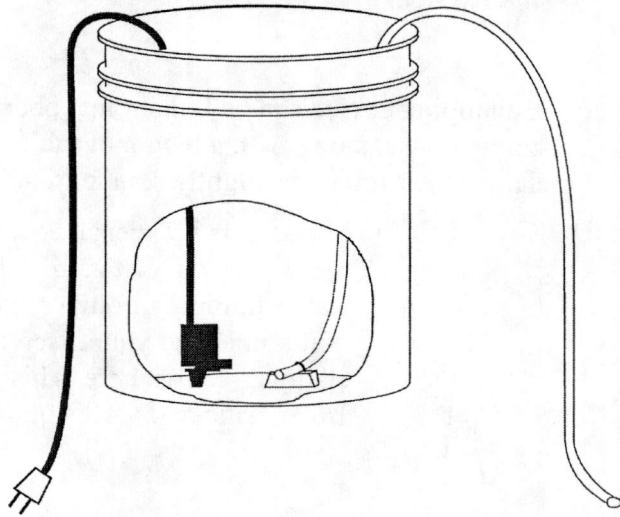

Calculating water volume in the sump:

You should calculate the amount of water in the sump. Multiply the sump's length (in inches) by its height (inches) by its width (inches), and divide by 231. A gallon contains 231 cubic inches of water, so this calculation will give you the gallon volume of the sump container.

Now you can divide the volume (in gallons) by the height of the sump (in inches), which will give you gallons-per-inch in your sump. Now you can place a new mark, at approximately 5 gallons below the "working water level" in the sump. This mark can be a useful reference. **Amounts and time frame for adding make-up water to different-sized tanks:**

> *Calcium hydroxide has a pH of 12 or more and must be added slowly, especially with small tanks*

On a smaller tank (even a 55-gallon), 5 gallons of high-powered make-up water must be used with caution! Kalkwasser

has an extremely high pH. Pay close attention to the drip/dosing flow of water, to be certain that it is administered very slowly. For a 55-gallon tank, you should take a 48-hour period to administer 5 gallons of make-up water. Make sure you test-run your drip method, to be sure that it introduces the desired amount of make-up water over the correct period of time. Adding Kalkwasser too fast will cause pH shock, which can be fatal or, at the least, unnecessarily stressful to the livestock. Take the recommended precautions and do not let this happen!

On larger tanks, 125 gallons and up, 5 gallons of make-up water will not have as much of an effect as it will in smaller tanks. For a 125-gallon tank, the Kalkwasser can be added at the rate of approximately 5 gallons in 8 to 12 hours. In a 200-gallon or larger tank, the 5 gallons can be added without any clamping system, allowing the airline tube to empty the 5-gallon bucket unrestricted. This will take less than 1 hour.

Time of day to add:

Another suggestion is to add the Kalkwasser mix when the tank lights go out, or (ideally) first thing in the morning. While the lights are off, the pH drops, reaching its lowest level the next day just before the lights come back on. If you add the Kalkwasser during this reef "night," the effect of raising the pH will not be as significant as it would be during lighted hours.

There may be some questions and concerns about adding 5 gallons of Kalkwasser all at once. Yes, some critics may be correct that adding smaller amounts more frequently would be a less risky, less stressful, and more natural approach. However, I have used my method on tanks from 55 to 200 gallons, with no adverse effects, and I have not lost one creature due to pH shock. You do have to be careful on smaller tanks, but once you get familiar with this system, I'm sure you will find it to be very practical: (1) you will add make-up water less frequently, and (2) on larger tanks (125 gallons and up), you can add 5 gallons of make-up water at a time, which is a significant, convenient, easily measurable amount of water to add.

Adding make-up water is an important duty in maintaining a reef tank. It should not be an inconvenience. I have found that the method I have described works extremely well, and I would suggest that you follow it closely. *In particular, dosing with a natural siphon from a raised bucket simplifies matters greatly.*

It is never a problem for me to top off the tank with water that will greatly enhance the reef. I have

- no spilled water,
- no uncertainty about how the Kalkwasser has dissolved,
- no doubt about how much I am adding, and
- no unreliable "dosing systems" with float switches or pumps that can malfunction.

This method is
- practical,
- easy to implement,
- basically foolproof, and
- inexpensive.

By constantly adding Kalkwasser this way, I can be sure that the calcium in my tank is kept replenished, and the pH is kept elevated.

Here are some other ideas to help you use this system.

The accumulated undissolved product:

After you have mixed up a few batches of Kalkwasser, you will find that the bottom of the bucket contains an accumulation of undissolved mix. This accumulation is normal—it is product that will not dissolve. From time to time it has to be removed from the bucket. Ideally you should remove the sediment after every mixing; if you have the time, by all means do so. I remove it approximately every 2 to 3 mixings, with absolutely no ill effects.

Cleaning the bucket:

> *Kalkwasser may be the most beneficial additive to the reef system*

When the bucket needs cleaning, take the bucket, powerhead, and airline hose outside, to an area where the white calcium deposits will not be objectionable, and rinse everything off with a garden hose until all is clean. At this time, disassemble the powerhead, and thoroughly clean it. Calcium hydroxide is caustic, so it is advisable during this cleaning process to wear eye protection and rubber or latex gloves.

If you do not have the convenience of an outside hose, you will most likely have to clean this equipment in the bathtub or a large sink. Be careful not to contaminate the bucket with any kind of soap at all!

Let everything dry, and set the system up again.

> *Calcium hydroxide is caustic!*
> *Wear gloves and eye protection*
> *when cleaning the mixing equipment*

Alternative mixing methods?

Do not try to vary the mixing procedure! It is important to mix the Kalkwasser as described in this section. Do not mix with an airstone; this will add carbon dioxide and oxygen, which will reduce the effectiveness of the calcium hydroxide and defeat its purpose!

Do not mix make-up water in a shakable container, unless you plan to shake it for several hours! Also, if you pour the Kalkwasser out of a shakable container (rather than using the siphon technique I have described), sediment will pour out along with the fully-mixed solution, and that also will undermine the benefits of this process.

Maintenance and size of powerhead:

When you plug in and then unplug the powerhead, quite often the impeller inside the powerhead will stick. This is very common and can be easily remedied. If the powerhead is not operating, suspend it from the cord and bump it gently on the bottom of the bucket. This will usually suffice to get it going. If it doesn't, then lift the powerhead to the top of the bucket and knock it against the side with your hand. If this still does not work, tap the powerhead with a semi-hard object, such as a block of wood. After a few tries, you will find what works best for you.

As stated before, you should designate a powerhead to be used only for mixing make-up water. This small pump will take a considerable amount of punishment, and in my opinion it is better to keep one pump for this purpose than to distribute the wear and tear on other pumps.

The powerhead used for this should be powerful (at least 400 GPH). This will do a better job of dissolving the calcium hydroxide. It will not jam as frequently as smaller pumps, and will hold up better in the long run. (Smaller pumps will do the job, but not as well.) We are trying to dissolve a chemical in water as completely as we can, under the conditions that we have, and we should employ a pump that will do the job well.

Electrical safety GFI outlet:

Also, keep in mind that electricity and water do not mix! When you are handling the powerhead while it is plugged in, there is a risk of electric shock! Use caution! Use a powerhead that is new! Do not plug it in or unplug it with wet hands, standing on a wet floor, or touching the floor with bare feet! This is a sure way to get zapped! And if you get zapped, who will be dedicated enough to care for your reef? Use common sense and caution!

The electrical outlet(s) you are using for your reef setup should be GFI:

This stands for "Ground Fault Interrupter." GFI outlets act as small circuit breakers when the circuit is ground faulted (short-circuited) by water or anything else. In a fraction of a second, a GFI outlet will stop the flow of electricity, interrupting the circuit. Once the problem is corrected (wet wires, for example), the outlet can be reactivated with a reset button. Most kitchens and bathrooms have these, so you may already be familiar with the GFI outlet. If you do not have one for the tank setup, I would strongly recommend that you have one installed by a licensed electrician. A reef system has many electrical components, including your make-up water system: do not compromise your safety!

The level of safety you get from properly installed GFI outlets is immense and should not be underestimated.

Benefits of adding Kalkwasser:

You may be interested in why it is so important to add Kalkwasser. Some of the benefits are:

1. It adds calcium that is needed by most of the creatures in the reef.
2. It encourages the growth of pink and purple coraline algae.
3. It keeps the pH elevated. By adding Kalkwasser on a regular basis (make-up water) and doing water changes every 2 to 3 weeks, I have found my pH to be consistently between 8.2 and 8.4. Keeping the pH at this level makes it less likely that micro-algae will become a problem.
4. The reef just seems to love Kalkwasser.
5. There are many more scientific and chemical reactions that are beneficial. Take my word for it: adding Kalkwasser on a regular basis is one of the most beneficial procedures for maintaining a healthy reef and desirable water chemistry.

Kalkwasser versus other calcium additives:

There are many other calcium additives on the market today, besides the well-known Kalkwasser. Many of them claim to be more concentrated, easier to use, and less expensive. These products seem to offer some benefits. However, I have not been willing to experiment with them. From what I understand, they are not as chemically complete as Kalkwasser. It seems that they will do one thing, but not another. They may be the best product available—I don't know. However, I do know what has worked extremely well for my reef, and when I find something that works, I personally am very reluctant to change. Call me old-fashioned, too careful, or whatever else you like, but I have enough problems to overcome without experimenting with other calcium additives on my reef.

Of course, I do not speak for all reef keepers, and they may get good results by using other calcium additives. There are probably many ways to add calcium and keep the pH elevated. I am conveying what has worked well for me, and therefore I recommend the approach I have described here. *I find it easy, affordable, complete, proven, very practical, and generally foolproof.*

Some other thoughts on Kalkwasser:

Kalkwasser is a German word. Literally, it means "lime water." Kalkwasser is a trade name for calcium hydroxide. The terms "Kalkwasser," "limewater," and "calcium hydroxide" all mean the same thing in this hobby.

When purchasing calcium hydroxide (Kalkwasser), try to buy it in large quantities. Depending on the size of the tank you have, you may use a considerable amount of this product. As with salt mix, you don't want to have to run out to the store every other month to buy small amounts. Get at least the 450-gram containers, and if you have a large tank buy several of them. You will probably use it up quicker than you expect, and it is good to have a substantial supply on hand. *An important reminder: keep the product tightly covered. It will lose its effectiveness if exposed to air.*
Note: In the question and Answer chapter area of this book describes where and how to purchase food grade calcium hydroxide for a virtually insignificant cost.

Calcium hydroxide is a caustic chemical, and certain safety precautions should be followed, such as:

> *$$—$$*
> *When you buy in bulk*
> *the things you use often,*
> *you will save money!!*

- The calcium hydroxide has a talcum powder consistency. Do not breathe the dust. Keep your face away from the bucket and the open product container when adding the fine powder. Some people may want to wear a filter mask.
- Wear disposable gloves when handling the components. Wash your hands when you are finished.
- Treat the product with respect, and use common sense.
- When washing out the container, wear safety glasses or goggles to protect your eyes from flying particles.

This sounds like a lot of precautions. Actually, use your common sense while keeping in mind the idea of safety.

If you follow the method I have described here, I am confident it will work the same wonders for your reef tank as it has worked for mine.

DAILY: 4. FEED LIVESTOCK

What kind of appetite do your fish have? This is an important indication of their general health and contentment. This is true with all living

> *More than 90% of saltwater fish are taken directly from the wild*

creatures, including ourselves. Think for a minute of a sick person. Usually the appetite is missing, and there is a general feeling of discontent. The longer this goes on, the more we become concerned with the lack of appetite. It is a positive sign when that person asks for food; then with full recovery the appetite becomes hearty again.

Saltwater fish have a long, hard story to tell. I'm sure you can imagine it. Most of them (more than 90%) are taken from the open ocean, which is a virtually pristine environment. They are born there, and have become 100% dependent on the conditions that are present in their unique habitats. One day some of them have the unfortunate fate to be removed from their specialized surroundings, on which they have depended.

When this happens, a fish will have to go through a long, unfamiliar treatment that is nothing like what it has experienced up to that time. This process is extremely stressful, sometimes resulting in death to the more fragile species. The estimates can be alarming as to the percentage of fish that end up healthy in our tanks, compared to the numbers that were caught.

Again, it is our responsibility to provide the absolutely best conditions that we can (especially water quality and the availability of food). Very fortunately, the supply industry has a wide variety of foods that contain many of the essential vitamins and nutrients that will help to ensure the health and well-being of the captive fish.

As far as recommending actual brand names, I stick with the larger, better-known companies. When looking at fish food, I look at the list of contents. The contents listed first make up most of the food; those listed last are present in the smallest amounts. The more progressive companies show the specific percentage of each substance contained in a product. This is helpful when you are choosing among the various products available. It is a good practice to find what the fish seem to like best, settle on that product as a staple diet, and then introduce other beneficial foods as time goes on. In fact, a variety of different foods will provide the fish with a more interesting, balanced, and nutritionally complete diet.

Types of food:

Freeze dried foods (flakes, pellets) are the easiest to handle, although they don't stay fresh for long. Each time you open the container to feed your fish, the product is exposed to air. Over time this depletes some of the vitamins and minerals in the food. Buy these products in smaller quantities, so you will use up each container while its contents are still relatively fresh.
Nori is a dried seaweed product that is an excellent vegetation supplement. It can be purchased in just about any health food store.

Frozen foods in small plastic containers are a convenient, more natural food source, and are relished by the fish. Frozen foods also have a certain nutritional shelf life: look for a manufacture date stamped on the package.

Record the date in your record-keeping book, each time you buy frozen food and store it in your freezer. This way you will know exactly how old it is as time goes on. If too much time passes, freezer burn will occur, and the food, I'm sure, will not be as nutritionally beneficial as intended. To ensure maximum freshness, use common sense: find as current a manufacture date as possible, and use the food within a reasonable period of time.

Live food, in my opinion, should be avoided. Brine shrimp can contain certain parasites that would be hard to eradicate once they got into the tank. I have been told not to introduce live brine shrimp. Apparently they are bred in conditions that are not that clean. I personally have had no luck at all in breeding brine shrimp (which is probably fortunate for my reef). Thus, I have come to abandon completely any idea of using live brine shrimp. Frozen brine shrimp are fine in moderation, but they are fatty.

Natural food consists of algae produced in the tank and other small organisms that are present in the live rock. Many "reef fish" (fish that will not bother corals) are algae eaters. Some will eat more than others. Some will eat all the algae they can find (yellow tangs, algae blennies, etc.), while others will just pick at it. Whether they pick or devour, it is a good sign to see them forage. It is desirable to have a manageable, natural supply of algae for them to eat.

Most of the micro- and macro-organisms that live in and on the live rock are not that obvious to the naked eye, and many of them only come out at night. It is my belief that as long as the reef has an abundant supply of oxygen, proper light, purified water, and trace elements added regularly with a high-quality salt mix during water changes, these almost invisible creatures will flourish, providing an additional natural food source for the fish and helping to keep the reef in balance. Having said that it is also important to occasionally supplement the reef inhabitants with, the home made food recipe occasionally fortified with Selcon (vitamin supplemental mix which is in liquid form). Note the Selcon will have a temporary detrimental effect on your protein skimmer.

Methods of feeding:

My fish always seem to be hungry. This is a very good sign. I feed them once a day, giving them only what they can eat in a few minutes. If I am feeding flake, I pinch a good bit (1/4 teaspoon) between my fingers, place it underwater, and then briefly remove it before releasing it into the tank. This way it gets water-soaked and will sink toward the bottom as it is being eaten. This method of presoaking the food ensures that it doesn't go into the overflow and out through the filter. This could cause problems by (1) providing a food source for undesirable algae, and/or (2) clogging your prefilter and overworking the skimmer.

Some foods (shrimp pellets and the like) are of the "sinking" variety. They will not cause problems by entering the filter, but they may sink too fast, and until they soften up from being underwater they will be difficult for most fish to eat. Also, if a fish does pick up a piece of this kind of food, and then drops it, the food can get trapped in the rock. Use sinking foods with caution, making sure they get eaten.

Presoaked flake food works best. If you have a good balance of livestock, any food that gets past the fish will be eaten by other tank inhabitants like cleaner shrimp, coral-banded shrimp, and small crabs (hermit, decorator). Leftovers provide nicely for the needs of these creatures.

Nutritional balance and a variety of foods are the goals in feeding the fish and keeping them healthy. You the keeper are responsible for fulfilling the dietary needs of your fish. Do not overfeed them! If they seem hungry, give them a little more food at the next feeding. If they are not overfed, they will forage on natural food (microorganisms and algae), which will get eaten instead of accumulating.

Feeding lettuce:

> *Do not introduce lettuce into the tank*

Some people have recommended feeding lettuce or the like to your fish. It has been strongly suggested to me by an expert I trust: do not feed your fish lettuce or any terrestrial base plants! Apparently there is a product in the fresh vegetation that is not removed by protein skimming and could induce an uncontrollable algae outbreak that will be most difficult to remove. Enough said.

Feeding the anemones:

Most of these creatures are photosynthetic, acquiring much of their sustenance from the lighting system. Some have a symbiotic relationship with certain types of clown fish: the fish will bring pieces of food for the anemone to ingest. Also, trace elements contained in a high quality salt mix provide much of their needs, along with nutrients in the water.

However, from time to time (every 3-4 weeks) most anemones appreciate a direct feeding of small pieces of clams, shrimp, or fish. This is usually done with tongs or with a thin long-handled stick, with the food placed on the end and directed to the *center* of the creature. *Lightly* place the small piece of food, and the anemone will "close up" around it. On occasion shrimp or fish will snatch up the piece of food and you will have to try again. Feed the anemones after you have fed the rest of the tank, so the other inhabitants will be less likely to take the food intended for the anemone.

Although feeding is important, and interesting to watch, do not overfeed these creatures. The size of the anemone will limit the size of the food pieces you can place in it. Under that limit, always err in the direction of underfeeding.

Feeding the corals:

My experience on the feeding of coral is that these creatures need a balance of proper lighting provided by specialized bulbs made for reef purposes only, with the correct wattage administered over the course of 9 hours a day. Most if not all corals will benefit from occasional feeding of prepared foods such as defrosted frozen fish foods or the home made food recipe contained in this book. Corals also receive essential minerals and other nutrients from a high-quality salt mix when water changes are performed, and when additional iodine, strontium, and calcium are added on a regular basis to replace what is consumed by the inhabitants of the reef and what is removed by adequate protein skimming.

A final note on feeding. See Questions and Answers in the rear of this book for a high quality, inexpensive, easy to make food recipe.

AS NEEDED: 1. REMOVE UNWANTED ALGAE (GLASS AND OVERFLOW PIPES)

Preventive measures:

You should not have a problem with algae if you have followed these recommendations:

- Purify your tap water with a triple carbon prefilter and reverse osmosis or deionizer system;
- Use Kalkwasser regularly to keep the pH between 8.2 and 8.4;
- Do water changes every 2 to 3 weeks;
- With water changes, vacuum off as much as possible of the debris in the rock crevices;
- Change your prefilter pad every week;
- Have the lighting on for no more than 9 hours a day, using the wattage recommended in Chapter 5;
- Do not use unnecessary additives (as discussed under "Biweekly: 2. Add Trace Elements,")
- Employ herbivorous livestock (turbo snails, small hermit crabs, hard starfish, and algae-eating fish such as yellow tangs, algae blennies, angels, etc.).

These procedures will ensure that your reef will not be overtaken by green, brown, or red algae that would cover desirable livestock and organisms (such as the hard pink coraline algae) that depend on water flow and light.

I cannot overemphasize the importance of following *all* the previous recommendations, as they will ensure that the undesirable algae do not have the conditions they need to survive, and *undesirable algae are the bane of reef keeping.* Follow the suggested procedures, and the algae should be manageable!

I can only say "should be manageable," because I cannot know the exact quality of your tap water or the specifics of your tank setup (whether it is too close to constant sunlight, etc.). At one time I had a major algae dilemma, but when I followed all of the above recommendations, the problem disappeared, never to return again at an unmanageable level.

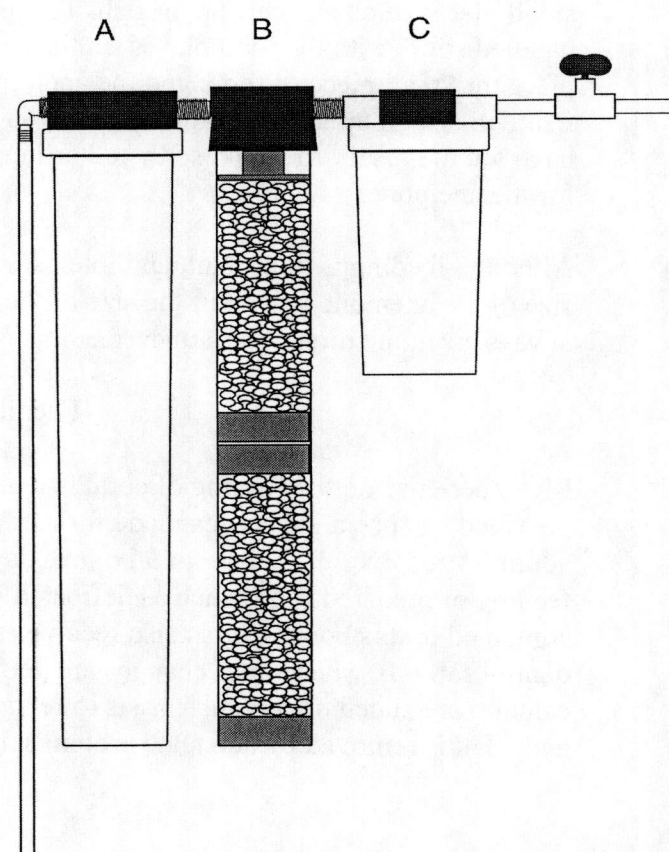

Micro-algae will grow!

The growth of micro-algae is a natural occurrence and will happen in most healthy tanks. It is only when the algae become unmanageable that we have a problem. Managing the growth of micro-algae means (1) limiting the conditions they need to thrive, (2) having livestock that will eat most of the algae, and (3) removing the remainder by hand with magnets, blade scrapers, and brushes.

In my tanks, brown and some green algae form on the glass on a regular basis. They do not thrive for long in other areas; they are only a problem on the glass and overflow pipes.

> *By following the recommendations here, you should be able to manage the micro-algae in your tank*

The glass is easily cleaned with an algae glass-cleaning magnet. When buying such a magnet, purchase the largest one you can find. Usually the larger the size, the stronger the magnet and the better the cleaning capabilities (pull) it will have. The magnet does a nice job for weekly or twice weekly cleaning. Little bright green patches will eventually form. These should be scraped off with a razor blade. You should only have to "blade" the glass about once a month at the most.

Algae growth—live sand vs. eggcrate setup:

The type of setup you have will determine the other areas where algae may accumulate in your system. If you use all eggcrate, algae growth will be less, because light will be blocked off from the back of the tank, as well as from the bottom surface and most of the sides. If you have a live sand filter, it is in your best interest to use less rock, because you want to be able to move the rock to vacuum the sand filter from time to time. Therefore, when you use a sand setup, parts of the back and sides of your tank will have some rock leaning up against the glass. The glass back of the tank will be exposed to light, and this will be an area for algae to form.

In these areas, lean the rock away from the glass and scrape off the algae with a razor blade (you can buy a blade holder extension handle for this purpose). This is not really a big deal, but it can get to be a nuisance. In my experience, the algae will spread to other areas if you let it grow on the glass for a while; if you keep scraping it off, it seems to grow only on the glass. For a tank with a live sand filter, I recommend having at least one yellow tang or other major algae-consumer (more than one for larger tanks).

With a live sand filter, the sand itself is likely to have algae growth. This is best managed with small hermit crabs. They constantly process the sand (a very interesting thing to watch), eating away algae and other organisms as they go along. With live sand, when you do a water change, it is recommended that you vacuum the gravel with gravel cleaner. This is another good way to interrupt algae growth on the substrate.

An enclosed reef set up on eggcrate, in my opinion, is going to have less algae accumulation, because the live rock blocks light from getting to the back of the tank. This setup seems to discourage micro-algae growth. The back, sides and upper eggcrate are covered with pink coraline algae as well as tube fan worms and other organisms. This, as we all know, is desirable.

I believe that the all-eggcrate system with covered tank sides is the way to go. It seems with solid sides (wood with black epoxy) that you don't get external light and/or a reflection of light from the lighting canopy onto the glass. On an all-glass aquarium, you can get the same effect by covering the back and sides with an opaque backing of some kind, removable for inspecting the tank.

WHY REEF STORES DO NOT HAVE AN ALGAE PROBLEM

Keep in mind that algae will grow and will have to be removed by hand on a regular basis. Do not be deceived when you go into your favorite reef store and observe that their tanks have no visible algae. You may think, "My tank has algae, why doesn't his?" The fact is that every morning someone cleans the glass and maintains the tanks so they will look absolutely pristine. This gives the impression that the people in the store know something about water quality that you don't. In fact, all they are doing is daily maintenance, in addition to the procedures listed above.

Having your hands in the tank:

> *Oils from your hand*
> *will temporarily affect the protein skimmer*

You should clean the glass every couple of days. I prefer to use a magnet. However, in stores a brush with a squeegee is used: the brush for the algae, and the squeegee for water spots on the outside of the glass. Stores have many tanks, and they are set up so that it's all right if they get some water on the floor. This method would not be practical in our homes. Again, I prefer a strong magnet. Another benefit of the magnet is that your hand is not in the water as much. Even if you wash your hands thoroughly (with water only), there are some oils that get in the water, and this will temporarily affect the protein skimmer.

> *Adding food to the tank*
> *will also affect the skimmer temporarily*

You will observe this when you put your hands in the tank. Look at the skimmer. Before your hands go in the water, the skimmer is foaming; the foaming will stop when you put your hands in. Fortunately, this is a temporary effect, which will last only 1 or 2 hours. Do not be overly concerned with this, as there are certain maintenance procedures that must be done with your hands in the water. Just be aware that you should not put your hands into the tank unnecessarily. To a certain extent the old adage, "Keep your hands out of the tank." is a good idea—but we do have to perform maintenance. Again, use common sense.

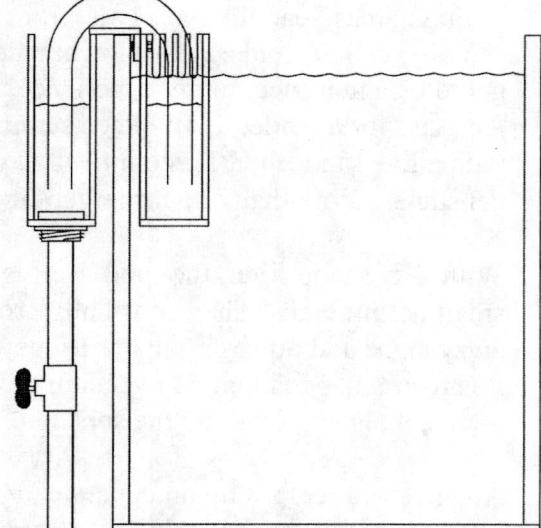

You will also find that simply adding food to the tank will temporarily affect the skimmer. Note the contents of any prepared food that affects the skimmer negatively. Try to use only those products that have a high nutritional content, and the least effect on the skimmer.

Removing algae on the overflows:

One other ideal spot for algae to grow is on any overflow, which will be close to the lighting and will have good water flow over it. Algae will definitely thrive if you have either (1) a solid dam-type wall overflow with a protector to keep tank inhabitants from going over, or

(2) drilled-through pipes with plastic screen protectors. From time to time you will need to remove the overflow with the protectors, and scrub off the algae. A good tool for this purpose is a bottlebrush, approximately 2-1/2" in diameter; this can be purchased in any domestic department store. Persistent algae in the tank can be scrubbed and then swirled into the brush and rinsed off in the sink.

Livestock to manage algae:

If you find algae growing in clumps on the rock, chances are you don't have adequate algae-eating livestock. Fish are the most aggressive consumers of algae (yellow tangs and algae blennies are good at this). Other algae management livestock are:

Turbo snails eat a fair amount of algae in tight areas, and can get around well in the tank. They usually will not eat clumps of algae. You cannot rely solely on these snails. Although they are an essential element of algae management, they have their limits. (On a side note - the name Turbo is the scientific naming of this creature, Turbo being spiral).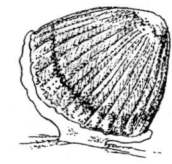

Hermit crabs also eat algae and cover a lot of area. They are especially good at sifting through the sand, constantly eating small bits of algae and picking at the rock as they forage. Hermit crabs are also limited as to the amount of algae they will consume. It seems they are not exclusively algae eaters, and they enjoy a variety of foods.

Hermit crabs are an asset to a reef tank with their constant picking at the rock and stirring of sand. When they are small (shell size 1/4" to 1-3/4"), they are great and generally do not damage other livestock. However, when they get larger than 2", they can cause extensive damage—and the larger they get, the more destructive their habits! As they grow, their appetites increase, and watch out! I have seen them firsthand open large clams and mussels, and eat just about anything alive. Keep your eye on the mid-sized crabs, and keep them well fed. Once they display destructive behavior, they will have to be brought to your reef store for someone else to handle. So when introducing them, put in relatively small ones. The smaller ones are an asset to any reef tank.

Sea urchins (pencil) are also algae eaters. However, they do not eat algae exclusively and cannot be relied on to manage algae in the reef. But having a few of them makes the tank interesting, and they will eat some algae. From my own observations, they are somewhat shy and do not seem to be fond of light. You will see them from time to time, but they prefer to stay relatively hidden and are slow moving.

Fish are the best algae consumers. Yellow tang, sailfin tang, hippo tang, algae blennies, and angels are constant algae pickers. By having exclusively fish that pick and eat algae, you will keep the algae totally manageable, providing you have followed all the preventive recommendations. Some fish at first will not readily accept commercial food, and will try to eat off the rock. After a while, they will begin to accept prepared food and will spend the rest of their time picking small bits of algae off the rock and anywhere else it crops up.

Keep in mind that we have an enclosed system. Even with our best attempts at processing the water (protein skimming), doing regular water changes, and keeping the pH in the proper range, a certain amount of nutrients will accumulate, and algae will grow.

The selection of livestock is important for successful algae management in a reef tank. In an enclosed system there will inevitably be nutrient buildup, which leads to micro-algae growth, to be controlled by algae-eating livestock of our choice. This, in my opinion, is a man-made environment in which we choose the elements. We can make choices of livestock that are favorable to managing algae in an enclosed system, or we can make choices that will make algae management nearly impossible.

Ratio of livestock:

I recommend that the largest population of livestock in the reef tank be shrimp, starfish, clams, urchins, snails, and harmless crabs. Next, in a lesser amount, would be the corals; they produce a minimum amount of waste, and in fact some of them will process waste. Finally, fish should be added, in the smallest numbers. They are the largest consumers of food, and therefore produce the most waste. Having only a few fish will mean that you will be putting in less commercial food. This reduces the risk of food going uneaten and accumulating in the prefilter, possibly becoming food for algae and/or leading to diminished water quality.

Your fish should be reef-compatible only; that is, they should eat algae but not coral. As I have mentioned in other areas of this book, nearly all of the creatures we put into our tank should be able to consume their fair share of naturally occurring algae. The selection of livestock is important for algae management.

I recommend that nearly all of the livestock in your reef tank be algae consumers—fish especially. To be allowed into your reef, just about every creature should consume its fair share of algae. This way, not only are the tank inhabitants interesting and beautiful, but they will serve an important function! They will manage the unavoidable, naturally occurring algae that would be a major inconvenience for you (the reef keeper) to remove manually. Let the fish, snails, crabs, and urchins remove it for you, naturally!

Manual removal of algae:

Then of course, the remaining algae will be removed by hand, particularly from the glass and overflow pipes. By using a strong magnet or a razor blade for the glass, and a bottlebrush for the overflow, it is not a problem to remove undesirable algae.

It is important to remember that we want to *remove* the algae, not just dislodge it. When using the magnet, after a few swipes you will feel the scrubber part of the magnet cleaner getting full of algae. Take this to the sink and rinse it off. Resume cleaning and repeat the rinsing process as often as needed. Rinse the scrubber when you are done. When using the bottlebrush, swirl it to trap the algae in the bristles, and rinse it out in the sink.

A strong algae magnet and Bottlebrush are useful tools

Some algae, of course, will get away from you. This cannot be avoided. Remove as much as you can, within reason. Algae that are dislodged and left in the tank will either reattach elsewhere, decompose into food for other algae, or get trapped in the prefilter (which needs regular maintenance to prevent it from getting clogged.

Summary of algae management:

I hope I have not scared you about managing algae. If you follow the suggestions I have given, it can be done easily. *Algae accumulation can be a serious threat to the enclosed reef system. Left unmanaged, it can become a problem that would test anyone's patience and sanity; it is not something you want to battle with!* However, if you select your livestock carefully and follow the other recommendations I have discussed, the naturally-occurring algae in your tank will be a good food source for the livestock, and what they don't eat can be managed with regular maintenance.

Remember:

You should run the tank.
The tank should not run you!

AS NEEDED: 2. CLEAN PROTEIN SKIMMER; CHANGE AIR STONES; ADJUST VENTURI VALVE

The protein skimmer is the most essential component for external filtration. Other than the prefilter, it is the only external filtration device that will need regular cleaning and maintenance.

Wiping out the inner neck:

It is important to keep the inner walls of the protein skimmer's neck clean and smooth, so that the foaming action and the actual skimming are efficient. If you have too much buildup on the inner neck, the foam will begin to cling to the sides, and the skimming action will be less effective. Manually remove the accumulated scum. Try wiping out the inside neck with a paper towel on a regular basis. This will facilitate the foaming, removing action.

You should frequently wipe out the collection area, where the overflowing foaming action takes place. Use a paper towel, and wipe off the brown scum so the skimmer is see-through again. Also wipe out the cover, and if your skimmer is air-driven wipe the air tubes. When doing this on a casual basis, you don't even have to shut off the pumps. Just uncover the skimmer, and wipe out any visible scum.

For a Venturi type skimmer, adjust the Venturi valve so the air bubbles are of the smallest size possible. Make sure the air intake tube is unobstructed. When taking the skimmer down, remove the Venturi valve, and make sure it is clean.

Counter-current system—replacing the air blocks:

The maintenance procedure for air-driven systems is to replace the air stones. Over a period of time they are a costly item. It is universally suggested that the wood blocks are replaced every 3 to 4 weeks, and over a period of time the cost can really add up. Most sizable skimmers have two wood blocks; at $3.50 each that comes to $7 a month, or $84 a year in disposable air stones! Personally, I have tried to use them for more than the 4 weeks (with poor results), and have even gone as far as to dry them out in the sun for many days and then belt sand the wear-off, so they could be reused (again, with poor results). Obviously, the next step for me will be to make my own. I have not had the time to pursue that endeavor as of yet! They are limewood blocks, cut to approximately 1" x 1" x 3", with a hole drilled in the block to accept the airline. The challenge is to find a supplier of dry limewood. The rest would be relatively easy. I just can't see them costing $3.50 each and lasting only a month!

Below is an idea of making your won from a piece of basswood located in any hobby supply shop. Basswood is the American equivalent of European limewood.

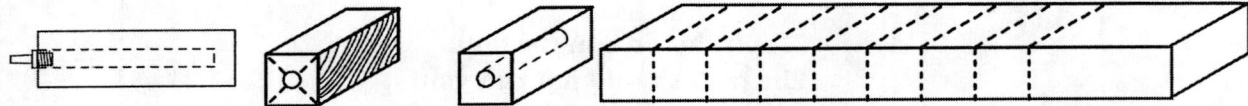

Counter-current system—air pump:

Another substantial cost in running an air-driven skimmer is the air pump! This pump will take a beating over a period of time. The constant driving of wood block air stones will take its toll on the best of air pumps. We are not talking about decorative bubbles here. The bubbles must be extremely small so that the particles of waste can adhere to them, foam to the top, and overflow. The air pump should be the strongest you can afford, and no matter what its quality, after about a year it will put out considerably less pressure. This will affect the efficiency of the skimmer.

Yes, air pumps can be rebuilt, but I personally have never had any luck with rebuilt ones. They never seem to work as well rebuilt as they did when they were new. This is an important factor when choosing your initial skimmer. Consider the long-term costs of running it: $85 for disposable air stones, $60 or so for a new air pump every year. This can be a significant cost, especially if you buy the skimmer without knowing this ahead of time. Then you may be stuck with a skimmer you want to get rid of, unless you are prepared for the long-term costs!

With all that said, air-driven skimmers work extremely well and use less electricity than Venturi skimmers (which require strong water pumps). Although a water pump will probably last longer than an air pump, water pumps also have to be replaced over a period of time—every 2 or 3 years. As I said from the beginning, this hobby is expensive, no matter how you look at it!

One other note on air-driven versus Venturi skimmers: you will rarely, if ever, see an air skimmer being used in a commercial (store) setup. Hmmm. I wonder why that is?

Note: *The downdraft skimmer is probably the most high performance, trouble free and easy to maintain skimmer on the market today.*

Nevertheless, if you have or plan to use an air skimmer, the air stones will have to be replaced on a regular basis (every 3 or 4 weeks) for the skimmer to be effective. When the blocks are ready to be replaced, you will see that they have a slime on them, and that they look shot. Throw them away, put on new ones, and keep an eye on the water level in the neck of the skimmer (it may have to be adjusted because of the new air blocks). You will always notice an improvement in the foam consistency when the blocks are replaced.

Flushing out the skimmer:

The last maintenance procedure is to disconnect the skimmer, take it outside, and blow it out with a garden hose. A combination of a large bottlebrush and a power spray attachment to the hose will get the skimmer looking good as new. Dry it off with a clean towel. Take it back to its station, and reconnect it. This should be done once a month, or every other water change. You really want to keep the skimmer clean and new looking, not for appearance, but for optimum performance—which is essential for the reef!

WEEKLY: 1. CHANGE PREFILTER PADS

For a discussion of this topic, see "Material To Use for Prefilter; Cleaning the Prefilter,"

BIWEEKLY: 1. CHANGE WATER

If the quality of the water becomes less than ideal, some livestock will suffer and possibly die. It is necessary to keep the highest quality of water we can manage. Over an extended period of time, this can only be done with frequent water changes (a minimum of 12% to 15% every 2 weeks).

Following a regular schedule:

You may, after a while, happen to skip a scheduled water change. The reef will seem to be fine, but when you do the next water change you may notice that certain corals have retracted. Sometimes they will never be the same again. This is a shock to the delicate coral, and it may lead to a slow death. This is not responsible reef management. Not only is it unfair to the delicate livestock; it is costly because of unnecessary losses. You must be willing to perform water changes every two weeks for responsible reef management and optimum results!

The water changes should be done on an absolutely regular basis; if you agree to a two-week schedule, stick to it! The livestock will get used to this and expect the change every two weeks. The problem is that sometimes we begin with two weeks, then skip a week and go to a three-week schedule for a while, return to the two-week schedule eventually, and so on—we keep fluctuating. This is not good for the reef. By keeping a regular schedule of water changes (every two weeks), you will maintain a higher quality of water.

You have most likely noticed that throughout this book it is emphasized that balance and stability are required to have a successful reef tank. Almost every procedure should be done regularly, using or installing the same products each time. Let me run off a quick list of such products:

- Salt mix
- Kalkwasser
- Trace elements (iodine, strontium)
- Light bulbs and timers for the lights
- Food for the livestock
- Prefilter material (optional)
- Livestock (purchased from the same supplier)

All these elements are needed to keep the reef alive and healthy. The reef will begin to depend on all these essential factors, and will expect the vital benefits they provide.

Biweekly water change—sequence of procedures:

1. First, calculate 12% to 15% of the tank's volume. Find a plastic container that will accommodate that volume, plus a little extra for a buffer. You will also need a powerhead with a 6- to 8-foot length of hose attached to it. Figure the gallons per inch of the tank, measure down from the very top of the tank, and put a mark there (leave this mark for future reference).

2. Fill the container with purified tap water, as described previously, to the

> *Spilling, overflowing buckets are unnecessary*

proper level needed for your tank. Bring the temperature of the new water up to the temperature of the tank. Do this by using a heater or by letting it get to room temperature naturally. Estimate the amount of salt mix: 1 cup salt will make approximately 3 gallons of saltwater with a salinity of 1.024. Add the salt, plug in the powerhead, and mix for about 6 to 8 hours. Observe the water. It should be clear, indicating that all the salt has dissolved. If it is not clear yet, continue mixing until it is. Then test the water's salt content with a specific gravity meter. Make the necessary adjustments to get a reading of 1.024. Continue mixing for a couple of hours until the salt is completely dissolved and you are confident that the water is at room temperature or within 5 degrees of the temperature in the tank. *I usually let the water acclimate to room temperature for a day, add the salt, let it mix for a day, check it again, make adjustments, and then use it.*

3. Drain the water. You will need a system to drain the wastewater into. I do not recommend buckets, as they are too messy to use. Spilling, overflowing buckets that have to be carried out and dumped will make changing the water a very unpleasant task. I use an old pool skimmer vacuum pipe. This is a plastic, ribbed, flexible tubing that is 1-1/4 in diameter by approximately 25 to 30 feet long. Keep your eye out for one of these pipes. Sometimes they get thrown out, or they can be purchased from a pool supplier. They work very well.

> *Place a reference mark on the tank, representing how much water is to be changed. This will be an extremely helpful reference mark for future water changes*

4. Shut off the water coming out of the tank. Prior to removing any water from the tank, we want to fill the tank to the absolute top. This will eliminate unnecessary exposure of the live rock to air, when we drain out the water we are going to replace. Let the pump fill the tank to the very top. Then shut the pump off. (You may need a shutoff valve on the pump to prevent water from siphoning back into the sump). The tank should now be filled (topped off) with water, and all the pumps should be shut off.

The drain system for your water changes will need some thought and consideration. I have mentioned the pool skimmer vacuum pipe that I use; a large diameter garden hose may also work. You will need a safe area to drain the waste water: either outside onto the ground, or into a sink, tub, shower or washing machine drain *(lower than the tank, so a siphon can be employed)*. The drain hose should be of a large enough diameter so it will not become clogged with sand or debris. The main drain hose will be temporarily fastened to the stand below the tank, so that the vacuum hose with which you will be cleaning the tank can drain directly into it.

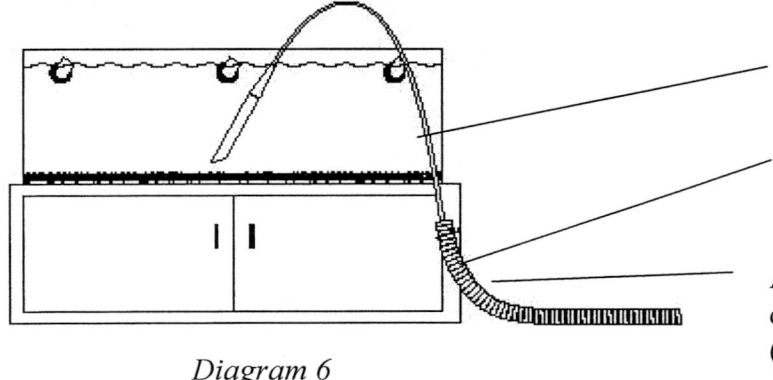

Pinch the hose here to control water flow

A small hook to keep the drain hose in place

A 1.5 – 2" pool drain hose to a safe waste disposal area.
(salt water will kill grass)
A shower drain may be a good choice

Diagram 6

Once you have a drain system, you are ready to proceed. Keep in mind that saltwater is not good for your lawn or garden and will most likely kill any type of delicate vegetation it comes in contact with. The water should be drained to an area where this will not be a problem. Also, if you drain into a sink or tub you will need to clean and rinse a significant amount of debris.

5. Now we need 5 or 6 feet of clear vinyl tubing, 5/16" inside diameter. You can find this size along with many others at a good hardware store or home improvement center. It is important to use a small diameter hose for vacuuming the rock, so the water does not siphon out (drain) too fast! This small hose will give you adequate suction, and time to vacuum all the debris on the rock, without worrying about removing more water than necessary, or going below the reference mark on the tank before you are done cleaning all the rock crevices.

6. The last item you need is a gravel vacuum. These come in many sizes, and you want the smallest one available: 1-inch diameter. This item will help you to start a siphon easily, and will also clean the sand or the front bottom area if you are using eggcrate. The smallest size will give you better control of cleaning without removing more water than necessary. This item is found in pet stores or by mail order supply.

7. How to start the siphon. (The following explanation may be long, and I apologize if you already know how to start a siphon this way. But those who think they have to suck on the tube to start a siphon will welcome this information.)

Lay out the main drain hose, and temporarily fasten one end of it to the stand (below the tank) using cable ties. Attach the gravel cleaner to one end of the 5- to 6-foot, 5/16" diameter hose. Place the other end of the hose into the main drain fastened below the tank. Take the gravel cleaner in your right hand, and using it like a scoop, place it in the tank sideways, filling it

Common gravel cleaner, used to start the siphon

with water. With the cleaner tube filled with water, raise the cleaner above the water line. Water will begin flowing down the tubing. With your left hand about 4 feet down on the tubing (below the water line), begin to crimp the tube as the water drains to the area of the crimp. Because the tube is being crimped, and is below the water level, the water will fill about 1/2 of the tubing (see diagram 6). Again, fill the cleaner, raise it above the water line, and release the crimp with your left hand. Water will flow out of the cleaner, filling the tube completely from the area where your left hand is, to the base of the cleaner. Crimp the tubing again. Place the cleaner underwater in the tank, sideways (letting any large air pockets escape from the cleaner chamber), release the crimp with your left hand, and you have a siphon going.

8. Vacuuming the live rock. Now that we have the siphon going, water will be draining out of the tank. Control this by crimping the tubing with your left hand. This will stop the water from draining when you are not actually removing waste.

Start at one end of the tank. Remove the gravel cleaning attachment from the tubing, and leave it in the tank. *Using only the tubing as a vacuum*, place it on the rock, and remove any loose debris and sediment from the rock. Be extremely thorough, paying particular attention to the crevices and nooks and crannies. When you have done the face of the rock, stick the tubing behind, under, and into areas you cannot see. Use the tubing as a probe. When you see a lot of debris getting sucked up, hold the tube in that area until the water flowing through looks clear. You should be impressed with the amount of waste and sediment being removed.

Work your way very thoroughly, top to bottom, from one end to the other. Keep an eye on the reference mark on the tank, so you know how much water is being removed. Use the crimping action to stop the water when you are not vacuuming. By allowing water to flow through the siphon only when you are vacuuming, you will have enough time to clean all the rock and bottom area thoroughly before the planned amount of water has drained out of the tank.

9. Cleaning the gravel or bottom. When all the rock has been cleaned, attach the gravel vacuum.

> *The 5/16" tubing can vacuum the small nooks and crannies of the rock*

Do this underwater, or you will have to start the siphon again. Use the gravel cleaner to vacuum the bottom area. With an all-eggcrate system, the spraybar should push most of the debris to the front of the tank. Here you only have a couple of inches to clean. Working from one end to the other, place the cleaner on the bottom. If you have some sand on the bottom, it will swirl up into the cleaner, and the debris (because it is lighter than the sand) will get sucked out. Use the crimping action on the hose to control the rate at which water is draining through the siphon. If you do not control the flow, sand will get sucked out as well as debris. I place the cleaner on the bottom, let debris and sand swirl around, and when the sand starts to siphon out, I crimp the hose. When the sand and debris have settled, I release the crimp and repeat the process. After a while, you will become comfortable with this technique and develop your own feel for it. Complete the cleaning this way, keeping an eye on the reference mark on the tank.

10. For a live sand or all sand bottom, proceed as described above. The only difference is that from time to time you will have to move the rock so you can clean the sand underneath and behind it. For an all sand bottom, it is most desirable to have large pieces of live rock that are flat, wide, or long. This makes it much easier to move the rock from one side to the other, out of the way, or back into place. If you vacuum the sand thoroughly, you will end up with little piles of sand where you cleaned. You can smooth these out with your hand or let the hermit crabs do it. Vacuum the sand up to the rock, move the rock, vacuum there, replace the rock, and so on until you complete the bottom.

Again, keep an eye on the reference mark on the tank. If you happen to finish the cleaning early, you can just let the water drain to the mark. But if the water reaches the mark before you are finished vacuuming, you will need to replace more water than originally estimated.

11. Refilling the tank: If you have not gone to the reference mark, drain the water to the mark. The water in the mixing vessel should be mixing all along. Check the salinity of the tank, compare it to the new water, and if needed make adjustments at this time. Check that the temperature of the new water is within 5 degrees of the tank temperature. You should have a hose connected to the powerhead to provide a more thorough mixing in the vessel. Take one end of the hose and place it in the sump. Fill the sump to near the top, and then plug in the main pump while the new water is still pumping into the sump. Open the valve on the overflow from the tank. If you have done everything correctly, the water volume should be perfect. If not, you may have to make some adjustments now and for the next time you do a water change. Follow this method, and I don't think you will be disappointed.

12. Conclusion: It takes me about 1 hour to vacuum my 200-gallon tank. It has approximately 350 pounds of rock in it, set up on eggcrate. Twice a month I use 35 gallons of purified tap water, mixed with high-quality salt mix. I drain the old water outside to a wooded area. I keep a powerhead with a hose attached to it, in the mixing vessel (covered when not in use), and I use this equipment only for water changes. I prefer to do the change when I am not hurried, and if time allows I disconnect the skimmers, take them outside, and clean them as well. The skimmers usually take me an hour to do; this includes disconnecting, cleaning, drying, and reconnecting them.

Summary—water changes:

Regular water changes with a high quality salt mix will

- Dilute the waste products in the water,
- Remove accumulated debris on the rock and substrate,
- Replenish essential trace elements, and
- Reduce guesswork about which trace elements to add and how often to add them.

A high-quality salt mix introduced regularly is all that is required to provide the reef with what it needs to thrive, without having to be concerned with adding unfamiliar elements (not in the salt mix) that could possibly encourage the growth of micro-algae or add undesirable substances to the reef!

BIWEEKLY: 2. ADD TRACE ELEMENTS

As previously discussed, adding elements to the reef with confidence can be problematic at best. With the wide variety of products on the market today, it can be very difficult to know with certainty exactly what to add to the reef to supply the coral, the anemones, and the organisms on the live rock with the elements found in their natural habitat.

I have studied just about all I can on this subject, and have yet to formulate a list of products to add. Many of the recommendations on methods, amounts, qualities, and availability of specific trace elements have been vague at best. Some products are labeled "trace elements," but do not provide specific information on what is in the container. I stay away from any product that does not list its ingredients, and show how much of each one it contains.

I get the best results by performing regular water changes with a high-grade salt mix that has been specifically formulated for use in an enclosed reef. *A quality salt mix does not mind informing me of its contents.* By replacing water in the reef with a high-grade salt mix, I am replenishing the needed trace elements in regular amounts on a regular basis. This eliminates most of the guesswork and potential problems that can be caused by adding questionable products in questionable amounts.

The primary additives that I use are:

- **Calcium hydroxide (Kalkwasser)**, for water make-up;
- **Iodine**: 2 tablespoons every two weeks, between water changes (for a 200-gallon tank);
- **Strontium**: same dosage as above (for a 200-gallon tank).

Scarlet cleaner shrimp

These are the only additives and amounts I use regularly, and the ones I have found to provide an additional benefit to the livestock. The iodine and strontium are quickly used up, and are also removed by protein skimming. I add them the week in between water changes, again to distribute the benefits on an alternating basis: water change one week, trace elements the next.

Of course I do not speak for all reef keepers. I can only describe what I have found to be necessary and beneficial for my own reef. My corals grow, millions of life forms are thriving on the live rock, and the tanks look fantastic; so why would I consider adding products of uncertain composition?

A problem I have found can arise when a hobbyist reads an article that discusses the necessity and hypothetical benefits of adding a certain element. One can then think, "I should add this to my tank." But perhaps the store or supply house does not have the specific product discussed in the article. Something else is available, which contains the supposedly beneficial element, but combines it with others. The hobbyist adds the substitute product anyway, and problems result. Then the question is, "What is wrong with my reef?"

I have become very suspicious of introducing any new, unproven product into my reef tanks. Once it's in, it's in. It may be harmless, or it may not. I just don't like to experiment. Up until now, my reef has proven to me that all it needs to thrive and grow is:

- Regular water changes with purified tap water and a high-grade salt mix;
- Adding Kalkwasser on a regular basis to compensate for evaporation while maintaining calcium levels;
- Biweekly additions of iodine and strontium; and
- Proper lighting.

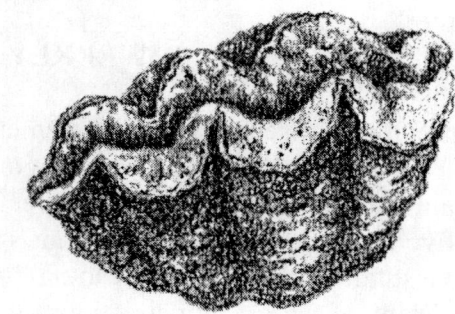

> **Products that will encourage micro-algae:**
>
> - **Phosphate**
> - **Iron**
> - **Silicate**
> - **Molybdenum**
> - **Liquid nutrient food source for filter feeders (must be refrigerated after opening)**

MONTHLY: 1. TEST WATER

Chapter 6 provides a detailed discussion of water testing.

MONTHLY: 2. CLEAN THE TANK COVER

The glass or plastic tank cover has been an area for concern among hobbyists. Covering the tank tightly will protect it from contaminants in the air, and will minimize evaporation; but neither of these effects is desirable in the modern reef.

Evaporation makes it necessary to add Kalkwasser regularly, which is very desirable. In fact, having substantial protein skimmers, and considerable turbulence in the sump box, encourages evaporation. Also, if your light canopy covers the whole top of the tank you will need at least one 2- to 4-inch fan, to disperse the heat generated by the high-intensity lighting. During semi-hot weather spells you may also want to run these fans when the lights are off, to facilitate cooling the tank, with or without using an air conditioner.

I recommend covering the tank approximately 1/2 to 2/3 with plate glass or Plexiglas. Avoid using Plexiglas in pieces longer than 24 inches, as they will gradually sag under their own weight. Glass is also better than Plexiglas at letting light through, and will allow a higher quality of light to reach the photosynthetic creatures. By covering 1/2 to 2/3 of the tank you will prevent most objects from falling in and splashing water onto the light bulbs, and you will reduce—but not eliminate—evaporation. *You will have an open area where the reef can "breathe" gas, and where temperature exchange will occur. The reef will benefit from this approach.*

Advantages of partial covering:

1. It allows some evaporation, giving you an opportunity to add Kalkwasser regularly.
2. It allows temperature exchange, keeping the tank at a more stable temperature.
3. It allows gas exchange (nitrogen gas released by de-nitrification and oxygen released by photosynthesis).
4. It protects the light bulbs from splashing water
5. Minimizes objects falling into the tank.

The fact is, evaporation and air/gas/temperature exchange are vital for the design of the modern reef, and the tank should be 1/2 (minimum) to 2/3 (maximum) covered with plate glass, at least 1/4 inch thick.

The maintenance involved is keeping the glass cover clean so the lighting will be most efficient. One problem will be with common dust. Here simply remove the glass cover and wipe it off. If you have a wave maker, water can splash onto the top of the glass cover. This should be avoided at all costs. It will eventually lead to a buildup of dried salt covering the glass and blocking most of the vital lighting from entering the tank. If you find that this is happening, remove the dried salt and correct the problem so that there is no salt buildup on the glass covering.

At times it may be helpful to take the glass panels to a sink or outside to a hose to clean them. Wipe them dry with a paper towel.

MONTHLY: 3. WIPE THE LIGHT BULBS

One other important monthly maintenance item is to take a slightly damp paper towel and wipe off the individual light bulbs. Do this of course when the lights have been off for some time. Wiping the light bulbs will remove dust particles and minor salt splashes. This will keep the spectrum output of the bulbs at their peak performance, and should be done on a monthly basis. Metal halide bulbs should only be wiped with a clean, soft, alcohol dampened cloth. Do not touch halide lamps with your bare hands! Always use a clean cloth.
If you are forced to handle them.

EVERY 3 MONTHS: 1. CLEAN THE COOLING FAN(S)

The cooling fans are workhorses, constantly moving air through the light canopy box. You will definitely notice a buildup of dust in and on the fan. For optimum performance of the fan and to prevent dust balls from getting into the water, carefully remove the fan from its location and thoroughly clean it. I have found 3-month intervals most effective for this maintenance job.

EVERY 3 MONTHS: 2. INSPECT AND CLEAN THE WATER PUMPS

The water pumps run continuously. They will last longer if you inspect them periodically; by temporarily removing them from the system and disassembling them to view the inner moving parts. Small problems can be observed, parts ordered, and any problems corrected while the pump is still working. Parts such as impellers and O-rings can wear, and may need replacing. This should be done on a 3-month preventive maintenance schedule. If you're adding calcium regularly there will be a significant build up of calcium deposit. *If this goes unchecked, when the power goes out and comes on again the pump may seize! If you are not at home when the power comes on the pump will be trying to start and finally burn out. So a word to the wise is clean the inside of the pump at regular intervals.*
Soaking the pumps internals in plain white vinegar will loosen the calcium deposits so they can be removed without un necessarily scratching the internal parts.
Dust will also accumulate on the motor. This should be cleaned so that the exterior of the pump is also kept in optimum condition.

EVERY 6 MONTHS: TAKE DOWN AND COMPLETELY CLEAN THE SUMP

At the 6-month mark your sump should be disconnected, taken outside to a garden hose, and thoroughly rinsed out with fresh water and a rubbing action from your hand and a new plastic brush designated for this purpose only. This will remove sediment that has accumulated on the bottom of the sump box. This is an extremely important maintenance procedure, as sediment can contain nutrients. If the sediment is left to accumulate it will contribute to nutrient buildup, possibly encouraging micro-algae and diminishing the water quality. I find that every 6 months there is *significant* sediment buildup that must be removed. You may take the sump down more frequently if you prefer.

EVERY 6 MONTHS: TAKE DOWN AND SERVICE THE PUMP

This procedure is similar to the 3-month inspection of the water pumps. The difference is that you now want completely to disassemble the inner workings of the pump impeller O-rings. Replace defective or questionable parts. Clean all parts of the pump, being as thorough as possible. Lubricate if applicable. Remove all dust and dirt from the motor casing. Get the pump up to optimum operating capacity as it was when it was new. Once it is placed back in service you should be confident that all the moving parts have been inspected, cleaned, and/or replaced.

If you keep an eye on the water pumps, your system will be less likely to have an unpredictable malfunction that could seriously affect the reef. Most progressive reef keepers replace the main pump and the skimmer pump after about 2 years of use. By keeping the older pumps, you have backup in case of malfunction and down time while waiting for parts to arrive, or in the event of actual pump failure. I recommend replacing your first pumps after 2 years. Then observe the life span of the new pumps, servicing them at the 3- and 6-month intervals recommended here. I have main pumps still operating very well after 5 years, while others have been replaced. Be prepared with a backup. Pumps will usually go at a very inopportune time, as I am sure you can imagine.

EVERY 6 MONTHS: REPLACE LIGHT BULBS

Refer to Chapter 5 for a full explanation of the reasons for changing bulbs. Reef bulbs last from 6 months to a year. I am aware that this is quite a range. It will really depend on your livestock. If you do not have creatures that expect absolute full light potency, you may be able to stretch the life span of the bulbs to almost one year. This is not recommended. As previously stated, unlike any other type of aquarium, a reef and all of its organisms will need a high-quality, life-providing bulb that is specifically designed for this purpose.

When you first install the bulbs, they will obviously be putting out the highest quality of vital illumination. As time goes on, month after month, the *quality* of illumination diminishes. You will not be able to observe this with the naked eye, but I assure you that the life forms in the tank will be affected by the difference. When you change the bulbs everything in the tank will *perk up and come alive.* Once you have observed this you will better understand the need to replace the bulbs regularly. I have found that replacing the bulbs every 6 months is the best way to maintain proper lighting so the reef creatures can photosynthesize, reduce nitrate, and grow.

Refer to Chapter 5 on lighting and Chapter 10 for information on purchasing replacement bulbs.

COMPLETELY TAKE DOWN, CLEAN, AND REBUILD THE REEF
Warning! If your reef tank is doing well this procedure is not necessary!

Typically new reef aquariums are just getting completely established at this point. Only use this technique as a last result to reinstate the tanks environment that may have become drastically out of balance.
The following instructions are also useful if you plan to move and are forced to relocate the tank. Despite your best planning and effort positioning the liverock as it was prior to the takedown will be next to impossible. The rebuilt reef will take 6 months to a year to develop the lush coraline growth it had before disassembly cleaning and re arrangement.

Occasionally, unexplained problems result in the enclosed reef. The remedy and preventive measure is to take the reef down, thoroughly clean the areas that cannot be serviced, and do a substantial water change (40% +).

In nature there are often upsetting storms that rip apart reefs, destroying and rebuilding. This is nature's way. We as reef keepers need not be as violent as Mother Nature, but we still need to act as if nature is present. Unfortunately this takedown and rebuilding has the possibility for some losses. Problems will result if sediment-rich deposits accumulate; they can lead to diminished water quality and an uncontrollable outbreak of micro-algae.

Doing a takedown with a major water change, paying close attention to where sediment is found and taking appropriate corrective measures, insuring proper operation of the spraybar and water flow in the tank—all of this will have positive, long-lasting effects on the reef. The takedown will also eliminate many potential problems. This in my opinion will determine the long-term future success or failure of the reef tank. *If this is not done, and problems such as micro-algae or diminished water flow occur after a period of time, you will be forced to play the undesirable and equally unfortunate "guessing game."* Let's not take chances: do it right, eliminate problems, improve water quality, and know with certainty what is going on with your reef tank.

We can compare this procedure with what we would do if we were moving from one residence location to another. The reef would have to be taken down, cleaned, and set back up. (Of course during an actual move the livestock would be making the trip as well, and would be at considerable risk from problems that can result in loss of life.

The goal is to do this procedure without any loss of livestock or major shock to the system.

What you will need:

1. Time. Allow yourself one whole day for this project.
2. Assistance. If possible, have an understanding and/or experienced person to help you.
3. Containers to hold replacement water equal to 40% of the tank volume.
4. Separate containers (at least 5) for coral, inverts, and different qualities of live rock.
5. Brushes of the correct diameter to clean the spraybar and plumbing supply to the tank.

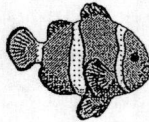

6. Cable ties.
7. Wire cutters.
8. Exterior garden hose.
9. Drop cloths to catch dripping water from live rock, corals.
10. Net for inverts.
11. All the apparatus for a water change.
12. Air pumps with airline and stones to administer oxygen to the containers of livestock while they are out of the tank.
13. New light bulbs: plan on installing them with the water change. This will help the photosynthetic creatures adjust and thrive in the new conditions.
14. Several 5-gallon buckets: have these on hand to wash off live rock as it comes out of the tank.
15. Disposable latex gloves (several pairs).

Before you begin:

- Double check and be certain you have more than enough containers for the live rock and invertebrates.
- Prepare and mix the new water at least one day in advance.
- Check temperature, salinity, and volume of water that you will change.
- Lay down drop cloths and/or newspaper to catch dripping water from the live rock.
- Set up drain system for wastewater (siphon hose, gravel cleaner, as for a water change).
- Plug in and check operation of air pumps, airline, and stones: one for each bucket of livestock.
- Be prepared to supply air to all containers holding livestock while they are out of the tank. This includes the live rock. Granted, when shipped it is out of water for many hours; but this contributes to the die-off on the live rock that takes so long to cycle out. When we perform this annual task of cleaning and rebuilding the reef, it will be the goal to have minimal (*if any*) die-off that would lead to an ammonia/nitrite cycle. *Make sure you administer oxygen to all the containers holding livestock!*
- Ideally begin this project in the morning, after the lights have been out and the reef is somewhat dormant. When everything is in place you are ready to begin.

Shut off the water overflow from the tank and let the tank fill to the absolute top. Then shut off all water pumps. Drain water from the tank to fill 2 or 3 of the containers that will hold the corals, anemones, and premium live rock. Fill the containers approximately 2/3 full of water from the tank, allowing for displacement when you add livestock. It is unnecessary to fill all containers with water from the tank at this time, and doing so would just expose more of the reef life to air.

Put on your latex gloves. Very carefully remove all of your corals and place them in a separate container; arrange them in a normal upright position where they are protected. Of course do not stack them. Many corals will need a waving motion of water to close up; if necessary, provide this motion with your hand (wearing the latex gloves).

Next remove all anemones. It is a good idea to place them in plastic bags filled with water. This will prevent the creatures from stinging each other, thus minimizing their stress during this ordeal. Try to place the anemones in a smaller, separate 5-gallon container from the delicate corals, even though they will be in bags. There is still a risk of releasing water that contains the anemones' stinging chemical, which would affect the coral.

Next remove the more delicate life forms (clams and sponges) and place them in the coral container until it is full.

Remove and place very carefully all of your premium ricordia live rock in a container designated for premium live rock only. As you remove pieces, vigorously wash sediment off the rock, as suggested for adding new rock. Dunk and swish each piece around several times. This will dislodge most sediment, and it will collect on the bottom of the 5-gallon wash-off bucket. As needed, fill containers 2/3 full of water from the tank and fill them with premium live rock. When all the quality rock is removed, proceed with the lesser quality in separately designated containers.

Continue to wash off sediment briskly from the rock in a 5-gallon wash bucket. If you have quite a bit of rock (more than 50 pounds) it will be more effective to use additional rinse buckets with clean water from the tank. You can use 2 buckets, allowing the sediment to settle in one and later pouring the clear top water into a clean bucket.

The goal is to dislodge sediment from the crevices of the live rock by briskly dunking and swishing the rock in water from the tank. Sediment buildup can be rich in nutrients, which contributes to diminished water quality, and can encourage growth of micro-algae.

When you have removed all of the live rock and it is in separate containers with airstones to provide oxygen for the life forms, you can proceed to remove the eggcrate material. This will usually require cutting cable ties and disassembling the framework so the bottom of the tank and the spraybar can be thoroughly cleaned, inspected, and set up again in the shortest amount of time possible.

Begin cutting the cable ties that hold the eggcrate, and remove the material. Try not to disturb sediment on the bottom under the eggcrate. At this point the water level will be quite low: approximately 1/2 of the water, and all of the live rock, has been removed.

As you have noticed, the fish, shrimp, and other highly mobile invertebrates are still in the tank. This is fine. I feel it is unnecessary to chase them around with a net and disturb the sediment. Most of them will stay to the side opposite where you are working.

Once all the eggcrate has been removed, begin to remove sediment with a large (3/8") hose and gravel cleaner. If you encounter large chunks of sediment, remove them with a net. Thoroughly clean the entire tank bottom, removing *all* sediment. Dislodge and remove any lumps or chunks of material adhering to the bottom and 6" up the sides of the tank. If they are not removed, these small barriers will restrict sediment flow to the front of the tank once it is set up again.

At this point you can begin adding the new saltwater to the tank. This will slowly acclimate the fish and inverts to the new water while you remove the spraybar. Add approximately 1/3 of the new volume of water. Do this as you would with a water change. A powerhead with a 6-foot garden hose will add the water nicely.

Remove the spraybar, take it outside to a garden hose, and thoroughly clean it with a combination of hose spray and bottle brushes. Reattach it to the pump return, and securely attach it to the bottom "anchor" devices. Pay particular attention to the direction of the bar. Position it correctly and securely fasten it in place.

Install the bottom eggcrate pieces, securely reattaching them to the rear anchors. Proceed with the back, then with the sides (as you did when you set it up originally). Install plenty of cable ties: they give the frame its structural integrity. Be sure to cut off and remove any excess cable tie material.

Refill the 5-gallon rinse bucket with clean saltwater and dunk, swish, and wash off the live rock piece by piece as you re-position it in the tank. This second washing provides a substantial benefit by dislodging more sediment. Position all the live rock as you did when you originally set up the tank: bottom base rock first, overlapping the eggcrate; then working up the sides, etc. For reminders of exact positioning, see "Placement of Live Rock on Eggcrate." Reinstall the rock and livestock in the reverse order of how they were taken out. Work up to ricordia and corals, clams, and sponges absolutely last. Of course add new water as needed, to keep the rock always covered.

Once everything has been placed back in the tank, add the rest of the water and turn on the pumps. Check for leaks on the spraybar attachment. Also be sure that the tank is operating with the proper water level.

Ideally there should be ample new water available. If there is extra new water, calculate how much there is, remove that amount of water from the tank (by estimating gallons per inch), and add the remaining new water. Discard old water, carefully checking the bottoms of the containers for desirable life forms. If you are lucky, some bristle worms may have fallen out and can be discarded at this time.

The last thing to do is to replace all light bulbs.

Observe the tank. In about 3-4 days check for ammonia, nitrite, nitrate, and pH, and record the test results. If you have followed the procedure here, ammonia and nitrite should read zero. Nitrate should be well below 10, or detected in only faint amounts. The pH should be 8.2 to 8.4 during the day after the lights have been on for 6 hours or more.

NOTES:

Chapter 10

Supplies

Chapter goal:
To direct the reader to the many practical alternative money-saving methods the author has found useful

As someone who has spent several thousands of dollars on reef keeping products, I consider myself an expert in this kind of purchasing. I have bought supplies in virtually all areas of this hobby, and on all experience levels. I believe that my expertise can be extremely valuable to you, as you purchase supplies for a new or existing reef tank.

How and where you purchase supplies will have a substantial effect on your budget, and on the overall cost of your reef

When I first started in this hobby, I was so eager to have a reef tank that I bought whatever I was told I needed. I trusted the suggestions of my retailer to steer me in the right direction. This, however, led to many expensive and unnecessary purchases of all kinds. Although several products available on the market today are vital to operating a reef tank, many others are inadequate or unnecessary. Because of my previous experience, one of the goals of this book is to inform the interested hobbyist about what I have found to be essential, what works best, and where to find it. *This information, I believe, is extremely valuable.*

I will break down the necessary items into separate categories. They are:

1. Tanks and stands
1. Sump box
2. Protein skimmer
3. Water purification equipment
4. Lighting
5. Expendable items
6. Live rock
7. Livestock
8. Unconventional products used in reef keeping

My suggestions on buying these items can help to make this hobby more practical and affordable.

1. TANKS AND STANDS

Know what you are looking for. The chapter on types of tanks can help you make your decision. Have a definite size in mind when you are ready to purchase a tank. If you want to buy new, call your local stores, and make a list of the prices they give you. Get to know what a particular tank is going for, with its stand. Shop around by phone. Always get the name of the person you speak with, so you can refer to them when you call back. Ask questions about the stand. (Is it open or does it have doors on it? What type of finish does it have? Etc.) Once you have a list, you can compare prices without actually having to go to individual stores. This will help you avoid making an impulsive decision.

If you want to buy a new tank and stand, and have shopped by phone to get the best price, then you are ready to visit the store to see what the components look like. If you like what you see, and it is within your budget, you are ready to buy. Larger tanks may have to be ordered. In this case, your retailer should be able to show you some photographs of what the tank and stand will look like. You may have to make a deposit, so be sure the particular tank you are ordering meets your needs.

Alternative approach #1: Buy someone else's tank. If buying new is not that important to you, consider a used tank. I have purchased many a tank this way, and have not had any problems. The cost is considerably less, because the owner *wants to sell*. Using this approach, you can *save a lot of money* on items that someone else paid top dollar for at one time, and now wants to get rid of. There are special newspapers that cater to people selling used items of all kinds, and you can save money by using these publications. Also, many people who belong to an aquarium society have tanks that they want to sell. Here, also, you can find some deals.

Alternative approach #2: Make your own. There is a section in this book on how to make your own tank. If you want a tank larger than 125 gallons, it may be worth your while to make it yourself. Again, I have used this approach with excellent results, and have saved money. Chapter 4, "Types of Tanks," will help you make your decision. See also Chapter 12, "Fabricating Components."

2. SUMP BOX

If you want to buy new, this component may be a bit hard to find. Know what size you need: that is, its gallon capacity. A trickle filter container may be the best bet, but be sure it will perform its function properly. Unfortunately, you may also have to buy the media with a trickle filter. Talk to your retailer, and tell him what you are looking for. See if he will accommodate your needs. If he values your business, he will. If not, you may have to use alternate methods.

Keep in mind the sump box is a very important component in your system, and you don't want to buy just anything. It must serve your needs and fulfill the desired function adequately. Get very familiar with what a sump box should do, so you will know exactly what you are looking for. It may be in your best interest to make your own, or find someone to make it for you.

Chapter 12, "Fabricating Components," will show and explain how to make your own sump box. If you are not mechanically inclined, a carpenter or a good glass/Plexiglas store should be able to fabricate one for you. This can be done with epoxied wood and a glass front, or with all Plexiglas. If someone else is going to make your sump box for you, you will have to draw a plan or design of what you want. Shop for prices, experience, and enthusiasm in the person or company who will do the project, and choose the person in whom you have confidence. If you have patience, this approach can ultimately provide a superior product.

If your circumstances allow enough space, a modified fish tank can also do the job. It will be more fragile than Plexiglas or wood. This may be a risk factor in the event of breakage. However, if conditions allow, a modified fish tank can be a reasonable, cost-effective alternative.

Some important ideas regarding other alternatives for a sump: A square container will hold a much greater amount of water than a cylindrical one of the same height and width (diameter). Also, in a square vessel it is easier to retrofit the two compartments for clean and dirty water. It is very desirable to have at least one side of the box transparent, so you can observe what is taking place inside. When you use a sump, this is where you will observe the changes in water level caused by evaporation, etc. So, an opaque cylindrical container is not really what you want.

3. PROTEIN SKIMMER

This component is of equal importance to the sump. You'll want the best you can get. Know what size you need, and whether you prefer air or Venturi, before you start looking around. I recommend cutting the factory rating in half. Skimmers are priced according to their size. The larger and taller the skimmer, the higher the price. In retail stores, you can expect to pay $250 to $350 for a decent-sized skimmer (6" in diameter, 24" to 36" high). This cost does not include the air or water pump that will be needed to drive the skimmer. Buying a used skimmer is usually the cheapest way to go. If you do not care to shop around for a used skimmer (it usually takes quite a bit of time to find the one that will serve your tank best), you may want to purchase this item from your retailer. He should have several to choose from, and you can actually see the product. However, this is the most expensive approach.

> *Purchasing a used skimmer is the least expensive approach*

Alternative approach #1: If you shop around and get some brand names and styles, you can also purchase this by mail order. By doing so, you can save a considerable amount of money. The only drawback with this is that you may not be able to see the product before you buy it. If you do use the mail order approach, I recommend that you speak to someone at the company who can thoroughly explain the skimmer to you. You'll want to know whether it is air or Venturi, how tall it is, what the diameter is, and how much water it will process. Remember my suggestion that you cut the factory rating in half. Also, you'll want to know what size pump the skimmer will need, whether it comes apart for a thorough cleaning, whether it is clear or tinted, its operating principle, whether it pumps in on top and is drained out by gravity on the bottom, whether it's the hang-on-the-back type (least desirable), and the size of the inlet and outlet.

Alternative approach #2: The design of a skimmer is no big mystery. It is actually quite simple. There is a description in Chapter 12 about how to build your own skimmer, which I'm

> *In deciding whether to make your own components, you will be choosing between convenience and effort*

sure you will find helpful. If you have any type of skill with power tools and cutting and fitting materials, you can build your own skimmer. Basically, what you will need is a source for the basic material, namely clear plastic pipe. Among plastic distributors, it is referred to as "rigid tubing." A good look in the Yellow Pages will lead you to some suppliers. After a few phone calls, you will find one who has exactly what you are looking for. With luck, the supplier will not be too far from your home.

If you plan to use air blocks, the skimmer will be relatively inexpensive to make. The 6" tubing costs about $8 a foot, and the 2" is about $3 to $4 a foot. The flat 1/4" plexi is about $3.50 a square foot. The other important item is glue for fastening the material. Your plastic supplier can provide the correct adhesive . The cost of the glue is insignificant. If you opt for a Venturi, which is the preferred skimmer design, you will also need to buy a Venturi valve. A one-inch Venturi valve costs about $40. These can be found in many of the national hobby magazines. They also list a major plastic distributor for tubing, in the event you cannot find one in your area. As with any self-made product, time and patience are essential. You will be investing them, to make up for what you save in money. The choice is convenience or effort.

4. WATER PURIFICATION EQUIPMENT

Don't worry about making your system for water purification. Here you will need a specific product—either a deionizer or reverse osmosis water purifier. The question will be: which one? They both have their advantages and disadvantages.

An R.O. unit may provide a higher quality of water. It is usually a 3- to 4-stage system (a membrane and 2 or 3 resin containers with a bypass for waste water). The main drawback is that it wastes a lot of water. With an R.O., a considerable amount of water bypasses the filtering membrane and goes into a drain as waste, so the drain will have to be near the unit.

Also, you will need good water pressure from the main supply of the house. It is generally recommended that you have about 120 pounds of water pressure to operate this type of unit properly. City water is usually at 120 pounds of pressure. Well water pressure is usually less than needed for operating an R.O. unit. Check this requirement with the manufacturer's specifications. R.O. water is thought to be a higher quality than deionized water. I have used both, and for my needs I have found no difference. R.O. water is extremely slow to get, and for a tank larger than 55 gallons, I would recommend a deionizer.

Drawbacks of reverse osmosis:

Here we should think of the application over the long run. Not only will you require water often for water changes, but you will also need water fairly regularly for evaporation. This means filling up a container to hold the purified water. As it is filling, the container needs to be monitored so that it does not overflow. The R.O. is so slow that it usually has to be left on when you are not home. If something happens to delay you for some time, or it slips your mind, the container can overflow in your absence. The easiest remedy is to have a large enough container, and to monitor it daily or as needed. This will allow you to have a constant supply of water on hand, but you will have to transfer the water from the large container to your make-up system, where you mix the Kalkwasser. This can be inconvenient unless you have space to keep this large container near the make-up system and the tank.

A Reverse Osmosis Unit:

The advantage:

> *A carbon prefilter will greatly extend the life of resins used in R.O. or deionizer purification systems*

- It supposedly produces a higher quality water.

The disadvantages:

- It processes water slowly.
- It must be near a drain for the waste water.
- The water supply from the house has to be on for extended periods of time.
- The unit may have to be left unattended while it is on.
- It will need a certain water pressure to operate properly. City water is usually okay, but a well pump may provide insufficient pressure. (Check the manufacturer's recommendation for water pressure.)
- The water may have to be transferred from a large holding container to the make-up mixing system near the tank.
- There are more fittings on the unit that could malfunction (strip if over-tightened, need replacing) or leak at some point.

A Deionizer:

The deionizer is a much simpler design than the R.O. unit. It operates on a one-stage principle, using a container filled with a resin material that removes contaminants. I find that the quality of water it produces is perfectly acceptable for my reef.

The advantages:

- A ready supply of water. A deionizer can produce 5 gallons in 1/2 hour.
- There is no bypass waste water, so no need for a drain.
- It can be set up right near the tank and make-up system, if there is a water supply nearby.
- It does not have to be left on for extended periods unattended.
- It has fewer fittings than an R.O. unit (fewer opportunities for something to malfunction).
- It is easy to service.

The disadvantage:

> —$$$—

- It is considered by some to produce a lesser quality of water than reverse osmosis.

When selecting purifying resin for the deionizer, try to get the "indicating" type. This resin will change color when it needs to be replaced. This can help you avoid replacing it prematurely, or waiting too long past the life span of the resin's contaminant-removing properties.

Water purification products are rated by the amount of water they will process in a certain period of time. Determine how much water you will be using for setup, bimonthly water changes, and evaporation replacement. Compare the rating versus the price. Then purchase equipment that is slightly larger than you absolutely need. If you have a good relationship with your retailer, and his prices are competitive, purchase from him. Usually, he will stand behind the product he sells, and have the parts and resin when you need them.

Prefiltering the R.O. or deionized water

> *$$—Extend the life of the resin—$$*

Prefiltering the tap water is extremely beneficial and economical! Placing one or more quality carbon filters before the water enters the R.O. or deionizer will remove many harmful contaminants and impurities *before the water goes into the expensive stage of purification*. This will extend the life of the resin, which is costly. A quality carbon water filter is relatively inexpensive. A large, two-cartridge, carbon, home water filter is about $60. The replacement cartridges are about $12 each, and they will last 6 months easily. Small versions designed for the home can be purchased for less.

My setup has a small single-cartridge unit connected to a larger double-cartridge unit, which then runs into the deionizer. My thought is that the first (single) unit is used as a prefilter, and ideally traps the bulk of impurities and sediments. This initial single cartridge is replaced every 2 months. The second, double-cartridge carbon prefilter handles what the first has missed, and is replaced at 4-month intervals. The final deionizer resin lasts approximately 5 to 6 months. I use 70 gallons a month for water changes and approximately 20 gallons to replace evaporation; this makes a total of 90 gallons a month, or 1,080 gallons a year.

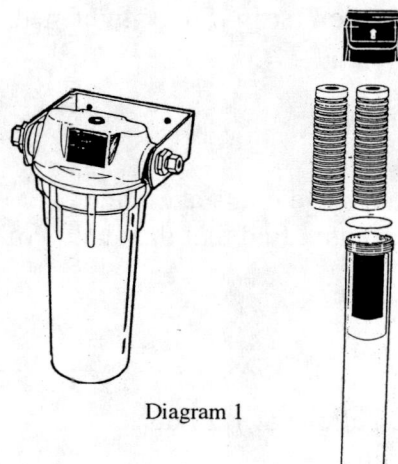

Diagram 1

Here is a per-year price breakdown for triple-carbon-filtered, deionized tap water:

1. Small single carbon prefilter cartridge: $5 each, replaced 6 times a year

    $ 30

2. Large dual carbon cartridges: $12 each = $24 a pair, replaced 3 times a year

    72

3. Deionizing resin: $60 a gallon, 2 gallons a year

    120

    Total per year: $ 222

This comes to approximately 20 cents a gallon ($222 divided by 1,080 gallons). This figure does not take into account the initial cost of the R.O. or deionizer unit. They range from the smallest R.O. unit at approximately $170 to a commercial grade deionizer at about $270. These new units come filled with resin.

When purchasing a home water filter, size is again a factor. It is better to have a large carbon prefilter. This will help to purify the water and extend the life of the resin. This type of prefilter can be purchased economically in many home improvement centers. However, if you are interested in a quality product, I recommend visiting a major plumbing supply house. There you will find large, heavy-duty carbon water filters priced not significantly higher than the smaller units in ordinary stores. You end up getting more for your money from a plumbing supply outlet: higher quality will outweigh any increase in cost. Wherever you purchase the carbon filters, make sure the company will be there for some time, so you can easily obtain replacement cartridges. (See Photo 19 and Diagram 1 for carbon prefilters).

Water Purification System

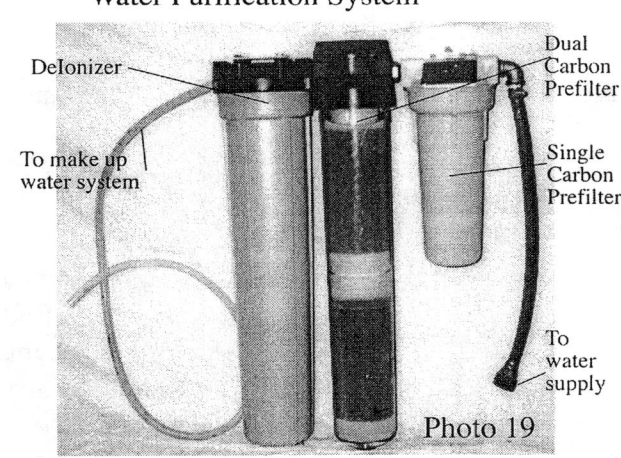

Photo 19

| A plumbing supply house can provide a quality carbon filter |

5. LIGHTING

Lighting requirements for the reef are very different from those for common fish tanks. Keep in mind that you want to have a minimum of 3 and a maximum of 5 watts per gallon, activated in increments, with timers for 9 hours a day. Most common retail pet stores will not have the proper lighting setup for a reef. The components for lighting the reef properly are:

1. The correct number of bulbs for the desired wattage (minimum 3, maximum 5 watts per gallon);
2. The correct spectrum of light from specialized bulbs used for a reef;
3. Special ballast's ("high output" or "very high output");
4. An internal reflector and cooling fan(s).

The main specialized item of reef lighting is the bulb. *It is necessary to deal with companies or retailers who have these special bulbs.* Since they are designed for a special application, and provide vital benefits, they are costly. Find one good source, and stick with it. I prefer to deal directly with the manufacturer, because when I do so the bulbs come right from the source, and I can be more confident about their quality. It's important to be sure of the bulb's quality. I have tried to substitute other types of commercially available, high quality bulbs, but they are not the same and will not meet the requirements of the reef inhabitants, as will these special bulbs made specifically for reef lighting.

If ordered from the manufacturer directly, the bulbs are delivered via U.P.S. in a special box, and you don't have to be as concerned about them being handled or banged around in a store's display. These bulbs are expensive, about $30 for a 4-foot and $35 for a 6-foot bulb. I

purchase six at a time, twice a year. There are many companies involved with reef lighting. The magazines for our hobby are filled with their ads.
You can purchase bulbs or a complete lighting canopy or setup from them.

I have more peace of mind purchasing reef lighting directly from the manufacturer

An alternative: You can fabricate your own custom light canopy. Basically, this consists of a nicely finished box to house the bulbs, end caps, reflector, and fan(s). Ballast's must not be in the box. They generate a considerable amount of heat and should be mounted on a remote ballast board, well separated from the canopy and in an area that is not enclosed. The ballast's (H.O. or V.H.O.) and bulb holders are available from any large electrical supply house. An H.O. ballast costs about $60, and a V.H.O. sells for approximately $120. The bulb holders are about $7 a pair. The fan and timers can be purchased from Radio Shack. For reflector material you can use white aluminum "coil stock" or sheet aluminum for waterproofing roofs, sold in home improvement centers as "rolled roof flashing." (See Chapter 12 on fabricating light canopies. More information on lighting is in Chapter 5.)

When deciding what will be most practical for your needs, the choices to weigh and consider are: (1) make your own, (2) buy from your reputable dealer, or (3) purchase direct from the manufacturer.

6. EXPENDABLE ITEMS

Products you will use often and have to replace frequently are considered "expendable items." They are:

1. Salt mix;
2. Kalkwasser;
3. Prefilter pad material;
4. Food for the livestock;
5. Trace elements (iodine, strontium);
6. Wood air blocks (if your skimmer is air driven).

The size of your tank will dictate the quantities you will use of each of these items. The larger your tank, the more frequently they will have to be replenished or replaced. If you have a 55-gallon or smaller tank, you may just want to purchase these items from your local retailer. For larger tanks, this is simply not practical. I have been a big fan of mail order supplies, and have had excellent results with this approach. I am particularly fond of Mail Order Pet, and have dealt with them for years. (See "Suppliers Reference Section,")

This is definitely the most economical approach for the serious hobbyist. Mail order sources supply all the products in quantity (something usually not available in retail stores), with savings that really make a difference! Not only money is saved, but aggravation as well. You don't have to drive out for salt or Kalkwasser every time you change your water or prefilter. I usually buy a 300-gallon salt mix, several 450-gram containers of Kalkwasser, 3 or 4 packages of prefilter material, a few containers of food, some trace elements, and 20 air blocks at a time. This will last about 4 months. In that 4-month period, I am never panicking for missing elements, paying retail prices, or going without products that my reef needs. Get the phone number of a mail order supplier, and request their catalog. Compare prices, and you won't be disappointed.

7. LIVE ROCK

Where you purchase your live rock will have a substantial impact on the cost and quality of what will go into your reef. With a small tank (up to 55 gallons), purchasing locally may be acceptable, but it will be expensive. *There is a tremendous markup on live rock.* One reason is that most retailers have to absorb any losses or damage incurred in the handling of the livestock. They also have to keep the creatures alive and in good shape until they are sold. (I am sure there are many more reasons for the exorbitant prices.) Personally, if I had to pay retail prices for live rock, I would not be in this hobby to the extent that I am. I have seen Florida live rock sold for $14 a pound. For a 55-gallon tank using 83 pounds of live rock, that would come to $1,162. For a 200-gallon tank using 300 pounds, the retail cost would be $4,200. At these prices, I would stick with fish only, and I'm sure very few others would be able to afford a large reef.

Depending on the area in which you live, there may be only one or two nearby retailers handling live rock. Also, because the hobby is relatively new, there is not an excessive demand for this commodity. When a retailer has little or no local competition in a rapidly expanding hobby, the conditions for exploitation abound. Fortunately, there are hobbyists like myself who persisted beyond the local market, and have found a way to pay reasonable prices for live rock.

Money saver:
How to purchase live rock

The magazines dedicated to our hobby publish countless advertisements of businesses that supply live rock. However, anyone would be skeptical about paying for something without seeing it first. I pursued many of these advertisers. Usually I was greeted with an answering machine, and I would leave a message. Very few suppliers called me back. This allowed me right off the bat to rule out the credibility of the people who did not return my calls. A few high-priced suppliers called back, offering to sell for local retail prices. I ruled them out, too. Of the 12 calls I made, two seemed promising. One actually answered the phone himself, while the other faxed some information after a long discussion of the product.

I requested references from these two suppliers. I wanted to talk to customers who live outside the supplier's area. After a long discussion with a few satisfied hobbyists who purchased live rock from these suppliers, I was certain of the company to deal with. Still, being slightly skeptical and concerned, I placed a small order, for about $400. The terms were C.O.D. at the airport. I was asked what day I would prefer to receive the shipment. Later the wholesaler called me back to confirm; he reviewed my order, told me the total amount that would be due, and gave me the flight number and approximate time when the packages were expected to arrive.

The day came when I was to receive the shipment. I called the airline, gave them the flight number, and they told me when they expected the plane. I drove to the airport, paid for the packages, loaded them in the van, and quickly drove home.

The best way I can describe my excitement when I arrived home and opened the boxes, is to say it was like opening gifts at Christmas. The rock was excellent and of the quality I was promised, and it had cost me less than $5 a pound. I was elated. I quickly unloaded, rinsed, and placed the rock. As I did this, I found other packages that were not in the order. I noticed some snails, starfish, and some small hermit crabs that were thrown in as a bonus. This whole experience bolstered my confidence in, and genuine appreciation for, this supplier. I had been paying $14 a pound for live rock; this experience opened a new door for me, and enhanced my participation in this hobby.

Since then, I have placed many orders with the same supplier, and have never been disappointed. Although collection of live rock has been restricted in Florida (starting in 1996), I have been assured that a supply will be available from other areas, at a slightly higher price but still affordable. Prices range from under $5 a pound for premium rock, under $9 a pound for ricordia, and under $2 a pound for live sand. The shipping costs are approximately $30 per hundred pounds, with a $6 box charge for the Styrofoam shipping container. The boxes hold approximately 35 pounds of rock. So, it totals about $14 a box after everything is added up. This is not unrealistic for shipping anything, let alone reef rock!

> *Finding a reputable wholesaler is a primary method to save money*

Important reminder: This is one of the areas where you will save the most money! Shop around by phone. List the companies and prices. Find a business you feel you can trust. This will take time and effort. Get references. Call and talk to their customers. Make sure you are confident with your choice. Place a small order first, and see if you are satisfied with the quality of the product. A reputable, affordable wholesale dealer is worth his weight in gold. He will save you considerable money, lessen your aggravation, and supply you with some beautiful live rock.

8. LIVESTOCK

> —$$$—

While we are on the subject of wholesalers: you can purchase your livestock this way too. Invertebrates, corals, and fish will be available for you at considerable savings. A reputable dealer will not sell you something he would not buy himself, as his reputation will be on the line. However, sometimes losses occur. You may ask for an item, and it will not be available, or the supplier may be reluctant to ship the special request with your order. This is the supplier's judgment call, and, of course, should be respected.

Usually you can save by purchasing invertebrates, coral, and live sand from a wholesaler. With other common livestock such as fish, the prices may not be very different from those at your retail store. Fish fare the worst in shipping anyway, and I personally prefer to see the fish before I buy them. The cost of shipping fish is increased by the weight of the water in which they are shipped. Use this approach to purchase only the unusual fish that your local supplier cannot get for you.

Your local supplier. You should use the same care and concern when purchasing locally as you do when buying wholesale. Usually there are a limited number of local suppliers for reef livestock. When I found my retailer after much trial and error, I realized that he was genuinely concerned with having me as a customer. He appreciated my business, and I valued his willingness to help me in my hobby. A good relationship developed between us, based on trust and respect. Thus, I have no doubt where to buy additional livestock.

> *A retailer who is experienced, and treats you well, is worth traveling some distance from your home*

Everything I have purchased from my retailer has been totally healthy and long-lived. Because of his many years of experience in the hobby, he was able *to answer my questions, simply and directly.* His initial advice has had much influence in getting me to where I am in the hobby today. He is not offended when I purchase my rock directly from the wholesaler, as he knows I will spend enough money with him, and he wants me as his customer. He will often give me special prices and point out items I may be interested in. On occasions when I didn't have the money, he has gone as far as to say, "Take it and pay me the next time you come in." He is happy to see me coming, and it is a genuine pleasure to do business with him.

I hope you are lucky enough to find such a retailer. Once you do, the idea is to purchase there exclusively. When something works, don't fix it. I would absolutely not consider purchasing livestock at any other store. Dealers have different approaches in handling their livestock. If you stick with the one who will treat you well and has experience at keeping everything healthy and in optimum condition, you will run less risk of introducing sick, diseased, or questionable livestock into your established reef. Also, you will not be paying more than you should for your purchases.

To sum up about livestock dealers: *Don't be intimidated! You will be spending a considerable amount of money! Select a dealer who treats you right. If he doesn't, find one who will. You may have to travel some distance, and spend some time, but in the long run it will be well worth it. And when you find the right dealer, you will know.*

A summary of purchasing: *Buy from someone who wants to sell.* This may seem obvious, because you may think, "Of course suppliers want to sell!" *But having things for sale, and wanting to sell, are two different mind sets.* For example, you walk into a pet store, and they

> *Two different mind sets:*
> *(1) Having items for sale;*
> *(2) Wanting to sell*

have 100 tanks for sale, each with its own value to the owner of the store. This is "having items for sale." The other kind of situation would involve a person who has been in the hobby and now wants out, or is moving at the end of the month. He "wants to sell." He is tired of looking at the tank, or afraid he will have to take it with him when he moves, or in need of the money he has invested in it. In any event, he is willing to take a loss in comparison to what he paid for the setup when it was new.

This is opportunity shopping. Remember, for everyone who is getting into a new hobby, there is someone getting out! As enthusiastic as you are about participating in the hobby, there are others who are just as eager to depart from it. If you can locate those who are exiting or expanding in the hobby, you will find some excellent deals. The quality of your sources for finding these people will determine how patient and investigative you will have to be.

> *Avoid impulse buying at all costs!*

Impulse buying is just what is says. You go into a store, see something you want, and buy it without knowing the competitive price of the product. In this hobby, impulse buying will leave you broke and angry, with many unneeded and overpriced items. Ninety-nine out of 100 of us cannot afford to purchase items in this manner. This is why, from the beginning, I have suggested interaction with other hobbyists to share your knowledge and experience regarding what works, where to shop, who the good suppliers are, etc. This networking will save money, time, and aggravation.

Plain old good will in business. Notice how your retailer treats you. Does he know your name? Does he care? If I am going into someone's store to buy live rock, a water purification system, a protein skimmer, or a pump, we are talking

> *Considering the amount of money spent in this hobby,*
> *I expect good treatment!*
> *I recommend that you do the same*

about my spending several hundred dollars at a time. Multiply that by several times, and you have a couple of thousand dollars. When I am spending money like this, I expect good treatment, and I recommend that you do the same.

When you are making an expensive purchase, will your retailer "throw in" an unexpected item for you, or give you a few dollars off, showing that he values your business? We are not talking about buying a few goldfish or some gerbil food. The items we need are very expensive, and they have a high enough markup to allow the store owner a little room for good will toward good customers. If you plan to frequent a store and spend a substantial amount of money, demand proper treatment.

9. UNCONVENTIONAL PRODUCTS USED IN REEF KEEPING

As we proceed to set up and maintain our reef, it will be extremely helpful to find and use some products that were never intended for our particular needs. Most of these items, because they are not "reef intended," are inexpensive and very practical to use. Here is a list of them, and where they may be found.

Abbreviations used in this list:

- **HIC = Home Improvement Center**
- **PSH = Plumbing Supply House**
- **ESH = Electrical Supply House**

Air conditioner (powerful). Used to keep tank at desirable temperature in summer months or in warm climate. Preferable to an expensive tank-chiller that does nothing to comfort the aquarist. *Highly recommended!*

BAGS: Synthetic nylon bags. Used to hold carbon in place in the sump if desired. These are found as paint strainers in 1- and 5-gallon sizes. Less than 50 cents each at a good paint store.

Baking soda, bicarbonate of soda. Used to raise alkalinity. Although I don't add this product frequently, it can be used as an alternative if the alkalinity must be raised. Usually by performing regular water changes with a high quality salt mix, the alkalinity can be kept at acceptable levels.

Bottle brush. Used to clean skimmers and to remove unwanted algae from live rock and overflow pipes. Many sizes to choose from. Plastic or plastic-coated recommended. Available in most department stores.

BUCKET: The all-important and valuable 5-gallon bucket. This item should really be #1 on this list. Have several clean 5-gallon buckets on hand at all times. Use one for make-up water, and have one or two connected for a surge bucket. Their applications are endless.

Bulkhead fittings. Gray, schedule 80, large: PSH. Less expensive PVC: pool supplier.

Cable ties. Used in many temporary or permanent applications. Have plenty of these on hand. Buy them in bags of 50. They can be used to clamp flexible vinyl tubing or to insert fittings where high pressure is not used. Use only black cable ties (they are less noticeable). The 10" length seems to be the most all-around practical size; they can be connected together to make longer ties. Available at most HIC, ESH, or PSH.

CLAMPS: Stainless steel hose clamps. Many sizes to choose from. Used for clamping hose under relatively high pressure. Can be removed easily for disconnecting and service. HIC, auto supply, PSH.

Containers for mixing saltwater. Depending on size, they can be found in department stores as large plastic storage containers for clothing, etc. Or, you can use new plastic garbage cans.

Eggcrate lighting diffuser material. Normally used in suspended-ceiling light fixtures. Has many uses in setting up live rock and supporting prefilter. Baffles to quiet cascading water, etc. White: most HIC. Black: special plastic supplier. Check Yellow Pages.

Epoxy resin (premium), hardener, tinting color (usually black). Fiberglass reinforcement cloth, inexpensive applicator brushes. Used to fabricate tanks and waterproof sump boxes. Find a good boating supply store.

Extension cords. Depending on the size of the tank and your needs in a power outage. Usually two or three 50-foot cords for an emergency.

FANS: Cooling fans, timers. Radio Shack.

FILTERS: Carbon water filters. Smaller models: HIC. Better quality: PSH.

Generator. A must in the event of an extended power outage. Good HIC or power equipment supplier.

GFI ("ground fault interrupter") outlets. A must for electrical safety around the reef tank. HIC, ESH.

Glass. Plate glass for fabricating tank fronts, tank covers. All sizes: shop by phone. Get best prices. Check the Yellow Pages.

GLUE: Special glue for plastic. For fabricating protein skimmers, sump boxes, and drip plates. Available in a variety of sizes from a good plastic supplier. Check the Yellow Pages.

Gutter guard, plastic. These are used to keep the leaves out of the gutters on a house. They can be cut and cable tied to the overflow pipes to keep livestock from getting into the plumbing system. HIC.

HOSE: Garden hose. Many slightly different sizes available. Can be a substitute for more expensive clear vinyl tubing when clear is not essential. Inexpensive. Most affordable at HIC.

HOSE: Plastic hose (large, flexible, inexpensive). For drain systems. Pool supplier.

Insert fittings. Used for connecting flexible vinyl tubing. A good PSH.

Light reflectors. Look for white aluminum "coil stock" or aluminum roof flashing in rolls of different widths. HIC, good hardware store.

Lighting ballast's, bulb holders, wire connectors. High output (H.O.) or very high output (V.H.O.). ESH.

Marine Tex. A type of epoxy "fix all." Excellent, quality product. Most boating stores or a good hardware store. See "Suppliers Reference Section."

PIPE: Water pipe and fitting. Hard or flexible. Most sizes, depending on supplier. PVC (polyvinyl chloride) or clear vinyl flexible tubing. Most HIC or large PSH.

Plexiglas. Used for sump boxes and drip plates. Shop around for prices. Glass store or a good plastic supplier. Check the Yellow Pages.

PLYWOOD: marine grade, 3/4". Used in fabricating tanks and sump boxes. A good lumber yard.

Power strips, multi-outlet. For adding several electrical devices onto one plug. Has a switch for shut-off. HIC, Radio Shack, ESH.

SCREWS: Stainless steel or galvanized Phillips head or square drive wood screws. Usually 1-3/4" or 2" length, used in fabricating tanks and sumps. A good lumber yard.

SEALER: Premium quality clear silicone sealer. Used to set and waterproof glass, and sometimes for added protection and reinforcement adhesion of Plexiglas to dissimilar materials, like epoxied wood. Make certain that the sealer is for underwater use, safe to use in saltwater, and non-toxic when cured. A good boating supply store.

TUBING: Rigid, clear plastic tubing. Most sizes, for fabricating protein skimmers. A good plastic supplier. Check the Yellow Pages.

VALVES: Ball valves, water shutoffs or regulators. Up to 1/2": HIC. Larger size: PSH. Affordable, large, 1-1/2" gate valves: pool supplier.

VALVES: Venturi valve. For protein skimmer. From your retailer, by mail order, or from magazines.

Chapter 11

Power Outage

Electricity is a critical need for the creatures and organisms in a reef tank. One usually does not give this vital element proper value until it

is not available. However, I'm sure the time will come when your tank is up and running, and the power goes out. *If you are not prepared, you will risk losing all that is alive in the tank in a relatively short period of time, and that is a fact.* Yes, you need a generator. I'm sure you have spent enough money by now to question your own sanity, but this is necessary.

I was told to have a generator on hand to protect my substantial investment. Although I understood the reasoning that went with that suggestion, I put off getting one for many months. Unexpectedly, a strong wind storm came into my area one night, and the power went out at 1 AM. I actually awoke just before it happened. Based on previous experience, I thought the power would be out for only a couple of hours, so I went back to sleep. I awoke at 8 AM, and still no power.

A generator is like insurance on your reef tank: one day you will need it!

Fortunately, I have a friend who had a generator, and he brought it over in about an hour. Meanwhile, I was on the verge of panic. I began a manual bucket siphon (see Diagram 35) to try to introduce oxygen back into the water. This is just about all you can do without electricity. After doing this for 45 minutes, I realized I had been foolish not to purchase a generator in the first place. Here was a very complex, delicate, valuable, and expensive environment that I had spent hundreds of hours working on, and it was about to perish because I was not prepared. Don't let this happen to you and your reef tank.

As radical as this may sound, I suggest you have an emergency plan to implement in case the power goes out. It may seem like going to extremes. However, when the electricity goes off, and while others are panicking, you will calmly put your plan into effect, and life in your reef will not miss a beat. You will be very happy about that! Here are some ideas to consider.

THE EMERGENCY PLAN

1. Buy a generator. *Don't count on your rental store. All the generators may be rented when you need one. Don't count on people you know. They may not be home, or they may need their generators themselves. In some emergencies, travel may not even be possible.* Purchase a large-capacity generator, at least 2,250 watts and 18 amps. This will run four water pumps (one 1,100-GPH, one 800-GPH, and one 500-GPH), two large air pumps, a couple of incandescent light bulbs (so you can see what you're doing), and your refrigerator. Although this seems like a large generator, this size is powered by a relatively small gas container that lasts only 2 hours, and therefore needs to be refilled frequently.

Look for a generator with a large gas tank. The power may be out for a couple of days, and you would probably rather not have to monitor the generator frequently. Also, the larger the generator, the more home items you could run for your own

> *As radical as it may sound,*
> *an emergency plan*
> *will save your reef*
> *when the power goes out*

convenience. Consider this as insurance on your tank. You have to pay for something that you don't use all the time, but it's there when you need it and will easily pay for itself by saving your reef. When the time comes (and it will), you will not regret your purchase.

2. Have an emergency plan. Do you have enough extension cords? Gasoline? Motor oil for the generator? Do you have an alternate heat source? What if travel is not possible? Take the time to do a simulated outage. This way, you will find out exactly what you are missing. Consider the "worst-case scenario," so you will be prepared. You cannot be over-prepared!

> *What exactly will you do*
> *when the power goes out*
> *and stays out for a day or so?*
> *Do you have*
> *an alternate power source?*

3. Keep all emergency items in one place, so you don't waste time getting them. Time can be important in an emergency!

OXYGEN LOSS DUE TO POWER OUTAGE

One of the main elements needed for life in the reef is a substantial amount of oxygen. This is provided by your large protein skimmer and the water traveling through the prefilter drip plate. Also, the turbulence that takes place in the sump introduces oxygen. When you have a large skimmer and a lot of turbulence, the water in the tank becomes "oxygen saturated," which means that when the system is in operation, the water cannot hold any more oxygen. This is also known as "oxygen potential" or "redox potential," which is a measurement of how much oxygen is in the water. As I have stated in the section about water testing, I do not test the water for oxygen. Rather, I know that by having large skimmers and a lot of turbulence in the sump the water is saturated with oxygen, which is a very important goal in the design of the water system.

In the reef tank, there are millions of living organisms, and most of them (with the exception of anaerobic bacteria) desperately need an abundant, constant supply of oxygen to survive. And oxygen is just what you lose when the power goes out!

When the equipment that introduces oxygen into the tank shuts down, the oxygen already in the water gets used up fairly rapidly. All the organisms are accustomed to a steady, abundant supply of oxygen, and have built themselves up in its presence. When that supply gets used up, and is not replenished, things begin to die.

The first to die are the bacteria that you cannot see. They are the most fragile. When they die, they set off a chain reaction, causing other things to die, and so on, until the whole tank crashes. Actually, this is what it means to have the tank "crash."

As you can see, you need to have a constant and abundant supply of oxygen to keep things alive and in balance. *When I say "abundant supply" and "in balance," I mean you need to have the power (electricity) the tank is accustomed to.* Anything less and livestock will begin to die. This is why I do not recommend the manual siphon method, battery air pumps, inflatable air pumps, or anything less than what the reef is used to.

Obviously, in an emergency a little is better than nothing. But don't depend on a little to keep your reef in balance and alive. Be prepared!

I hope you see the importance of (and the responsibility for having) a reliable, readily

> *The millions of life forms*
> *in the reef*
> *all depend on oxygen*

available, alternate power source—along with gas, oil, plenty of extension cords, possibly an alternate heat source, and an emergency plan. Your reef, your wallet, and your peace of mind will all be saved when the power goes out.

SOME OTHER COMMENTS ON POWER OUTAGES

1. Oxygen gets used up more slowly when the lighting is off. The creatures that photosynthesize are not as active without light.

Before I got my own generator, my tank (200 gallons) experienced an 8-hour outage in the middle of the night. I hope your tank never goes through this. By the time an emergency generator arrived, most of the oxygen in the water was used up. Fortunately the only thing that happened was a small ammonia cycle that balanced out in a day or so. I believe my tank was saved by super-saturation of oxygen in the water, due to large water pumps. I would never take that chance again. I now have a generator, and an emergency plan to follow.

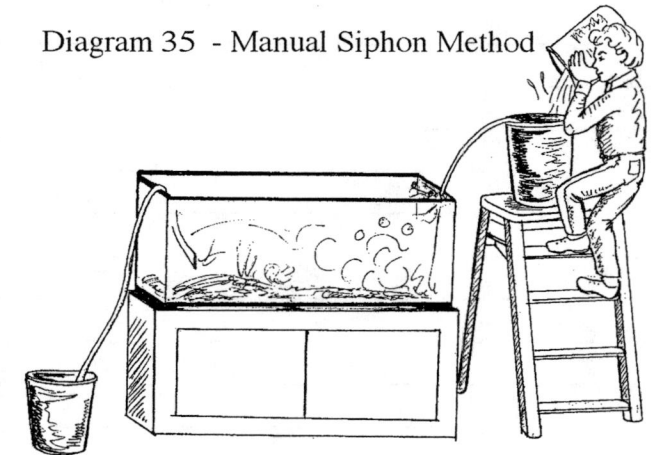

Diagram 35 - Manual Siphon Method

NOTES:

Chapter 12

Fabricating Components

Chapter 4, "Types of Tanks," will serve as an introduction to this chapter.

CONSIDERATIONS OF A LARGE TANK

To begin making your own tank, it would of course be helpful to have a size in mind. If you decide to make a large tank, you should consider the weight factor. Saltwater weighs approximately 8.5 pounds per gallon. Taking into account the sand, rock, glass, etc., I use the figure of 10 pounds per gallon. You do not want to *underestimate* the weight of the proposed tank; by using the 10-pound figure, you can be confident of your estimate. Ten is also an easy number to multiply.

The first question will be, "Can your floor hold the weight?" Having a 55- to 125-gallon tank will not usually present a structural concern in the average home: the floor will generally support the weight. It is only when you venture into sizes larger than 125 gallons that you should take a close look at exactly what all that weight will be resting on.

STRUCTURAL CONCERNS

Tanks set up against a wall usually have better support than they would in other locations, for example in the middle of the room. The length of the tank should be perpendicular to the floor joists, which are usually 16" apart. Placing the tank perpendicular to them (rather than parallel) ensures that the tank's weight will be distributed over several joists. If the tank is parallel to the joists, only one or two of them will support it. With a large tank this would be inadequate.

Positioning the tank perpendicular to the joists will not only provide superior support; it will also make it relatively easy to add reinforcement if necessary. If you have access to a basement or crawl space, the support for a tank on the first floor can be reinforced with additional carpentry work that is not that difficult to do. See the next diagrams for a description of structural terms and illustrations of extra reinforcement.

If you are not confident of your own knowledge of building, you can call in a home improvement contractor to

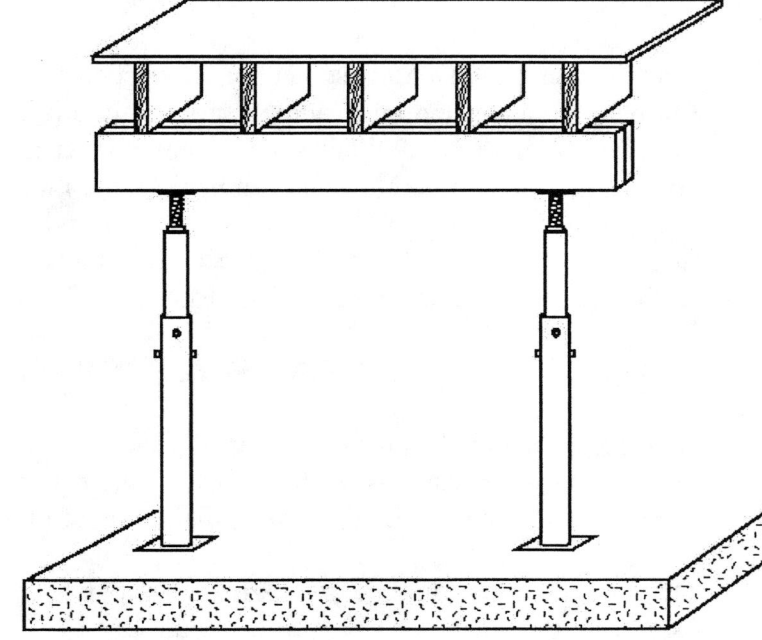

assist you. For a reasonable cost he could install a temporary beam with metal telescoping posts for extra support. Or, he may tell you that it is not a good idea to have the tank in a certain area, and give you the reasons why. Usually small, reputable home improvement contractors will share your enthusiasm and concern for proper structural support. Take advantage of what others may offer as suggestions.

Having a tank larger than a 125-gallon on the second floor is usually not a good idea. This is particularly true of homes built more than 40 years ago. During that time, builders relied more on "joinery" than practical weight transfer (which is the method of home building today). It is much more difficult to add additional support if the tank is located over a finished living

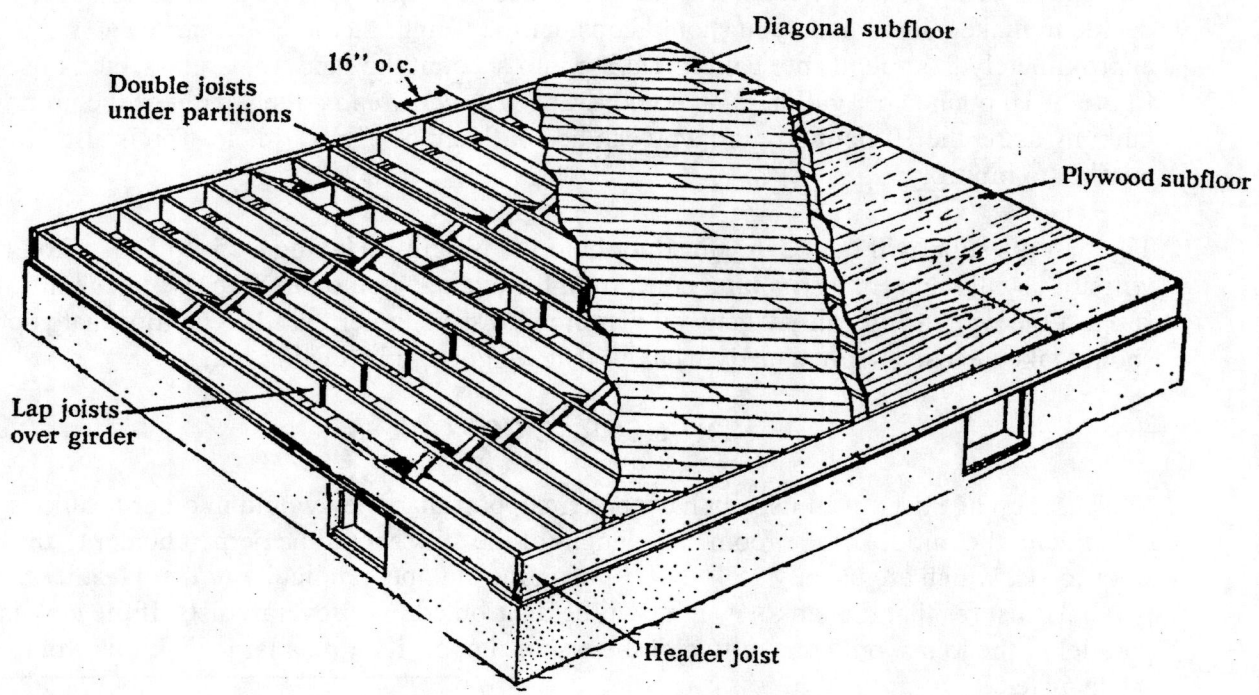

space, rather than over a basement or crawl space.

From a practical standpoint, adding support for a large second-floor tank would not be worth the effort in materials and labor, or the potential risk of loss or damage. Again, if you insist, you can talk to a contractor who can inspect and judge your individual situation. Usually the floor joists for the second floor are not as wide and strong as the ones supporting the first floor. As the house goes up, the lumber gets smaller. Homes are not really designed to have 2,000 pounds of water in a 16 square foot area. Get professional advice!

SIZES AND STYLES OF SELF-MADE TANKS

As I mentioned in Chapter 4, "Types of Tanks," it is not practical to make a tank smaller than 125 gallons, as this size is relatively affordable ready-made. Tanks larger than 125 gallons are expensive. If you want a large tank, "making your own" can be practical.

The only method of making a tank that I am familiar with and personally have done involves using epoxy-coated marine plywood. This style of tank is only open for viewing from the front, as the back and sides are plywood. In certain circumstances, tanks have only the front exposed anyway: for example, if the filtration sump box and skimmer are on the sides, as they should be. In such a case, the filtration components would be covered with a door that was finished in the same manner as the tank. Or, in an ideal setup, the tank would be recessed into a wall with a room behind it, allowing all the apparatus to be out of sight, with plenty of room to service the tank. This would be my next type of setup. The disadvantages of not being able to view the tank from the sides and back are, in my opinion, minimal in comparison to the advantages of having the tank size you want.

LARGE TANK, LARGE COST

Many people would love to have a large reef tank. The larger the tank, the more dramatic and "natural" it will look. This is true to some extent. Yes, a large tank can house more livestock, giving you and others a wider variety of creatures to view. And yes, a large setup will look more like a "natural" reef, and will be extremely beautiful! *However, the fact is, a large tank is still a tank—an enclosed system.* If you choose a large size, everything connected with your system will be larger—especially the expense!

- A large tank will take up more space in your home or apartment.
- It will need stronger pumps.
- It will require larger-volume water changes.
- It will need larger protein skimmers that require substantial height.
- It will take more electricity to operate.
- You will need more live rock and livestock; just the cost of stocking a large tank can be intimidating.

Review the planning and cycling method described in Chapter 3 of this book. Then

> *It is not practical
> to make your own tank
> if it is smaller than 125 gallons*

write a plan, and list everything you will be using and needing to buy. Are you willing to commit to that extreme? A large reef tank is very beautiful; however, it is also very costly and it commands a lot of initial, as well as long-term, work.

If you are prepared to go on, welcome to the group of over-the-edge extreme hobbyists! I will be describing how to have a large tank for the least amount of money. This will require you to get involved in

- wood working,
- plumbing,
- minor engineering, and
- major problem solving!

The challenge is immense, but the results will be impressive! You will have to visit

- lumber yards,
- large plumbing suppliers,
- pool suppliers,
- glass shops,
- large plastic suppliers,
- the airport,
- etc…

Yes, it seems like yesterday when I did all these things, but since my tank has been set up, all I have had to do is maintain it (which is a breeze compared to the initial effort it took to do everything myself). And, as I have said before, when I do it again, I will use the same methods and approach I have in the past, only on a larger scale!

CALCULATING THE VOLUME OF A TANK

As an example I will use a tank size of 24" x 24" x 96," or 55,296 cubic inches. Remember from the section on calculating the volume of a sump in chapter 7. One gallon of water has a volume of 231 cubic inches. This is the magic number. In other words a square box measuring 6.14" x 6.14" x 6.14" equals approx. 231 cubic inches. So a tank with a volume of 55,296 cubic inches will contain 239 gallons of water when it is completely filled (55,296 / 231 = 239).

This magic number, 231, can be used to calculate the water volume of any tank, container, sump box, etc. Of course when you are figuring tank volume, you should measure the *inside* dimensions to obtain an accurate result. You will find that many "stock" tanks are really smaller than the manufacturer's claim. The volume of such tanks may have been calculated using their outside dimensions.

> *The magic number is*
> ***231:***
> *1 gallon of water*
> *has a volume of 231 cubic inches*

CALCULATING GALLONS PER INCH

It is also helpful to familiarize yourself with calculating gallons per inch. First find the volume of the tank in gallons, then divide that number by the height of the tank (measuring inside). In the example I am using, the volume of the tank is 239 gallons and its height (inside) is 24 inches. 239 / 24 = 9.96, so there are 9.96 gallons in each inch of this tank's height.

This is useful for estimating the overflow of the tank in the event of a power outage, and when calculating the estimated water going into the sump under the outage conditions. It is also used for estimating the volume of water needed for a water change.

The desired amount for a water change (for example, 12-15% of the tank's volume) is first determined. With the 239-gallon tank I am using as an example, 15% of the tank's volume is 35.85 gallons (239 x .15 = 35.85). During a water change I will want to remove this amount of water from the tank, and then replace it with make-up water. To make it easy to drain this same 15% amount from the tank for every water change, I can make a mark on the glass showing where the water level should be after 35.85 gallons have been drained out. I know that there are 9.96 gallons in each inch of this tank's height, so draining 35.85 gallons will lower the water level by 3.6 inches (35.85 ÷ 9.96 = 3.6). I make a mark on the glass 3.6

inches below the full operating water level, and drain the tank just to that mark whenever I am doing a water change.

These useful water volume estimating methods will allow you to calculate quickly and accurately:
(1) The amounts of water in your existing or proposed tank, and
(2) The amount of water removed from the tank, whether it is drained out manually (during water changes) or by gravity (to supply the "working water" of the sump, or through overflow pipes or during a power outage).

TANK LOCATION

First determine the tank size you would like. This, of course, will first depend on the tank's location in your home, where the tank and filtering components will fit in with the other furnishings, etc. This location is extremely important to the long-term success of your tank! *Do not underestimate the proper placement of the tank!*

> *Good access
> for servicing the equipment
> will pay off over and over*

A good common location would be with the back of the tank close to a wall. You can have your spraybar hidden. This will also allow for using the eggcrate method without having to be concerned with the back of the eggcrate being seen. This also allows some room for a wave maker, and the overflow drains can be hidden.

Ideally the absolute best location would involve installing the tank in a wall with a room behind it (such as a utility room) for the sump box, skimmer, lighting, and water supplies. From the viewing side, the tank would be even with the wall and would not take up any floor space in the living area. All the unsightly components would be hidden, and there would be convenient access for maintaining the tank. This type of setup would be ideal, and in time, when I expand, it will be my next approach. If you have such a room, behind a wall in which you would like to position the tank, give some thought and planning to the carpentry work that would be involved. You might end up with an ideal location for your reef.

My recommendation is: do not be overly concerned with viewing the tank from as many sides as possible. *Do not sacrifice practicality for vanity!* If you have the proper

> *The location of the tank
> will have a long-term effect
> on its success*

location in the first place, the tank will be most beautiful from the front. This will allow space for the components that make up and enhance the reef. No one ever said to me, "If only I could see the sides and back, it would really be nice." No, most people just stare in awe at the front of the tank, asking many questions. They know there is more going on than meets the eye—that all the action of the wave maker and the high flow rate come from somewhere out of sight.

> *If the quality of water diminishes,
> the tank will not be much to view anyway!*

In other words, it is more important to have a properly functioning tank system than one that is viewed from all sides. Over a period of time, with the tank and components set up in a poor location, the quality of the water will suffer, and the tank will not be much to look at anyway. When the quality of water diminishes, there will be a persistent algae problem and loss of livestock—occurrences that can make this hobby very unpleasant! At that point, you will have to relocate the tank and/or its components to a more practical and serviceable location. Some of these locations are suggested in this book.

SYSTEM NEEDS

Proper placement of the tank and its components will determine whether it is easy or difficult to:

- Set up the live rock;
- Perform regular maintenance for the optimum health of the reef and its inhabitants;
- Clean and maintain the skimmers;
- Make and add water to compensate regularly for evaporation;
- Position the spraybar so that it pushes sediment to the front of the tank, where it can be easily removed; and
- Add a wave maker if desired.

A helpful idea is: if it seems difficult when you first start to perform these procedures,

> *If maintenance seems difficult when you begin, it will become more of a nuisance as time goes on.. Plan accordingly!*

don't expect them to get easier. If they are difficult at the beginning, they will become more and more of a nuisance over time. This may lead to total neglect of the tank, with fatal results. I can speak from first-hand experience of having to deal with cramped conditions, not having a water supply close by, and having the skimmer jammed in under a tank stand cabinet so that it was practically impossible to service it, let alone get it to operate properly.

If you plan ahead so that you have ample area to service the external equipment, you will perform maintenance tasks more easily when they need to be done. This will help to guarantee the success of your reef tank.

> *Don't sacrifice practicality to vanity*

In my opinion, the worst location for a tank would be in the middle of a room. The reasons for this are obvious. Although you can get around and service the entire perimeter of such a tank, all the equipment is exposed and would be unsightly. Also, you could not use the eggcrate system I have described for setting up the rock, and your spraybar could not be concealed.

Another bad location would be near direct sunlight. This could cause problems with the lighting cycles of your system. On bright sunny days, there will be too much sunlight, and that could cause algae problems. Also, a sunny location would provide a longer duration of lighting than the recommended 9 hours a day. This could also encourage the growth of micro-algae.

> *Pay particular attention to the location of the tank. If it is very large, you will not be able to relocate it easily.*

Once you
- have decided on an ideal location,
- have a size in mind as far as the length, width and height of your tank, and
- have taken into consideration the structural factors in your home or apartment,

COMMITMENT AND DECISION FOR A LARGE TANK

Now that we have discussed several preliminary issues on building your own tank, let's briefly review these concerns and make a decision.

1. Can you afford to stock and maintain a tank larger than 125 gallons?
2. Do you have the space and structural support for such size and weight?
3. Can you have a water supply and a temporary drain system near the tank?
4. Is there enough room near the tank (preferably next to it), to locate the sump properly and to allow for the height of the skimmer?
5. Are you willing to build the system yourself?

If you answer yes to all of the above questions, you are ready to proceed with building your own large tank.

WORK SPACE

Have a place to perform the work. A garage or barn might do well. Wherever you will be working, take into consideration that there will be a strong odor when you apply the epoxy. It will be most definitely out of the question to do this inside your home; you will need a well-ventilated area. The workspace temperature should also be above 50 degrees for epoxy application (or follow the manufacturer's recommendation on the product label).

Here is a list of tools and materials recommended for building a tank.

RECOMMENDED TOOLS

A set of saw horses.

A circular saw with a sharp blade (preferably carbide tipped).

A straight-edge, and clamps to make long straight cuts with the circular saw. (This can be a straight piece of 3/4" lumber used with two C-clamps that will accommodate 1-3/4" thickness of wood. This is to allow 3/4" for the plywood material and 3/4" for the straight-edge, plus 1/4" for free play.)

A cordless drill or variable speed drill. (This will be used for tightly driving the screw fasteners and installing the dowels to fasten the "picture frame" oak material.)

1/4" x 8" drill bit for doweling the corners of the oak.

A table saw. This is not essential, but it would be most useful for a variety of purposes. For example, it could be used to bevel the top brace pieces slightly, so that water will not accumulate on them. Also, you could use it to custom rip the oak "picture frame" material.

A belt sander would be useful for making extremely smooth outside corners on the tank. This is where excessive glue gets squeezed out, and the cut edges of the plywood can be seen. Using a belt sander on these outside corners, as well as on any exposed edges, will give you a smooth, flat surface that will blend in with any finishing process. Internal surfaces will be epoxied; external surfaces will be painted (usually black).

A router with a carbide "rounding over" bit would be used to round the edge of the "picture frame" oak material. This takes away the hard square edge of the oak frame, and gives a smoother, professional, more pleasant look to the front of the tank.

A caulking gun will be used to apply construction adhesive to the wood joints, and to apply the silicone sealant.

A plastic, 1-gallon milk container. Cut in half, this makes a good container for mixing epoxy. The container is flexible, so it can be reused: you can easily break up any epoxy that has hardened. Plastic milk containers can also be cut into approximately 4" x 4" squares, for use as squeegees for applying and smoothing out the epoxy.

SUPPLIES FOR A CUSTOM TANK

Refer to Chapter 10 for information on where to find unconventional supplies.

- 3/4" marine grade plywood.
- 1-5/8" to 2" galvanized or stainless steel screws, Phillips head or square drive.
- Plate glass for front of tank. You may want to measure and order the glass after the tank box is built. This is a safer approach for the beginner, and it will give you "a margin for error" while putting the box together.
- 1" x 3" oak. Used for the front "picture frame" to hold the glass in place.
- Construction adhesive tube for a caulking gun. Buy a quality product that is compatible with marine plywood.
- Epoxy resin with (black) tint and hardener. Shop around, and buy the highest quality available.
- 1" x 5" oak for the top braces: three 2-foot pieces.

Do not use the lesser-quality fiberglass resin. The high-quality epoxy resin should cost about $60 a gallon. You will most likely use 1 gallon. This product is also sold in quarts. However, if you are building a large tank, it will take more than one quart to do the job.

The tinting material is sold in 1-ounce tubes. Normally, one tube will be enough. It is extremely important to tint the first coat applied to the wood.

The hardener will come with the gallon of epoxy. It is definitely advised to purchase extra hardener. Sometimes I have found it helpful to add slightly extra hardener, to ensure proper drying and curing. Don't overdo it with the hardener; adding significant extra amounts may cause cracks in the epoxy that will have to be filled in with the next coat.
Fiberglass reinforcement cloth can be found on rolls in 3- or 4-inch wide strips, and will be used to reinforce the inside corners. Estimate how many feet you will use, and buy a little extra. This may save you a trip to the store during the application.

Clear silicone tubes for a caulking gun are used to set in and waterproof the glass panel.

1/4" wood dowels. These will be used for added strength on the corners of the "oak picture frame." Two 3-foot pieces should be more than enough. You will use eight 6-inch pieces, two for each corner.

Two 3" disposable brushes for applying the epoxy.

One quart of acetone. If you want to reuse the disposable brushes, you will need this solvent. One quart will cost about $5, and the brushes are approximately $1 each. If you use the acetone, only one brush will be needed. If you don't, the brushes will harden and become useless. You will be applying 4 or 5 separate coats, so the acetone will come in handy.

PUTTING IT ALL TOGETHER: BUILDING THE TANK

At this point, you have a place to do the work, and all the tools and materials are in one area. Ideally there will also be someone available to assist you. An assistant can be very helpful for some people, and a real nuisance for others. Determine which approach best suits your needs.

Making the plywood shell of the tank:

The plywood comes in 4' x 8' sheets, and the tank used here as an example (239 gallons) will measure approximately 24" tall, 24" wide, and 96" long. For this tank, there will be 4 pieces of plywood. They are:

- The bottom (24" x 96");
- The back (24" x 96"); and
- The two sides, or end pieces (24" in height, 23-1/4" in width). The 24" height will actually come out slightly less than 24", because when you cut the 4-foot sheet exactly in half, the width of the saw blade (the "kerf") will be removed from the wood. The only time you will have to allow for this is when measuring the width and height of these side pieces.

Cut the bottom piece first, the back second, and the sides last. See Diagram 21.

To begin, place one sheet of plywood on the saw horses. We want to cut the sheet exactly in half to end up with two 2' x 8' pieces. Measure 24" on each end of the sheet, and with your straight edge, make one straight pencil line connecting the two marks.

Now, begin cutting with the circular saw along the center of the line. When you have cut in approximately 3 inches, stop the saw, and mark the plywood where the edge of the saw table is on the opposite side of the motor, usually on the right-hand side of the saw. Measure from the edge of the sheet to this new mark, and make a corresponding mark at the other end of the sheet. This new mark will give you a guide for the saw, compensating for the "saw table." Using the C-clamps, fasten the straight-edge to the plywood sheet so that it will guide the saw table on a straight line between the two new marks as you cut the sheet. It may help to add a small finishing nail in the center of the straight edge, so it doesn't bow out while you are pushing the saw against it. This little hole will have many coats of epoxy over it, so don't be concerned about leaks. The nail should be small (#4 finishing nail), and should only go into the plywood 1/4"—just enough to hold the straight-edge in place.

Now, with the straight-edge accurately clamped on the plywood (and secured in the middle with a finishing nail), resume cutting with the saw. Cut the plywood sheet in half, using the straight-edge as a guide for the saw table, and keeping an eye on the original pencil line to ensure that there are no errors.

You should now have two 24" x 96" plywood pieces. One is for the back of the tank, the other is for the bottom. Using a small broom, remove any sawdust from the wood. The back piece is going to sit on top of the bottom piece. You will place screws through the bottom, up into the back piece.

Select the factory edge of the bottom piece (this is the edge you didn't cut), and place that in the direction of the front of the tank. Along the back edge of the bottom piece, where the back piece will sit, run a 1/4" bead of construction adhesive. Determine the factory edge of the back piece, and place that edge into the adhesive. Position the two pieces so that the corner is even (flush) where they meet, and hold the assembly in place. (This is one time when an assistant can come in handy.)

Using the cordless drill with the screwdriver bit, begin one screw going through the bottom and into the back, approximately 3" in from the end. Drive it in tightly. Go to the center of the 8-foot back and bottom assembly. Line up the pieces, and drive another screw through the bottom and into the back. Do the same at the remaining end.

Now place pencil marks every 6" along the area to be fastened. A helpful trick is to extend your tape measure to the length of wood that you plan to mark at 6" intervals. Looking at the tape increment of one foot, you can plan the layout for 6" increments and "center" the tape measure from end to end so there will be an equal space at each end.

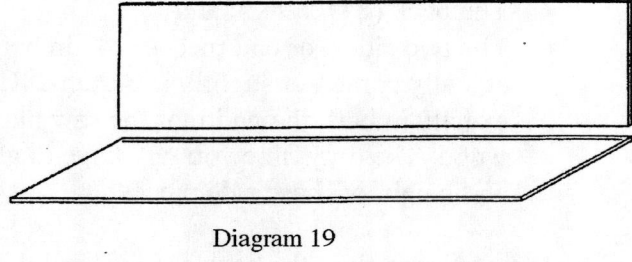

Diagram 19

Install screws at the pencil marks. The back and bottom are now fastened.

Measure the width and height of the side pieces as accurately as possible. There may be a small discrepancy caused by the saw cut ("kerf"). Keep in mind that these side pieces will attach to the *inside* of the back and bottom pieces. This will provide superior strength, as opposed to attaching the side pieces onto the outside ends of the bottom and back.

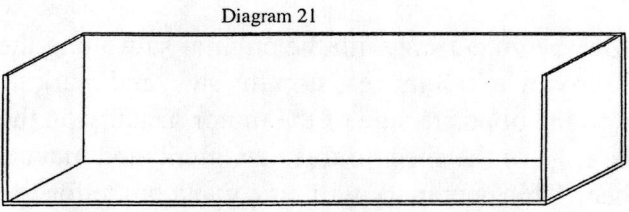

Diagram 21

Lay out the sizes for the side pieces, and make certain they are square. These pieces are smaller, and you can probably cut them fairly straight with a pencil line and a saw; however, the straight-edge method will give more accurate results.

Take one of the end pieces and place a 1/4" bead of adhesive along the two edges that will meet the back and bottom plywood. Position the side piece into the corner, lining it up so that it makes flush edges with the back and bottom pieces. Pushing downward on the side piece and keeping it lined up, put a screw through the back piece and into the side near the corner where the three pieces of wood meet. Install another screw through the back piece, near the top of the side piece.

Now place a screw through the bottom piece upward into the end piece, near the corner where the three pieces of wood meet; then another screw through the bottom into the end piece, approximately 3" back from the edge where the glass will be. Make pencil marks at 6" intervals between the pairs of screws you have already installed, and add screws there.

Follow the same procedure for the other end of the tank.

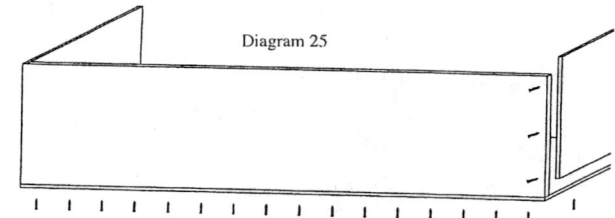

Diagram 25

You should now have completed the plywood installation. Check to see that all the screws have been installed at 6" intervals, and that they have been driven in snugly. Construction adhesive may have gotten squeezed out at the seams. Let this harden, and remove it later when it has dried.

Now, lay the assembly on its back, so that the future front of the tank is facing upward. You will be preparing the plywood edges for the oak "picture frame" that will surround the glass. Check to see if the edges are even where the plywood pieces meet. A belt sander is very useful for evening out small differences. A sharp plane will also work, or in the worst case you will have to use rough sand paper with a flat wood block. Go over all the end-grains of the plywood, so they are smooth and even.

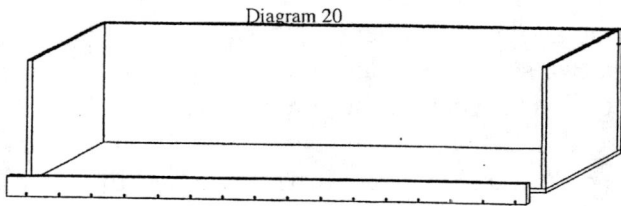

Diagram 20

The oak "picture frame" for the front of the tank:

The next step is to add the oak "picture frame." First measure the bottom piece. If you have used a full 8-foot bottom piece of plywood, and the sides are resting on top of it (as in Diagram 20), the bottom measurement for the oak will be 8 feet. Measure your bottom piece left to right, and cut two pieces of 1" x 4" oak material to that length. One will be for the bottom edge of the tank's front, the other for the top edge. They should be the same size. This will ensure a square, parallel finished product.

Oak is an extremely hard wood. It is also very strong. For these reasons, I have used it for the purpose of holding in the glass securely—with very good results. Because it is such a hard wood, you will have to pre-drill and countersink the holes for the screws that will secure it to the plywood.

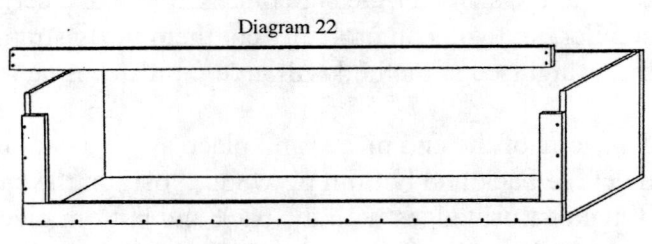

Diagram 22

Work first on the bottom piece of the oak frame. Starting approximately 2" from one end of the oak strip, measure and mark out 6" increments for the screw holes. Then, so that each screw will be centered in the narrow plywood edge, place another mark for each screw, 3/8" in from the outside edge of the oak. This will provide the most accurate placement of the screws.

Put the countersink bit in the drill, and place the oak piece on a work table. Drill the holes for the screws. Countersink the holes approximately 1/8" below the surface of the wood. This will allow space to fill in the screwhead hole with a putty filler, once the screws are in place. You only need to drill the oak, not the plywood. Once the screw holes in the oak have been drilled and countersunk, run a bead of adhesive along the edge of the plywood. Position the oak piece and fasten it with screws.

Once you have attached the bottom edge of the oak frame, cut the two oak side pieces, deducting for the width of the top and bottom pieces. As you did for the bottom oak piece, mark the locations for the screws, drill and countersink the holes, and apply glue to the plywood edges. Also apply glue to the bottom end of the oak side pieces, so the end grain will be glued to the bottom piece of oak. When you screw the side pieces into place, be sure that they fit snugly against the bottom piece.

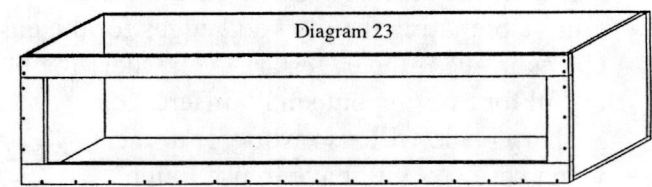

Diagram 23

The top piece of the oak frame does not lie along a plywood edge; it is fastened with just two screws on each end. Pay particular attention to where these screw holes are placed in the oak. You want to get the screws into the plywood without splitting or cracking the plywood side piece. It will help to drill 1/8" pilot guide holes in the plywood. Working with the oak piece, mark out the location of the screws; then drill and countersink them in the oak. Next, position the oak strip where you will want it on the plywood assembly, and use the screw holes in the oak as guides to make pilot holes in the plywood, using a 1/8" drill bit. Glue the ends of the oak strip well, and install the two screws on each end.

Reinforcing the oak frame:

Now that the oak frame is complete, we will want to take further steps to reinforce it. The first job will be to install two dowels (1/4" x 6") in each corner of the frame. This will lock the corners together permanently.

The size of oak strips we are using for the frame is called "1 by 3"; they are actually 3/4" x 2-1/2". We want to install two dowels at each corner of the frame, going through the 2-1/2" dimension of the long (top or bottom) oak piece, and at least the same distance into the side piece (or slightly more). This dictates a hole depth of at least 5". The drill bit will also have to go into the chuck of the drill about 2", which is why you need a bit length of 8" or longer.

The dowels should be cut to approximately 7" to 8" long. The extra length allows for any peening over of the dowels (damage caused by tapping them in with a hammer). This will be cut off later and become scrap.

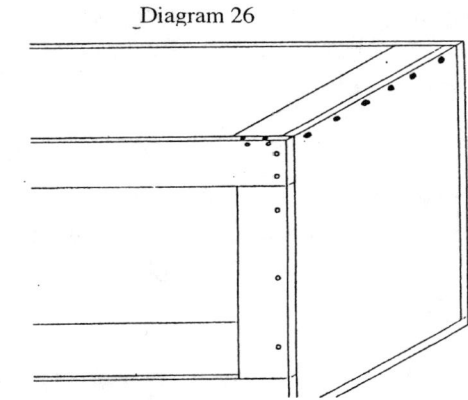

Diagram 26

Using a 1/4" x 8" bit, set up the drill to make a hole that is the desired length of the dowels, approximately 5" to 5-1/2". Mark the location for the dowel holes carefully. They should be centered relative to the 3/4" dimension of the oak strips, and should not hit the screws that were just installed. I would mark the locations centered on the narrow edge of the top or bottom oak piece, and positioned so the dowels will enter the side oak pieces 3/4" in from each edge.

Drill through the top or bottom piece of oak, into the side piece. Remove any shavings that might affect the depth of the holes. Cover the dowels with carpenter's wood glue, and very gently tap them in with a hammer. If the first two holes work well, apply the same procedures to the other corners of the frame. If the first corner did not work out, review the instructions above and adjust your procedure so the other corners of the frame will come out well.

Once a dowel bottoms out in the hole, some of it may be sticking out. Don't worry about this, as it will be cut off and sanded later. Drill, glue, and tap in two dowels in each corner of the oak frame. Once that is complete, you can cut off the protruding ends of the dowels. Use a small hand saw for this.

The last step of woodworking will be the top reinforcement braces. These are three oak pieces, 3/4" thick by 3-1/2" wide, which will be installed as braces going front-to-back: one at the top right corner, one at the top left corner, and one in the top center. These braces will reinforce the tank well, and will give you something to rest the light box on.

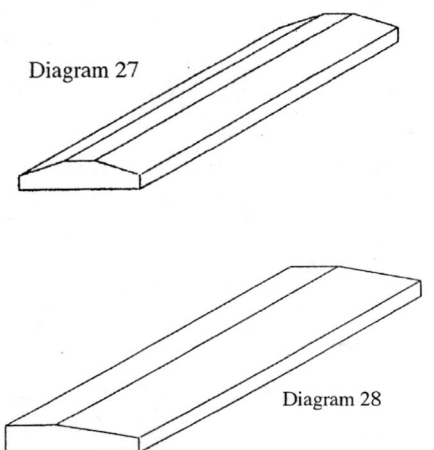

Diagram 27

Here the table saw will come in handy, because you want to have a slight bevel on the top of these braces so that water will not rest there (see Diagram 27). Measure the length of the braces, and cut them all to the same length. You will not install these pieces until after the glass has been set in. Bevel them as shown in Diagrams 27 and 28, using a table saw or a sharp wood plane.

Diagram 28

Preparing to apply the epoxy:

We are now ready to prepare the inside tank area for the epoxy. Using a sharp knife or chisel, remove any construction adhesive that has oozed out during the fastening process. Take your time when removing this excess, as you will probably find it adhering tightly. Remove all the excess glue.

Go over all the ends of the wood to make sure they are even. The top of the plywood and the inside edge of the oak frame should also be smooth and even. Do a thorough job, because no further corrections can be made once you install the epoxy. Finally, sweep and blow out any sawdust or other foreign material inside the tank. Once you have all this done, proceed with the epoxy.

Before working with the epoxy, read all the following material, down to "Finishing the outside of the tank."

Pour approximately 2" of the epoxy into the cutoff bottom half of a plastic gallon milk container. Add a small squeeze of tinting material from the tube. A squirt 1-1/4" long will be about right for this amount of epoxy. Mix the tint thoroughly with the epoxy, using a small scrap of wood.

The epoxy will not begin to harden until the catalyst is added, but once it is added you will need to work quickly. Therefore before you add the catalyst, be sure you have everything you need to work with the epoxy, such as the applicator brush, some square pieces of cut-up plastic milk container to use as squeegees to spread the epoxy, and some inexpensive cotton gloves to protect your hands. Flexible rubber gloves may also be used.

Applying the epoxy:

Set the tank so the bottom is flat and level. Add the recommended amount of catalyst to the epoxy/tint mixture, and mix very thoroughly and vigorously for a full minute. When using epoxy, you have to work quickly and add the correct amount of catalyst. There is no room for making corrections later. Read the directions for the particular product you are using, and get very familiar with them so you can work confidently.

You will be applying many coats of epoxy, so this procedure of combining the epoxy resin, the tint, and the catalyst, and mixing them thoroughly for 60 seconds, will be repeated numerous times. Determine a batch size that you are comfortable handling. For a large tank (200 gallons or more) I usually mix slightly less than a quart at a time.

> *Be sure to tint
> the first application of epoxy*

One very important recommendation is to add the tinting material with the first coat of epoxy! If the first coat has not been tinted, the other coats will **not** give you a solid color—no matter how many coats of tinted material you apply! Make **sure** to tint the first coat. That way the tint will get into the pores of the wood, and subsequent coats will give you a nice solid color. If the first coat is not tinted, it will seal in the wood's natural color, which will then be impossible to cover with the desired (black) tint.

To review: first you add the tint to the epoxy resin *without* the catalyst, and thoroughly mix it in. Then you add the catalyst. Once the catalyst has been added to the tinted epoxy, you can apply it to the inside wood of the tank.

Pour about 1/3 of the material from the container onto the floor of the tank. Work quickly and methodically from one end of the tank to the other. Be generous with the epoxy, and only be concerned with the bottom and about 4" up the sides at this time. Pay particular attention to the inside of the oak picture frame area, making sure it is covered.

Don't try to paint the epoxy on with the brush only; use the brush and squeegee together to spread it around as evenly as possible. The material by nature will find its own level, and will adhere permanently to the wood. You should have plenty of mixture to cover the bottom, and if you have some excess at the end of the application, just pour it onto the bottom and spread it out. Now let this application dry. Depending on the temperature and humidity level, it should take an average of 12 hours to completely set up. Leaving it to dry longer will not be a problem.

When the bottom has dried, lay the tank on its back, and repeat the application on the back area. Again, work about 4" up the adjacent vertical surfaces. When the back has dried, set the tank on its end, prepare a smaller amount of the mixture, and apply it in the same way. When it has dried, do the other end. You will also want to apply epoxy to the top end grain of the box. This will ensure that no moisture will get into the wood.

Adding the fiberglass reinforcing cloth:

Use a brush soaked in epoxy to push out all air pockets and bubbles under the fiberglass cloth

Now the tank has one coat of epoxy on it.
Next you'll be applying fiberglass reinforcing strips to cover along corners where two pieces of wood meet. Using sharp scissors, pre-cut the pieces of fiberglass cloth to accurate lengths, especially the pieces for the bottom corners, which must be a definite length. (The vertical side corners may run past the top of the tank and can be cut off when dry.) It will be most helpful to burn the ends of the cut cloth, to prevent strings from coming off the material while you are applying it. With the pieces accurately cut and the ends burned, you can apply the reinforcement cloth. (Note: you don't have to maneuver the tank around when applying the reinforcing strips.)

Mix the epoxy and apply it with the brush along the corner where the cloth is to be installed. Place the end of a cloth strip at the end of the corner. Try to get it centered over the corner, so the middle of the cloth strip follows along the joint of the two pieces of wood. Working along the strip, use the brush to force the cloth into the corner, while keeping the rest of the strip out of the wet epoxy until it is pushed into position with the brush. After completing one corner, *use the brush with wet epoxy on it to push out any air bubbles that may have been trapped behind the cloth.* Then go over the strip with one full application of epoxy.

Continue with the remaining corners, using the same method. Keep in mind that any strands of material can be removed later by sanding, but they will be more easily removed when wet. Burning the cut ends of the cloth strips will minimize this "stranding." Complete all the inside corners, and let the material dry.

Coating the top braces:

You should also apply epoxy to the three top brace pieces of oak, which have not yet been installed on the tank. You can be working on them while you wait for the various applications of material to dry on the tank and the reinforcement cloth. Apply epoxy to all but the bottom side of these braces; when that application is dry, flip the pieces over and do the bottom side. This will totally waterproof the oak braces, and you can then install them with complete confidence after the glass has been set in. It will also be helpful to lay these brace pieces on some scrap strips of wood, so you can brush the edges thoroughly. Apply at least 4 or 5 coats of material to these braces. Don't forget to coat the "end grain" cut surfaces.

Sanding the epoxy:

Once the reinforcement strips have dried, sand the epoxy surface by hand with a sanding block or a small orbital sander. Use 80 grit paper, and change it often. This is to rough up the hard shiny epoxy surface; it will ensure a good bond between coats, and will remove any noticeable protrusions of cloth. Pay particular attention to any spots where reinforcement cloth overlaps onto the inside of the oak frame. This is where the glass will rest, so the whole inner surface of the frame should be very smooth, with no irregularities.

When the inside of the tank has been sanded slightly to rough up the surface, apply at least two more complete coats of epoxy as you did at the beginning, sanding between coats to rough up the surface for a good bond. Do the bottom first and let it dry. Then do the back and the sides. By positioning the tank flat and level, you will allow the epoxy to even out naturally, while you continue to apply it approximately 4" up on any adjacent vertical surfaces. This will give a good buildup of material, and I'm sure you can see by now that this container will be permanently waterproof and exceptionally strong.

Summary of steps for epoxy application:

1. Apply one *tinted* coat to the complete interior of the tank.
2. Apply the fiberglass reinforcing strips to all the corners, using tinted material.
3. Sand the high spots and rough up the surface after the epoxy has cured.
4. Apply an additional 2 or 3 coats, sanding for a good bond between coats.
5. Of course you don't need to sand the last application.
6. Pay particular attention to sanding off "high spots" on the interior of the oak "picture frame," where the glass will rest.

Some other tips on working with the epoxy:

1. Keep the project out of the direct sun. Heat can make it set up almost immediately.
2. If you can, do the project when there is low humidity. Dry air will enhance the curing process.
3. Tinting the material will make the inside of the tank a pleasant uniform color. I don't think anyone would like the look of plywood grain. Add tint to all coats, especially the first one!
4. To use acetone solvent: cut a 1-liter plastic soda bottle down to about 6" tall, and pour in about 3" of acetone. After each application of epoxy, swish the brush vigorously around in the acetone, and immediately shake off the excess solvent.

The brush will be ready for the next application. The acetone can be reused many times.

5. Wearing cotton gloves will protect your hands from the wet epoxy in case you brush against it. After a while the gloves will accumulate an epoxy buildup and get stiff. They will still offer protection, but they will not be very comfortable. Rubber gloves may be a better alternative, depending on which type you get. Epoxy disintegrates some rubber and plastic.

6. If you get epoxy on your skin, it is easiest to remove it before it dries. Wipe it off using a rag with acetone on it. Then wash the acetone off your skin with soap and water. If the epoxy does dry on your skin, it can be peeled off.

7. Pay particular attention not to get epoxy in your hair. If you have long hair, wear it back, and use a hat. If you get this material in your hair, it will have to be cut out.

8. Do not add excessive tint. A little goes a long way. *Adding too much tint may affect the drying process* of the coat you are applying. Use only the recommended amount of tint.

9. When sanding and sweeping out the material, use a dust mask.

10. Do not waste any epoxy mixture to which you have added catalyst. If you have some extra, pour it on, and level it out or brush it onto the sides. It should not be necessary to throw away any epoxy material.

11. Use the correct amount of tint and catalyst (hardener). You may use slightly more hardener than called for. If you do not add enough hardener (or if you add too much tint), the material may not set up. This is about the worst thing that can happen with epoxy—that an application doesn't dry. Pay close attention to the amount of catalyst you use. Add the correct amount, or just *slightly* more. If you add too much more hardener, the mixture will set up very quickly and then develop cracks that will have to be filled in with the next coat.

12. The average "working time" for a mixed batch of epoxy is about 20 minutes. After that time, the material will not spread well.

13. Work quickly and confidently with the material. Apply it, and then let it dry. Don't waste time being fussy about the look of the material. As long as it is one color and is applied generously, the finished look will be fine.

Finishing the outside of the tank:

So now the tank is built, and the epoxy has been applied to the interior for waterproofing. We will now proceed to the external finishing.

The oak frame edges should be routed with a carbide rounding-over bit to give the frame a smooth look. Fill the countersunk holes with a carpenter's wood filler. After that dries, sand it smooth.

You will have to decide on what kind of finish you want on the outside of the tank. Whatever look you prefer, the finishing should be complete before the glass is installed. The two areas to consider will be the oak and the plywood. On my tank I painted the plywood with a black satin enamel paint, and lightly stained the oak with a finish coat of polyurethane.

Keep in mind that all the viewing will be done from this side of the tank, so it makes sense to spend some time on the appearance of the oak frame. Once it is finished with paint, stain, and polyurethane, you will be ready to set in the glass.

The size of the glass front:

When measuring the size of the glass there are a few factors to consider, such as:

1. Do not make the glass too tight. The sealing and waterproofing are done with the silicone sealant, and if the glass is too tight there will not be enough room for the silicone. Also if the glass is too snug it will be difficult to install, and may break. You want a *buffer* of silicone to *cushion* the glass.

2. To get the length of the glass: carefully measure the inside length of the epoxied tank. Take two measurements inside the tank, not just one. Measure the inside length along the top, and then along the bottom. Write down and use the smaller of these two numbers.

   Then deduct 1/8" from the measurement you have written down. The result is the correct length to order for the glass. The 1/8" deduction is to allow for the silicone sealant, so you will not have too tight a fit between the glass and the wood that holds it. This 1/8" allowance will be split in half when you center the glass in the frame, so there will be 1/16" of play on each side. This space will be filled with silicone.

3. To get the height of the glass: carefully measure the inside height of the epoxied tank. As with the length, use *two* measurements (one at each end of the tank); write down and use the smaller of the two.

   Then deduct 3/4" to allow for the top braces that will be installed after the glass is set in. Also deduct 1/8", as you did for the length. This 1/8" will be made up with silicone.

GLASS THICKNESS COMPARED TO HEIGHT OF TANK

Taller tanks require thicker glass, because they contain more water and therefore create higher pressure on the sides of the container.

For this tank height	Use this thickness of plate glass
15" to 22"	3/8"
24" to 30"	1/2"
30" to 36"	5/8"

Glass is priced by size and thickness. The thicker the glass, the more expensive it will be. As you shop around by phone, you will quickly learn the relationship between thickness and cost. The above recommendations are accurate; I personally have used glass in all thickness listed above, for tanks up to 30" tall.

I do not recommend trying to save a few dollars by using thinner glass, which may not be as strong as the more expensive, thicker glass. Once the glass is installed it is relatively permanent, and changing it would be a major project. If you use the recommended glass thickness for your tank, even though it *may* possibly be slightly thicker than you need, you will be making a wise investment in the tank's long-term integrity. Consider too: if you move and the tank has to be transported, thicker glass will hold up much better.

To set the glass you will need two people to position it correctly, and to minimize the risk of breakage. One of the most important factors to consider when setting the glass is to make absolutely sure that there are *no high spots of epoxy* on the inside of the oak frame. These high spots will act as pressure points against the glass, and could cause breakage. Minor irregularities will not be as much of a concern, considering that a hefty 3/4" bead of silicone will be installed in this area. Not only will this be a water seal and adhere the glass to the frame, it will also act as a buffer to cushion the glass. Just be certain to remove any high spots and irregularities of epoxy around the inside area of the oak frame.

Select a silicone sealer that is non-toxic when cured, and made for underwater use. Use a clear material: it will not be as noticeable as sealers with color in them. Also make sure that you have enough silicone. Once you begin applying the material you don't want to run out or have to skimp on the desired 3/4" bead. For the tank described here, the glass measures 24" x 96". I recommend having at least 4 tubes of silicone on hand to seal this size glass front. Have a caulking gun that operates properly and is ready to go.

Here is how to set the glass

1. Place the tank on a flat bench with the oak picture frame facing down.
2. Remove any high spots, dust, and debris where the glass will go.
3. Wipe the area with a clean damp rag to remove any dust particles, and let all surfaces dry.
4. Using two people, carefully "dry fit" the piece of glass in the tank on the oak frame, making sure it fits in freely, with no restrictions. Make any needed adjustments by working on the glass. Small amounts can be removed from the glass using a belt sander. *Do not force the glass into the wood frame.* When you are confident of the fit, remove the piece of glass and place it in a safe location.
5. Cut the caulking tubes of silicone at a 45-degree angle and puncture the seal of two tubes. Run a silicone bead 3/4" thick along the center of the oak frame, completely around the perimeter. Don't skimp with the silicone.
6. Using two people again, very carefully place the piece of glass back into the wood frame. Set the long bottom edge first, and then slowly lower the whole glass panel flat onto the silicone.
7. Using your hands, carefully press the glass down into the silicone bead. You should see the bead spread out between the glass and the oak.
8. Let the material dry for at least 24 hours.
9. After the material has set up, carefully run another (smaller) bead to fill the space between the edge of the glass and the side walls of the tank. You are aiming for a complete seal, and also for a concave bead that goes slightly up onto the wood that surrounds the glass. Pay particular attention to getting sealer into the four corners, filling any spaces with silicone. Go over the material *once* with your finger to smooth it out and provide the concave bead. Let it dry for 24 hours.
10. If necessary repeat Step 9 to seal the edges of the glass completely. Do not put on unnecessary material. Repeat Step 9 only if the seal between the glass and the wood looks as if it could use another application. You should end up with a 3/16"

thick, continuous, concave bead of silicone along all four inside edges of the glass, curving up a small distance onto the surrounding wood.

11. Leave adequate time for the silicone to dry, with the glass in the horizontal position. This will use gravity and the weight of the glass to insure a good bond of the dissimilar materials, as well as an absolutely waterproof seal.

INSTALLING THE TOP BRACES

We will complete the tank by adding the 3 top braces. These oak braces are going to be the primary supporting components of the self-made tank. The side braces will hold the right and left corners tightly in place, and the center one will keep the middle of the tank from bowing out. Unlike the rest of the tank, these pieces are not glued in with construction adhesive. They are sealed in with silicone sealant and screwed in place securely with galvanized or stainless steel wood-screws.

The side braces should have a slight bevel on the top, so that water will not accumulate there. The center brace should have a bevel along both sides, with a flat ridge approximately 3/4" wide running along the middle of the brace.

You have already coated the braces with several applications of epoxy. All edges and ends should be coated. As you install the braces you may need to trim them slightly; aim for a snug fit, but do not fit them so tightly as to force existing wood out of place. If you have to trim one of the braces, cut only one end of it and then cover that end with silicone sealant. This will waterproof the end grain and thereby extend the life of the container.

Oak is an extremely hard wood, and it is out of the question even to think about installing a screw through it without first drilling a small "pilot hole." Therefore the braces and the front "picture frame" will have to be pre-drilled. Use a 1/8" drill bit, and space the holes in such a way as to get maximum power from the screws. It is not necessary to make a pilot hole where a screw is going to go through plywood, only where it is passing through oak.

Trim one side brace to fit, drill the pilot holes, and countersink them where necessary. Seal the cut end of the brace with silicone and position the piece. Install the screws in through the side plywood first, using 1-3/4" screws. This will pull the oak brace into position tightly against the plywood. Next screw through the front "picture frame," and finally do the back. Proceed to the other side brace and repeat this sequence.

The center brace must be placed exactly in the center of the tank. This will distribute the pressure of the water evenly against the front and back of the tank. Carefully countersink the screw holes through the oak "picture frame" and then follow through with the 1/8" pilot hole into the brace. Seal the cut end with silicone if needed, and install two 3-1/2" screws into the front and two 3-1/2" screws through the rear of the brace.

Finally, go over all the areas where the brace meets the side walls of the tank and run a 3/16" bead of silicone sealant. This will seal the braces in, thereby sealing and protecting the screws. See Diagram 24.

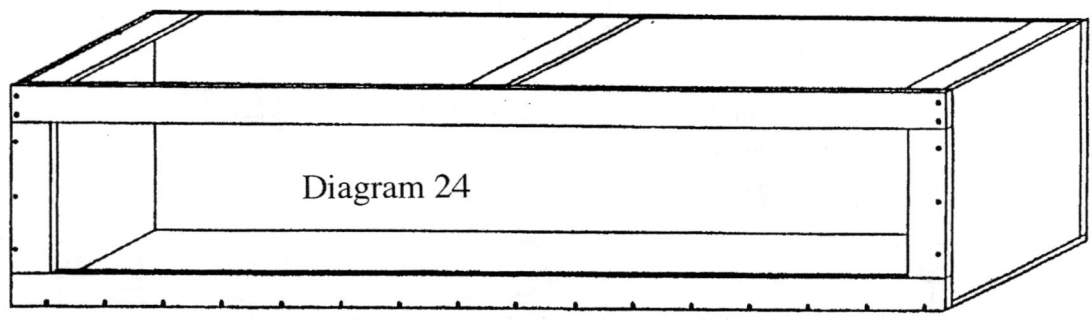

Diagram 24

COMPLETING YOUR SELF-MADE TANK

Now you have your custom tank. Most likely it is of an impressive size. My description of how to build it may be more complex than necessary if you already have woodworking skills. I have provided detail for people who may not have much experience with this kind of work, and especially for those who are building their first tank. Once you get familiar with the epoxy and the fundamentals of creating a large vessel to hold water, it is not that big a deal (although it does require quite a bit of work). I know, because I have built several tanks—and when I expand I will build yet another one, only larger!

After a few days to let all the materials cure sufficiently, and before you bring the tank into the house, remove foreign material by washing the tank out well with plain water and a clean rag. Any excess silicone can be trimmed off with a razor blade, and the glass can be cleaned with white vinegar and rinsed off thoroughly with fresh water. The tank should now be ready to be brought into the house and placed in its location.

TANK STANDS

A stand for a tank larger than 55 gallons will have to be very strong. As previously discussed, saltwater weighs approximately 8.5 pounds per gallon. When estimating the weight of a tank, I use a figure of 10 pounds per gallon. This allows for the weight of the live rock, the sand, and the tank itself. The figure of 10 pounds per gallon is generous; I think most of us would prefer to figure on the more cautious, heavier side when estimating the tank's weight, to be sure that it is well supported.

Load Capacity of Common Lumber

Rather than go into a long discussion on the structural capabilities of different species of wood, I will concentrate on using readily available common lumber. This lumber can be found at any home improvement center or lumber yard.

The common lumber sizes used horizontally for supporting a tank are:

Lumber size	Number of pieces	Will support	Spanned	Tank size
2" x 4"	3 (installed with the 3-1/2" dimension placed vertically on edge)	550 pounds	4 feet	55 gallons
4" x 4"	2	550 pounds	4 feet	55 gallons
4" x 6"	2	1,250 pounds	6 feet	125 gallons
4" x 6"	3	2,400 pounds	8 feet	239 gallons

The above sizes of lumber can be spanned the length of the tank without the need for a center support. If you place a vertical support in the center of the stand, the weight is transferred to two additional support points. This decreases the span and increases the capabilities of the materials used for support.

The common lumber sizes used vertically for supporting a tank are:

Vertical size:	Used with horizontal size:
2" x 4"	2" x 4"
4" x 4"	4" x 4" and 4" x 6"

So there are basically two types of stands:

1. **The conventional stand.** This is an independent one-piece reinforced box, with doors of some kind under it for filtration equipment or storage. Usually, the largest commonly available store-bought stands are for tank sizes up to 125 gallons. This type of stand would not be practical for a large self-made tank, such as the 239-gallon I have been using as an example in this chapter. The stand would be too heavy and bulky to transport, and might have to be disassembled to some extent to be moved.

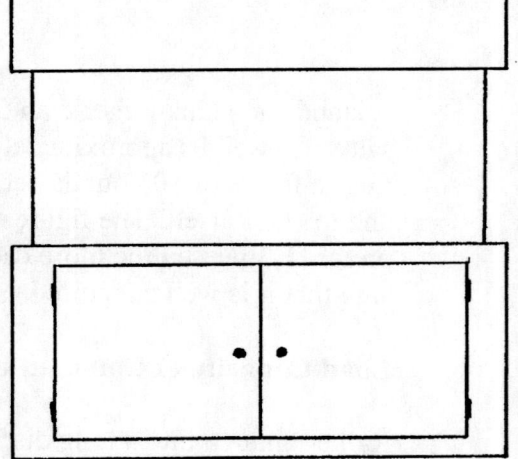

Conventional stands are usually made out of wood. Some are made from steel angle iron that is welded together, and most often covered with removable finished wood. These steel stands are exceptionally strong.

2. **A custom stand, or supporting platform.** This is a supporting system made up of several components that could be easily disassembled and transported: for example, wood planks and cinder blocks. A supporting platform like this could be finished with a removable sliding or hinged cover of 1/4" luan plywood, stained or painted. The doors could be in a removable face frame that would be a separate component of the stand. This type of stand is for the do-it-yourselfer. It is the most practical approach for supporting tanks larger than 125 gallons.

A very common mistake when considering the stand is to plan to have the sump and the skimmer under the tank. As I have explained in the chapter about filtration, the sump should be very easily accessed so you can change the prefilter, and the skimmer needs enough height to operate properly. The skimmer should be above the sump box, so that gravity can drain it into the sump and prefilter. If you plan to have the skimmer under the tank, this will be most difficult to accomplish! If need be, the sump may be under the tank; but then the skimmer should be on the side of the tank.

The drawing below shows the proper location for the skimmer and sump. I very strongly recommend following this design for the location of the sump box and the skimmer.)

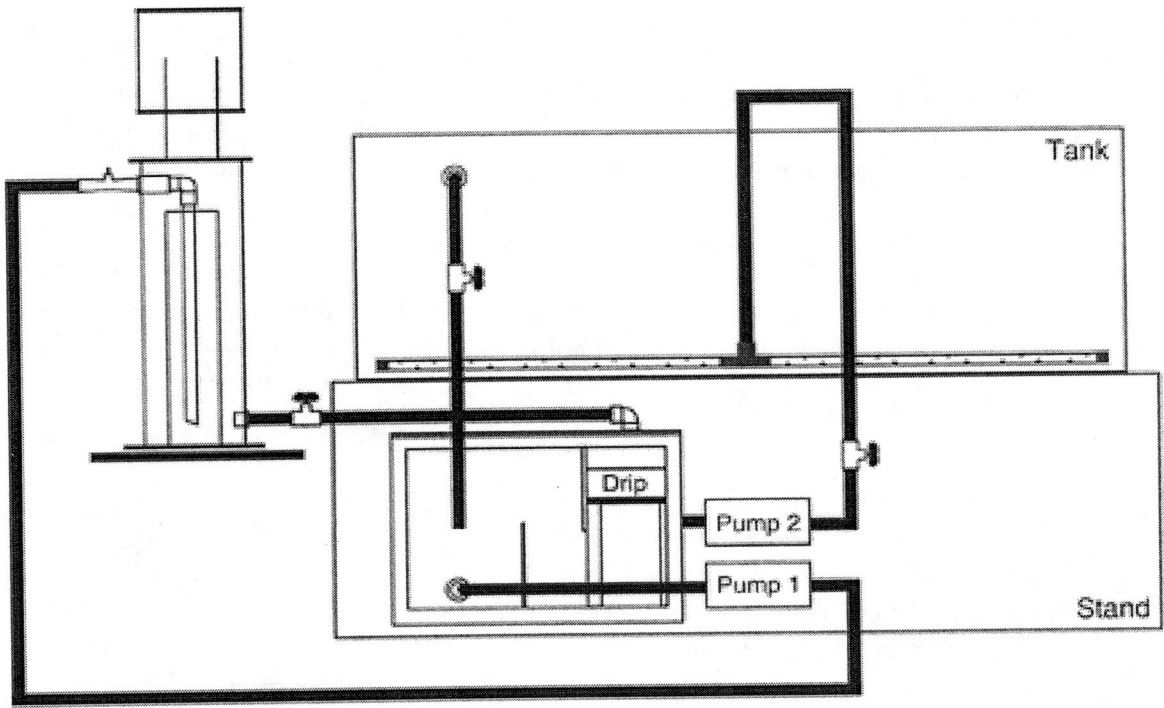

Methods of attaching the vertical supports to the horizontal ones will depend on whether the stand is a one-piece unit, or just components positioned together so that they can come apart easily. An example of a component stand would be cinder blocks with two 4 x 4's resting on top. You would first position the blocks, then place and level the 4 x 4's, and finally position the tank on top of them. In this system, nothing is fastened together, so if you had to move the "stand," it would disassemble for easy transporting, storage, and reassembly.

This type of components stand will be referred to as a "K.D.," meaning it comes apart by disassembly or "knock down." A front cover could be sliding 1/4" wood panels that are mainly decorative, used as sliding doors for access to the space under the tank. Or a door face can be made that is a separate unit by itself, fastened with a few screws. This 1/4" material is sold as luan plywood, in 4' x 8' sheets. It is inexpensive and can be finished nicely. It can also be used to cover the sides of the structural material. Fastened with a few 3/4" screws, it will be easy to remove if and when take-down is necessary.

In the K.D. approach almost everything is free-standing, and there is very little if any lateral (side to side) pressure from the weight of the tank. The pressure (weight) is vertical (directed downward). The amount of lateral movement depends on how high off the floor the tank is, and how wide the vertical supports are. This movement can be observed as wobble or sway of the supporting platform.

There would be little if any lateral movement if you used a K.D. method with cinderblocks that are 16" tall, on which you place horizontal supports that are 4" x 4" or 4" x 6". The top surface of this support platform would be only 20" or 22" above the floor. By contrast, there would be a considerable amount of lateral movement if your tank were on vertical 2-by-4's, with a cabinet underneath for a 36" tall sump box. This type of stand would have to be reinforced. Lateral movement, sway, or wobble can be removed by screwing a back piece and side pieces of plywood to the support frame.

Stands can be purchased ready-made, or they can be put together by someone who knows how to support the weight of the tank. I use cinderblocks and planks for my lower tank. The upper tank has 4-by-4's attached to 4-by-6's, fastened with large angle-iron brackets in the corners. Triangular pieces of plywood are used in the back where access is not important. Using common sense and common materials, find what works best for your needs.

THE SUMP BOX

Making a sump box will be very similar to constructing a tank. First, determine the volume of water the sump box will need to hold (see "Calculating the Size of the Sump Box,"

You will need:

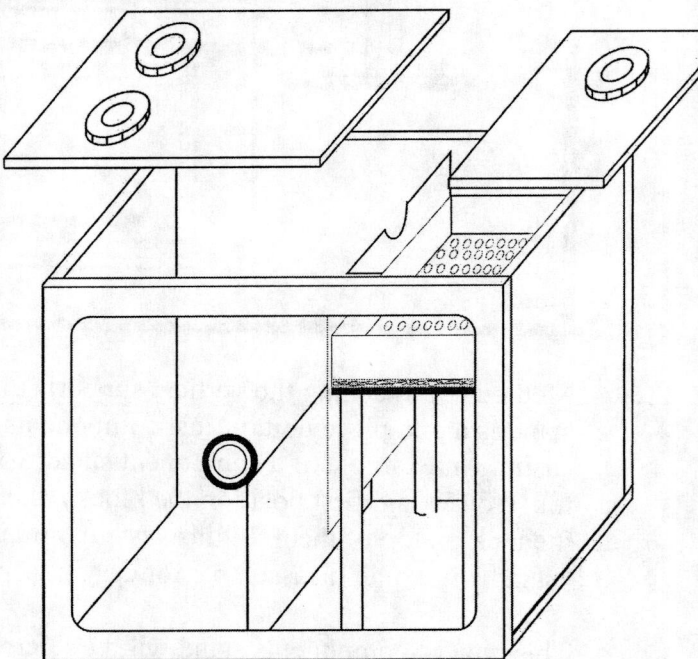

- 3/4" marine grade plywood, including enough for the top cover of the sump box.
- Epoxy resin with (black) tint and hardener. Find and buy the highest quality.
- Plate glass for the front of the sump box. As with the tank front, you may want to measure and order the glass after the box is built.
- Plexiglas to form two separate areas in the sump, "clean" and "dirty."
- 4 bulkhead fittings.
- 4 PVC standoffs (1-1/2"), for the drip plate.
- Eggcrate, sized for the drip plate and prefilter areas.
- Silicone sealant.
- Plexiglas to form the drip plate.
- Plexiglas knife cutter for scoring and cutting the material to size.
- Power tools recommended for fabricating a tank.

Sequence of building the sump:

- Determine the size.
- Draw your plan.

- Fabricate the box, following the same procedures described in "Putting It All Together: Building the Tank," starting on p. 143.
- Apply several coats of epoxy, including the fiberglass corner reinforcements; allow time to cure.
- Measure and purchase the glass for the front observation panel.
- Set the glass in, as described for the tank front.

- Once the glass has been set and sealed, and the sealant has had time to cure, it may be a good idea to bring the box outside and completely fill it with water to check for leaks. It may be difficult to trouble-shoot for leaks after the Plexiglas has been installed. If there are no leaks, drain the box and proceed.
- Cut and fit two Plexiglas panels as shown, using temporary support pieces to hold them in place.
- Determine the size of the drip plate; make it slightly smaller than the compartment, so removal is easy
- Cut and place the 1-1/2" PVC standoff pipes to support the eggcrate.
- Cut and fit the eggcrate material; as with the drip plate, make it slightly smaller for easy removal.
- Cut and fit the prefilter material to size (slightly larger than the eggcrate, so that all water flow goes through the material).
- Determine the location of the two lower bulkhead fittings: one to the main pump and spraybar, the other to the protein skimmer. Drill, test fit, apply sealant to, and install the lower bulkheads.
- Note: on one bulkhead fitting you may want to install a plumbing T, so that a drain hose may be connected later. Use a fitting with the center T threaded so it can either be plugged or have a drain hose attached. This will be helpful in completely draining the sump when cleaning is needed.
- Position the sump box in its location and determine where the skimmer outflow will enter. Drill, seal, and install a bulkhead fitting through the top of the sump cover.
- Keep in mind the skimmer should be above the sump box. Locate and secure the skimmer with the drain going through the top of the sump, with a bulkhead fitting on the prefilter side.
- Determine the location of the overflow(s) from the tank, with a control valve shutoff going into the "dirty" side of the sump box. Locate, drill, and seal a bulkhead fitting though the top of the sump box in that area.
- Once all the drilling and sealing is complete, and after the sealant has had adequate time to cure, bring the box outside and thoroughly rinse out all debris with a garden hose. Let the box dry.

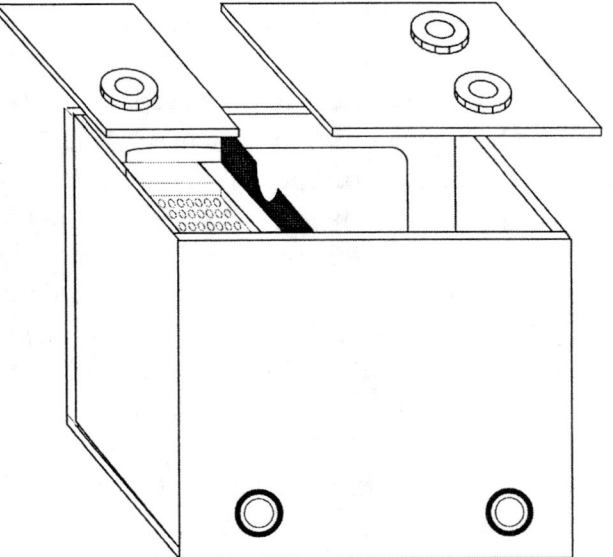

BACK

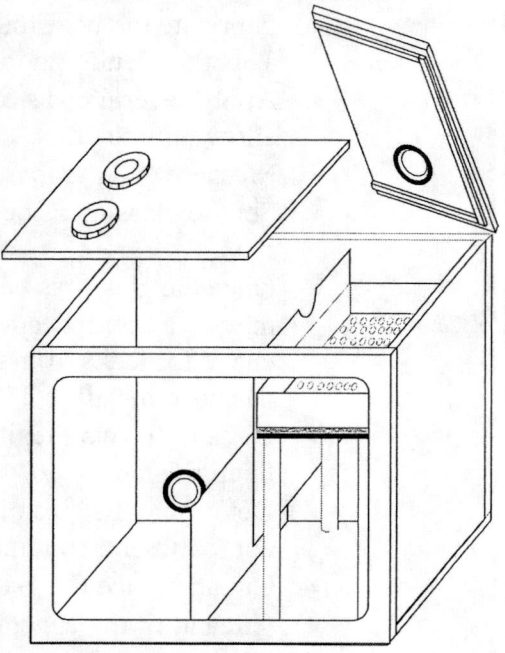

- Place the sump box in its operating location. Make the connections for the two pumps (skimmer and main), the drain from the skimmer, and the overflow drain from the tank.
- Position the PVC standoffs, the eggcrate, the prefilter material, and the drip plate.
- Complete all connections.
- Fill the box and test all fittings for leaks.
- The sump box is now up and running. Make necessary adjustments to the flow of the skimmer, and to the overflow from the tank.

FABRICATING A PROTEIN SKIMMER

Most people are not familiar with Plexiglas or plastic tubing, this leads them to believe it is a difficult product to work with. Actually it is very simple and relatively easy to work with. Besides the tools listed here, the main element you need is *patience*.

To build a "Venturi" skimmer you will need:

The Tools:

- A plastic laminate knife.
- A table saw, with a triple chip tooth pattern. This will ensure a very smooth cut without unnecessary chipping of the flat surfaces.
- A jigsaw, with a blade for cutting plastic.
- Some masking tape to hold pieces in place while the glue cures.
- Safety glasses to wear when cutting with a power saw.

The Materials:

- Rigid plastic tubing for the outer column: 6" diameter, 40" long.
- Rigid plastic tubing for the inner column: 2" diameter, 30" long.
- 3 flat Plexiglas pieces, 16" x 16" x 1/4". Black is common, although not necessary. Clear may be used..
- 1 container of thin, instant-set glue.
- 1 container of thick, slow-set glue.
- 1 Venturi valve, 3/4" to 1" depending on the size of your pump. A 3/4" valve will take up to 800 GPH pressure. Use a 1" valve for pumps larger than 800 GPH.
- 2 bushings, 1" x 3/4", for feed and drain through the side of the box (Part K).
- A 1" threaded female adapter (Part L).
- 3/4" rigid PVC pipe, 30" length (Part N).
- Marine Tex (approximately 8 ounces).
- A 3/4" STREET 90° fitting (Part M).
- 8 nylon bolts with wing nuts, 1/4" x 1-1/2".
- 1 O-ring from pool supplier, 6-1/8".
- 1 shutoff valve, 3/4".

- 1 insert fitting, 3/4" for waste drain of the collection cup (Part N).

To Begin:

(See Diagram 53 for reference.) Cut carefully on a table saw:

- 6 square pieces of Plexiglas, 8" x 8" x 1/4" (Pieces A, C, E, G, I, J).
- 1 main column, 6" x 32" (Piece D).
- 1 collection cup, 6" x 8" (Piece H).
- 1 inner column, 2" x 28" (Piece B).
- 1 upper neck, 2" x 6" (Piece F).

Drill carefully:

- 2 holes, approximately 1-1/4" diameter, through the side of the main column (D). Test your bushing in a piece of scrap material. The fitting should thread in snugly without forcing. Position one hole 1-1/4" down from the top, the other 1-1/4" up from the bottom.
- 1 hole, 3/4", in the upper collection plate (to install an insert fitting for the collection cup waste drain, N).

Determine the center of the bottom square piece of Plexiglas (A). Center the 2" x 28" inner column (B). Check for evenness of the cut. Sand or file the column to fit flat onto the bottom Plexiglas piece. Glue with thin, fast-set glue. Set aside.

Determine the center of the top square piece of Plexiglas (C). Draw a circle around this center point; the circle should be the *inside* dimension of the 6" column (D), so that the flat Plexiglas sits on top of the 6" column. You can draw the circle with a magic marker and compass, or by centering the 6" cylinder on the center mark and tracing a mark around the inside of the column, using the cylinder as a guide.

The three most common types of protein skimmers

Venturi **Downdraft** **Counter Current**

Diagram 53 - Protein Skimmer

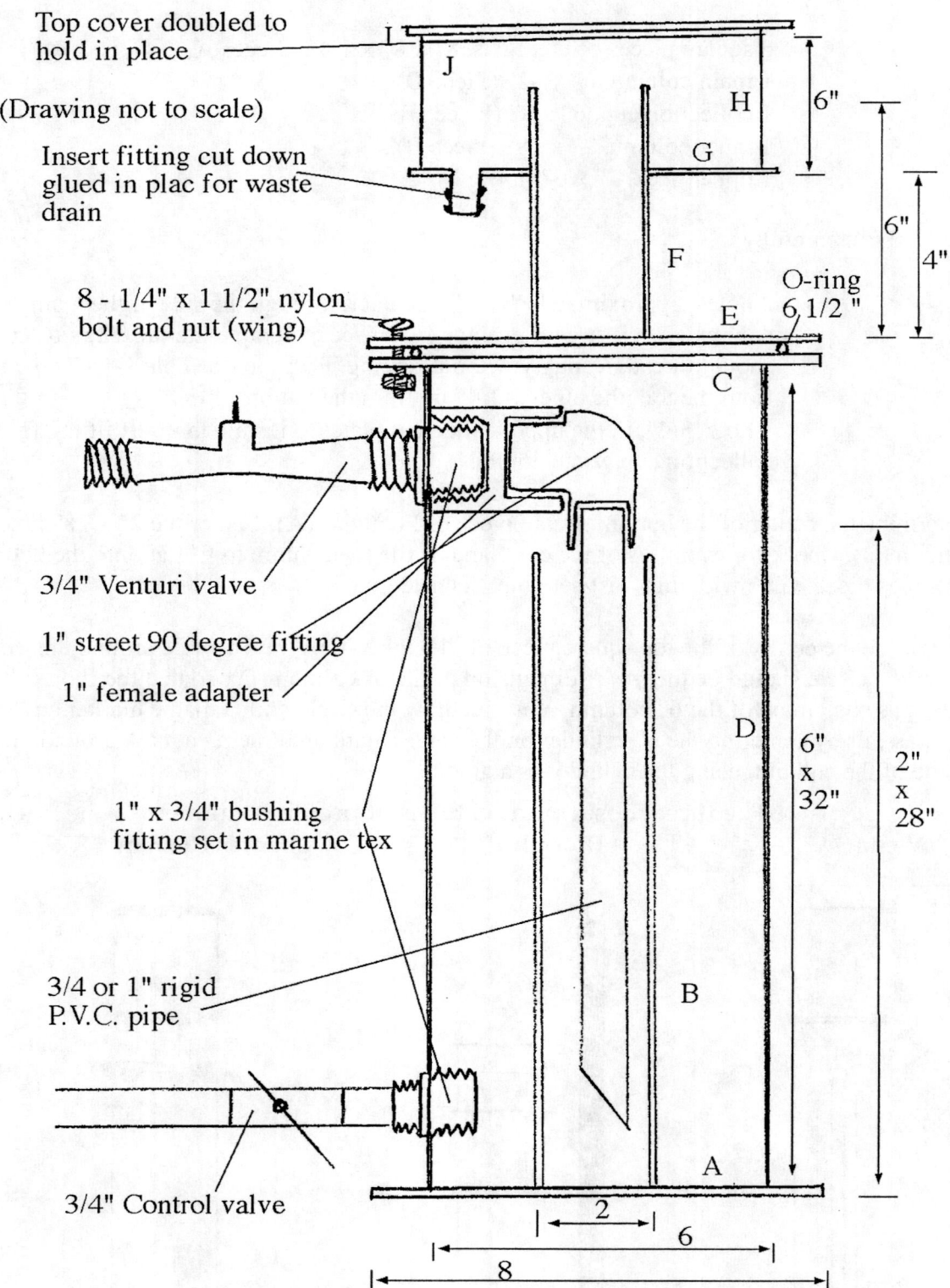

Top cover doubled to
hold in place

(Drawing not to scale)

Insert fitting cut down
glued in plac for waste
drain

8 - 1/4" x 1 1/2" nylon
bolt and nut (wing)

3/4" Venturi valve

1" street 90 degree fitting

1" female adapter

1" x 3/4" bushing
fitting set in marine tex

3/4 or 1" rigid
P.V.C. pipe

3/4" Control valve

O-ring
6 1/2 "

6"

6"

4"

6"
x
32"

2"
x
28"

2

6

8

A B C D E F G H I J

Drill a 3/4" starter hole for the jigsaw. Then use the jigsaw to cut along the inside of the circle you just drew. If the jigsaw blade is moving too fast, you will find that the plastic will melt back together where you have just cut it. To remedy this, use a variable speed jigsaw and cut slowly. You may have to go around the cut twice to get the waste out of the way.

Once you have cut this circle out of piece C, test the fit on column D. Piece C should sit *on top* of the column. Use rough sandpaper, rasp, or file to remove any rough edges from the circular hole. This piece is designed so the top of the collection device can be removed for cleaning. You will later bolt the upper collection device to this lip you are now installing. Ideally the inside edge of the circle in piece C should be smooth, although this is not critical.

If the fit is good, center the piece over the column and lightly glue in place with the thin, fast-set adhesive. Set aside to set up and cure.

Take the third square piece of Plexiglas (E) and mark the center. Draw a circle, the inside size of Piece F, around this center point; this circle should be the *inside* dimension of the 2" x 6" upper neck piece (F). As above, you may use a compass and magic marker; or by using the cylinder as a guide you can mark the required size directly. The neck piece will sit *on top* of the flat Plexiglas square. Drill a starter hole and carefully cut out the hole for this piece. Smooth the edges, glue the piece, and set the assembly aside.

Piece G has the drain hole previously drilled for waste measure. Find the center and use the 2" column as a guide. Mark the *outside* size, as this upper neck (F) will go through Piece G. This cut should be very smooth, although some differences can be made up gradually with the thick adhesive. The neck piece should be glued approximately centered, with 2" up in the collection chamber, and the remaining 4" separating the upper collection chamber from the lower chamber.

After the glue has set up initially, add the collection cup (H). This piece is cut out of the 6" diameter stock, and will be approximately 8" in length. The length is not critical, as long as it is at least 8"; that will allow enough room for foam collection. Fit the piece, glue lightly, and set aside.

Cut the cover cap (I) to
approximately 7" diameter, so it will

Diagram 55

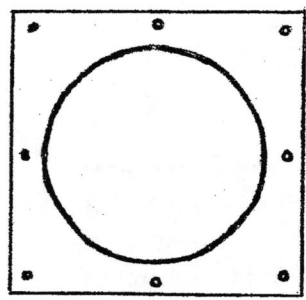

Main Column Cap PC-C

Diagram 54

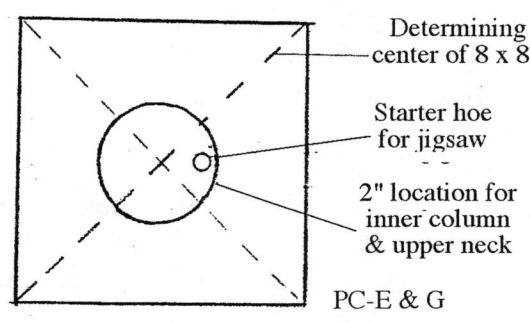

Determining
center of 8 x 8

Starter hoe
for jigsaw

2" location for
inner column
& upper neck

PC-E & G

Note: F rests on top of E / F goes through G
Slightly different hole sizes

overhang the collection device, giving you something with which to pull the cover off. Then cut another circle (J), slightly smaller than the inside of the 6" column. This will keep the top cover from getting knocked off of the collection cup. Test Piece J for a slightly loose fit; center and glue it to the upper 7" cover.

Once the glue has set (approximately 2-4 hours), you can run a bead of the thick-bodied adhesive along all connections on all the pieces that have been set aside. Once the thick glue has dried (4-6 hours), inspect all joints and connections. Where necessary, touch them up with a small amount of the thick glue to insure absolutely welded joints.

Note: do not overdo it with the glue. When you apply this type of glue on top of itself it temporarily softens up the previous layer. Use only what is needed. A joint may not look sealed, but it doesn't take much of this glue to make a waterproof connection between pieces of Plexiglas.

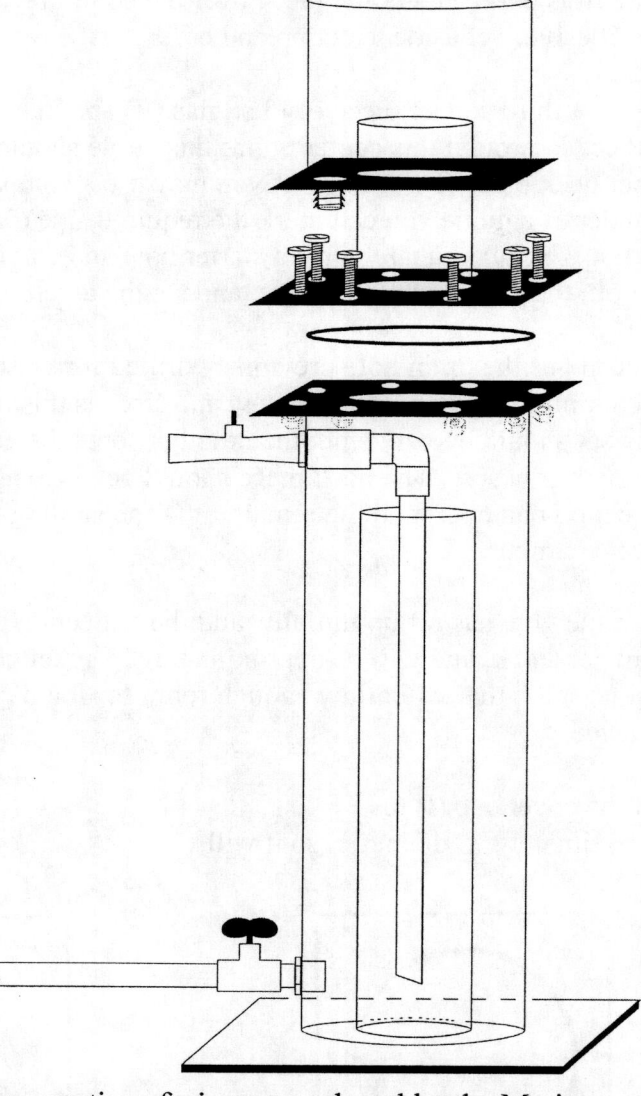

Once you have touched up the joints, set the pieces aside and proceed to the main column (D). We are ready to set in the bushing fittings through the side wall holes that were previously drilled. The bushings should of course be snug: not loose, but not too tight. Ideally they should thread into the hole you have drilled. Use the bushing to test hole sizes in some scrap material. When you are confident of the hole size, mix up a couple of teaspoons of Marine Tex and place it on the threads of the fitting where it will thread through the main column.

You don't want this epoxy material on the inside end of the fitting. Other connections will have to be made on the upper fitting, and Marine Tex would contaminate the threads. Apply the material only as described, and thread the fitting through the wall of the column. Once it is in, add a sufficient amount of Marine Tex to "build up" the outside of the fitting. Lay the assembly down with the connections facing upward, and let the Marine Tex cure for at least 24 hours. Once the piece has cured, inspect the inner wall where the fitting goes through it. If there are any gaps, carefully fill them with a small amount of Marine Tex. Again let dry.

Now you are ready to attach the already glued A + B section to the main column, D + C. First, carefully align and glue Pieces A and D together with the thin, fast-set glue. Then build up and reinforce with the thick, slow-set adhesive around the perimeter of column D where it joins base A. Let the glue dry for 4-6 hours.

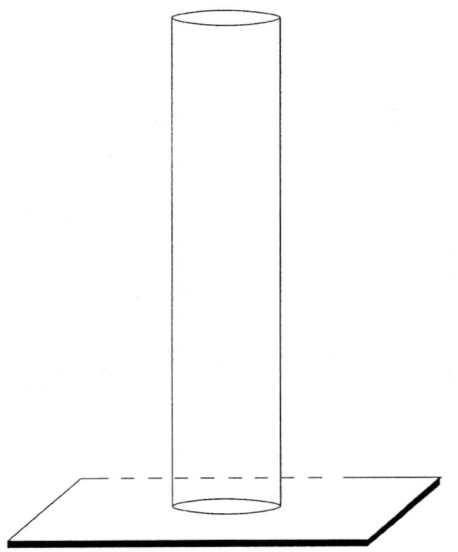

You should have 2 sections of the protein skimmer, upper and lower. Align Pieces E and C together evenly on top. Check the location of the O-ring. You will be installing 8 nylon bolts; they should be on the outside of the O-ring, and should not interfere with it.

See Diagram 54

Start at one corner of the Plexiglas covers (E and C). About 7/8" diagonally in from the corner, drill a 1/4" hole and install a nylon nut and bolt. Next drill and install the nut and bolt at the opposite corner. Installing these 2 bolts first will keep Pieces E and C together while you are drilling the remaining holes. Lay out the locations of the remaining 6 bolts evenly; mark, drill, and install them.

Remove the nylon bolts, install the O-ring, and reinstall the bolts snugly.

Complete the skimmer by installing the female adapter fitting with a 90° elbow, and the piece of 3/4" or 1" rigid PVC going into the reaction column. Install a connection with a shutoff regulator valve, onto the lower bushing. Screw in the Venturi valve and connect it to your pump.

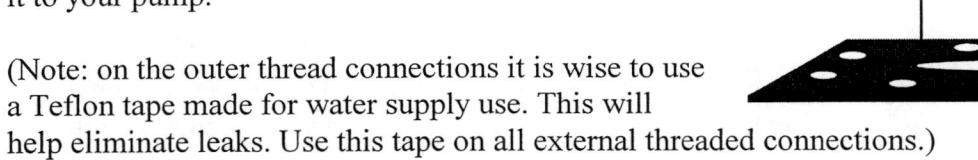

(Note: on the outer thread connections it is wise to use a Teflon tape made for water supply use. This will help eliminate leaks. Use this tape on all external threaded connections.)

Lastly, connect the upper waste drain tube. You can run this to a collection bucket, but there are advantages to connecting the skimmer drain directly to a sink drain. This is what I have done (see Chapter 6 photo, under sink connections). This setup eliminates the risk of the skimmer overflowing, and there is no collection device to empty.

Once you have the skimmer in the proper location (above the sump box) and adequately supported, recheck all the connections and then turn on the pump. There should be a control valve *before and after* the pump from the sump box. This is so that the pump can be removed, and water coming out of the pump can be regulated as well. Do not underestimate the need for valves to regulate water *going in or coming out* of the skimmer. It is extremely important to be able to *fine-tune the water flow* so you will get optimum performance from the skimmer.

BUILDING A COLUMN DENITRIFIER

For the aquarist who would like to experiment with additional approaches for denitrification, a column denitrifier may be of interest. It is very simple and inexpensive to make, and if it is placed in the proper location it will work without the need for any type of pump or electricity!

The design involves a section of PVC pipe, 4" in diameter and about 36" to 40" tall, which is capped off at each end with removable FURNCO caps (see Glossary for description of FURNCO connectors; also see Photo 21). Two holes are drilled through the side of the plastic pipe: one about 1 1/2" up from the bottom, the other about 1 1/2" down from the top. The size of the holes will be dictated by the actual size of the fittings you can find.

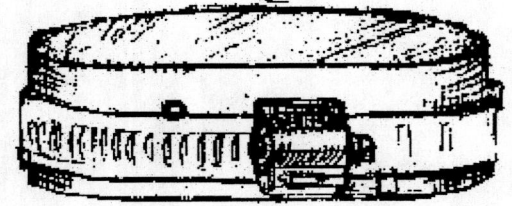

FURNCO Cap

Fittings and connections:

1. For the top fitting use a connector from an old wooden air block. The kind of plastic connection that has a male threaded end that screws into a wooden block would screw into a hole that you will drill through the plastic pipe. A 4-foot section of airline tubing will slip onto the exposed end, and will siphon water from the tank into the top of the plastic column. Once the fitting is epoxied in place and waterproofed with Marine Tex, you can insert a short 1-1/2" piece of rigid plastic airline into the inside of the fitting. This will direct the flow of water to the center of the column.

Cut away view of wooden air block

2. The lower fitting should be a larger size, preferably 3/8" to 1/2" inside diameter. You want to find a fitting that is just like the one used for the top, but larger. On one side this fitting has a threaded male end; on the other side it has an insert fitting with a 3/8" to 1/2" inside diameter. Once you have the larger fitting, find a drill bit that is the same size as the threaded end of the fitting and drill through the PVC pipe. Test the drilled hole with the fitting, and when satisfied of a proper fit epoxy it in place with Marine Tex. Allow the recommended curing time for the epoxy to set up thoroughly. I recommend waiting a full day; this will insure proper bonding and curing.

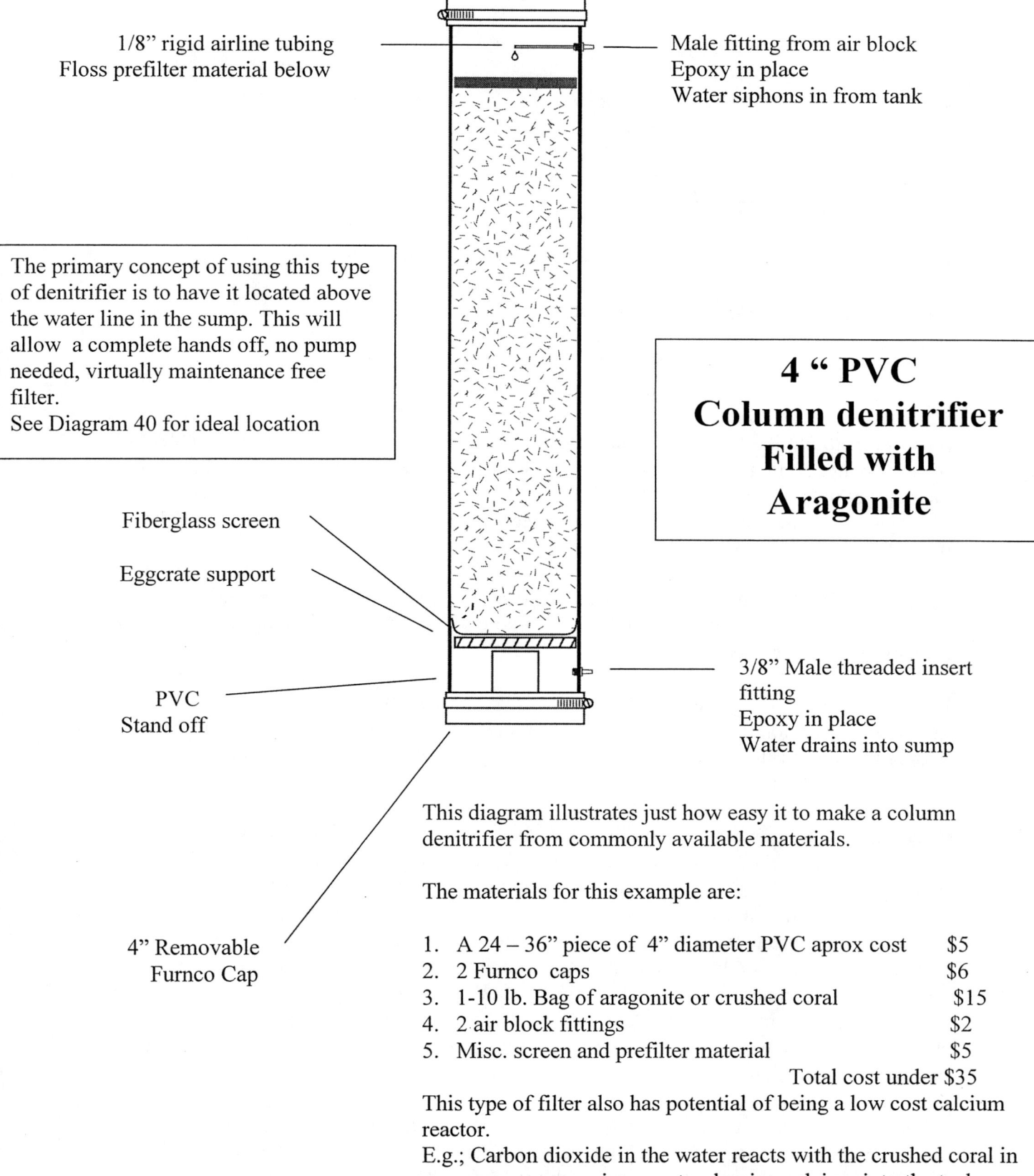

1/8" rigid airline tubing
Floss prefilter material below

Male fitting from air block
Epoxy in place
Water siphons in from tank

The primary concept of using this type of denitrifier is to have it located above the water line in the sump. This will allow a complete hands off, no pump needed, virtually maintenance free filter.
See Diagram 40 for ideal location

**4 " PVC
Column denitrifier
Filled with
Aragonite**

Fiberglass screen

Eggcrate support

PVC
Stand off

3/8" Male threaded insert fitting
Epoxy in place
Water drains into sump

4" Removable
Furnco Cap

This diagram illustrates just how easy it to make a column denitrifier from commonly available materials.

The materials for this example are:

1. A 24 – 36" piece of 4" diameter PVC aprox cost $5
2. 2 Furnco caps $6
3. 1-10 lb. Bag of aragonite or crushed coral $15
4. 2 air block fittings $2
5. Misc. screen and prefilter material $5
                                    Total cost under $35

This type of filter also has potential of being a low cost calcium reactor.
E.g.; Carbon dioxide in the water reacts with the crushed coral in an oxygen poor environment, releasing calcium into the tank

The reasons for two different diameter hoses are

- The top hose is airline and will provide a small but steady stream of water.

- The bottom hose is larger so that there will be no restriction of the water that will accumulate in and be drained out of the plastic pipe.

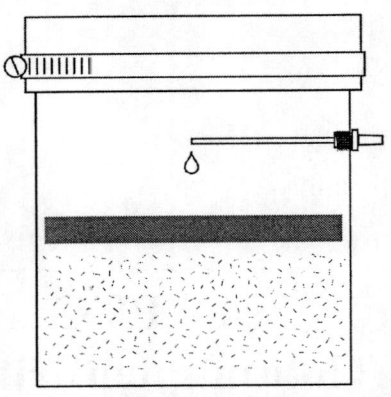

TOP   BOTTOM
The Contents

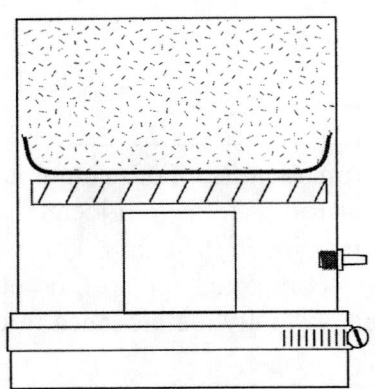

The plastic pipe will be filled with aragonite substrate material to encourage the growth of denitrifying bacteria. On the bottom inside of the pipe you will have to install a standoff area, made with a smaller piece of PVC pipe—something like 1-1/2" to 2" diameter. This piece of standoff pipe will be slightly taller than the bottom outlet in the 4" pipe. Cut and fit a piece of eggcrate material for the inside diameter of the 4" pipe. Set it on top of the 1-1/2" standoff. Cover the eggcrate with fiberglass screening material. This standoff piece will insure proper flow by keeping the outlet from getting clogged with sand particles.

First cut and fit the materials for the standoff. Carefully place them on the inside of the FURNCO connector. Then set the 4" column into the FURNCO and fasten. Then install the bottom FURNCO connector.

Using a flashlight, look down the pipe and make certain the standoff and screening are snugly in place and positioned above the bottom outlet. Now fill the pipe with the aragonite material to approximately 1-1/2" below the top inlet. Cut a piece of prefilter material to fit the inside of the pipe. This will be taken out and cleaned every 2 months or so.

Once the prefilter material is in place, install the small piece of rigid plastic airline inside the upper fitting to direct the water to the center of the pipe column. Before installing the top FURNCO cap, take the section of airline tubing that you will use for feeding water to the denitrifying column. It should be about 4 feet long. Place the tubing in the tank. This will fill the tubing with water. When you are confident that the tubing is filled, crimp one end of it; keeping the other end under water, raise the crimped end out of the tank and bring it down to where it is lower than the water level in the tank. When the crimp is released a siphon should occur (water will drain out of the tank). Connect this to the upper fitting, and observe the flow of water into the center of the plastic column. The operational tubing in the tank should be placed to a depth of 2" below the water line.

When you are confident of the flow (the small piece of airline is firmly in place in the tank and is directing water onto the prefilter and the center of the pipe), you then can install the FURNCO cap. An important reminder with the FURNCO cap, as with any FURNCO connector, is to make sure the cable clamp is fastened tightly. The clamps can be tightened with either a flathead screwdriver or a 5/16" socket wrench. The socket will do a superior job at getting the clamp tight and leakproof. Use the socket, and keep it nearby for whenever you use removable FURNCO connectors.

The location of the column denitrifier:

Proper location of the column denitrifier will insure that it will operate totally naturally, by a constant siphoning and draining of water. You will not need any type of pump or electrical connection.

1. The top of the column must be below the water line of the tank.
2. The top of the column must be at least 6" above the sump box.
3. The bottom drain fitting of the column is connected to flexible tubing (3/8" to 1/2"), which passes through a hole in the top of the sump box to drain into the prefilter area of the sump.

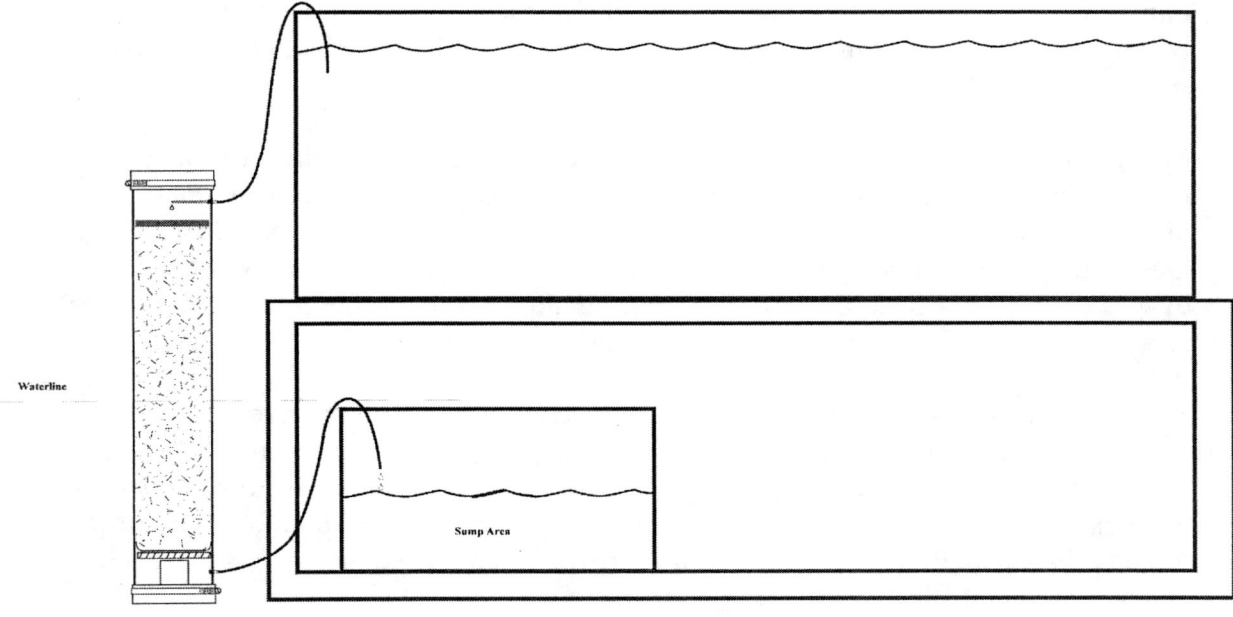

Diagram 40

How it works:

1. The water siphons out of the tank through the airline tubing into the column.
2. The column fills with water from the tank.
3. When the water level in the column rises to above the top of the sump box, the drain tubing fills with water and begins to drain out into the sump.
4. The column is at all times filled with water being siphoned out of the tank to the level above the sump box where the drain tubing is inserted.
5. Because the column is capped off and air tight, external oxygen is not available to the inside of the denitrifier. Although the water passing into the column is oxygen saturated, the oxygen gets quickly used up by aerobic bacteria inhabiting the top area of the column. As the water passes down the column, oxygen in the water gets used up. Denitrification takes place in that middle to lower area of the column. The airline tubing allows only a small flow of oxygen-rich water to pass through the sand material; therefore, the oxygen gets used up quickly, reducing oxygen in the column and encouraging denitrification.

Feeding the Denitrifying Bacteria:

This is a highly debated topic. In many of the commercially available denitrifying systems, a constant food source is of paramount concern. This has always deterred me from considering a commercially available system. The debate has been about exactly what kind of food source should be used, how it could be regularly administered, and so on. It seems apparent that very little is known, but the speculation is great. My thoughts are, "What happens if I run out of this special type of food? Would all my precious denitrifying bacteria die? What if the company went out of business or demanded an outrageous price for the food? How would it be shipped? What is its shelf life?"

The Column Denitrifier and Denitrification:

My observation has been that denitrification definitely takes place in my tanks. Therefore I think it is fair to assume that there are denitrifying bacteria present, and I am sure these bacteria are eating something. In other words, they are finding a naturally occurring food source in the enclosed environment.

My primary concern is to provide favorable conditions for the bacteria to colonize. Denitrifying bacteria occur and thrive in oxygen-poor conditions, which are found in the core of the live rock and in other semi-dense substrates. The outer layer of these substrates is inhabited by oxygen-requiring, nitrifying bacteria. These bacteria consume the available oxygen on the outer substrate, and they produce nitrate. The level of nitrate in the water increases, giving you measurable nitrate readings.

We can create low oxygen conditions for denitrifying bacteria to colonize: for example in the core of live rock, in dense sand, or in a separate oxygen-poor setting such as a denitrifying column. Denitrification occurs, indicated by substantially low nitrate readings. I have found that this takes place in my tanks without my having to add special food for the denitrifying bacteria. I am sure that if you implement the methods suggested throughout this book you will also see denitrification occurring in your reef.

My nitrate reading is well below 10 PPM, which is extremely low. I attribute this to having 1.5 to 1.75 pounds per gallon of live rock in the tank.

BUILDING A WAVE MAKER

A wave maker is a device to provide alternating water flows for the reef tank. During my time in the hobby I have observed several kinds of self-made wave makers in operation. The type I will describe here works best, and is the easiest to build. It is very inexpensive to make, and it works extremely well. It uses 5-gallon buckets to hold the water, and they can be connected together to create larger sizes if desired, in 5-gallon increments. The example here is for a 10-gallon version, to illustrate the possbility of connecting two buckets together.

The materials to use:

- Two clean 5-gallon containers with lids.
- One 1" diameter hard plastic siphon tube

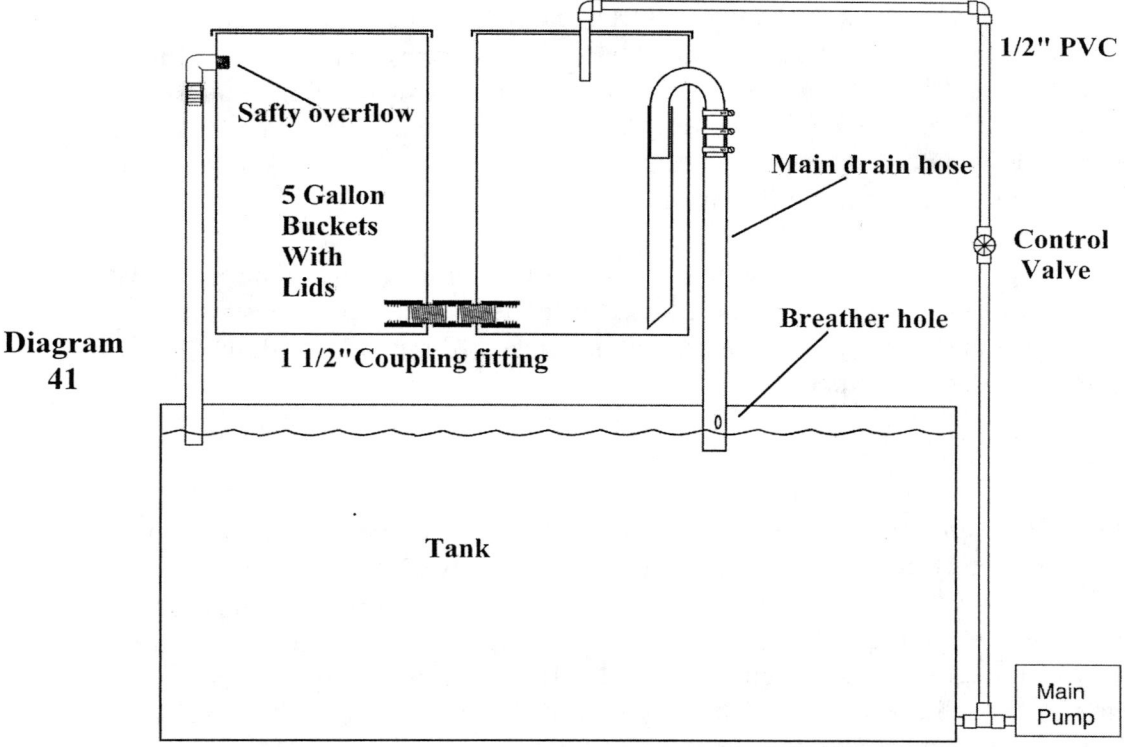

Safty overflow

5 Gallon Buckets With Lids

1/2" PVC

Main drain hose

Control Valve

Breather hole

Diagram 41

1 1/2"Coupling fitting

Tank

Main Pump

- One 1" 90° threaded male X insert fitting (for safety overflow).
- Two 1" male "close nipple" plumbing fittings, approximately 1-1/2" length (for bucket connections).
- Three 1" x 1" female coupling plumbing fitting (for bucket connections).
- One tube silicone sealant for underwater use, non-toxic when cured.
- Six to eight feet of clear vinyl tubing, sized to fit the outside diameter of the siphon tubes (buy from plumbing supply house).
- Three or four stainless steel hose clamps, 1-3/4", to fit over the tubing (for an external airtight fit).
- 1/2" rigid PVC water line, to feed containers from a T-fitting and valve, coming off the main pump.

Tools needed:

1. Two drill bits: one the size of the siphon tube, and the other for the "close nipple" fitting.
2. Electric drill.
3. Caulking gun to apply the silicone sealant.
4. A 5/16" socket or flat screwdriver for the hose clamps.

You will also need an outside location with a garden hose, where you can test run the system.

Once the wave maker is operating properly it will work again and again for an indefinite period of time. However, getting it to operate trouble-free will take some time and patience. It must be tested and run in, to check for leaks and to be sure the siphon works reliably.

This testing should be done outside with a garden hose, filling the bucket at different flow rates. You will have to find the correct amount of water that will fill the bucket and make the siphon occur. If the flow is too slow, water will trickle out of the main siphon tube as fast as it enters the bucket. In this case, the flow should be slightly increased so that it is a little faster than the draining trickle. However if the flow is too fast, it will cause the bucket to overflow. Once the proper flow rate is attained, water will fill the bucket, and then fill the siphon tube, triggering a natural siphon. The siphon effect will drain the bucket, the siphon will stop, and the bucket will start to fill again.

A one-inch diameter siphon hose will drain 10 gallons of water in about one minute. That's *fast*! This provides a good wave effect in the tank. Once the correct flow rate is established, the siphoning occurs about every 10 minutes; that is, it takes 10 minutes to fill up the two 5-gallon buckets and trigger the siphon.

How It Performs:

To get an idea of the siphon's performance, let's do some math. It operates every 10 minutes, or 6 times an hour. 6 x 24 hours = 144 times a day, x 7 days a week = 1,008 times a week, x 52 weeks = 52,416 times a year! That's performance! I have a 10-gallon wave maker in operation, and can attest to these figures. Since the day it was set up there has never been a problem. Over and over the siphon occurs flawlessly. The main trick is to work out any bugs of the system in a area where it won't matter if you spill water, and where you can clearly see the water flow and make adjustments.

Putting It Together:

Photo 20 and Diagram 41 will give you a good idea of how the wave maker is designed and put together.

First the drill bits: when you have the "close nipple fitting" and the siphon tube, test the drill bit you think will work on a piece of scrap plastic material (preferably another bucket). Once you have drilled the correct size for the upper siphon hose, it should sit in the hole evenly so that one side is not higher than the other. The primary siphon hose should connect to the bucket just below the level at which the ends of the wire handle join the bucket. You will have to add a length of flexible tubing from the siphon tube down to the inside bottom of the bucket so that the siphon will empty all the water out of the bucket.

The Safety Overflow:

This is used to keep the bucket from overflowing onto the floor, in the event of improper water flow. When the overflow is connected and the hoses are in the tank you may from time to time observe water trickling out of this safety tube. If this takes place too frequently or for a long period of time, you will have to speed up or slow down the water flow to the bucket.

This extra overflow allows correct operation of the wave maker, and must be included. The bottom of the safety overflow fitting is located approximately 5/8" above the level at which the wire handle joins the bucket. The safety overflow does not have to be a siphon tube. It can be a 90° male threaded insert fitting, for which a hole is drilled and which is then secured in place with silicone sealant or Marine Tex. It would take an extremely fast water flow to make the bucket overflow in spite of two 1" drain holes, but this may happen as you experiment with the garden hose.

At this point drill the holes for the siphon tube and the safety overflow. Dry fit the parts, making sure they fit properly. You may have to enlarge the drilled hole slightly with a razor knife for an absolutely proper fit. Then, using the other drill bit, drill the hole for the close nipple fitting that will connect the two buckets together. This hole should be close to the bottom of the bucket, but not too close: allow for the fact that you will have to rotate the female coupling with your hand and a wrench.

Before siliconing the parts in place, add the length of flexible tubing inside the bucket to the siphon tube. *This is the most crucial connection: attaching the vinyl tubing to the outside siphon tube.* If this connection is not airtight, you will get a very small air leak that will prevent the siphoning from taking place. To avoid this:

1. Get the tightest-fitting flexible tubing to match the siphon tubing.
2. Apply a small amount of silicone to the outside of the siphon tube, where the vinyl tubing slips over it by approximately 6 to 8 inches.
3. Install 2 or 3 cable clamps to compress the tubing's together firmly.
4. Determine the location of the buckets. The bottom of the buckets should be above the top of the tank. You may need to make a small platform to keep the buckets in this position (remember they will be filled with water, and will be heavy).
5. *Install a breather hole in the tubing.* The main hose should be in the water of the tank about 3 to 4 inches. This will eliminate unnecessary splashing. *On the hose above the water line there must be a small hole (1/8") to allow air to escape, and to allow the hose to drain completely.* This hole should be directed down toward the surface of the water in the tank. If it is not pointed down, water will spray onto the light box and/or the glass cover (if you are using a cover), and you will get a substantial salt buildup in those places.
6. Cut and dry-fit the vinyl tubing from its operating location on a small stand into the tank. By planning ahead for the correct length of vinyl drain tubing, you can make adjustments for length and positioning *before* you hook everything up and seal it in place.

The Location Of the Wave Maker: (see diagram 41)

I recommend having the siphon hose enter the tank from the top center of the left or right side. This will provide the most benefit by directing the water flow across the entire tank, from one end to the other. Keep in mind that you should have the hose angled slightly toward the front glass area. This will help keep sediment pushed to the front of the tank, where it can be seen and removed. Avoid having this device push waste where you will not see it. Once it is set up in the proper location you may have to lengthen the hose with a coupling insert fitting; or if the hose is too long, it can be cut back. (Pre-fitting and positioning will make these adjustments unnecessary or minor.)

Other Important Considerations:

In between siphons, the wave maker will gradually take water out of the tank to fill the bucket (or buckets). This will have the most noticeable effect in the sump, where you will see a decrease in the water level. The water in the tank will also go down, but only slightly. *However, when the bucket discharges, it will rapidly drain through the siphon into the tank. This surge of water will have to be absorbed by a dam type overflow, or by overflow pipes that are large enough; otherwise the tank may overflow.*

I recommend erring on the side of having more overflow drainage capacity than you need, rather than not having enough. On my 200-gallon tank I have four 1-1/2" PVC overflow drains. (See Chapter 14 on plumbing fixtures and water flow for more information.) If you include *more* than enough overflow capacity in the design of your system, you can always adjust the flow downward with control valves, and you will be able to incorporate a significant wave generating system without changing anything else on the tank.

Once you have decided on the location of the wave maker, have dry fitted the tubing, and are confident of the positioning and length of the hose, take the bucket to a work area and prepare to make the connections. First, determine the correct drill size for the plastic nipple to connect the buckets, as previously described. Test the hole and fitting in a piece of scrap material if necessary, to insure a proper snug fit.

Attach the buckets with coupling fittings and 1-1/2" nipples. Apply silicone to all male threads. Tighten securely, and silicone the areas where the coupling adjoins the bucket. Connect the safety overflow insert fitting by applying silicone to the male threads, and screw in the fittings. Complete the connection with silicone on the outside area where the fitting has gone through the bucket.

Proceed to the siphon tube. Place the tube through the correct-sized hole in the bucket. Connect the inner flexible vinyl hose to the bottom of the container. Note: the end of this hose should make a 45° angle with the bottom of the bucket; this will prevent a gurgling sound as the hose sucks the bucket empty with substantial force. Attach this piece by placing a small amount of silicone onto the siphon tube and sliding the piece on. It should overlap the siphon tube by at least 4".

Attach the outer main drain tube in the same manner, but add 3 stainless steel cable clamps where the flexible tubing overlaps the hard vinyl. At this point be certain the hose is in the proper direction, as flexible vinyl has a tendency to "roll" in the direction in which it has been coiled.

Once the above attachments have been made, generously apply silicone both inside and out, to insure a leak-proof seal and support to the siphon tube. Let the silicone dry for at least 1 day. Now you can test run the system.

Test Running the Wave Maker:

Run this testing in a location where water spillage is not a concern. With the wave maker firmly supported on a table about 3 feet off the ground, place a garden hose into the container, and fill it with water at a moderate flow rate. Observe what happens when the bucket has filled up:

Troubleshooting the device:

If water trickles out of the siphon tube, but a full siphon does not start:
  * *Increase the water flow.*

If water overflows the bucket:
  * *Be sure water can flow freely through the siphon hose. Remove any kinks. If necessary, lift up on the hose and provide support for it in the new position. If water can freely flow through the hose, and the bucket is still overflowing, decrease the water flow from the garden hose.*

If a siphon still does not occur:
  * *There may be a small air leak. Recheck the outer connection, tighten the cable clamps.*

If a siphon does occur, but the main drain hose does not empty completely:
  * *Be certain the breather hole is installed, approximately 4" to 6" from the end of the drain hose.*

If there is an unpleasant gurgling sound when the siphon completes:
  * *The hose should be cut to a 45° angle relative to the bottom of the bucket. (Some of this noise cannot be avoided. Using a cover placed lightly on top of the container will reduce the sound.)*

Once the siphon does occur, note:

- The position of the drain hose;
- The approximate rate of water flow entering the bucket;
- How often the siphon occurs (a stopwatch will make noting this for future reference easier).

Let the hose run in the bucket for an hour or so, to be sure the siphon is performing reliably. Once you have the wave maker running, it will be a very rewarding addition to your reef tank.

Bring the device inside and place it in its location, approximately 6 to 12 inches above the water line in the tank. Place covers on top of the containers; one cover should have a hole in the center to receive the water supply.

Supplying Water to the Wave Maker:

In the main pump line going to the spraybar, install a insert X 1/2" threaded T fitting. The insert connections go in line from the pump to the spraybar. Attach a 1/2" close nipple fitting to the T; to this fitting add a 1/2" threaded PVC stop valve. Then run a length of 1/2" PVC water supply pipe to the cover of the bucket. At the bucket end of this pipe, glue on a 90° elbow and a 4" length of pipe to direct the flow down through the cover of the bucket. Because the plastic water supply pipe is rigid, it will remain stable and in place going into the bucket.

Turn on the stop valve with approximately 2/3 of a full turn, by approximating the time you previously recorded. Using the valve, adjust the water flow to get the same frequency of siphoning that you had during the testing. Check for leaks and make minor adjustments to ensure smooth operation. Pay particular attention to the *breather hole* at the end of the main drain. Remember it should point downward, and should allow the siphon hose to drain completely after each cycle. Observe how the water level in the tank rises when the wave maker drains through the siphon. Adjust the overflows if necessary.

When you add a surge device to your reef tank, you will observe corals swaying in the flow of water. You will see that fish take pleasure in getting unexpectedly pushed by the current created by the wave maker, and your whole reef tank will seem to be more *alive*.

FABRICATING A LIGHT CANOPY

A custom light canopy can be made from the wood of your choice. First determine the actual width and length of the top of your tank. These dimensions, plus 1/4" to compensate against too tight a fit, will be the *inside* size of the box you will make. To get the outside dimensions of the canopy, you have to *add* to the box the thickness of the side pieces, normally 3/4" each.

So, on a 55-gallon tank that measures 48-1/4" long by 12-3/4" wide, the top piece (outside dimension) will be 50" by 14-1/2":

50" long:

48-1/4" + 1/4" clearance + 1-1/2" for the side pieces (3/4" for each) = 50"

14-1/2" wide:

12-3/4" + 1/4" clearance + 1-1/2" for the side pieces (3/4" for each) = 14-1/2"

At this point compare your actual bulb length with the holders. Determine how long the bulb/holder setup will be. It is possible you may have to increase the length of the box slightly, and this will mandate that you also increase the width of the "support cleats" inside the box. Check these dimensions *before* you proceed.

The height of the side pieces will be determined by how many bulbs you plan to house. With this particular setup, using two sets on HO ballast's and one set on a standard ballast, the height of the side pieces of the box is 8-1/2". By using VHO ballast's you could decrease this size.

Keep in mind that the desired wattage range is 3-5 watts per gallon.

3 watts per gallon x 55 gallons = 165 watts

4 watts per gallon x 55 gallons = 220 watts
5 watts per gallon x 55 gallons = 275 watts

A 48" standard ballast produces 80 watts
A 48" HO ballast produces 120 watts
A 48" VHO ballast produces 230 watts

These figures will help you determine the height of the light canopy.

Determine the size and cut the
top piece.

Determine the height of the
side pieces and cut them to
length. For the end piece the
ends should be cut to a 45°
angle to make a finished
corner. Attach the end piece to
the top with glue and #6
finishing nails through the top.

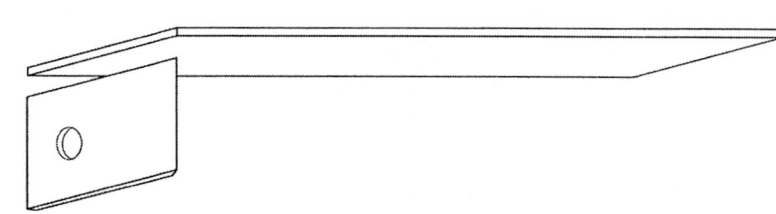

Continue cutting and fastening
the side pieces around the perimeter of the box, gluing and then nailing them with #6
finishing nails

Once the box is complete, we need to add "support cleats" inside it. They will rest on the top
of the tank and support the box . They should be strips of wood 1/2" x 1/2", placed so that
their bottom edge is 1/2" up from the
bottom edge of the canopy. Cut, glue,
and nail these support strips inside the
box.

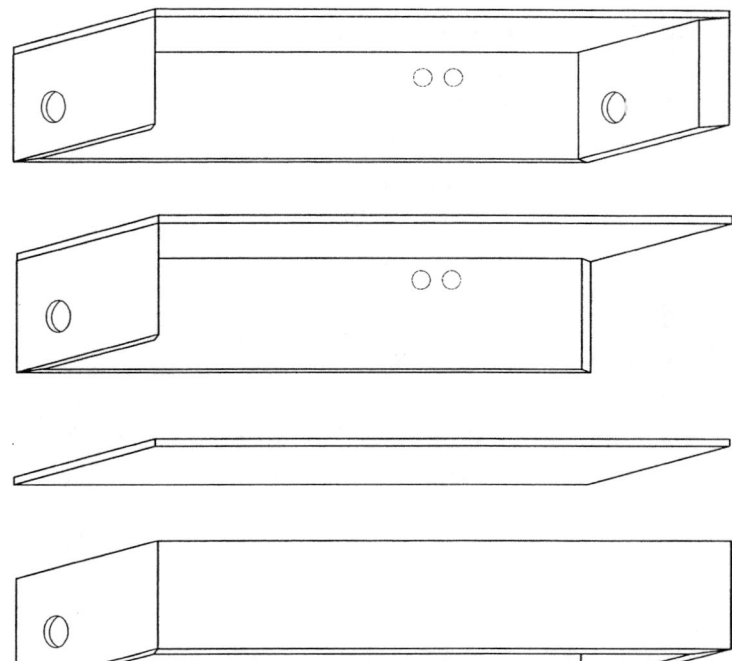

Determine the best-looking side of the
box, and designate that as the front.

We will now cut the box into two parts
and install a piano hinge, so you can
raise part of the canopy to access the
tank. Determine 1/3 of the width of the
box. Mark and carefully cut the box
along the line.

Use a 5/8" x 48" piano hinge. Locate its
position on the top of the box and notch
in each side of the wood to accept the
hinge. Carefully line up the box and
hinge, and temporarily fasten them

together with a few screws. Check the functioning and alignment of the hinge. When you are satisfied, install the remaining screws.

The two holes that are side by side are for wires coming off the fan and bulbs, going to the remote ballast board Depending on your situation, 3/4" to 1" holes are usually sufficient.

Determine the size of fan you will be using, and drill or cut corresponding holes, one for the fan and one for the exhaust At this point you will need to attach the reflector material inside the box. Use either roll aluminum or white aluminum (see supplies). Cut, fit, and attach the reflector material with small screws, so as to cover the entire inside of the light box. This will give maximum reflection of the light into the tank.

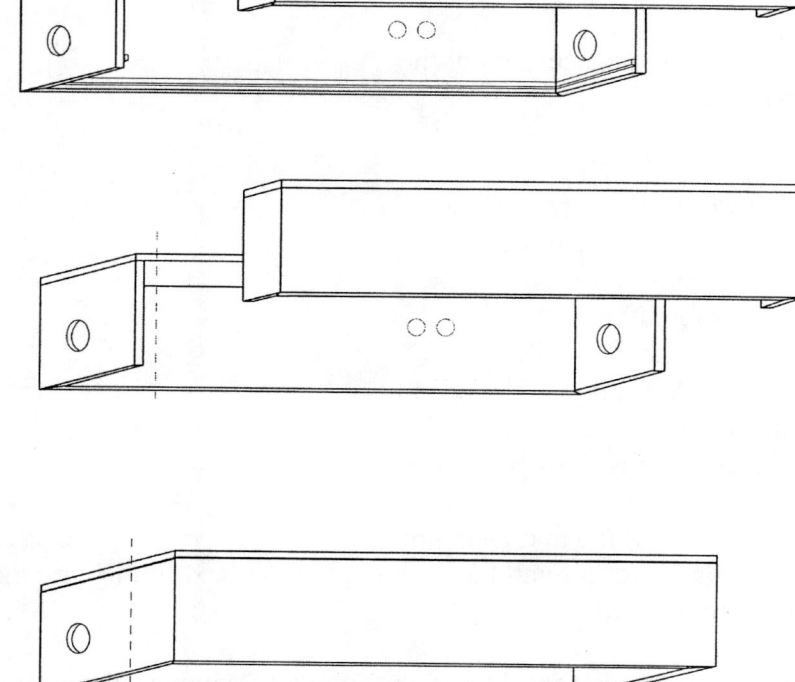

Now is the time to sand, stain, and finish the wood box, as it is still easily maneuverable at this point. Complete the finishing before continuing to the next step.

Attach the bulb holders. It is usually best to do one end, install the bulb as a spacer, and then fasten the other holder. This will give proper spacing. Determine the lengths of wires needed to reach from the bulb and fan to the remote ballast board. Cut the wires, tape them together, and attach them to the correct connections. At this point you may need someone familiar with electricity to make safe, correctly grounded connections. Connect the fan to the primary set of lights so that when the light comes on with the timer the fan will also be activated. Use the correct gauge of wire, with corresponding wire nuts taped securely. Make the connections to the ballast board.

Then attach a cord (4 to 6 feet long) to the ballast, with a plug end that will connect to the timer and wall outlet. The last step will be to attach a "clasp" to each side of the box where you cut. This allows a snug fit so the box doesn't get knocked off its support. Check at your local lumber yard or home improvement center for two clasps that suit your needs. The light box is now complete.

Overview of a high wattage light canopy

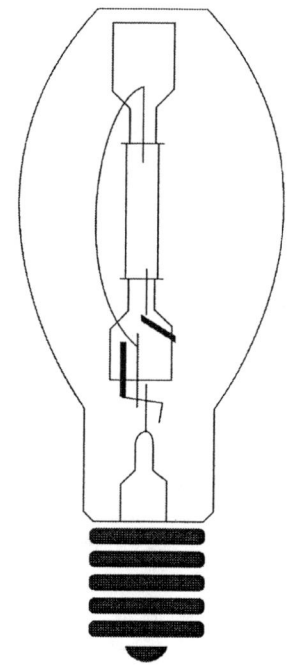

Close-up of a metal halide

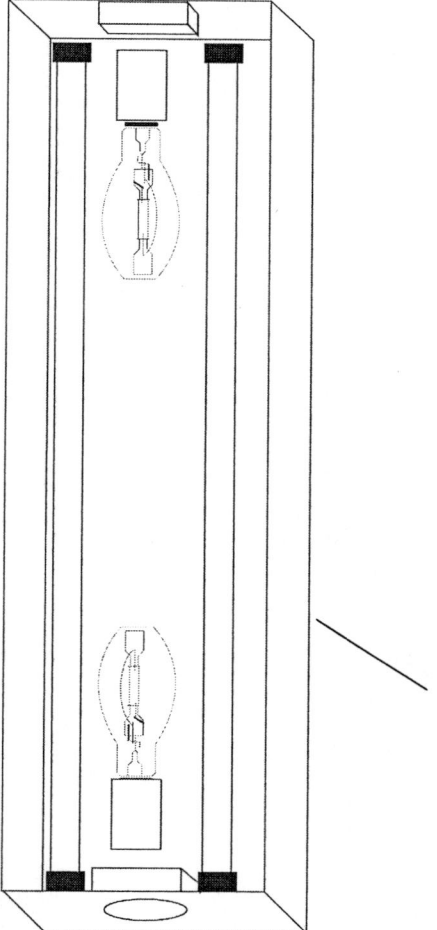

3 – 4" cooling fan

3 Fluorescent lamps are shown to illustrate a high intensity light canopy

3 halide lamps
note: the highest intensity would be in the center of the box

Note: cooling fans may be needed on both ends of the box. One blowing in and the other blowing out.
In a less intense lighting canopy, one may opt for only one fan exhausting air along with an opening in the opposite end for intake.

Here is a less intense combination consisting of
dual halides and fluorescent.

Note: Wattage's will vary among halide lamps. Be sure to calculate accordingly for the wattage you plan to use.

FABRICATING A DRIP PLATE

What you will need:

- 1/4" Plexiglas
- Fast-set adhesive for Plexiglas
- A laminate "knife" or table saw
- Protective eye wear for when you are cutting the Plexiglas

1. Make the bottom piece first. Determine and cut the size you need. (Note: this bottom piece is the actual size of the drip plate. The side pieces sit on top of it, so no allowance is needed for them in the dimensions of the bottom.) Mark out and drill 1/4" drain holes, spaced approximately 1" apart.

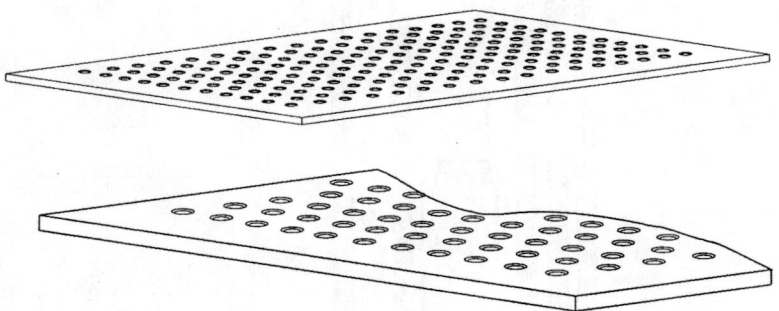

2. Measure and cut the side pieces. Mine are approximately 1-1/8" high. Fasten them with fast-set adhesive. Allow each piece a few minutes to set before gluing another one.

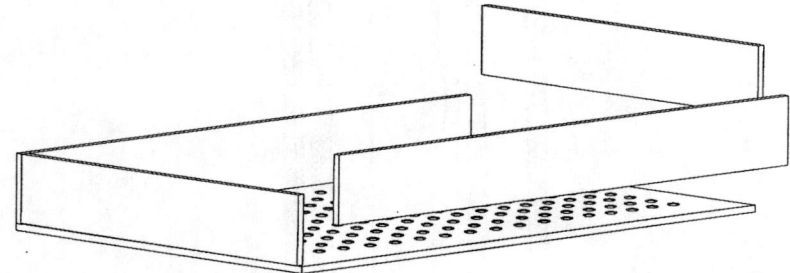

3. Measure and cut the top pieces. I used 1-1/2", keeping uniform widths as "stock" pieces. These pieces are splash guards, and are important for keeping the water inside the box. Allow each piece a few minutes to set before gluing another one.

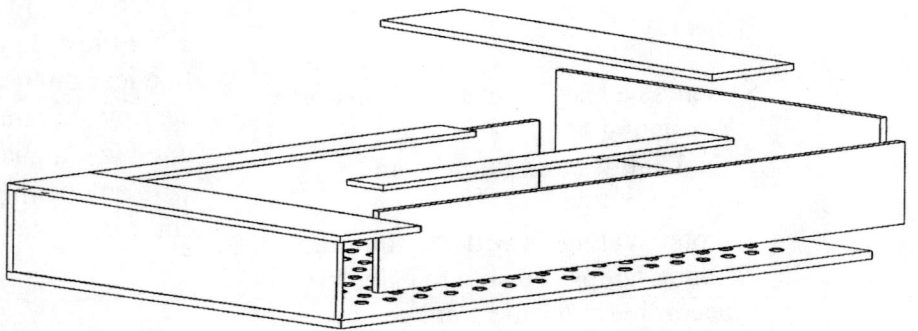

The finished box should look like the illustration below. The prefilter material goes under this box eggcrate to support the prefilter PVC standoffs under the eggcrate to the bottom of the sump box.

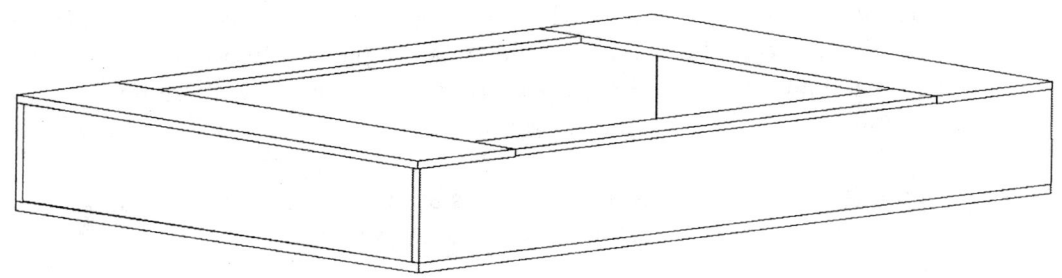

Homemade Airlocks

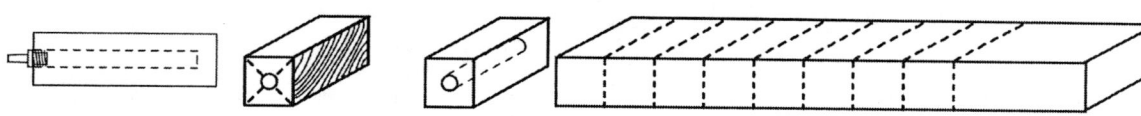

If you are running a counter current skimmer you are well aware of the high costs of replacement airblocks. These little items cost around $3 each if purchased retail, this expense can add up quickly in a relatively short period of time. Fortunately they are easily made.

Most airblocks are made of European limewood but you will have a difficult time finding that although bass wood is the American equivalent to the hard to find limewood.
Hobby shops and small wood workers supply houses carry basswood and for about $6 you can easily make 15 or more airblocks.

What you will need

- A 1x4x36 inch piece of American basswood
- Plastic threaded nipples (These can either be salvaged from old airblocks of purchased in a good hardware store)
- A drill bit corresponding to the size of the plastic nipples
- Either a tap threader or steel bolt corresponding to the size of plastic nipples
- Table saw (A hobbyist shop may be able to cut these to size for you)
- Electric drill

Note that not all plastic nipples are threaded, some are tapered and simply wedge in place although this may seem easier to use, its worthwhile to find the threaded nipples as they tend to hold much better.
Once you get the proper drill bit and bolt to thread the hole, the whole process will be easy.

The piece of basswood will be ¾" x 3 ½" x length, so we want to crosscut this piece of wood to ¾" x ¾" this is best done on a power table saw. Cut the whole length of wood to ¾" x ¾" blocks.

Next place the blocks in a vice or jig that will hold it securely while you drill the holes for the plastic nipples. Test your drill bit and bolt threader for proper size corresponding to the plastic nipple.

Once you're confident of the fit proceed to drill the holes in the center of the wood block. Drill the hole to within ½' from the end of the block. If the piece of wood is in fact 3 ½" set the drill depth to 3" using a piece of tape wrapped around the it as a depth gauge. Drill out all the blocks, insert the nipples and your ready to use you homemade airblocks.

One last note, you don't need nipples for all the blocks at once. You only use 2 at a time so really you only need 4 or maybe 6 at most and keep reusing them.

The Downdraft Skimmer

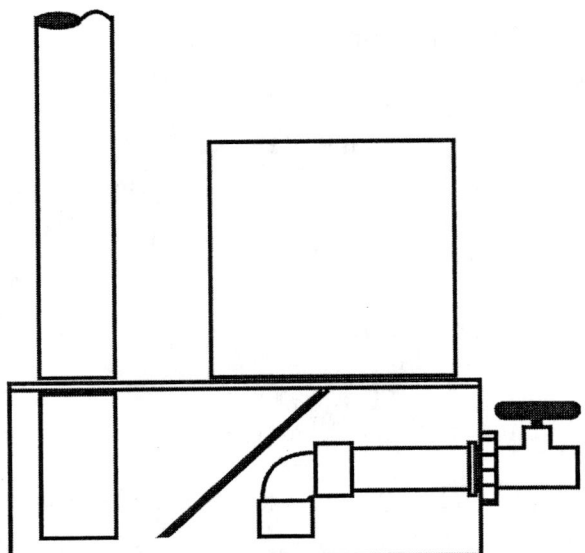

This is the inner working's of a downdraft skimmer. The following diagrams will give you an idea of how to fabricate this component. Let me describe the basic principals of the downdraft.

- The narrow column on the left is approximately 2" in diameter with an air intake hole on top of the column this is filled with bioballs.
- Water then gets forced down this tube by the water pump and through a fairly narrow nozzle.
- As the water streams down the column it pulls air with it and gets further turbalated by contact with the bio-balls.

The water air mixture becomes a frothy mix and crashes into a rectangular Plexiglas box where any particulate laden foam rises to the larger collection column on the right.

- Inside the collection box is a diagonal piece of Plexiglas this is to direct the foam and allow water to pass beneath it and returned to the tank.

I like to think of his type of a skimmer as a free flow where as there are really no restrictions commonly found with other types of skimmers. The water just gets pummeled through the bioballs, picks up air, crashes into the box and flows out of the skimmer drain and into the sump. All that is left behind is the foam.

Originally this skimmer was designed to be very tall approximately 5'. For most hobbyists this size would be impractical so shorter, dual columns were designed and are able (barely) to fit under a tank.

If you plan to build one of these skimmers I would first *recommend determining a definite height* and work from there. Also be aware that the cap and nozzle has to be removed fairly easily, this usually adds about 4 or 5 inches to the overall height of the skimmer.

Here is how to build a full size downdraft skimmer. The skimmer will be 5' tall.

You may tailor the dimensions to suite your needs, be sure to dry fit the pieces before gluing them. Note: This is a difficult project. The following instructions are only general guidelines

Materials needed
(1) For the base – 2 – ¼ x 7.5" x 12" top & bottom (base A & B)
(2) For the base – 2 - ¼ x 7" x 12 " sides (base C & D)
(3) For the base – 2 – ¼ x 7" x 7" front and back (base E & F)
(4) For the base – 1 – ¼" x 7" x 9" internal baffle (base G)
(5) For the base – 1 - 1.5" through wall bulkhead (base H)
(6) For the base 1 – a 1.5" to 1 ¼ " reducer bushing (base I)
(7) For the base – 1 – 1.5" x 4" PVC pipe (base J)
(8) For the base – 1 - 1.5" 90 degree elbow (base K)
(9) For the base – 1 – 1 1.25" ball valve (base L)
(10)   Bioball tower – 1 – 2.5" x 60" (column 1)
(11)   Main reactor – 1 – 6" x 20" (column 2)

(12)   Upper neck –1 – 4" x 18" (column 3)
(13)   Collection area – 1 – 6" x 9" (column 4)
(14)   Joining pieces – 3 – 7" x 7" (join 1 to 3)
(15)   Cap 1 –1 sufficient size to cover the 2.5" bioball tower (fitting 1)
(16)   Insert fittings aprox 6 to connect from the pump to to the bioball tower
(17)   Bioballs – aprox one gallon
(18)   Misc. plexi glues to bond the plexi (Weldon) purchase with the Plexiglas
(19)   Approximately 8' of 1" flexible vinyl tubing

Approximate cost of the above materials $150

Begin by cutting and laying out and dry fitting pieces for the base as follows. It is helpful to use masking tape to hold the pieces together insuring a correct fit.

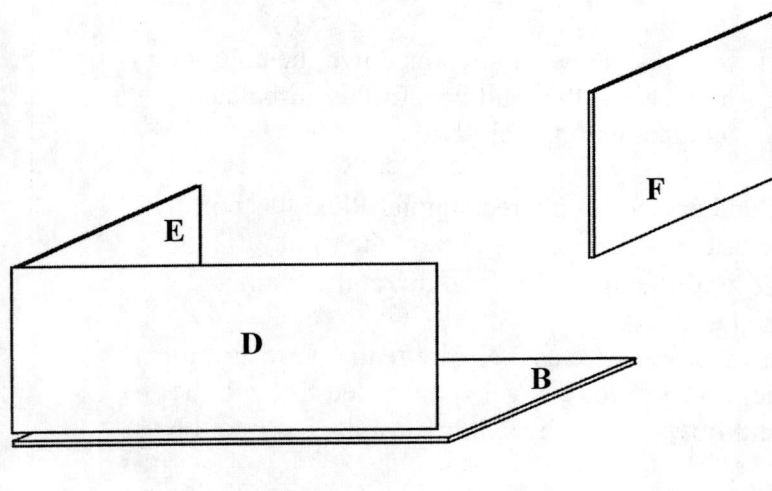

Note: Piece A & B are the largest

Piece C & D sits on top of B and the same length as B

E & F are the smallest sitting Inside C & D

Piece A the top is the same size as B (the bottom)

The small holes should be drilled, while the 6" diameter will need to be cut with a jigsaw.

Pay particular attention to drill this hole to the –**inside** - dimension of the bioball cylinder. This is so the cylinder will sit on top of piece A
Be sure the same is true for the large cylinder

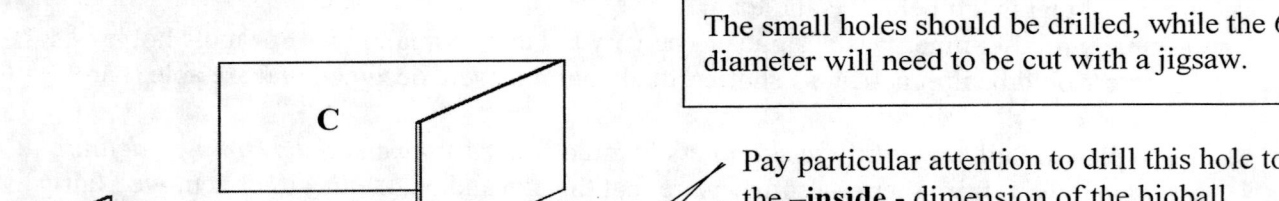

You will drill a hole here for the 1 ½" bulkhead fitting. Find the center by connecting the diagonals.
Be sure to have the bulkhead on hand to obtain the actual dimension of the hole needed.

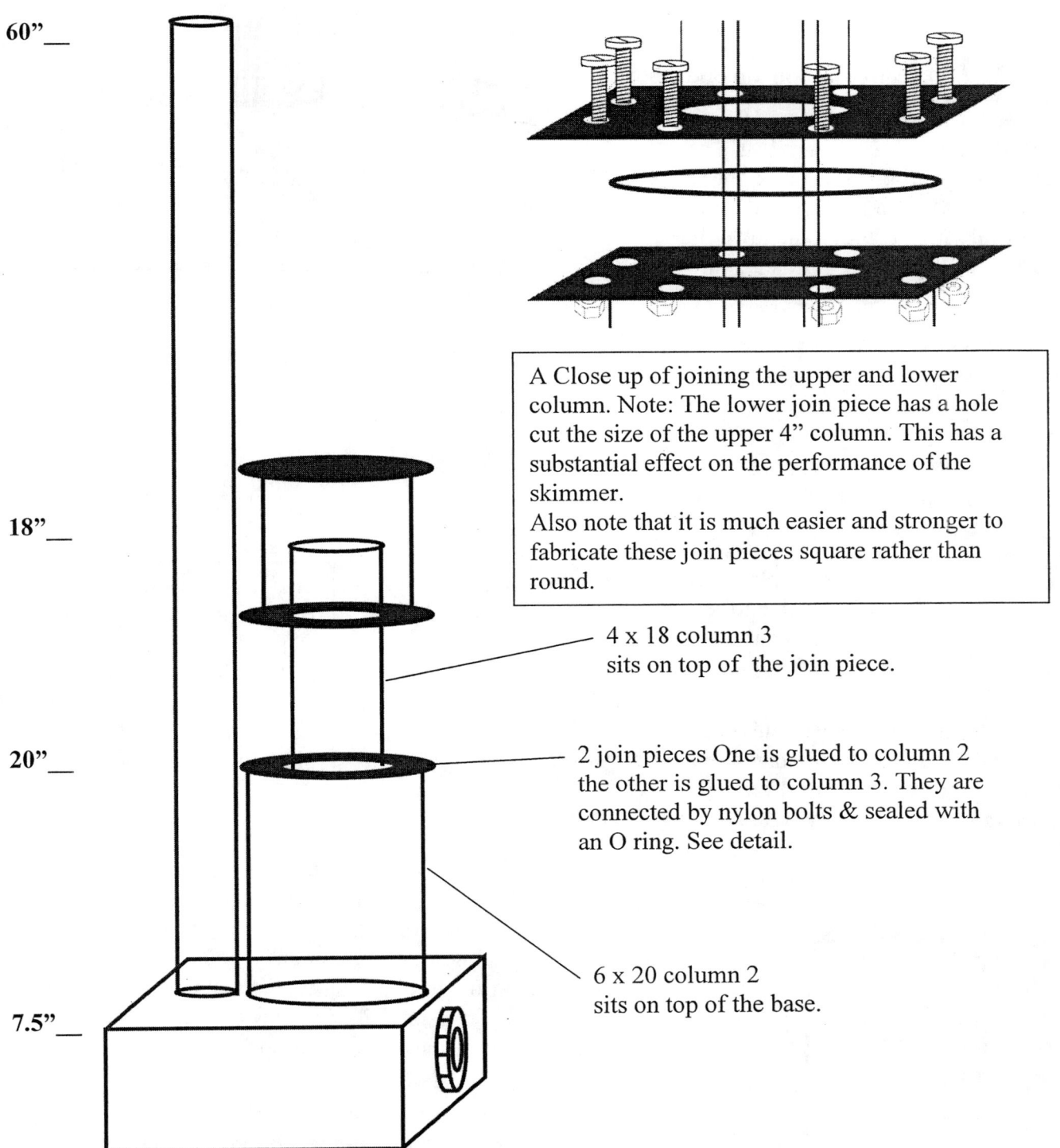

60"—

18"—

20"—

7.5"—

A Close up of joining the upper and lower column. Note: The lower join piece has a hole cut the size of the upper 4" column. This has a substantial effect on the performance of the skimmer.

Also note that it is much easier and stronger to fabricate these join pieces square rather than round.

4 x 18 column 3
sits on top of the join piece.

2 join pieces One is glued to column 2 the other is glued to column 3. They are connected by nylon bolts & sealed with an O ring. See detail.

6 x 20 column 2
sits on top of the base.

Dry fit all connections before gluing with WELDON. Use 2 different type of glue: One thin and one thick. When purchasing the glue be sure to get an applicator which is a small container with a needle like dispenser. Use a small drop of thinset to position the piece , then fill in with thickset. Work on one piece at a time allowing ample drying time before moving on. Recommended sequence: Base box first, join pieces second, attach the lower join then the upper so we have 3 separate components. The base, the large column, and the upper column. Make the collection connection and bioball chamber last. The inner baffle does not go to the bottom, it is positioned aprox ¾" above the bottom. This is a critical area of the skimmer. Water must be allowed to pass below the baffle and an ample exit e.g.: the 1 ½" bulkhead fitting. You will control the water flow with the 1 ¼ ball valve.

This piece sits on top of the box.

You will to glue in a small strip of Plexiglas aprox .25 x .75" x the ID of the bioball cylinder. This will prevent bioballs from entering the lower box.

This is a separate piece glued inside the box, It is set ¾" above the bottom.

The internal baffle is lightly glued to the – **sides** – of the box before piece A (the top) is glued on.

The 1.5" PVC is not glued in place but rather a slip on connection. You will be able to remove and clean this area by reaching in through the 6" column with your hand.

This is a 1 1/5" through wall bulkhead fitting, with a reducer bushing to accommodate the 1 ¼ ball valve. It's threaded on one end for the valve and a slip connection on the opposite end to accommodate the PVC pipe.

The diagram below is to remind you of specialized fittings needed. Depending on your location they may be difficult to find. Nevertheless they can be found Check you yellow pages for plumbing supply houses.

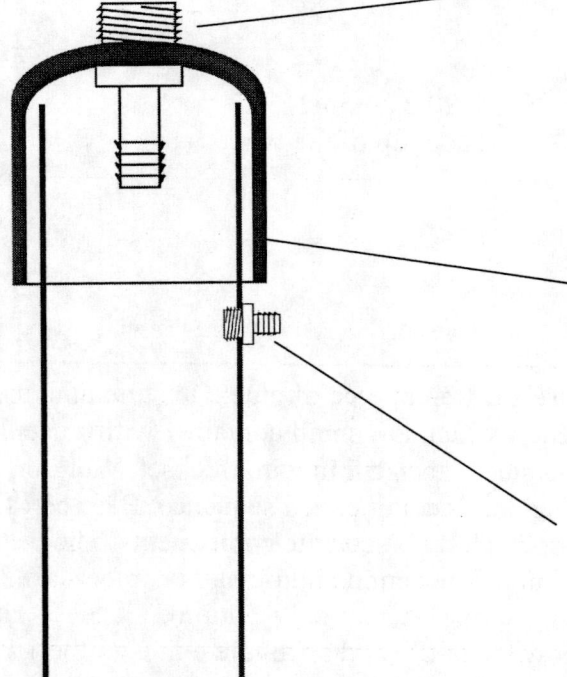

¾" nylon insert fitting. Note: The lower barbed portion must be reduced to 3/8" or less. This allows important restriction of the water, somewhat like a nozzle. You are taking water flow from a 1" hose and reducing it to 3/8" or preferably ¼". You may have to spend some time looking for this special fitting.

This is another specialized fitting. It must simply slip over the cylinder column. You will have to match this up with the cylinder. Then drill a hole and Marine Tex in the nylon insert fitting.

This is a 3/8 barbed insert fitting. It is need to induce air into the column as the water is pumped downward. These areas are susceptible to salt creep and will need to be cleaned to insure proper air flow. Drill and marine Tex in place.

Nylon insert fittings needed to connect to your pump. These will typically be 1". Use Teflon tape on the threaded fittings.

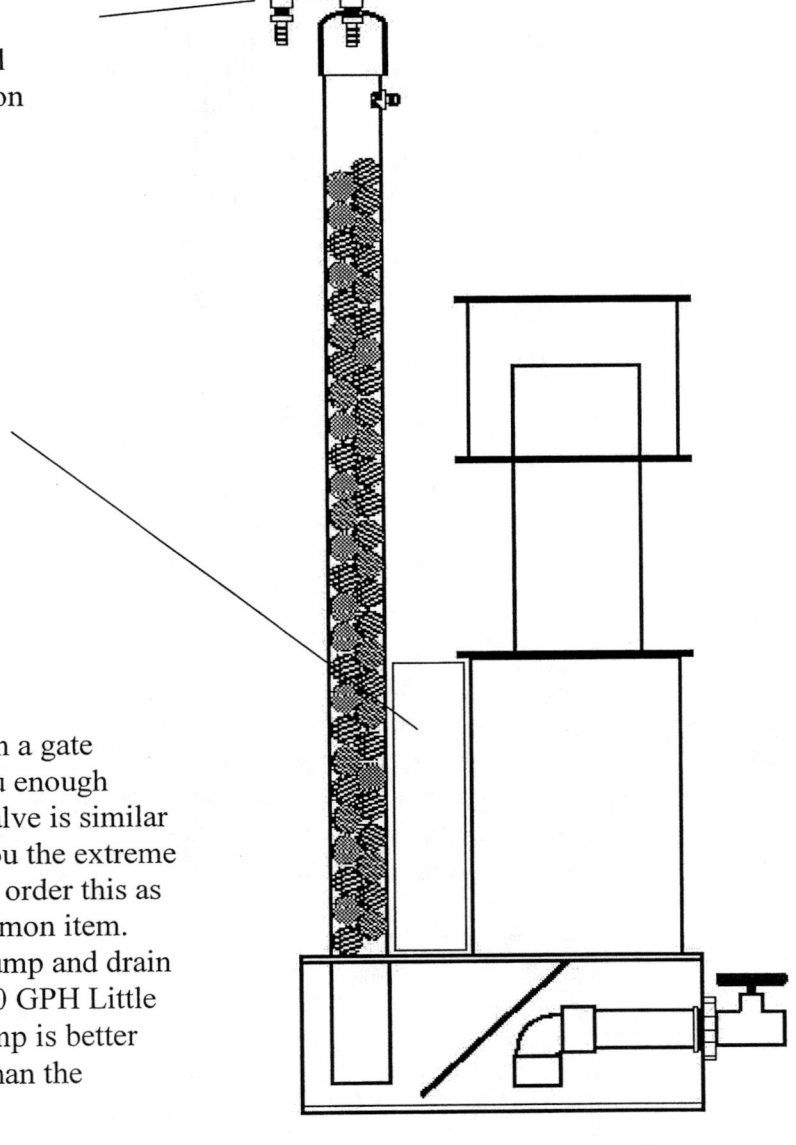

Consider gluing in a piece of ¼" Plexiglas here to support the tall column. This will add substantial strength to the unit. Measure cut and fit accordingly.

Be sure to use a Ball valve rather than a gate valve. The gate vale will not give you enough control of the water flow. The ball valve is similar to your garden spicket, it will give you the extreme fine tuning needed. You may have to order this as a 1 ¼" plastic ball valve is not a common item. This skimmer should sit above the sump and drain by gravity into the sump. I use a 1200 GPH Little Giant pressure pump. A pressure pump is better designed for this application rather than the common flow pump.

This is what your downdraft skimmer should look like. You can tailor the design to fit your needs, creating shorter dual main bioball columns if needed. The principle is still the same. This is probably the most difficult skimmer to make however it's a workhorse for removing proteins and super oxygenating the water. It's far less prone to failure and overflowing as other conventional skimmers.

Many people think this skimmer to be so efficient that they only run it occasionally. I run mine constantly as I fin it easier to add trace elements rather than to be concerned with elevated proteins in the tank.

As a final note: Drill in an insert fitting to the bottom of the collection cup, connect a 1" drain dose either to a waste container or permanently to the house drain as illustrated in previous chapters (under sink connections).

Building an Overflow box:

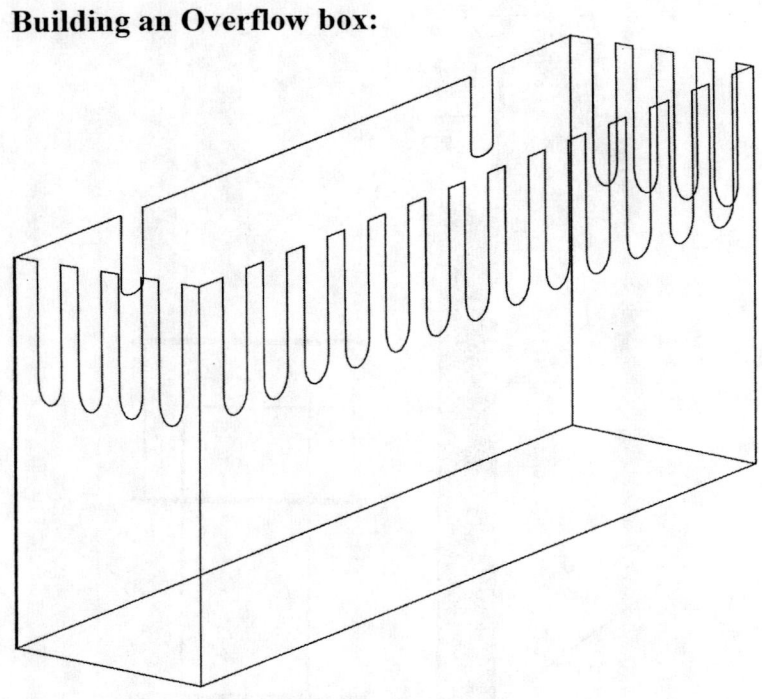

For sake of brevity, study the other areas of working with Plexiglas to determine your size requirements for this box.

By carefully looking at the close ups here you will develop your own approach to build this project.

Probably the most difficult aspect of building this item is cutting the Plexiglas in the dovetail fashion. This can be minimized by sandwiching the Plexiglas between 2 pieces of plywood. Cut the plywood about 2 inches larger than the Plexiglas temporarily screw the together, mark the layout on the wood and then cut the Plexiglas, Another alternative is to just drill ¾ - 1 inch hole at the area where the water would flow in. This will greatly simplify the project.

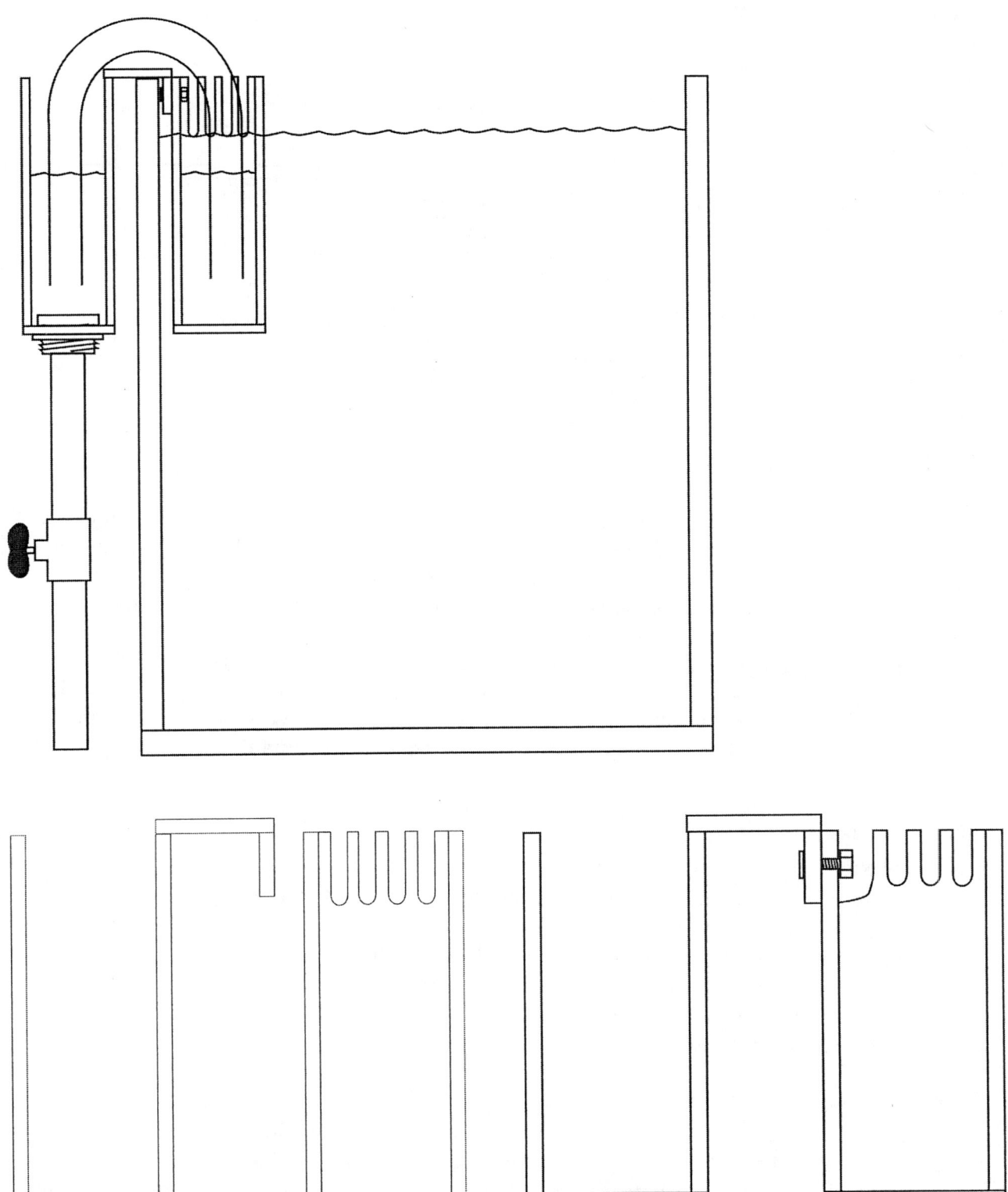

Building a poor mans chiller:

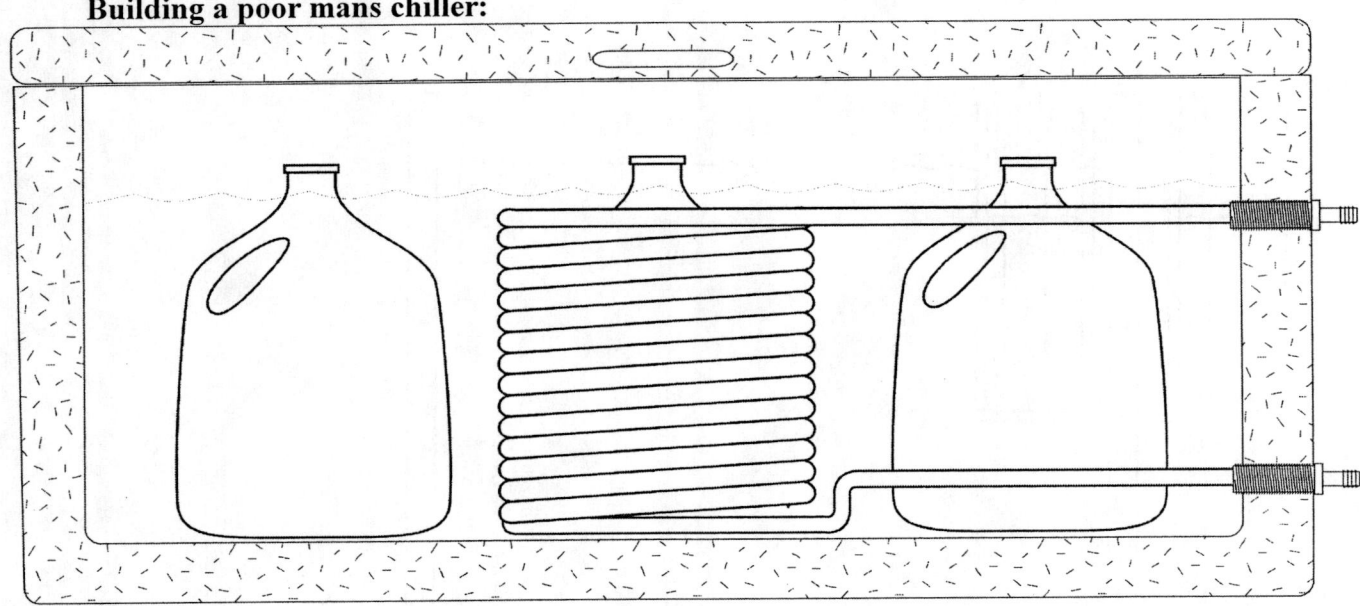

Many times hobbyists need a means to cool their tank and either don't have the money for a commercial chiller or their temprature swings are brief (for a month or less). In this case a chiller or if you prefer a "cooler" can help to reeduce the temprature of your tank. The diagram above illustrates the general idea. The insulation material shown is actually common plastic picnic cooler. The cooler should be able to hold 3 1 gallon plastic milk containers. The milk containers are frozen and placed in the cooler. While they are in place you would have another 3 containers freezing to replace the ones in the cooler. You would simply keep rotating the plastic frozen milk containers as needed. While this cooler cannot replace a commercial version, it will reduce the temprature of your tank

Materials needed:
- One plastic picnic cooler.
- 6 plastic 1 gallon plastic milk containers.
- Aprox 50' or more of 3/16 plastic tubing (typically sold for connecting an ice machine to your refrigerator).
- The necessary plastic connectors to pierce the cooler and connect the tubing.
- Ideally the connectors would be thruwall and have a nut on the inside so it could be tightened – insuring a leakproof device.
- Sealant for the thruwall connectors (silicone is ideal).

How it works:
The cooler is positioned in the same manner as the column denitrifier. This eliminates any need for extra pumps. It needs to be above the sump and is fed by gravity – water siphoning from the tank, through the tubing then into the sump. The water flow is restricted by using a relatively small diameter tubing in this case 3/16" if you use larger tubing an inline valve would be useful to control the water flow. Building the cooler is fairly self explanatory however here are some principals of its usage. It's important to have at least 50 ft of tubing inside the cooler. The more tubing used, the longer the water from the tank has a chance to cool. This example would be useful on a short term basis for a tank up to 55 gallon. On a larger tank you would need 100' of tubing and a larger cooler. How much will this cooler affect your tank depends on the temprature and amount of tubing used.

Protein Skimmer muffler:

The diagrams below illustrate an inexpensive "muffler" to quiet that noisy protein skimmer. Attach it to the skimmer with flexible vinyl tubing

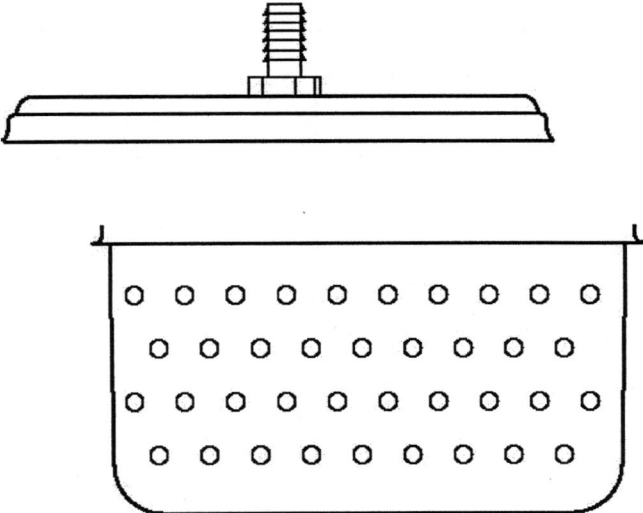

This "muffler" uses a cool whip container filled with either filter floss or pieces of sponge. Insert a nylon insert fitting to make the connection

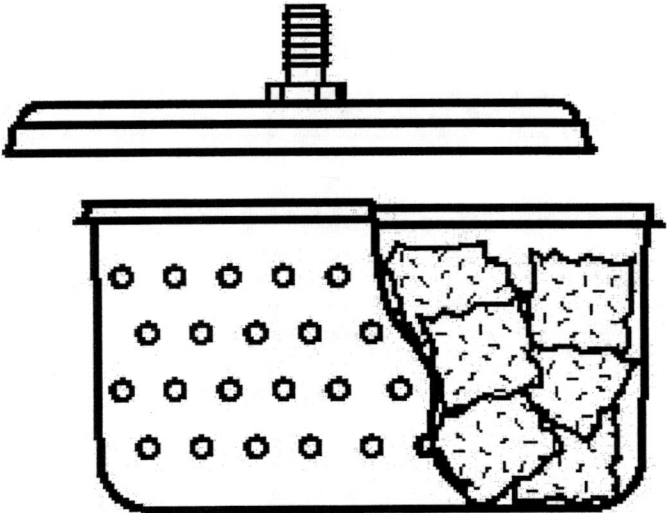

NOTES:

Chapter 13

Reef Livestock

HANDLING FISH

**Rule #1:Purchase fish from an experienced, reputable dealer.
This will eliminate most problems.**

When purchasing fish from your retailer, carefully look the fish over:

- How adjusted does the fish seem to be in captivity? Swimming freely with other fish is a positive sign. On the other hand, staying in a corner or near the surface of the tank is a sign of stress, caused either by the other fish or by the creature acclimating to being shipped, being in new water, etc. I would resist buying a fish that was not fully acclimated to a captive environment.
- Look for small white spots or pimples, the size of the head of a pin. This is a sign of Cryptocaryon (saltwater "ICH," or Ichthyophthirius). Never purchase a fish with any white spots.
- Do not buy fish that have frayed fins.
- Do not buy a fish that has a dramatically shrunken stomach. This is another sign of stress, implying the health of the fish is questionable.
- Ask your retailer about the characteristics of the fish. What does it like to eat? Is it overly territorial with other fish? Will it eat corals or shrimp? Make certain the fish is "reef compatible."
- Some fish are more prone to saltwater "ICH" than others. Tangs, "Powder Blue" and "Powder Brown," are particularly susceptible. Again, consult with your retailer.
- Ask to see the fish eat. A good appetite is usually a good sign.

Once the fish is purchased and bagged, it will be up to you to take precautions to insure its health and its successful acclimation to its new home.

The trip home. Get home as soon as possible. Avoid exposing the bagged fish to noticeable temperature changes. Try to keep the bagged fish at a constant temperature. Sometimes placing the bag in a cooler is helpful in extreme temperature conditions, such as during the winter or summer. While in the store, wrap the bag in a large towel and place it in a cooler. This is the safest way to transport fish. They will be protected against dramatic temperature differences that stress the fish and often cause an outbreak of "ICH" or subject the fish to radical temperature shock, which is usually fatal. Take all precautions against temperature changes when transporting your fish.

When you get home. My preference is to place the bagged fish in a 5-gallon bucket, using a few clothespins to position the bag so that it is open at the top, but will not spill into the bucket. Once the bag is secure, I pour approximately 1 cup of water from the tank into the bag. I note the time, or use a timer, and add 1 cup of water from the tank at 30-minute intervals:

> 1 cup initially;
> 30 minutes later, another cup of water;
> at 1 hour add another cup;
> at 1-1/2 hour add another cup (total of 4 cups added).

At 2 hours, pour the water from the bag into the bucket. Then use your hand or a net to support the fish, and place it in the tank.

Note: Take precautions not to introduce water from the bag into your tank. Often captive fish are in water containing copper to minimize outbreaks of disease, and you don't want any copper water in your reef.

Quarantine. Many hobbyists use a quarantine tank to hold the fish for observation, and for treatment if necessary. This is considered to be the safest approach to handling new fish. The quarantine tank is usually 10 to 20 gallons, and has the same water as your main tank, with a small carbon bubble-up filter or an airstone to oxygenate the water. Here the fish can be acclimated or observed without jeopardizing your healthy reef. This tank can also double as a "hospital" tank for sick fish if needed. Although many regard a quarantine tank as essential for the safe introduction and acclimation of saltwater fish, it also has its drawbacks:

- Although the water in the quarantine tank is from your reef, you may find it quite a challenge to keep the smaller tank biologically and environmentally stable, and to duplicate in it the most significant aspects of your reef, such as lighting, temperature, territorial arrangements, etc.

- A quarantine tank is one more stressful step for the fish. Consider how many times the fish has to acclimate to a new environment:

  1. Going from the wild into the boat;
  2. From the boat to the wholesaler;
  3. From the wholesaler to the retailer;
  4. From the retailer to you;
  5. (Optional:) In a quarantine tank;
  6. In your reef.

Using the information above, as well as getting recommendations from others, will help you make a decision on whether you will quarantine or not.

A reminder: once you have your reef set up with live rock, inverts, and corals, it will usually be a big deal if you have to remove a fish. Most of the rock will have to come out, and then be set up all over again. For these reasons it is important to

- purchase from an experienced, reputable dealer;
- avoid fragile, delicate specimens;

- acclimate new fish as suggested above, adding 1 cup of water from the tank at half-hour intervals over a 2-hour period;
- observe fish prior to purchasing them, looking for positive health signs: they should eat well, be active swimmers, and seem well-adjusted to a captive environment.

Disease. There are many books specifically dedicated to the diagnosis and treatment of the diseases of fish. It is recommended that you have at least one complete guide in your collection of books, as a reference on this subject.

The reef tank is extremely delicate, and cannot be treated with conventional medications designed for fish-only tanks. When there is disease in the reef tank, there are two options:

1. Remove the sick fish, place it in a "hospital" tank, and diagnose and treat it accordingly.
2. Rely on nature to take its course. The live rock and invertebrates are usually not susceptible to common forms of disease. When the fish is removed from the tank, any "ICH" spores will not have the "host" they need to reproduce, and they will die off in approximately 2 weeks. Increasing the tank temperature to 85° will speed up this process.

Cryptocaryon (saltwater "ICH," Ichthyophthirius). The most common activation of saltwater "ICH" is a sudden temperature change, usually caused by improper transporting or acclimation. The most commonly-used remedy is to raise the temperature of the tank to approximately 85° for 6-8 days. This speeds up the reproductive cycle of the parasite, and will usually wipe it out (although in advanced stages fish losses are very possible). Cleaner shrimp in sufficient population will pick off parasites, providing the fish wants to be assisted in this way.

Following the suggestions given previously will dramatically reduce the outbreak of diseases.

HANDLING INVERTEBRATES AND CORALS

Before adding any invertebrates, be certain to record zero ammonia/nitrite levels with a reliable test kit.

Most of these creatures, as delicate as they are, seem to require minimal acclimation compared to fish. The primary concern in acclimating inverts is to get the water temperature in their shipping bag as close as possible to the temperature in your tank. You can

- either acclimate the creatures as described above for fish, adding a cup of water from the tank every half hour for 2 hours;
- or, more simply, "float" the bag in the tank for approximately one hour. This will bring the temperature of the creatures and their shipping water approximately to the temperature of the tank. *Never* introduce foreign water into your tank—dispose of it. Some suggestions:

Anemones. These should be handled with latex gloves and "purged." This is done by removing the creature from the bag and water. Place it on a clean dinner plate (no soap or residue), pour off any remaining water. In about 5 minutes you will notice more liquid on the plate; again, pour this off. Let the anemone "purge" one more time; after 5 minutes pour off any liquid. Then place the creature in the tank, positioning it according to its light requirements.

Corals. Handle with latex gloves. Place on a secure area of live rock or tank bottom, in a location where the coral will not get "knocked over" by snails or urchins. Consult your retailer about the coral's light requirements, and place it accordingly.

Snails. Float to the temperature of the tank. Remove and place individuals flesh downward. This will prevent them from being "picked on" by fish.

Starfish, shrimp, urchins. Float to the temperature of the tank. Dispose of shipping water.

Clams. As above. Position according to light requirements. (Tridachna clams usually have a high light requirement, and should be placed close to the light canopy.)

Sponges. Acclimate to the temperature of the tank. With these creatures the most important precaution is *not to expose them to air*. The transfer from bag to tank must be done *underwater*. Also, most sponges have a low light requirement, and therefore should be protected from intense direct lighting. This can be achieved by placing the sponge under an overhang of live rock. Sponges are very colorful filter feeders. Some aquarists have good results keeping them, while others cannot keep them alive. I recommend that you attempt a hardy specimen before considering a substantial population. Sponges also must be kept free of sediment. This is most often done by delicate vacuuming during water changes; it may also be done more frequently by "blowing off" the sediment with a turkey baster.

LIVE AND DECORATIVE ROCK DESCRIPTIONS

1. **Fresh rock.** Fresh multi-colored coraline reef rock. A limestone rock encrusted with pink and purple coraline algae. Fresh rock is collected just prior to shipping. This takes from 2 weeks (minimum) to 6-8 weeks (maximum), depending on the amount of die-off in and on the rock. Stay away from fresh rock, unless you are prepared to cure it yourself. Often this is not worth the slightly lower cost.

2. **Cured rock.** This is the same as the above, but has been cured for approximately 3 to 8 weeks.

3. **Premium live rock.** Purple coraline encrusted with multi-colored micro-algae, tunicates, colorful sponges, and other sea life. Cured, top quality.

4. **Plant rock.** Plant rock is fresh rock that is covered with various types of green caulerpa macro-algae. Try to purchase it cured.

5. **Premium live rock.** With some encrusting gorgonia (octocoral). Reddish brown polyps.

6. **Premium live rock.** With top 90-100% covered with encrusting gorgonia (octocoral). It will contain branch gorgonians, branch sponges, tube worms, feather dusters, small anemones, and small invertebrates, and will be encrusted with pink and purple coraline algae.

7. **Premium live rock.** With gold or green sea mat (zoanthid), heavily encrusted.

8. **False Coral Gorgonian on rock.** False Coral Gorgonian is a type of encrusting gorgonian that takes the shape of the objects it comes in contact with. When the polyps are closed, the objects take on the appearance of whitish stony coral. When the polyps are open, the objects look like they are covered with a pink shag carpeting.

9. **Oyster rock.** Oyster rock is the home of small black purse oysters. These oysters range in size from a penny to a quarter, and are in clusters.

10. **Florida Ricordia.** Florida Ricordia is a colonial anemone that is attached to coraline encrusted reef rock. The large, thick polyps are either green or golden in coloration with tiny bright green dots. This beautiful decorative rock is collected beyond Florida state waters and thrives in tanks with good lighting and water quality. This is considered to be very desirable rock, and does extremely well in captivity.

INVERTEBRATES: DESCRIPTIONS

Anemone:

Handle all anemones with latex gloves. They come in all different colors. Some are compatible in a reef system; others should not be put in. Consult with your dealer. They need medium to high light. Feed them with very small pieces of shrimp, squid, and fish. Always remember not to over-feed.

Many anemones can move around in the tank. If you plan to keep both coral and anemones, select anemones that are primarily stationary. See "Anemones," p. 196, under "Handling Invertebrates and Corals."

- Carpet (Atlantic)—Semi-hardy. Symbiotic with clown fish. Moves around. The carpet anemone has the most powerful sting, which usually results in a painful rash that lasts for a day or so. Wash the affected skin area with soap and water.

- Colored Carpet—See above information.

- Colored Tube—Intolerant of ammonia and nitrite. Interesting feeder. Fairly stationary.

- Condylactus—Florida. Very hardy, inexpensive. Can move around.

- Curlique—Very hardy. Same as above.

- Haitian—Purple tip tentacles, orange base. Does well.

- Long Tentacle—Does well. Host to clownfish.

- Rock—Very hardy, inexpensive. Caribbean. Doesn't move around much. Very desirable.

- Saddle Carpet—Can get big. Can move around. Symbiotic with clownfish.

- Sebae—Symbiotic with clown fish. Reasonably hardy.

- Sebae Purple—Symbiotic with clown fish. Does well. More expensive. Beautiful.

- Sebae Yellow—Symbiotic with clown fish. Not as hardy.

- Tube—Intolerant of ammonia and nitrite. Can kill naive fish. Peach, lime, dark purple. Doesn't move much.

Filter feeders. Easy to take care of. Need low light. Available in many colors.

It is important that sponges not be exposed to air. They must be kept underwater at all times, particularly when being unpacked. They must also be kept free of sediment, either by shaking them underwater or by using a turkey baster to blow off sediment. It is also important to purchase sponges that are collected with a base, not simply cut off. Algae must also be removed, by gently rubbing them off with a soft brush. Sponges should be placed in a shaded area of the tank.

Commonly available sponges are:

- Green Barrel
- Orange Tree
- Purple Barrel
- Red Ball

- Red Clumo
- Red Tree (Deep Water)
- Yellow Clumo
- Yellow Tre

Crabs:

All crabs listed are hardy. Most are scavengers.

- Anemone—Small, interesting.

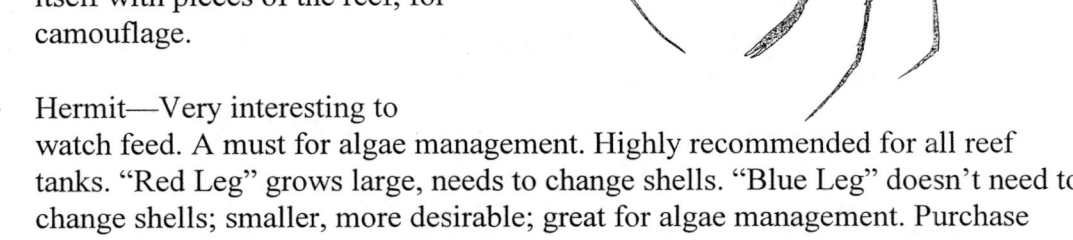

- Arrowhead—Very interesting spider-like creature, with an arrow-shaped head. Thought to eat bristleworms.

- Decorator—Extremely interesting. Likes to "decorate" itself with pieces of the reef, for camouflage.

- Hermit—Very interesting to watch feed. A must for algae management. Highly recommended for all reef tanks. "Red Leg" grows large, needs to change shells. "Blue Leg" doesn't need to change shells; smaller, more desirable; great for algae management. Purchase "Blue Leg" small (1/4" to 3/4" shell size).

Feather dusters:

Hardy filter feeders. They live in a soft tube and open up like flowers.

- Atlantic—Hardy. Nice in a reef tank.

- Cluster—Small, very hardy. Commonly reproduces in a healthy reef.

- Hawaiian—Hardy. Larger than the "Atlantic," also more expensive.

Gorgonian (octocoral):

Very hardy. Comes in various colors. Nice decoration for the reef tank. Needs medium light.

- Common—Low light.

- Corky Sea Finger—Low light.

- Orange with red polyp—Deep water. Needs low light.

- Purple—High light requirement. Very hardy.

Mollusks:

Herbivores, algae eaters. Scavengers.

- Colored Sea Cucumber—Filter feeder. Extremely slow-moving. Does well.

- Cowry—Algae eater.

- Flame Scallop—Beautiful orange color. Great addition to the reef. Inexpensive.

- Flamingo Cowry—Eats gorgonians. Not recommended.

- Red Tulip Snail—Grows large. Can climb out of the tank.

- Tridachna Clams—High light requirement. Place in the upper area of the tank. These clams do well in captivity. Very desirable.

- Turbo Grazer / Astrea Snail—A must for algae management. Hardy, although intolerant of ammonia. Use one per gallon. Place flesh side down to prevent them from being picked on by fish. They can get large, and may knock over loose areas of the reef.

Shrimp:

The shrimp listed here are all very hardy. They are scavengers, and have beautiful colors. Be careful not to put in fish that will eat the shrimp. All shrimp molt from time to time. Do not be alarmed to find a shell of your favorite specimen.

- Anemone—Tiny. Commonly found in anemones.

- Coral Branded—Very hardy and long-lived. A must for an interesting reef tank. Beautiful, hardy. One per tank, unless a mated pair. Highly recommended.

- Gold Banded—See above.

- Mated Pair—Usually they are not compatible with each other; this is a pair that gets along.

- Peppermint Pistol—Inoffensive, good, hardy.

- Red Fire—Expensive. Also eats parasites off of fish. Beautiful creature.

- Scarlet Cleaner—Very hardy. A must for an interesting reef tank. Beautiful, graceful. A natural remedy for saltwater ICH. Removes parasites from fish, clams, scallops, etc. Highly recommended.

Starfish:

Excellent scavengers. Compatible with invertebrates in the reef tank. Starfish are intolerant of ammonia or nitrite.

- Brittle—Shy. Good scavenger. Rarely seen. Interesting hairy legs that are very brittle and break easily.

- Chocolate Chip—Most colorful. Shy, rarely seen once it is in the tank.

- Hard Spiny Green—Very desirable. Algae eater. Moves around the tank well, is less shy. My personal favorite starfish.

- Red Serpent (Deep Water)—Low nitrite; has to be acclimated slowly.

- Serpent—See information above, under "Brittle."

Urchins:

All are hardy. Handle them carefully. Good algae eaters.

- Algae Eater—hardy

- Pencil—A harmless, wonderful addition to any reef.

- Pincushion—They can get large, and have a tendency to knock over coral or live rock. Purchase small.

- Pink Pincushion—nice color, hardy.

CORALS: DESCRIPTIONS

All corals should be placed in a secure position, to minimize the risk of their getting knocked over by snails, urchins, etc.

Low light =   3 watts per gallon or less, or a semi-shaded area of the tank.
Medium light =   4 watts per gallon.
High light =   5 – 7+ watts per gallon.

- Asst. Mushroom Rock—Hardy. Low light.

- Blue Mushroom Rock—Hardy, easy to maintain. Low light.

- Brain—Hardy. Medium light.

- Branch Soft Coral—Hardy. Medium light.

- Bubble—Semi-hardy. Medium light.

- Cup—Semi-hardy. Medium light.

- Elegant—Hardy. Needs room: grows well and expands. Medium to high light.

- Elephant Ear Mushroom Rock—Needs room: expands. Medium light.

- False Brain—Hardy. Medium light.

- Finger Soft Coral—Hardy. Medium light.

- Fox—Semi-hardy. High light.

- Giant Mushroom Rock—Hardy. Medium light.

- Green Plate—Semi-hardy. Needs room. Must be placed flat. High light.

- Hammerhead—Fragile, delicate. Difficult to keep. High light.

- Leather Soft Coral—Hardy. Medium light.

- Metallic Green Mushroom Rock—Hardy. Medium light.

- Open Brain (Green)—Hardy. Needs high light.

- Open Brain (Rose)—Hardy. Needs high light.

- Pearl—Semi-hardy. High light.

- Red Mushroom Rock—Hardy. Medium light.

- Red Plate—Semi-hardy. Needs water current. Must be placed flat. High light.

- Red Polyp—Multiplies easily. Low light.

- Red/Orange Soft Coral—Hardy. Low light.

- Staghorn (Acropora)—Delicate, probably the most difficult to keep. High light.

- Star Polyp (Green)—Hardy. Multiplies easily. Medium light.

- Striped Mushroom Rock—Hardy. Medium light.

- Sunflower (Goniopora)—Does well initially, but not recommended. Usually not long-lived. Has needs unique to its natural environment. High light.

- Xmas Soft Coral—Hardy. Low light.

FISH: DESCRIPTIONS

Species in this list are generally suitable for most reef aquariums. Note that all are not completely trustworthy with certain corals and polyps. Consult with your supplier as to suitability with your reef.

Angels:

- Coral Beauty—Good for reef tanks.

- Flame—Good for reef tanks.

- Flameback—Hardy, good for reef tanks.

- Pigmy—Hardy, nice color.

- Resplendent—Hardy.

- Swallow Tail—Not recommended for reef tanks.

Anthias:

All good for reef tanks. Should be selected by sex: one male, with several females. Plankton feeder.

- Flame
- Lyretail (female)
- Lyretail (male)
- Orange

- Purple Queen
- Square Pink—Nice color, highly recommended for reef tanks
- Tri-Color

Basslets / Dottybacks:

One per tank. All hardy and good for reef tanks, but do not place more than one of the same kind.

- Bicolor Pseudo
- Black Cap Gramma
- Diadema Pseudo
-
- Purple Pseudo
- Royal Gramma

Blennies / Gobies:

- Bar Goby—Good cleaner.

- Barber Post Goby—Good cleaner.

- Bicolor Blenny—Picky eater.

- Blue Dotted Jawfish—Rare.

- Catalina Goby—Good jumper. Possibly undesirable unless the tank is properly covered. Likes cooler water, about 72°-74°.

- Clown Goby—Good cleaner.

- Mandarin Goby—Beautiful, but picky eater. Usually not long-lived. Eats mostly from the live rock. Has needs unique to its natural environment. Although beautiful, **not recommended!**

Clowns:

All hardy and easy to take care of.

- Maroon—Grows large. Can be aggressive.

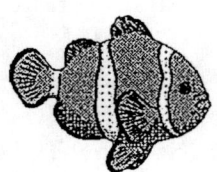

- Percula—A good hardy fish.

- Sebae—Symbiotic with anemones.

- Tomato—A good hardy fish. Symbiotic with anemones.

Imported:

- Allardi—Rare.

- Blue Stripe—Rare.

- Orange Skunk—A little bit more sensitive to the water than the skunk clown.

- Pink Skunk—Easy to take care of.

- Saddleback—Gets large. Can be aggressive.

- Xanthurus—Rare.

Chromis / Damsel (most are territorial, and become more so as they get larger):

- Black/White—A little on the aggressive side. Basic hardy reef fish.

- Domino—A little on the aggressive side. Basic hardy reef fish.

- Electric Blue—Hardy. Nice color.

- Fiji—hardy. Good for reef tanks.

- Green Chromis—Hardy. One of the best damsels. Likes to "school." Best if purchased in groups of 4-8.

- Stark's—Hardy.

Cardinals:

Good in reef tanks, although you should consult with your dealer.

- Flame—Will eat small fish.

- Red Spot Cardinal (a.k.a. "Pajama" or "P.J.")—Excellent fish.

Miscellaneous:

- Coral Catfish—Not recommended for reef tanks.

- Dusky Jawfish—Good cleaner, good for reef tanks.

- Firefish—Good cleaner, good for reef tanks.

- Flame Goby—Good cleaner, good for reef tanks.

- Flame Hawkfish—Some are odd and rare. Good for reef tanks.

- Flashing Tile Goby—Good for reef tanks.

- Forktail Blenny—Good algae eater.

- Gold Neon Goby—Good cleaner, good for reef tanks.

- Golden Head Sleeper—Good cleaner for the gravel.

- Lizard Sand Goby—Moves quickly. Very interesting fish.

- Longnose Hawkfish—Good for reef tanks. Very interesting fish.

- Mandarin—Good scavenger for reef tanks.

- Marine Betta—Calm, graceful. However, they will eat small fish.

- Mated Pair Neons—Excellent reef fish. Will pick parasites off of fish.

- Neon Goby—Good reef goby.

- Orange Spot Sleeper—Hardy.

- Pearly Jawfish—Easy to keep. Makes its home in the gravel.
- Purple Tile Goby—Good jumper. (Tank must be well covered.)

- Red Lip Blenny—A little bit aggressive.

- Red Scooter Blenny—Good scavenger.

- Sailfin Blenny—Good algae eater.

- Spotted Mandarin—Good scavenger for reef tank. One per tank.

- Stripped Goby—Good cleaner, good for reef tanks.

- Watchman Goby—Good cleaner.

- Yellow Tail Blenny—Good cleaner, good for reef tanks.

Tangs:

- Chevron—Rare.

- Powder Blue—Not recommended. Susceptible to ICH.

- Powder Brown—Not recommended. Susceptible to ICH.

- Purple (Red Sea)—More expensive than yellow tang.

- Sailfin Desjardini—Hardy. Excellent fish. Good algae eater. Considered a must for a reef.

- Yellow—Hardy. Excellent basic saltwater reef fish. Good algae eater. Mandatory for algae management.

- Yellow Eye—Good algae eater.

Wrasse:

OK for reef tanks, but be careful with your invertebrates. May not be desirable in your reef.

- Japanese—Hardy.

- Ornate Leopard—One per tank.

The following identification list is quoted from *A Practical Guide to Corals*

By Ed Puterbaugh & Eric Borneman
ISBN 0-945738-99-4 Crystal Graphics Lexington KY
Published by Crystal Graphics
2891 Richmond Rd. Suite 102
Lexington Kentucky 40509
1-606-266-4888

Their website is located at http://members.aol.com.octocoral/corals.htm

A Practical Guide to Corals is definitely a book worth having!

It contains stunning pictures and useful descriptions of most corals available on the market today.
I also feel it worth noting here that Eric Borneman has be one of the hardest working authorities in the online reef keeping community today. He can be found on certain mailing lists and discussion boards where he tirelessly answers questions and continually enlightens the reef community with his knowledge and experience. I'm quite sure history will note Mr. Borneman's dedication to the hobby.
I would highly recommend purchasing a Practical Guide to Corals

The following list is humbly quoted from their book.

Common Name	Scientific Name	Lighting	Current	Aggressiveness	Difficulty
Acropora, Blue tip	Acropora loripes	7-10	M-H	M	6-9
Acropora, Brush	Acropora cytherea	7-10	M-H	M	6-9
Acropora, Bushy	Acropora aspera	7-10	M-H	M	6-9
Acropora, Cats Paw	Acropora palifera	7-10	M-H	M	6-9
Acropora, Cluster	Acropora digitifera	7-10	M-H	M	6-9
Acropora, Delicate	Acpopora pulchra	7-10	M-H	M	6-9
Acropora, Gem	Acropora gemmifera	7-10	M-H	M	6-9
Acropora, Green	Acropora valida	7-10	M-H	M	6-9
Acropora, Noble	Acropora sp.	7-10	M-H	M	6-9
Acropora, Pine Tree	Acropora sp.	7-10	M-H	M	6-9
Acropora, Purple	Acropora tenuis	7-10	M-H	M	6-9
Acropora, Purple Tipped	Acropora cerealis	7-10	M-H	M	6-9
Acropora, Staghorn	Acropora formosa	7-10	M-H	M	6-9
Acropora, Table	Acropora sp.	7-10	M-H	M	6-9
Acropora, Yellow	Acropora selago	7-10	M-H	M	6-9
Anchor	Euphylllia ancora	4-9	L-M	H	5
Birds Nest	Seriatopora hystrix	8-10	M-H	M	4-10
Blue Coral	Helipora coerulea	6-10	H	L	8
Blunt Finger	Lobophytum sp.	2-9	L-M	M-H	2
Boulder (Brain)	Montastrea curta	4-9	M-H	L-M	4
Boulder (Brain)	Montastrea magnistellata	4-9	M-H	L-M	4
Branching Anchor	Euphyllia parancora	4-9	L-M	H	5
Branching Hammer	Euphyllia parancora	4-9	L-M	H	5
Bubble	Plerogyra sinuosa	3-9	L-M	H	4
Bubble Mushroom	Discosoma sanctithomas	2-6	L	L	2
Button	Cynarina lacrymalis	3-6	L	L	5
Button Polyps, Brown	Zooanthus sociatus	2-8	M	L	1
Button Polyps, Green	Zooanthus pulchellus	2-8	M	L	1
Button, Red	Cynarina lacrymalis	3-6	L	L	5
Cabbage	Lobophytum crassum	2-9	L-M	M-H	2
Cactus	Pavona decussata	6-10	M-H	L-M	7
Cactus, Frilly	Pavona varians	6-10	M-H	L-M	7
Candleabra	Eunicea mammosa	5-10	M-H	L	4
Candycane	Caulastrea furcata	3-8	L-M	L	4
Carnation, Gold	Dendronephthya sp.	1-4	L-M	L	9
Carnation, Pink	Dendronephthya aurea	1-4	L-M	L	9
Carnation, Red	Dendronephthya rubeola	1-4	L-M	L	9
Cauliflower	Pocillopora damicornis	6-10	H	M	8
Cauliflower, Pink	Pocillopora verrucosa	6-10	H	M	8
Chili	Alcyonium sp.	3-8	L-M	M	5
Christmas Tree Worm Rock	Porites lutea	7-10	H	L	8
Clove Polyps	Clavularia sp.	2-8	M	L	1
Club Finger	Alcyonium sp.	2-9	L-M	M-H	2
Club Foot	Stylophora pistillata	7-10	M-H	M	9

Common Name	Scientific Name	Lighting	Current	Aggressiveness	Difficulty
Colt	Cladiella sp.	2-8	L-M	M	2
Corky Finger	Briareum asbestinum	4-9	M-H	L	5
Crystal	Galaxea astreata	5-9	L-M	H	8
Cup	Tubinara peltata	4-9	M	L	6
Cup, Yellow	Tubinaria frondens	4-9	M	L	6
Daisy	Alveopora sp.				
Daisy Polyps	Clavularia sp.	2-9	M	L	1
Dented Brain	Symphyllia radians	4-9	L-M	L-M	5
Devil's Hand	Lobophytum pauciflorum	2-9	L-M	M-H	2
Devil's Finger	Lobophytum sp.	2-9	L-M	M-H	2
Disk	Fungia sp.	5-9	L-M	H	6
Disk, Purple	Fungia danai	5-9	L-M	H	6
Doughnut	Scolymia australis	2-6	L-M	M	6
Doughnut, Red	Scolymia vitiensis	2-6	L-M	M	6
Elegance, Brown	Cataphyllia jardinei	3-8	L-M	H	3
Elegance, Green	Cataphyllia jardinei	3-8	L-M	H	3
Elegance, Purple Tipped	Cataphyllia jardinei	3-8	L-M	H	3
Elephant Nose	Mycedium elephantotus	4-7	M	L	7
Elephant Skin	Pachyseris rugosa	6-9	M-H	L	7
Elephant's Ear Mushroom	Rhodactis sp.	2-6	L	L	2
Encrusting Boulder	Briareum sp.	3-9	M-H	L	7
Encrusting Carpet	Erthropodium sp.	3-9	M-H	L	7
Fat Finger	Lobophytum sp.	2-9	L-M	M-H	2
Finger Leather, Green	Lobophytum sp.	2-9	L-M	M-H	2
Finger, Gold	Sinularia sp.	2-9	M-H	M	2
Finger, Green	Sinularia sp.	2-9	M-H	M	2
Finger, Mauve	Sinularia sp.	2-9	M-H	M	2
Finger, Purple	Cladiella australiensis	2-9	M-H	M	2
Fire, Branching	Millepora alcicornis	6-10	L-M	H	7
Fire, Plate	Millepora platyphyllia?	6-10	L-M	H	7
Flat Brain	Lobophyllia hemprichii	4-9	L-M	L-M	5
Florida Mushroom	Discosoma carigreni	2-6	L	L	2
Flower Leather	Sinularia dura	2-9	L-M	M-H	2
Flowerpot	Goniopora lobata	4-8	L-M	M-H	10
Flowerpot, Branching	Goniopora eclipsensis	4-8	L-M	M-H	10
Fluted Galaxy	Galaxea sp.	4-9	L	H	8
Fox	Nemenzophyllia turbida	2-6	L	L	6
Frogspawn	Euphyllia divisa	4-9	L-M	H	5
Galaxy	Galaxea fasc+C91icularis	5-9	L-M	H	8
Giant Anthelia	Anthelia glauca	5-9	M-H	L	6
Giant Brown Mushroom	Rhodactis sp.	2-6	L	L	2
Giant Cup	Amplexidiscus fenestrafer	2-6	L	L	2
Giant Mushroom	Rhodactis sp.	2-6	L	L	2
Glowing Ember	Distichopora irregularis	2-4	L	L?	?

Common Name	Scientific Name	Lighting	Current	Aggressiveness	Difficulty
Grand Polyp	Palythoa grandis	2-8	M	L	1
Grape	Euphyllia paradivisa	4-9	L-M	H	6
Grape, White	Euphyllia yaeyamaensis	4-9	L-M	H	6
Grooved Brain	Oulophyllia crispa	4-9	L-M	L-M	5
Hammer	Euphyllia ancora	4-9	L-M	H	5
Helmet	Halo+C118mitra pileus	4-7	L-M	M	7
Horn	Hydnophora rigida	7-10	M-H	H	8
Horn	Hydnophora exesa	7-10	M-H	H	8
Horn	Hydnophora grandis	7-10	M-H	H	8
Jeweled Finger	Porites cylindrica	7-10	H	L	8
Jeweled Toe	Porites antennuata	7-10	H	L	8
Kenya Tree	Capnella sp.	2-6	L-M	M	5
Knobby Sea Rod	Eunicea sp.	4-10	M-H	L	4
Lace	Distichopora sp.	1-4	L-M	L	6
Lace, Delicate	Stylaster sp.	1-4	L-M	L	6
Lettuce, Antler	Pectinia alcicornis	6-10	M-H	L	10
Lettuce, Frilly	Pectinia lactuca	6-10	M-H	L	10
Lettuce, Palm	Pectinia paeonia	6-10	M-H	L	10
Long Tentacled Plate	Heliofungia actiniformis	4-7	L-M	H	7
Maze (Brain)	Platygyra sinensis	4-9	L-M	L-M	5
Medusa	Sphaerella krempfi	2-5	L-M	L	5
Moon Polyp	Palythoa sp.	2-8	M	L	1
Moon, Brown	Favites abdita	4-9	M	L-M	4
Moonstone	Favia sp.	4-9	M	L-M	4
Moonstone, Green	Favia speciosa	4-9	M	L-M	4
Neon Green Tree	Nephthea sp.	2-6	M	L-M	6
Octobubble	Plerogyra symplex?	3-9	L-M	H	4
Octopus	Turbinaria petula	4-9	M	L	6
Open Brain, Green	Trachyphyllia geoffroyi	4-8	L-M	L	6
Open Brain, Red	Trachyphyllia geoffroyi	4-8	L-M	L	6
Orange Finger	Diodogorgia nodultfera	2-6	M-H	L	7
Pagoda	Turbinina patula?	4-9	M	L	6
Pearl	Physogyra lichtensteini	3-9	L-M	H	4
Pineapple	Favites flexuosa	4-9	M	L-M	4
Pipe Organ	Tubipora musica	3-10	L-H	L	4
Porous Sea Rod	Pseudoplexaura sp.	4-10	M-H	L	4
Purple Corky Finger	Briareum asbestinum	4-9	M-H	L	5
Red Finger	Diodogorgia nodultfera	2-6	M-H	L	7
Ricordea	Ricordea florida	2-6	L	L	2
Ricordea, False	Actinodiscus sp.	2-6	L	L	2
Rose, Caribbean	Manicina sp.	4-8	M	M	5
Rose, Pacific	Trachyphyllia geoffroyi?	4-8	M	M	5
Rose, Pacific	Wellsophyllia sp.?	4-8	M	M	5
Ruffled	Merulina amplicata	7-10	M-H	L	10

Common Name	Scientific Name	Lighting	Current	Aggressiveness	Difficulty
Ruffled	Merulia scabricula	7-10	M-H	L	10
Sea Blade, Gold	Peterogorgia anceps	6-8	M-H	L	7
Sea Blade, Purple	Peterogorgia guadalupensis	6-8	M-H	L	7
Sea Mat, Blue	Palythoa sp.	3-9	M	L	2
Sea Mat, Gold	Palythoa sp.	3-9	M	L	2
Sea Mat, Orange	Palythoa sp.	3-9	M	L	2
Sea Mat, Red	Palythoa sp.	3-9	M	L	2
Sea Plume, Purple	Pterogorgia bipinnata	5-10	M-H	L	6
Sea Plume Yellow	Pterogorgia bipinnata	5-10	M-H	L	6
Sea Spray, Red	Leptogorgia sp.	3-9	M-H	L	8
Silver Gorgonian	Muricea laxa	3-9	M-H	L	7
Slipper	Polyphllia talpina	4-8	L-M	M	6
Slit-Pore Sea Rod	Plexaurella sp.	4-10	M-H	L	4
Snake Polyps	Isaurus tuberculatus?	2-8	M	L	1
Star Polyps, Brown	Clavularia sp.	2-8	M	L	1
Star Polyps, Flowering	Clavularia sp.	2-8	M	L	1
Star Polyps, Gold	Clavularia sp.	2-8	M	L	1
Star Polyps, Green	Clavularia viridis	2-8	M	L	1
Starlet	Solenastrea bournoni	2-10	L-M	M	3
Stick Polyps	Parazoanthus swiftii	2-8	M	L	1
Sun	Tubastrea faulkneri	1-3	M	L-M	6-7
Sun, Black	Tubastrea micrantha	1-3	M	L-M	6-7
Swollen Brain	Blastomussa wellsi	4-9	L-M	L-M	5
Toadstool, Common	Sarcophyton trocheliophorum	2-9	L-M	M-H	2
Toadstool, Fancy Yellow	Sarcophyton sp.	2-9	L-M	M-H	2
Toadstool, Gold Crowned	Sarcophyton alcyonidae	2-9	L-M	M-H	2
Toadstool, Green Leather	Sarchophtyon sp.	2-9	L-M	M-H	2
Toadstool, Pin Leather	Sarchophyton sp.	2-9	L-M	M-H	2
Toadstool, White Fairy	Sarchophyton sp.	2-9	L-M	M-H	2
Toadstool, Yellow	Sarchophyton sp.	2-9	L-M	M-H	2
Tongue	Herpolitha limax	4-8	L-M	M	5
Torch	Euphyllia glabrescens	4-9	L-M	H	5
Tree	Lithophyton arboreum	2-6	M	L-M	5
Trumpet	Caulastrea echinulata	3-8	M	L	4
Umbrella Mushroom	Discosoma neglecta	2-6	L	L	2
Velvet Finger, Green	Montipora digitata	8-10	M-H	L	8
Velvet Finger, Purple	Montipora digitata	8-10	M-H	L	8
Velvet Finger, Yellow	Montipora digitata	8-10	M-H	L	8
Velvet Stone	Montipora spongodes	8-10	M-H	L	8
Warty Soft Coral	Scleronepthya sp.	2-4	L-M	L	7
Waving Hand	Anthelia sp.	5-9	M-H	L	6
Whiskers	Duncanopsammia axifuga	2-9	L-M	H	3
Xenia Pom-Pom	Xenia sp.	5-9	M-H	L	6
Xenia, Silver Tip	Xenia sp.	5-9	M-H	L	6
Xenia, Thin Bar	Xenia sp.	5-9	M-H	L	6
Xenia, Tree	Xenia elongata	5-9	M-H	L	6

Common Name	Scientific Name	Lighting	Current	Aggressiveness	Difficulty
Xenia, Umbrella	Xenia umbellata	5-9	M-H	L	6
Yellow Encrusting Leather	Alcyonium fulvum	2-9	L-M	M-H	2
Yellow Polyps	Parazoanthus gracillis	2-8	M	L	1
Yellow Scroll	Turbinaria reniformis	4-9	M	L	8

NOTES:_____

_____

_____

_____

_____

_____

_____

_____

_____

_____

_____

_____

_____

_____

_____

_____

_____

_____

_____

_____

_____

_____

_____

_____

_____

_____

_____

_____

_____

_____

_____

_____

Chapter 14

Plumbing

Plumbing is a field from which many make a complete career. With the limited space here I will try to explain the very basics of water flow and the various types of fittings, and give you some tips on connections. It will be a very good idea to have at least one good plumbing book in your library to illustrate further and assist you in the basic principles of plumbing.

PIPE AND FITTINGS

Use only non-metallic materials. Avoid using A.B.S. black plastic pipe. It is suitable only for waste drains. PVC schedule 40 and 80, gray or white insert fittings, and clear flexible vinyl tubing are all acceptable and saltwater safe.

Plastic pipe and fittings are very inexpensive. When purchasing the items you need it will be wise to buy several of each, as well as extra pipe and fittings in different sizes and styles. This way you will be more likely to have the right fittings on hand when you need them. Most plumbers carry at least one, if not several, of the most common sizes. If you have to modify your original plan, it will be a snap if you already have several different styles of pipe and a variety of common fittings. The cost of standard plastic fittings and pipe is (for the most part) insignificant.

Common available sizes. 1/2", 3/4", 1", and 1-1/2" are the most common. 1-1/2" will probably be the largest size fitting you will use. 1/2" is usually for water supply. 3/4" or 1" are used for water returns to the tank. 1" and 1-1/2" are used for overflows from the tank. Note: 1-1/4" is an "uncommon" size.

Cutting plastic pipe. The saw of choice is called a "power miter box." If you have one, by all means use it. This type of saw will make extremely square, smooth cuts. If you don't have this equipment, a common hand saw will easily cut the pipe; just about any hand saw will do. A hacksaw may also be used, although the teeth of the blade are finer than needed for cutting plastic. Whichever tool you use, take your time and cut the material as "even" and "square" as possible.

CONNECTIONS

You will use three methods of making plumbing connections: gluing, threaded male-female, and an insert used with flexible vinyl tubing.

Gluing. Always use "primer cleaner" to prepare the pipe or fitting for the glue. Most leaks in glue fittings will be eliminated by using "primer." Dry fit all the pipe and connections before applying any primer or glue. Using a heavy pencil or magic marker, draw a reference mark from one piece to the other. When you are gluing the connection, this simple mark will allow you to align the pieces exactly as they were when you dry fit them.

213

When measuring lengths of plastic pipe, add approximately 1/2" to each side of the fitting where the connection is made. This is to compensate for the pipe fitting into the connection. After cutting the pipe, always "dry fit" all pieces. Then place your reference marks on all pipe/fitting connections.

Beginning at one end of the system, glue one connection at a time. Apply primer to *both* pieces being connected together. Then apply a liberal amount of glue to both pipe and fitting, and quickly join the two, giving the pipe a twisting motion with your hand to be sure the glue is distributed in the connection.

The PVC glue will weld the plastic pipe in about 30 seconds, so work deliberately and confidently. If you happen to make a mistake don't worry about it; simply cut, fit, and glue another one. As you will find out when you purchase the materials, their cost is virtually insignificant, so you can afford to discard some if you make a mistake.

Types of common fittings:

1. **Coupler.** Used to join pipe in a straight line. These are handy if you make a mistake: you can use this type of fitting to repair a small area.
2. **90° elbow.** Female both ends. Used to make a 90° turn in the pipe's direction.
3. **45° elbow.** Same as above, but makes a 45° change in the pipe's direction.
4. **90° and 45° "street" elbow.** Has male on one end and female on the other. The male end is used to join into another fitting without the need for a short connecting link of pipe.
5. **T fitting.** Used to connect in line with a branch.
6. **Cap.** Used to cap off, end a run of pipe.
7. **Union, male.** Glue one end, threaded male other end.
8. **Union, female.** Glue one end, threaded female other.
9. **Bushing.** Used to increase or decrease the size of a threaded fitting. Threaded female inner size, male outer size.
10. **Nipple.** Plastic pipe, threaded at both ends. Lengths: "close" (approximately 1-1/2"), then 2", 4", 6", 8", 10", and 12". Note: threaded fittings are easily disconnected for re-use in other applications. Glue fittings, on the other hand, are usually unusable once they are disassembled, and have to be thrown out. Threaded fittings are prepared by wrapping the male threads with a vinyl tape designated for use on drinking water connections. Wrap the threads so that two layers of tape are on the fitting. When the fitting is tightened the tape makes a waterproof seal.

Valves and shutoffs. Valves are usually used "in line" to control the flow of water passing through. They are normally either "ball" or "gate" valves. Gate valves are considered to control the flow of water better, where minute adjustments are needed. Because of their design, they are also more likely to become fouled with marine growth over extended periods of time. This fact by no means eliminates their usefulness, but it is important to remember.

Ball valves, on the other hand, completely wipe off their closing surface of marine growth when they are opened or closed. When performing maintenance it is advisable to open and close all valves completely several times, to dislodge marine growth on the inner surfaces.

A spigot or sillcock shutoff is commonly found on the fixture that supplies water to your garden hose. This type of fitting is used with common garden hose attachments when connecting a water supply to a purifying system near the tank.

FURNCO Connectors. These connections are also very useful because they are removable. They are found in couplers, 90°, 45°, T, Y, and reducing "one size pipe to another." FURNCO fittings are made from rubber and have hose clamps to make a waterproof seal. The hose clamp uses either a flathead screw driver or a 5/16" socket. (I prefer to keep a 5/16" socket driver handy for this purpose.) These can be used where you connect PVC pipe to the sump and may need to disconnect for service, etc. If you place a shutoff valve on the stationary "water" side of the FURNCO, you can then disconnect, service, and reconnect with ease. The only drawback of these fittings is that the smallest commonly available size is 1-1/2", although you may find them in smaller sizes. Insert fittings have the same removable qualities in smaller diameter applications. FURNCO fittings can be removed and reused, making them very practical. Larger sizes up to 8" are common, although expensive. These can be used in a protein skimmer application.

A tip on valves. Purchase valves with threaded connections. This way if your system is ever modified or changed you will salvage the valves and can use them elsewhere. Valves cost more than pipe or fittings, so connect them to the pipe with male unions.

Bulkhead fittings. These are for going through material such as glass, Plexiglas, wood, etc. They are a more specialized item, and are found at larger plumbing supply houses. These fittings command a premium price, as they are not that common. Sizes range commonly from 1/2" to 1-1/2". When installing a 1/2" bulkhead, you will have to drill a much larger hole to accommodate the "fitting" itself. One end has a female glue fitting, which goes inside the tank or underwater area. The other end has a threaded female inner and male outer, where a large nut is attached. There are two rubber washers: one goes on the inside of the wall the other goes on the outside. When the nut is tightened, this sandwiches the gasket, making a waterproof seal. I would recommend placing silicone sealant on the underwater side of the gasket. Then you will not have to over-tighten the nut; it should be tight, but not over-tight.

Bulkhead fittings are extremely useful as overflows from the tank, feeds from the sump to the pump or through the top of the sump box, etc. One reminder with bulkheads: always try to use one size larger, if the application is questionable. This way it will be easy to "downsize" with a bushing, rather than having too small an opening for your water flow.

Insert fittings. For me, these are absolutely *the* most useful fittings, because they are the most adaptable to "odd circumstances." The insert design allows you to use flexible vinyl tubing for the water pipe. The tubing slips onto the barbed insert. The fitting can usually be turned, to accommodate specific situations. By using flexible vinyl tubing you can eliminate extra connections, and the whole system will be more "flexible."

The size of the vinyl tubing going onto the insert fitting will dictate how you make a leakproof seal. Many times it is enough simply to slip the tubing onto the fitting all the way, covering the three barbs. If that does not make a waterproof seal, the next method would be to cinch cable ties tightly above the barbs. Two cable ties may also be used. For vinyl tubing under high pressure, a stainless steel hose clamp will make a reliable connection. Personally I have rarely used hose clamps. I have found them necessary only in the water supply area, where there is substantial water pressure.

When you find a good supplier of these and other plumbing fittings, you will be amazed at the variety of connections available. I usually can't resist purchasing extra fittings that might come in handy at some point.

Vinyl tubing, although very convenient, is expensive. As with most items, the larger sizes cost substantially more than the smaller ones. Always buy a little more than you think you need. The largest practical size of flexible vinyl is 1" diameter, which costs around $1 a foot. Anything over 1" costs $4 or so. If you need sizes larger than 1", use PVC instead of vinyl. 1-1/2" PVC pipe and fittings are very affordable, and can handle considerable water flow.

BASIC IDEAS ON PLUMBING

Besides not having leaks, the next most important consideration is to have a neat job with the fewest fittings possible. For the novice it is easy to add fittings or change pipe sizes. A more thoughtful, planned approach will give you a very simple, neat, streamlined job. This is what you want. Often the novice, not knowing what types of fittings are available, will end up with a "bird's nest" of connections and pipe. Besides being unsightly, this kind of system is more likely to leak somewhere; more importantly, it will have reduced water flow.

Again my recommendation is to get a basic plumbing book. Study the available fittings. Then go to the supply house and familiarize yourself with what they have in stock. Draw a plan of what you need. Buy extra fittings and pipe. Once you actually begin connecting, you may find that you need different fittings, or even a completely different approach, from what you originally planned. This is somewhat typical for the beginner. When we undertake this kind of work, we can begin to respect professionals and understand why they charge so much.

Basically there is a plastic plumbing fitting made to fit, adapt to, and function with almost any water flow need. The main tip is to find a good supply house.

Use the Yellow Pages. Call the larger supply houses and ask what size PVC insert fittings they carry. Ask if they have bulkhead fittings, and what sizes. If they carry these items, that is the supply house for you. If they don't carry them, ask if they know who does.

WATER FLOW AND VENTING

Controlling and directing water can at times be frustrating, but a good plumbing job will give you tremendous satisfaction once it is operating properly and without any leaks.

One important area is the overflow from the tank. Most tanks that do not use a self-starting box (which I never cared for) will have to be drilled; bulkhead fittings will be installed through the upper back wall of the tank, and a 90° "street elbow" will be placed inside the tank at a slight angle, to catch the overflowing water. This 90° fitting is very useful, as it can be turned to raise or lower the water level in the tank. A protective barrier is made with plastic "Gutter Guard," cable-tied in place, to prevent creatures going into the "overflow." On the back of the fitting, use a 90° male threaded X insert fitting. Run flexible vinyl to the "dirty" side of the sump, where the water will collect and be available to the skimmer pump.

This is also an area where you want to have a valve to control water flow, or completely shut off water flow and disconnect the sump.

For a 55-gallon tank I have used two 1" bulkhead fittings and a 500 GPH pump. This has been adequate, so I would assume it is safe to say that one 1" bulkhead fitting could easily process 250-275 GPH.

On my 200-gallon tank I have four 1-1/2" PVC bulkheads. Four are really not needed; I have shut one off. The remaining three 1-1/2" PVC bulkheads will handle 1200 GPH, which is 400 GPH each. It looks as if one 1-1/2" PVC will handle 400 GPH in an overflow situation.

An important reminder when considering draining water is that the plumbing will need a vent. This allows air to escape from the plumbing, ensuring a smooth water flow. In an unvented system, the water flow will be restricted by air in the pipe, and there will be a gurgling sound. All homes have a vent pipe going through the roof. If the plumbing system were not vented, our sinks, toilets, and tubs would not drain properly. This vent pipe is very important, and should be incorporated in your reef tank system. Water will drain without a vent, but the flow will be significantly less than in a vented system.

Here is an example for a 55-gallon tank with two 1" bulkhead fittings connected with insert fittings to 1" flexible vinyl. Connect the two overflows with a T pointed upward. Add enough tubing so it is a few inches above the water line of the tank. *This is the vent*. Cut in another T in line, pointed downward. Add a section of tubing going to the sump box and install a shutoff/control valve before the sump. The vent tube may gurgle because it pulls in air. You can then install a vent cap to minimize this sound. This fitting can also be found at a good supply house. It is called a "cap vent," or a "no-vent."

With a little trial and error experimenting, you will have your system up and running. After all the connecting and troubleshooting is done, it will provide years of trouble-free service. This is well worth the initial effort it takes.

On the next few pages are illustrations of useful fittings.

Schedule 80 PVC Pipe Fittings

FIPT	-	Female Iron Pipe Thread
MIPT	-	Male Iron Pipe Thread
SP	-	Spigot

REDUCER BUSHING
Flush Style
(SP x MIPT)

FLANGE
Solid Style
(FIPT)

UNION* O-RING TYPE
(FIPT x FIPT)

FLANGE
Blind

SPECIAL FITTINGS

30°ELL (Slip x Slip)

REDUCER BUSHING
Flush Style
(MIPT x FIPT)

(Slip)

WYE (Slip x Slip x Slip)

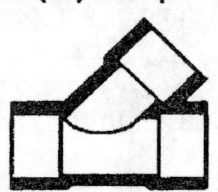

45° ELL
(FIPT x FIPT)

FLANGE Loose Ring
(Spigot)

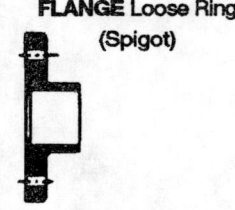

REDUCER WYE (Slip x Slip x Slip)

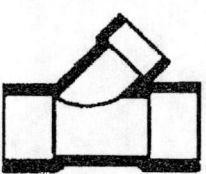

FLANGE
Solid Style
(Slip)

UNION* O-RING TYPE
(Slip x Slip)

VENT CAP

FEMALE REDUCING ADAPTER
(FIPT x Slip)

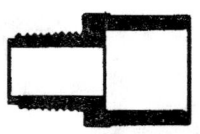

MALE ADAPTER
(MIPT x Slip)

MALE REDUCING ADAPTER
(MIPT x Slip)

REDUCER BUSHING
(SP x Slip)

REDUCER BUSHING
(SP x FIPT)

CROSS
(Slip)

REDUCING CROSS
(Slip)

COUPLING
(Slip)

THREADED COUPLING
(FIPT x FIPT)

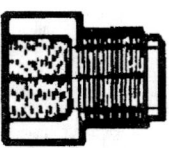

RISER EXTENDER
(FIPT x MIPT)

CAP (Slip)

CAP
(FIPT)

PLUG
(SP)

PLUG
(MIPT)

ADAPTER
(Slip to Insert)

NESTED COUPLING
(Slip)

Schedule 40 PVC Pipe Fittings
Schedule 80 PVC Pipe Fittings

TEE
(Slip x Slip x Slip)

REDUCING TEE
(Slip x Slip x Slip)

90° STREET ELL
(SP x Slip)

BULLHEAD TEE
(Slip x Slip x Slip)

TEE
(Slip x Slip x FIPT)

TEE
(Slip x Slip x FIPT)

90° STREET ELL
(MIPT x Slip)

90° STREET ELL
(SP x FIPT)

90° STREET ELL
(MIPT x FIPT)

90° SIDE OUTLET ELL
(Slip x Slip x FIPT)

45° ELL
(Slip x Slip)

TEE (FIPT x FIPT x FIPT)

90° ELL
(Slip x Slip)

90° REDUCING ELL
(Slip x Slip)

90° ELL
(Slip x FIPT)

90° REDUCING ELL
(Slip x FIPT)

90° ELL
(FIPT x FIPT)

INSERT FITTINGS
PVC & NYLON

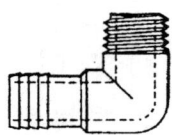

COMBINATION 90° ELBOW

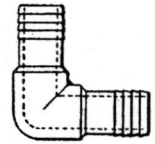

FITTING INSERT ELBOW

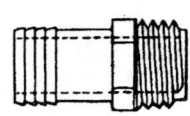

INSERT MALE ADAPTER

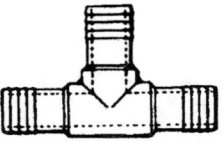

INSER T TEE

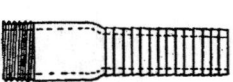

EXTRA LONG ADAPTER

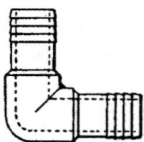

FITTING ELBOW

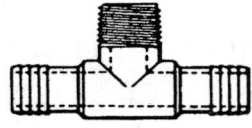

COMBINATION TEE

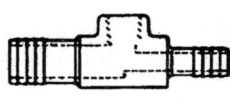

COMBINATION AND REDUCING TEE

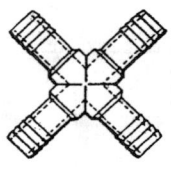

INSERT CROSS

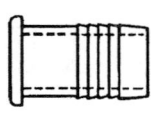

INSERT PLUG

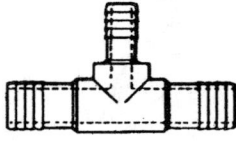

INSERT REDUCING TEE
INS X INS X RED

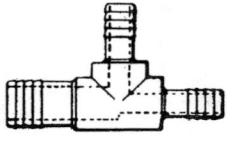

INSERT REDUCING TEE
INS X RED INS X RED INS

INSERT FITTINGS
PVC & NYLON

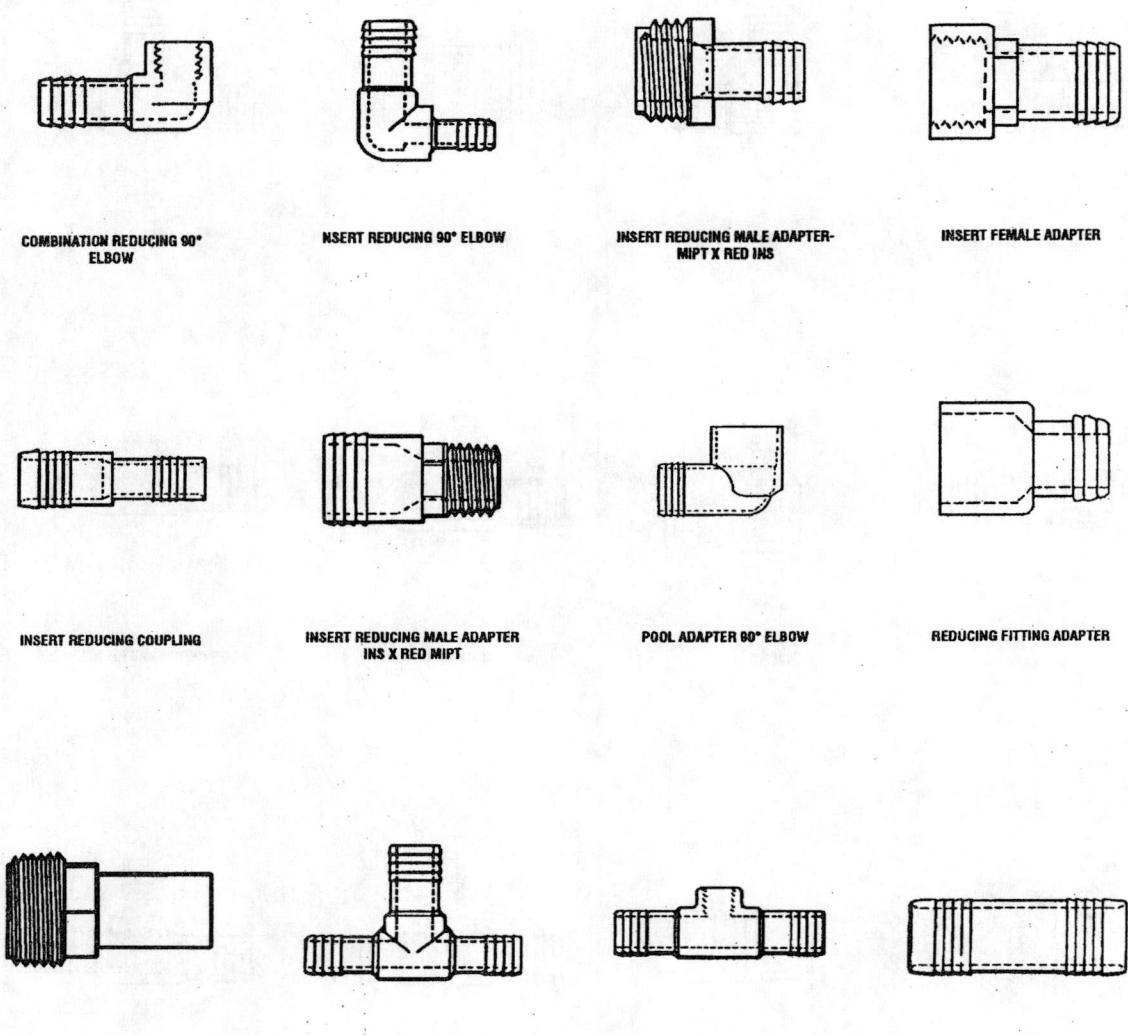

COMBINATION REDUCING 90°
ELBOW

NSERT REDUCING 90° ELBOW

INSERT REDUCING MALE ADAPTER-
MIPT X RED INS

INSERT FEMALE ADAPTER

INSERT REDUCING COUPLING

INSERT REDUCING MALE ADAPTER
INS X RED MIPT

POOL ADAPTER 90° ELBOW

REDUCING FITTING ADAPTER

SWIMMING POOL ADAPTER

BULLHEAD TEE

COMBINATION AND REDUCING TEE

NSERT COUPLING

Chapter 15

Questions & Answers

Adding chemicals

I add CaCl when my Ca++ is low.
I think calcium chloride is a bad idea. It is best not to try and "maintain" such high readings of Ca. The CaCl unbalances a system, possibly giving you an inaccurate Ca reading. Your reading/additives sound "picture perfect", except the calcium chloride and buffering of it. Try it without CaCl and cut back on the Lugols and see what happens. It's obvious we can't rely on "readings" all of the time. I'm sure you mix your Kalkwasser to "supersaturated levels." In my experience, adding plenty of kalkwasser only, combined with regular water changes using a high quality salt, will give excellent Coraline growth.

My other tank is a 30-gallon and I am having a difficult time elevating the pH up to 8.2 - 8.3. It is about 7.9 to 8.1. I have tried Seachem marine buffer without success.
First, use a good salt mix like Coralife or Instant Ocean along with RO or DI water. Mix and test the batch; it should be 8.2. Next, add Kalkwasser regularly for make-up water in order to elevate it. Then the Seachem buffer will maintain that level.

What is the most commonly used additive?
The additive I use most regularly is Kalkwasser, also known as calcium hydroxide. This is mixed and added for evaporation (makeup water), usually on a weekly basis. The only other two products are iodine and strontium, that are added biweekly in between water changes. Use a high quality salt mix, such as Coralife or Instant Ocean mixed with purified tap water. This mixture will replace the needed complex trace elements. Water changes performed on a regular basis, at two, three, or four-week intervals are important. The more frequent the water changes and maintenance schedule (vacuuming the live rock), the more optimum the conditions will be for the rock and live stock. Some reef keepers try to bypass water changes by adding a wide range of trace elements. I doubt if positive results can be reached with any certainty.

You said my red slime algae is most likely caused by the new Coral Vital I started to use. I am stopping addition of this today to see what happens.
Don't get me wrong It's a good product, but for some it can cause problems. It's a well-known fact that this product can produce algae. Myself I did not have any algae related problems but discontinued because I could not justify the cost.

As I mentioned before all the additives I am currently using are (Kent Iodine Strontium/Molybdenum - Coral-Vite & Seachem Reef Calcium). You said using Kalkwasser is the best way to go for maintaining calcium.
Yes, definitely.

I believe it is a polygluconate with some strontium and magnesium? Am I going to cause problems this way? I was going to start using the new 2-part calcium like Kent-

TectraCB or C-Balance but they also raise Alkalinity, which my Superbuffer should already be maintaining.

C balance is good and if you use it you won't need the buffer. However it is expensive over the long run. Kalkwasser is much more economical especially if you use a food grade Kalkwasser i.e. pickling lime $1.40lb

Algae

I have a brown layer of algae that is covering some of my Coraline algae. It's no thicker, but it is expanding. How can I control it?

It sounds like Diatom algae, the remnants of a new tank cycle. It is a possibility that you are feeding too much. Until it passes, control it with the usual methods such as manual removal with a bottlebrush. Hermits dislodge it and some critters will eat it. When did you last replace your light bulbs? Sometimes this can be an indication of failing lamps. This type of algae is the most common and "should" go away naturally if all other components are working such as the skimmer, the tap water, not overfeeding, and having herbivorous livestock.

Is it just a different kind of Coraline?

No, Coraline is a hard calcareous and usually either pink or purple.

I have a new problem. I have some hair algae that I assume has occurred from increase in light. I have bought seven hermit crabs and two turbo snails. One died in a week. I can't seem to keep snails alive very long.

Some snails are not long-lived and are sensitive to *any* cycling ammonia/nitrite. Some, believe it or not, are poisoned by the algae. One out of two isn't that bad. If it were 25 out of 50, then you may have a problem.

I am thinking of purchasing more snails, —45 for $45 deal. Is this a good idea?

Yes, that's a good idea. Snails will be good for the tank and will reproduce easily once they become acclimated.

Should algae settle down when it gets adjusted to the new light?

Are you using RO or DI water? You should. Also, be sure to dose Kalkwasser regularly. There are two things to keep in mind:
1. Be sure you dose Kalkwasser for all evaporation water, and
2. Use RO or DI water and your algae will disappear.

Do I need to purchase phosphate remover?

No.

Problem Algae

When was the last time you replaced your light bulbs? That sometimes can contribute to algae (shifted spectrum) Also, how old is the Spectrapure inner resin? You seem to have everything in order but do not mention the age of the above. Also, I would recommend using Kalkwasser only...for make up water it seems strange to me that the snails are dying. In my experience some snails can be fairly delicate however over a reasonably short period of time 1-year + they should begin to reproduce in your tank. Then you end up with a much hardier snail. Typically the asteras reproduce fairly easily, at least mine do.

I have been changing water one week then the next. Its a 30 gal with 30 lbs. live rock 2 inches of crushed coral substrate bak pak filter skimmer and 110 watt of light. I have huge bushes of hair algae and my nitrates are 70 or so. I have been considering a CPR wet dry filter would this help my problem or make it worse? Would I need a sump box? Please help I'm real frustrated...

The most common causes for algae are
- Using non purified tap water. Are you using RO or DI water? You should.
- Old light bulbs. I remember you had just installed a new light setup, are the lamps new?
- Overfeeding I would only feed every 3 days or so
- Inadequate skimming - What kind of skimmer are you using? A backpack is probably good for a 30.

How old is the resin in the RO/DI? You know that gets expended, maybe it has to be replaced. It sounds like the algae is getting a food source from somewhere, I have to think it's the source water. If you have high nitrates, you probably have some kind of biological media in a filter? That will produce nitrate. Usually the amount of liverock you have will easily de-nitrify the nitrate 1 lb. to 1.75 lb. per gal does it, you say you have 110 watts from what I remember you purchased a much more powerful setup than that.

Look into the source water. A wet dry with biological media will produce nitrate so I would definitely not use it.

My skimmer is the backpack. I have the blue biomaterial in the backpack and wash the sponge on the front out three times a week. Do I need to remove all of the biological material at once?

Remove it gradually, I bet that is where the nitrate is coming from. Remove it and then test the nitrate in a week or so. I bet you have zero nitrates.

I plan to test Nitrate again tonight the tank looks better overall tonight than previously. I did manage to get rid of some algae.

Ok it will probably take about a week for you to see noticeable drop in nitrate, but you should definitely see much lower numbers in that time span. You also *may* see an increase of ammonia (don't worry about it) as the bacteria relocate to your rock & sand. Again, without knowing your tank, I would suspect the water, silicates usually. Maybe its time for a re-doing the internals of your water purification system?

History: 62 gal. Plexiglas that has been up and running for a year and a half. Conditions have been real good until about a month or so ago. Brownish/clouded water has been plaguing it. I have a Fluval 303-canister filter and a CPR Backpack protein skimmer, 2 powerheads and a good heater. I do 30% water changes every month along with changing the carbon in the Fluval. The tank used to stay crystal clear but not any more! So far I have done extra water changes, bought two new bulbs (daylight and actinic) because the daylight was a year and a half old and the actinic 9 mos. old. There has not been much in the way of algae on the surfaces (no more than usual towards the end of the cycle) but there have been a lot of tiny bubbles in the water and many have been accumulating on the Plexiglas. I do NOT have an air stone and the protein skimmer does not seem to be putting many bubbles into the water. When I took a water sample out to show the local fish store, it was brownish/cloudy at first but then cleared up with just "dark brown cob web looking things floating around". All my water tests (pH, kh, nitrate, nitrite, and ammonia) have been great forever. I tried covering the

tank with blankets for a three day period to keep all light out in the hopes of killing a strange algae strain, but it didn't do much. My last water change was 50% about a week ago. I'm almost ready to take my fish into a store and drain my tank and start all over.

Any suggestions or question that I may answer would be greatly appreciated. --

This is a stumper

Do you use RO or DI water? If so when was the last time you replaced the resin? The resin has a certain lifespan depending on the impurities of your water. I would look into that. Your maintenance sounds very good so It leads me to believe the source water is suspect. Also, canister filters are not generally used on modern reef tanks. I would seriously consider getting rid of it or if you must, only use it for a pump and remove the internal media. The internal media becomes a nitrate factory this is something you *don't* want or need. Do you have a sump? Or an area where you could put a fairly large amount of carbon where the water doesn't have to flow *through* but around. Using sizeable amounts of carbon this way will generally strip most any questionable material from the tank. I would go to a paint store and ask for nylon pain strainer bags about .50 ea. And use them to holds the carbon. In a 60 gallon tank I would use aprox 3 to 4 oz of carbon at a time (in the bag) for about 3 to 4 days then replace and continue for 2 or 3 applications. If you see an improvement, continue if for some strange reason your corals react badly... discontinue use. They shouldn't but one never knows. Also, the small bubbles may be caused by not having enough skimming. It could be small particulate matter coming from the Fluval. I know a backpack is rated for a 60 gallon but that's probably pushing it to its limits. You may want to thoroughly clean the skimmer and possibly consider upgrading to a larger model.

I have been experiencing an algae bloom of sorts although all parameters test well. I have also just purchased a doser and intend to dose Kalkwasser. My Ca level is a bit low - in the 360-370 PPM range - but consistently there. Also, this is a relatively new setup that has cycled through and has minimal livestock at the moment.

I think the 360 range isn't bad... especially if you don't have a high calcium demand. Kalkwasser is very good to add, and a low cost alternative is Pickling lime used for canning. Ask for it in your local food stores or you can order it directly. It is food grade calcium hydroxide same thing as reef Kalkwasser the difference is the lime is $1.49 per lb. a case of aprox 12 lbs. will cost around 24 shipping included.

I have about 60lbs of Fiji Rock, a number of Turbos, some Red-legged crabs, a few Scooter Blennies, a Condylactis that we discovered hidden in a rock but is doing quite well. Initially I had some coral gravel as a substrate, but discovered it was leaching P04 in a serious way and removed it all. At the moment the bottom is bare. I had fought with lowering the P04 for a month or so and it is now down below 0.1 PPM. As I mentioned, all other parameters seem in good shape.

Are you using RO or DI water? That is usually a source of phosphate

I went through an algae bloom earlier on, which led to the discovery of the P04 leaching, but seemed to get that under control until some minor bubble algae began, and then green filamentous algae which grows literally, like a weed.

It sounds like the tap water to me

As a result, and because I felt overall the tank was doing well enough, I added a 3"
Yellow Tang in the hope it might consume some of the algae. After reading in your
book about canisters and plastic media in trickles I am concerned that may be more of
the source than anything else.

Possible, but again I'm more inclined to think of the source water. Its best to of course limit
all potential algae causes, as the problem usually becomes worse.

Bristle Worms

How much of a problem are Bristle Worms? How much devastation can they cause?

Their destruction is subtle for the most part. They aren't that bad, but it is odd... not all
creatures of the same species have the exact same habits. Generally, Bristle Worms are
considered to be destructive, especially when they become large. I'm sure they eat some
Polyps, Sea Mat, and Gorgonian, but you will find in the long run, some life forms disappear
and others take their place.

The best advice I can give is to remove what is obvious in shipping and to wash the rock.
Watch the tank as to what you have and what seems to be missing. If you begin to see life
mysteriously disappear, be sure to take corrective measures. For Bristle Worms, examine the
tank at night with a light to see them, and remove what you can by various methods. You can
use traps nylon stocking with bait, or employ a more drastic measure by removing the rock
cover and waiting until they fall out.

**I will be adding a few more LBS. of live rock this weekend and was hoping you could
tell me of any way to eliminate those unwanted guests "BRISTLE WORMS" before I
add the rock to my display tank. I have heard of a few of ways to do this. One way of
course is the trusty old Arrow Crab (I have already in tank), but I am hoping to resolve
this before the live rock goes into my display tank. Two other methods I have briefly
heard about are:**

1) Dip the live rock in fresh DI/RO water and this will force them out; or

**2) Dip the rock in some carbonated water, which the carbon dioxide gas will force them
out. Don't know of anybody that has tried these methods yet?**

**One concern is if these methods will work what problems might they cause if the live
rock is already "CURED". I guess it could kill coraline algae's or anything else, which
is beneficial for the rock?**

Ok those are bristle worms and a natural occurrence in live rock. They used to be considered
bad for the tank as they were thought to eat coral. The new thinking is that they are good and
serve a purpose stirring the sand and processing detritus. I'm fairly sure these are what you
have. They are a pinkish flesh color with whitish fury looking legs those are bristle worms,
they can get large! I have personally seen them 12 inches in length needless to say I got rid of
it. Smaller ones do a good service to the tank. Other similar looking worms but different
colors deep solid red are fireworms and will give you a very bad sting. These are more
unusual to have and I would get rid of them if I had one.

The opinion of bristle worms is changing... especially if you have sand. They are detrivores
and do a very good job churning the sand. A few years ago, they were thought to eat corals
etc. and it's a possibility that they might, but if you use sand it is considered good to have
bristle worms. (Also see removing crabs, bristleworms & mantis shrimp from live rock)

Do they reproduce in the tank?
Yes the reproduce very easily... one other suggestion is to look at the tank after the lights have been off for about 2 hours. Use a flashlight and try not to make vibrations on the floor when you walk. You should see creatures that you do not see during the day

Covering the tank

Do you use a cover for your tank?
I have used glass, Plexiglas, and no cover. I prefer no cover. I am of the opinion that cover glass cuts light output in the usable spectrum by at least 10%. I'm sure, but it probably cuts light more with the inevitable salt film that collects on the glass.

Wouldn't this help lower my evaporation rate?
Evaporation is good! It gives you an opportunity to add Kalkwasser to build calcium and raise pH. It contributes to substantial cooling in the summer months. In fact, you can increase your calcium levels with forced evaporation. Adding fans in the hood or blowing on the sump will require more top off water with Kalkwasser.

For a tank cover, would thin acrylic be better than glass?
Acrylic always ends up sagging. Flip it over, and it sags again. Brace it, and it will sag less, but inevitably it will sag again. Acrylic clouds over time. The main benefit is that a cover will protect your bulbs. They need to be cleaned and wiped periodically—approximately every two weeks. I find that there is no cover that works best.

Cycling

I have another tank that I have been cycling with live rock for two weeks. It's a 30-gallon with a plenum, 1inch of crushed coral, 1 inch of sand, and 1inch of live sand. I have 25 pounds of live rock. My question involves my observation on one side, where the crushed coral has a brownish-green substance growing that appears similar to algae. What is it is? Is it normal?
Yes, it is normal, although it's not occurring the way it is supposed to happen. I wouldn't be surprised if there were a small algae outbreak. It sounds like typical cyano bacteria caused by cycling.

I have not turned on the lights.
Well, it's been two weeks so I would think that it's probably about time.

Nitrate levels and cycling

My tank has been setup about a week and the nitrite level should start to drop, shouldn't it? Is something causing it to slow its cycle?
No, nothing is slowing it down (other than the lack of nitrobacter) which will occur naturally. Your first cycle is ammonia...then nitrite...and nitrate last. Usually ammonia takes the longest time. Nitrite takes less time about 1/3 less time than the ammonia. This is common and you just allow it to happen! Don't add any more livestock until you obtain zero ammonia and nitrite readings.

We are cycling for the first time. Do we need to get zero ammonia, nitrite and nitrate reading before adding creatures?
You need to add *all* the live rock and then obtain a zero ammonia and zero nitrite reading. The amount of die-off on the rock will determine the length of the cycle. Usually, it begins with a low ammonia reading; then it elevates to an extremely high reading; and then to zero.

The nitrite begins again from zero to extremely high and then to zero. You will get a faint nitrate reading that indicates a complete cycle. That's when you can begin to add your livestock. Providing you have enough live rock and/or sand (approximately 1.5 pounds per gallon) you should experience near complete denitrification on a regular basis. Normally, low nitrates are not a problem to maintain in a reef tank.

Cycling

My ammonia is 0 and I am not showing any nitrate either, but I don't think the tank is cycled yet.

Most likely you will experience a substantial cycle happening with lots of ammonia, followed by nitrite. Don't worry about it! Just let it happen! Usually it will take from two to eight weeks. Don't add any livestock until you obtain nitrate and the tank is completely cycled!

Damaged Corals

I have a question about my Colt coral. It dislodged from the rocks and wound up in the bottom of the powerhead!

I do not recommend powerheads in the tank just for this reason, among others.

Part of the ends were torn. Is there anything that I can do, or is it a wait and see game?

I recommend a wait and see strategy many times trying to help out a damaged animal causes more harm than good when it's trying to adapt on it own. Make sure the base of the coral is either attached with a "light" (not too tight) rubber band, or firmly wedged between the rocks where it can begin to feel secure and attempt to re-attach to base rock. The colt is a very hardy and beautiful species. I venture a guess that it will be OK.

I have a green star polyp that is about two weeks old. It has not come out since my last water change, about one week ago. Do you think it's a problem?

When you did the water change did you:

- Match the salinity?
- pH? Temp?
- Did you use a quality salt? (Such as Instant Ocean or Coralife?)
- Did you change anything else?
- If you answered yes to all but the last question, your polyps should be fine.

How long has it been since the last water change? How much did you change? It sounds like you probably changed at least 30% or more and that's why they are reacting as they are. Star polyps are hardy but they are giving you experience as to the sensitivity of corals. I recommend changing 12% every two weeks. That's a good maintenance schedule. If you don't follow that schedule, at least try to be consistent with smaller amounts. Water changes, are the best maintenance you can perform and help eliminate guesswork about adding trace elements, etc. I think your corals will be fine—just rethink your maintenance plan.

My leather coral didn't extend today during the light cycle. It's the first time its polyps haven't appeared. Should I be concerned?

This is typical. They go through a period of "sloughing" from time to time. I have two Sarcophyton—one at each end of the tank and it seems that one is always closed. One day one closes, the next the other. I believe this is a kind of regenerative process. That's a nice "easy to keep" animal.

I am able to grow Coraline for awhile… then it turns white.

I have only seen Coraline turn completely white when exposed to air. Particularly when doing a water change and having the rock exposed to air for a period of time.

Down Draft Skimmers

I was told that the downdraft skimmers could starve some soft corals. Was this bad information?

That all depends upon with whom you talk, what group you want to subscribe to, and what type of maintenance schedule is involved. One of the most significant agreed upon points is that there are as many methods of keeping a reef as there are people doing it. Personally, I have a large downdraft and almost all soft corals with no ill effects. A monthly water change of approximately 15% with a high quality salt along with regular calcium, strontium, and iodine additions, high turnover rates of water in the tank, and proper lighting does the trick for me.

What are you referring to when you say "downdraft"?

I consider a downdraft skimmer one that is fed at the top. Water flows downward, and the output (for figurative reasons) is at the bottom. There are three kinds of skimmers; a counter current that uses small pump and airstones; a Venturi that uses larger pump, and a Venturi valve restrictor with a small air intake. The downdraft has a TALL—approximately 5 foot x 2-inch "tower" filled with bioballs. The water is pumped into the top of the column under relatively high pressure through a small 5/16 inch or 3/8 inch piece of plumbing that fits like a tapered fire hose nozzle. The top of the 2 inch x 5 foot tower has a hole about 3/8 inch that allows air to be "downdrafted" into the bioball column. The turbulated, air induced foamed water then crashes into a small rectangular box about 8 x 8 x 12 inches. The foam drifts over to a LARGE, approximately 8 inch acrylic reaction foam collection accumulation riser, much like a regular protein skimmer. Bubbles burst, foam rises and overflows into a collection area like a regular skimmer. This works very well, as there is virtually no restriction to a high flow rate. Mine processes 1200 gph for the skimmer and another main pump (1200 gph) for the main.

Do you suggest that ETS skimmers kill plankton?

Because a downdraft skimmer is more efficient than conventional skimmers my answer is yes, depending if you have a refugia or not. If the refugia is sufficiently separated by reduced water flow in a separate area, this will not be a significant issue.

Eggcrate

What is supporting the bottom plate of the eggcrate that is raised off the bottom of the tank? Is it PVC piping? If so, how big is it in diameter?

Yes, PVC pipe. Either 1 inch or 1-1/2 inch.

Or is it small strips of eggcrate? Your description does not provide any detail. I like the idea of doing this, however I would like to have a more specific detail.

Yes, it works very well. See the third paragraph on page 84, "The Function and Layout of Eggcrate." Also, see pages 86 and 87, "Positioning and Fastening Eggcrate." The height/diameter of PVC pipe you use will be determined by the size of your tank. I would say one would customarily use a minimum of 1 inch to 1-1/2 inch pipe. Cut the front of the PVC at a 45 degree angle in order to visually minimize its presence from the front of the tank. Have another look, to get a better understanding.

How high should the top of the back support of the eggcrate be? How close to the top of the tank should it be? Does it matter?

The important consideration is to have eggcrate high enough to be useful (displaying the rock) having good water flow beneath the material so the spraybar can move the water in a circular motion and at enough of an angle so the rock naturally stays supported (not too steep of an angle). Usually this will be about 4 inches below the top of the tank and about 1-1/2 inches to 2 inches below the waterline. Try to follow exactly how it is explained in the book. It will be helpful to acquire a general idea by "laying it out" on a floor. By using either tape or light pencil marks, you can get a picture of the angle and lengths of pieces. Most vinyl tile floors have 12 inch squares to guide you for straight lines and increments in feet to help you with "dry fitting" the material.

The other questionable area is where you fasten the back to the bottom. Here you want to have the back sloped enough so the rock will stay in place with approximately a 70 to 75 degree angle. This leaves you with bottom pieces that appear *very* small. Do not be concerned, because that's normal. The rock "overhangs" the front of the material so it will be larger than it appears. Pay close attention to allowing enough room for future cleaning access in this front area of the tank. You will want *a minimum* of 2 inches from where the rock overhangs. There will be a temptation to stretch this, but don't. At your first and subsequent water changes, you will be very glad you left this space. Not leaving enough space will force you to fight with it and you will regret it. Be sure to remove all plastic clippings, which is another annoyance. I am pleased to see that you intend to utilize eggcrate. I think that once you have incorporated it, you will be pleased too! It's a great system.

I am concerned about my hermit crabs and snails falling off the eggcrate structure and not being able to climb up back on.

As far as creatures "walking out," that seems very logical, but I've not experienced it.

What exactly is the "eggcrate" material?

Eggcrate is a plastic grid like material sold in 2 x 4 foot sheets. White is very common. Black is more difficult to locate. This material is also known as lighting diffuser used in light covers in suspended ceilings.

Where do I purchase it?

White can be found at any home improvement center. Black is found only at a specialized plastic supplier. You can get it directly from Modern Plastics 1-800-243-9696 and ask for Raul Flores. I was there about 6 months ago and asked if he would be willing to ship eggcrate to my readers and he said he would be happy to. So give him a call. I think he gets about $8 for a 2x4 ft piece not including shipping. I'm glad to hear your going to use my eggcrate method I'm sure you will be happy with the results. Feel free to contact me if needed. Also, if your getting a order from Modern and plan to do any fabrication with Plexiglas I would suggest to also order a few tubes or containers of Weldon Plexiglas glue. It's only around $2 ea. and lasts a long time. Get one fast set and one slow set if you get the fast set tell them to include an applicator .99. You may also ask for a few 3/8 or 1/3in Plexiglas dowels they can come in handy to make small shelves in the eggcrate structure again they are only about a dollar for a 36 in piece.

Ethics

I am a marine biologist who would love to start a tropical reef tank, but do not want to buy reef animals who have been captured in the wild. I am sure you realize that for

every animal that 'makes it', 20 have perished. Also the methods that are used to capture these animals can be devastating to reef ecology.

I agree with the moral and ethical values of reef conservation. It's very interesting to observe that most hobbyists share this same belief. One of the main facts is that some creatures do extremely well in captivity, others do not. My recommendation is that by getting a better understanding of the needs of the less demanding creatures further enhances the hobbyists knowledge of husbandry n general, and therefor a good thing. A small example is the coral XENIX, a few years ago this creature was so delicate it could barely be shipped. Through the dedication of some hobbyists this coral today is easily tank raised, propagated and exchanged amongst hobbyists. Some say it "grows like a weed". This coral has become a tank-raised species something unheard of a few years ago.

Do you know of anyone that sells tropical fish in captivity?

You must mean captive bred. Yes, I'm all for captive raised species. In fact several companies are doing just that. Unless the hobbyist is very wealthy, deaths of fragile creatures put a damper on keeping a reef tank for most people, who wants to keep removing dead creatures from the tank? Not very rewarding. What does make the hobby interesting is... exchanging information amongst those who are experienced thereby minimizing costly mistakes. With the advent of the Internet, the hobby has, I believe, become as informed and conscience of the responsibility that goes along with keeping a reef aquarium. Hobbyists today are making their own liverock and propagating corals have you seen the GARF website? This is a favorite site of hobbyists http://www.cyberhighway.net/~algae/

Aquarius's should promote the use of these rather than animals from the wild. What do you think? Have we done enough damage?

I think more damage to the wild reef has been done in the past by inexperience and greed. My impression of the state of the hobby today is that most end users, hobbyists, are more informed than ever, and continue seeking out knowledge to expand their husbandry skills while also being aware of unethical practices by greedy suppliers.

Filtration Methods

My question is should I keep the biological media in the wet/dry filter during the break period for the live rock? Should I gradually remove the bioballs? Or do it when I add the live rock? Or remove the bioballs from the start? It seems to me that there would be some benefit to using the available bacteria that is well established in the wet/dry filter.

You don't say if this is an active tank, i.e.: existing fish, existing water, that you are considering reusing. If you have any fish, they should be removed when you add the live rock and complete the cycling process. At that point, I question the suitability or history of the water. Has it ever been treated with medication? Has it had problems with algae? High nitrate? My thought is to begin with known parameters. Use RO/DI water with a high quality salt mix. Remove the bioballs, as well as any existing sand, rock, decorations and (existing live rock). Add *all* the live rock, perform the complete cycle, add inverts (all or most), and finally add fish, (all or most). It is not advantageous to cut a corner here or there. It's best to start with a "known" and build from there. Finally, I don't see any real benefit from using the bioballs.

I have seen several references to the "Berlin Method." By inference, I believe this to be simply live sand/live rock with a protein skimmer. Is this true?

Yes. That is what I would call it, and basically it is known as that. Although, if investigate, I'm sure you will find information to the contrary. Below is my interpretation of the "Berlin."

The "Berlin" uses approximately 1.5 to 1.75 pounds per gallon of live rock and minimum sand covering for a substrate (just for appearance to cover the bare bottom). Strong skimming equals turning the volume of water a *minimum* of 6 times per hour—more would be better with 10 times per hour being about *maximum*. A prefilter is usually located in the overflow or in the sump. This is to minimize particulate matter either through the skimmer or the tank. It is basically a mechanical filter that is not allowed to turn biological. Proper lighting wattage and spectrum are used for the photosynthetic livestock to consume nitrate in the process of photosynthesis. This will handle the bioload of an "average" amount of livestock, i.e., not overstocked. The end results using this system are very low or zero nitrates. This is the preferred system algae and denitrification problems are minimal.

I was "guided" by a local fish store, which is actually an hour and a half from where I live, and purchased an Eheim Professional canister. I certainly cannot afford to shelve it and purchase an entirely different setup but wonder what, if anything might be suitable to use in it simply for mechanical filtration/circulation.
You could use it as the main pump. But I would not have *any* media inside as this will end up at some point producing nitrate as well as being difficult to maintain. I know Eheims are top of the line but in my opinion not for a reef (although they are good pumps). If you do use a mechanical prefilter and don't have a sump you could fashion some porous sponge near the intake of the pump and change that. Of course its not the ideal set up... best to have a sump box, or an old trickle filter without the media.

Is it possible to utilize the Eheim more as a mechanical only, and eliminate it's efforts at being biological and, if so, how would you suggest I attempt this.
I don't think I see what size tank you have but a sump is a good idea. It's really hard to work around a problem... although A sump is a good idea. I wish I could tell you more. I suppose that would mean either drilling the tank or buying an overflow box to drain into the sump. Then use the Eheim to pump back into the tank. Are you using a protein skimmer? *That* is *very* important. Some how I don't see it incorporated in your system.

"Fish only" tank?
The reason why I write to you is that I'm curious if your book will help Fish Only tanks. I understand that if I maintain the fish tank like a reef tank, the fish will be happy. However, fish create more waste than coral and invertebrate, so there should be slightly different approaches to operate a fish tank. I'm using 240 pounds of live rock to cycle my tank now and I don't see my tank as a pure Fish Only tank.
From your tank description, I think that trying to have both worlds—a "fish only" and "240 pounds of live rock" can lead to problems. Fish produce waste, Ammonia and phosphate. Ammonia will get broken down to nitrate and eventually nitrogen gas. However, the phosphate will still have to be dealt with by very strong skimming. If it is not dramatically reduced, you may have substantial algae that will cover the rock. If you have acquired the live rock, I suggest favoring reef principals (minimum fish) and lean in the direction of a reef tank. With that amount of rock in the tank, I don't see a lot of happy fish unless they are very small. Trying to have a lot of fish may result in ruining a lot of live rock.
Basic modern reef principals are:

- 1.5 to 1.75 pounds live rock
- RO or DI tap water, elevated pH and calcium via: Kalkwasser
- Strong lighting with proper spectrum

- Strong protein skimming
- Good turnover rate of water tank gallons six times per hour
- Minimum fish and mostly, if not all, algae eaters
- Photosynthetic livestock

The above conditions will yield zero nitrates, manageable algae, and a thriving reef tank. I hope this helps your decision.

HOME MADE FOOD RECIPE

I noticed you asking about what to feed your anemones, I would highly advise this home made food. It is a recipe from Dr. Sanjay Joshi and he is allowing me to include it. I did some feeding with frozen food but this has it hands down! One of the best food sources for your tank can be home made and when you try this I doubt if you will go back to any other type of food. The fish and corals absolutely love this. It is very inexpensive to make and for about $10 or so you can make at least a six months supply. Here is how.

This recipe comes from Dr. Sanjay Joshi of and is passed on with his permission.

- Go to an oriental food store and buy some nori (seaweed in sheets) unseasoned.
- From your favorite food store buy 1/4 lb. of fresh ea. of squid, clams, mussels, fish filleted, scallops, shrimp.
- Put the seafood in a blender and puree adding water to get a consistency of thick soup.
- Then take 2 or 3 sheets of nori cut into one inch strips and add to the blender, add more water to maintain the thick soup consistency.
- Then simply put about 3 tablespoons into a small sandwich bag, repeat until you use all the mix.
- Double bag the excesses and freeze. When you want to feed break off one third of the bag defrost slightly then add it to the tank.

I like to use a piece of plastic gutter guard shaped into a small cup, held together with cable ties. This makes a nice dispenser. Just add the mix to the holder and swish. The food is wonderful. Also nori is a good food for herbivores by itself and if you want to go further add a product called selcon. A vitamin mix for fish.

ICH

For the infection my approach is... Raise the temperature of the tank gradually to 85 degrees then increase slightly over time to 89 /90 this speeds up the lifespan of the parasite. Do this gradually over a period of 2 days when complete aprox up to 2 weeks possibly 1 week or when the infection seems to be subsiding, reverse the procedure gradually. *Along with the increased temperature* decrease the salinity to 1.017 (in that low range aprox) for the same 2-week period, again gradually and when reversed do it gradually. AND / OR Buy a few cleaner shrimp (scarlet cleaners) these critters eat parasites off of the fish also they are extremely hardy and beautiful retail 15 - 20 $$ get a few there a great addition I myself *would not* do any other approach (dips/copper/hospital tank or any thing else) My opinion is let nature take its course. These outbreaks are usually caused by temp change during transport or introducing sick fish that have been purchased from questionable sources.

I have a blue Damsel that's been in my main tank for since setup 8 mo.'s ago. Nothing to stress it- water quality is good, no new fish or anything has been added. Question: It has only two white specks (that look like ICK), on it's mid-body. The fish seems in perfect health. These spots have been on the fish for 10 days. No more have appeared. All other fish are fine. What should I do? I do have a quarantine tank if I could ever catch it.

I wouldn't try to catch the fish, as that will more stressful to it and the other fish. I would definitely purchase a few cleaner shrimp. They are a must in the reef as far as a solution to ICH. Also they are extremely hardy and very beautiful a "Must have" in the tank. I guarantee you won't be disappointed getting a few of these. On the other hand it may not be itch. In that case, still get the cleaners and then just let nature take its course in the tank. Too many times people try and get in there and "manage the situation" this IMO is not recommended. Make sure you always buy your fish from a reputable dealer that *knows* what he is doing. Buying livestock from a reputable dealer will eliminate many if not all problems health related.

Iodine dosage
What is your recommended dosage for Lugols? I have a 50-gallon tank.
First I would test the tank water to determine the level of iodine. Natural salt water has approximately 6 PPM. If the tank is below this amount, I would start with one drop every other day. Test the water to get the reading you desire, and increase if needed. Usually the recommended dosage is one drop per 20 gallons every other day or to achieve a test result of 0.06 PPM. I recommend to start slow, as each tank differs as to demand, skimmer removal, and maintenance (water changes). I believe one of the drawbacks of Lugols is that it is so economical that it's tempting to add too much. I have been using it for about six months and find that it works well as a supplement. However, I believe that frequent water change with a good salt will almost eliminate the need for adding iodine, unless you have corals that have a high demand. Also, I use the Salifert test kit, which is very economical.

Kalkwasser
How much should I start off with, considering I will be adding it daily?
Use it for all your make up water (evaporation). For mixing Kalkwasser, add approximately 3/4 to 1 teaspoon per gallon. Mix it for a few hours. Let it sit for four to six hours. Without disturbing the sediment in your mixing vessel, add the upper portion of water. Rinse the vessel and discard the sediment.

Calcium hydroxide and pickling lime.
What does pickling lime do for the reef tank?
Pickling lime is food grade calcium hydroxide. It elevates pH, adds and maintains calcium. And is an inexpensive replacement for the more expensive Kalkwasser.

From what I have heard Kalkwasser usually will not go over 300-350 PPM, so to raise it to 400-450 then you need to add additional calcium supplement?
Well it depends on who you talk to and what animals you keep. If you have an *extremely high demand* than yes you may want to add a reactor. Looking at your specs below I really don't see any calcium demand other than coraline. My point, Kalkwasser will be fine.

This is why I am starting to use Reef calcium. Seachem states this is 175x more calcium than Kalkwasser?
I doubt it. The chemical Calcium Hydroxide is the same.

Lastly, I am starting for the first time to add Kalkwasser. My tank does not evaporate much (maybe 1-gallon week).
That's not too good. Most believe in high evaporation to maintain calcium via Kalkwasser. I evaporation a minimum or 15 gal per wk in my 200 now a 255 with refugium. You should have fans in your hood, which will increase evaporation. Some people will go as far as

placing fans (sometimes very large fans) over the sump. Increased air movement = evaporation = more frequent or larger doses of Kalkwasser. I would say a 55 should do about 5 gal per week and added in 2 2.5 gal increments. You add the Kalkwasser in the AM when the pH is lowest. Mix in the PM let settle then dose in am

So I will be adding this probably once a week. What is the rule of thumb for adding how much in a period of time? Is it one drop per second?
Depends the size of the drop. Using an airline tube the drops are large, an IV bag they are small. I would recommend airline with a reliable clamp and dose the 2.5 gal in a 24-hr period you will be fine. The *main thing* is to make the adding water to the container/mixing/dosing as *easy* as possible so it is not a dreaded inconvenience. That's the main trick! I use a 5-gal bucket with a pump at the bottom and a water supply right in the bucket. Fill... add Kalkwasser... turn on powerhead...mix for 4 hours or so... unplug powerhead... let settle for about an hour... then drip in. I drip 5 gal in about an hour through airline w/o clamp

I need to be careful not to raise the pH too fast right.
Yes, add it in the am pH is lowest at that time.

I just started a 75 gallon reef tank its been running for 3 weeks with about 120 pounds of cured live rock in it. I have been testing the water and the Calcium readings are why high about 630 PPM is this normal and how do I get them down. I read that it should be 400 PPM to 475 PPM,
I seriously doubt if your readings are accurate. Its highly unlikely they are 630 which test kit are you using? Its easy to get inaccurate readings if your not familiar with the test kits, usually it will take some time to get familiar with the procedures. I always recommend judging your tank by how everything looks and not get hung up on keeping test readings exact all the time. Testing the water is mainly to get a general feel for where the tank is. If you use RO or DI water a good salt mix Coralife instant ocean use Kalkwasser for all your evaporation do regular water changes have reef lighting you don't *really* have to sweat the test readings. Your animals will be the best indication. More often than not damage or imbalance happens when the aquarist tries to keep the test reading tweaked. Take the suggestions here and you should be all set.

Where to find pickling lime
It depends on where in the country you are. A low cost replacement for over the counter premium priced Kalkwasser is food grade calcium hydroxide. This is sold as pickling lime and sells for about $1.49 per lb. I have personally used Knerrs brand. Also available is Balls. Some areas of the country this product is more readily available than others.
After checking all the stores in my area... Super Kmart, Super S&S, Big Y, etc. Locally, I've have not been able to locate this lime. I called Altrista Corp. makers of Ball products and they were happy to send it to me. Costs 16oz $1.30 or a 12 pack (master canner) for $14.20 + $6 for shipping. $20.28 for 12 lb. I told the woman she could be expecting a flood of calls 1-800-240-3340 she says "that's what I'm here for". They are in Muncie Indiana (apparently the canning capital of the nation). Check your local food stores, sometimes the larger Kmart's etc will have it. If not you can call the 800# and order a case of it. Personally, I had trouble finding it where I live (Connecticut) and had to call and order. It seems to me that some states every store has it while others never heard of it.

Lighting

Do you still favor fluorescent over metal halide lamps now that metal halide is available in high K values?
That is one of the changes that are going to be made. Yes, metal halide is OK depending upon the use. They definitely have their place and can be useful. They are particularly advantageous where high wattage is needed for stony polyp, corals, or clams. They are beneficial where space is limited and one desires higher wattage. I personally prefer fluorescent lamps and lower light-requiring creatures. It's more economical in the long term. Lower light = lower cost. A final suggestion is to select your creatures very carefully as to light requirements.

I have a couple of metal halide 175-watt Coralife pendants that I picked up used.
Well sure, if you picked them up used, go for it. They are nice lights.

What are the pros and cons of using pendants?
Pros:
- Nice clean looking light "shimmering" on the surface.
- Powerful and direct you can place high light corals directly under the bulb.
- Corals do well under metal halide light.
- Pendants give you an open top for ++ evaporation, good opportunity to add Kalkwasser.
- Gives a less cluttered look to the top of the tank and a more high tech appearance.

Cons:
- Possibility for excessive heating of the tank or making cooling difficult.
- More difficult to cool with a fan.
- Possibly higher wattage being more expensive to operate.
- More coral growth = higher calcium demand. Be aware of that. Calcium and alkalinity.
- Lamps are fairly expensive. They cost from $80 to $100 each, and need to be replaced yearly.

I'm setting a new 40 gal coral tank with dimensions 36"w x 18"d x 16"h. Do you think 2 95w VHOs would be sufficient to light the tank?
So that's 190 watts divided by 40 gal = 4.75 watts per gallon which in my opinion is adequate or slightly above adequate. *It really depends on exactly what type of creatures you plan to keep.* It would be minimum for allot of stony polyp corals or clams. Although, those are probably not the creatures you plan to keep. Most long polyp stony and *all* soft corals this arrangement would be great.

I'm thinking about getting the ballast from Coralife.
I would definitely not get the Coralife... I've never heard anything good about them, other than they are convenient because most local fish stores carry them. Your best bet would be to go with an icecap ballast they are much, much better. If you have time have a look at my survey to see what others use. Myself I have used standard supply house tar ballast's tar type. And have upgraded to icecap they are really nice the ballast is lightweight and runs extremely cool. Also I like URI bulbs URI stands for the company Ultraviolet Resources. They have ads in FAMA (although ordering direct from them will cost more than getting them online).

Live Rock
A friend gave me old, dry Fuji rock that had been stored in a box for a year after he no longer wanted a Salt Fish tank. My questions are can I clean and use this rock? Can I

put it in my wet/dry filter under the bioballs? Does this help in any way with the water dripping over it? This is a fish only tank.

You could use it as biological filter media if you don't have enough material in the sump. It will provide an area for bacteria to colonize.

Are there any benefits or drawbacks to adding this rock?

I doubt if there are any real benefits other than if you desperately need more area for biological filtration and have an excessively large sump. It depends upon how many fish you have and how much waste is produced. One drawback may be that because the rock is uneven, (unlike uniform bioball media) the aerobic action may be decreased. On the other side, your anaerobic (denitrifying bacteria) may increase, to possibly give you some denitrification. You do not say how much rock, or how many gallons of bioballs you have, or the size of your sump. My first inclination is to add it to the tank as decoration. It will give you some denitrifying properties without interfering with desirable aerobic action in the sump.

What does it mean to "cure" live rock?

Live rock contains millions of life forms when it is shipped or moved from one environment to another, a certain amount of "die-off" of these life forms occur. Consequently, uncured rock is usually ammonia laden. "Curing" it actually means to cycle it—ammonia to nitrite to nitrate. When you have zero ammonia and nitrite you will get faint nitrate readings indicating that it is cycled or "cured." Depending on how much die-off is present on the rock determines the length of time needed to complete the cycle. It can be anywhere from two to eight weeks, or even longer!

Is it necessary to place live rock in a curing tank for long periods of time?

If you don't have any other life forms in your tank you can, by all means, use your tank. If you have only a few creatures or fish you may want to temporarily relocate them. Definitely do not try to cycle with other livestock, as the ammonia readings will skyrocket. The best thing to do is just let it happen, and it will happen.

It would be difficult to supply a separate tank with filtering equipment to cure my rock.

You don't need filtering equipment to cycle the rock. It can be done in a new garbage can or a clean garbage can with several liners and a few good air stones. I prefer to use the tank without livestock.

I have added my live rock that was supposed to be cured, however there appears to be more life forms that are dying. Should I add hermit crabs or snails?

Don't worry about the die-off; just don't add *any* livestock *at all*—absolutely nothing, until you have a full cycle. When you have zero ammonia and nitrite with a faint nitrate reading, then you are ready for hermits or snails and adding the remaining livestock.

Substitute for live rock

My problem is the expense and the taking of live rock from the reef. I know that there is probably no real substitute for live rock, but can I compensate with better mechanical filtration and more frequent water changes? Which would be better, the fluidized bed filter or is they're a denitrification filter that changes the nitrate to nitrogen gas? Without live rock, what would be best for a substrate?

This is an excellent question, and frankly one I've never had before. I would think having enough sand *may* do the job, you'll have to experiment with it and see if you end up with zero or very low nitrate. Also, you could add the column denitrifier in my book (that works well). The main suggestion I have is to stay away from fluidized beds or other conventional aerobic and semi anaerobic filters as these are sure to *produce* nitrate. I suppose you may have the impression that I'm anti sand so that's why you didn't suggest it, but my feelings on sand have been changing so that may be your best bet. Usually when one thinks of a reef tank it has allot of live rock so it all becomes easy with that. Another point is if you invest in the sand say 3 to 4 inches of it then decide you want to add liverock, will that be a problem? I would try and shoot for 1.75 lbs. per gallon of sand or up to 2 lbs. Per gallon of rock and sand combined. Whether or not you use a plenum will be up to you. I would suspect a plenum being possibly better though, for what you're trying to do. Another idea is this will be a semi reef tank... meaning you have to be careful (not use) medications if your fish get ich. Cleaner shrimp are the best bet for ich. You may need some snails & hermits also. One other idea is to make your own live rock have you seen the GARF site? They have instructions to make aragacrete (homemade live rock) maybe worth a look http://www.cyberhighway.net/~algae/

Combined rock and sand weight
I've been reading that you advocate using the appropriate amount of LR & sand. It wasn't clear if this total is cumulative (sand + rock).
This topic generates huge controversy. My opinion is to use a min of 1 lb. to max of 1.75 lb. of live rock. I haven't been an advocate of sand as my system uses raised eggcrate wit a spray bar in the lower rear. However, my opinion on sand is changing. One can of course have sand, but in my experience, using more than 2 lbs. per gallon may make the system too biologically dense. I feel a 2 lb. per gal max of sand & rock to be a safe limit. Think about it... how much is too much? A tank *full* of sand & liverock would be too much, wouldn't you think? Using more than 2 lbs. per gal may lead to accumulated waste creating a food source for microalgae and causing other long term problems. One does not need more than 2lbs per gallon to be effective with denitrification

For a 55G tank I believe you calculated 82.5lb of Rock:
1.5 lbs. x 55 =82.5

1) Is this total rock? live and dead, when starting out what is the appropriate % of dead and live (seed) rock.
I never bother with dead rock or base rock. Use all live rock. Using eggcrate, one maximizes the display w/o the need to build up with un-necessary waste accumulating base rock

2) If using a plenum with 3" of live sand cover. What % should be aragonite Vs live (sand)?
Depends on your budget. If money is no object use all live sand. If you're trying to be somewhat conservative use 50/50 aragonite on the bottom, then live sand on top. Is all live sand necessary? No. Is all live sand better? Not necessarily. A 50/50 mixture is fine

Since I will be using a plenum (I haven't set this tank up yet), how much more rock should I add to the sand base?
I would calculate how many lbs. of sand you plan to use then make the balance up with live rock while trying not to overshoot the 2 lbs. per gal

Metal near the tank

Should I be concerned with any metal fittings in or near the tank?

Yes, metal of any kind in salt water is a definite "no-no." I recommend finding a large, high quality plumbing supply store. Check the yellow pages and make a few calls. There are plastic fittings made for more applications than metal. You need to find the right local supplier. Once you find the right store, you will be amazed at what is available. You have to be very careful with dropping small metal screws or clips while working over the tank. If you drop one in especially if its brass you may not be able to find it and metal rapidly breaks down in salt water releasing itself into the water. You have to be very careful with anything metal around the tank.

Mini Reef

I'm toying with the idea of setting up a minireef (20-L tank) using four 20-watt fluorescent bulbs for lighting and the Berlin method for filtration. I read your recommendation to keep no smaller than a 55-gallon tank. Since I lack experience, I will likely stay away from the harder-to-maintain 20-gallon tank for now. I'm still thinking through the lighting possibilities. One factor weighing in favor of a 20-gallon tank is that I would feel more comfortable moving a smaller tank when I relocate in approximately one year.

In actuality, a 55-gallon is not much different in terms of initial cost or physically moving the tank. I definitely recommend the 55-gallon over a 20-gallon, because once you have the 20-gallon you will wish you had the 55-gallon. Realistically, the main cost difference is the expense of the live rock and with affordable Internet merchants, that's not really an issue.

I am patient, so I may spend the next year learning, saving sufficient money for a nice reef system, and then set up a larger tank in a more-permanent place.

I suggest writing out a realistic plan as to costs and see if it is within your budget. In my opinion, if you can setup a 20-gallon—you also can setup a 55-gallon.

Moving

I moved last year. Here are some tips and questions.

- Get someone to help you this is definitely needed.
- Mix up plenty of new salt water a few days in advance for the new water change, spillage and oversights.
- Devote the entire day to the tank. Just you & a helper for the tank.
- Save 2/3 of tank water in clean plastic jugs, or a new or very clean trashcan 1/2 full double lined.
- Bag fish in individual bags and place in standard Styrofoam shipping box,

How do I protect corals from moving around?

I placed them the same as fish & inverts body up trying not to use an oversize bag will minimize movement.

I plan to drain tank down till only 1-2 inches of water above the livesand.

That's *risky*! If you don't drain the tank completely...its very east to break while moving it. I would take out as much water as possible and then use a piece of 3/4 in plywood approximately 6 in bigger all around to carry the tank with placed under the tank as a base stabilizer.

I am a believer in taking down the tank occasionally, originally I was of the thought to do yearly takedowns but that may not be necessary. Every 2 years or so will be fine. Nevertheless moving is an opportunity to clean your rock a bit. As you take out the rock have a 5-gal bucket of water from the tank and vigorously swish dunk the rock. You will be *amazed* at the detritus in the nooks & crannies that come out of the rock. As the water in the 5 gal gets disgusting looking after about 5 pieces dump it and siphon again from the tank. That way you are using up the 1/3 water you plan to change. The rock at the bottom will be the worst, when you do this you will see what I mean.

When you remove the rock take it out & *place it in the box good (coraline & life form side up.)* The most difficult part is getting the tank to look as it did before the move. *Also, label the boxes - base rock -good stuff- top decorative- this is very helpful.*

Have a tape gun handy to seal up the boxes

Have your new destination prepared for the tank placement. Power supplies, drop cloths, towels hoses for siphons a small pump for pumping in the new salt water.

I moved my 200-gallon reef tank. With 375 lbs. of rock set up with a custom eggcrate frame and spraybar 45 gallon sump 6 fish 12 to 15 corals and a bunch of inverts. It took 2 men working all day 10+ hours to take down move and re-setup. I only moved about 1/2 hour away, the biggest mistake was when I mixed up my new salt water the resin in my DI was expended and I didn't realize it. I did about a 50% waterchange with bad water, hair algae followed and so did more waterchanges with fresh DI unit. Double-check your resin before making up a large batch of saltwater!

Nitrate

My Nitrate levels float is between 10-15ppm. I am wondering how low Nitrates had to be before I attempt to add other inverts.
You have borderline acceptable levels now. However, you don't have the mechanism for denitrification. By adding more fish, etc., without having an export for nitrate, I would expect your levels to rise much higher.

I will only add another two fish, which will be approximately 3 inches each in length.
Adding fish will increase your nitrate.

I do not have any live rock or sand yet for two reasons:
1). All my LFS (local fish stores) told be not to bother.
2). The LFS that do stock it only stock very poor quality rock.
The live rock is used for the reef so denitrification can take place and to have a diverse population of micro-fauna. The basis of a reef tank is incorporating the proper amount of live rock.

I would like to introduce live sand but I am not sure if I can do this as my tank has live stock in it. I will be reading up on this subject during the following weeks, but in the interim if you have any advise, please let me know.
Yes, adding any biological material now, (either live rock or sand) will cause problems with high ammonia and nitrite during the cycling die-off process. Usually this process will stress out existing fish, corals or inverts. If you want to add new rock or sand, I would recommend relocating the livestock in the tank or cycle the new live rock in a new garbage can or similar container using a power head for circulation and airstone for oxygen. Go through the testing

of ammonia and nitrite once your new live rock cycles, you will know that it is safe to add to your tank.

What do you class as low nitrates? I am thinking of adding a few inverts to my aquarium but I have heard you need to have a zero reading of Nitrates to be successful. Mine is 15 PPM

Low is 10ppm or below. I doubt that 15 would be harmful, but I would have a look at your live rock situation. Using around 1.5 pounds per gallon usually will give you close to complete denitrification. I get the impression that your tank is somehow out of balance; either too many fish, not enough live rock, too much feeding, or improper spectrum of light for photosynthetic livestock who use nitrate in the photosynthesis process. In an established tank that is balanced, (ratio of waste producers to waste processors) zero nitrates are common and indicate a "balanced" system. However, during the process of attaining the state of balance, medium nitrate readings are common and not harmful. Even having 40 PPM nitrate reading will not be harmful

I have a Wet/Dry filter with bioballs. I have heard they produce nitrate. How do I remove them?

Providing you have enough rock, 1.5 pounds per gallon or the equivalent in sand and all parameters are OK, ammonia and nitrite, and the tank is fairly stable—remove approximately 15% every week until they are all removed. This will give the nitrifying bacteria an opportunity to relocate to the live rock or sand in relation to the tanks current bio load. You can remove larger percentages of the media at a time but more gradual and smaller amounts insure a seamless transition or bacteria relocation.

NNR Natural Nitrate Reduction

I would like your opinion on using a NNR system with it. Was this system preferred before the new high efficiency skimmers were available?

I believe it was found to harbor denitrifying bacteria and very low nitrates and then deemed a breakthrough for denitrification. Years ago, it was thought best to place as much live rock as could fit in the tank to achieve nitrification and denitrification, (a little is good—more must be better). The result was that hobbyist's tanks that were setup for one year to eighteen months experienced unexplainable and unmanageable algae outbreaks. These outbreaks were attributed to having too much rock where nutrients build up was unseen. It also turned otherwise good quality rock, to base rock, as lighting was unable to reach the stacked rock. This meant a complete takedown, a 75% water change, and removal of unnecessary rock. At that point, a rule of thumb was established.

Noisy overflow

My overflow is noisy what can I do?

If the noise emanates from the drainpipe of the tank, you may need to install a vent covered with a small piece of sponge as a muffler. What I suggest is to make a muffler out of small Tupperware or Rubbermaid products with small 1/4 inch holes in them. Fill the container with floss material connected with flexible vinyl tubing. Use a threaded X insert that fits the size of your tubing. Or, run a vent hose that is long enough to an area where the sound wont be noticed, (as much). If you are referring to noise in the sump, some eggcrate placed diagonally under the drip plate will minimize the sound and will act as a baffle.

Other filtration methods

I was wondering if you have tried other less popular filtration systems?

No, I have not tried them. Primarily I use the Berlin and have used the Jaubert. I am sure that the less popular set-ups have merit and I would love to set up a couple of tanks to experiment with those principals. However, during recent years I haven't had time.

In particular, I am interested in the Lee Chin Eng's (or Natural) system.

Yes, the Lee Chin seems to be the least technical and may work well for a very lightly stocked tank. As pointed out in TRA (The Reef Aquarium Dellbeek & Sprung), oxygen is probably the most essential element in the tank and I question how much realistically could be added with just an air pump.

There is also Dr.'s Adey's System.

Adey's uses the turf scrubber and surge device. This system is probably the most difficult to run properly. Additionally, there is significant extra cost of lighting, not only in operating (electricity), but the replacement costs of bulbs. (I'm less in a hurry to experiment with this one.) Also, the alga needs to be carefully managed. I am sure the system would work well, but I see it as being complex.

I'm curious since I don't have much room for my 55-gallon tank and the natural system doesn't require extra sumps and other components.

Of all the systems, the two most popular are the Berlin and Jaubert. Quite a few people who run a Jaubert also use a skimmer and that is called a NNR system. I frequently hear about algae problems associated with plenums over a period of time and it has happened to me. My recommended system is the Berlin combined with using eggcrate. Employing the spraybar and eggcrate makes it a "Glorified Berlin." It works extremely well and I highly recommend it. My observation is that because these systems never caught on, there must be a reason for it. Most hobbyists are economical and if a less expensive or bulky system would work, it would be more widely used. I gather that is the basis or your question. I wish I could be of more help. In the future, I may do some experiments with these systems in the future.

Overflow problem (surface algae)

I have a Dutch aquarium with a protein skimmer. The algae is green and grows so fast that I'm afraid that it will suffocate the tank. It floats on the surface and almost stops surface water flow. It's almost brought my operation to a halt.

That's not good at all. I strongly suggest adding a surface skimmer box. You should be able to find one at your local fish store. Until then you should manually remove the algae. You definitely need a surface skimmer box to improve your surface waterflow.

Is there an animal that eats surface algae?

No, you shouldn't have *any* surface algae! You should be *"surface skimming"*—meaning all the water to feed your protein skimmer or filter should be taken from the surface of the tank. This is usually done with an overflow box or the tank is drilled with a fitting through the top back wall. As the water is pumped into the tank, it will overflow into this fitting, or overflow box. The water that feeds the skimmer is removed from the surface and will eliminate your problem. This is the method used in 99% of reef systems.

Painting

I plan to do some painting. I know I should cover the tank. I was going to turn the pumps to the skimmer off to avoid injecting more fumes than necessary and covering the entire tank with a plastic drop cloth. Any other suggestions?

That sounds good. Use common sense. Here are a few more tips.

- Open as many windows as possible.
- Use as many fans as possible to exhaust out the window.
- Shut the entire tank down during painting and for 4 to 6 hours—maybe 8 hours after the job is complete.

This will keep your water less likely to "pick up" anything.

- *Tightly* cover the tank with plastic (duct tape if needed)
- Use a heavy blanket to deflect fumes.
- Also, *remember to cover the sump.*

Use as many precautions as possible.

Plenums

I would appreciate your opinion on using the plenum method in a reef system.

You have to ask yourself, why a plenum lives and a filter is useful? Most claim it to be a complete nitrification and denitrification system and basically it is, just that. However, so is an all live rock or Berlin system. The fact is, virtually complete biological filtration (nitrification and denitrification to nitrogen gas) will take place in both methods. Problems occur when one adds more than two pounds per gallon of sand or rock. My best expression of this is that the system becomes biologically dense; i.e., too much area for bacteria to colonize and detritus to accumulate without enough water volume ratio and turnover.

My suggestion is to have 1.5 to 1.75 pounds of sand or rock. This seems to be a good rule of thumb ratio—material to water. For example, a 55-gallon plenum system takes 80 pounds of sand for the required minimum thickness of 2-1/2 inches and comes out to 1.45 pounds per gallon. Using the rule of thumb of pound per gallon doesn't leave much for live rock. It then becomes a different looking tank. Even if you decide to overshoot the suggested pounds per gallon, and place rock on the sand and corals on the rock, you then begin to have dead spots under and behind the rock. Those are places where detritus cannot be removed without moving around animals. This is my opinion and what I have personally experienced. I have an aversion to detritus and believe constant removal of waste is important. This is best achieved by using my eggcrate method which is a framework of eggcrate material cleverly designed and incorporating a spray bar as the main return to the bottom rear of the tank which pushes all detritus to the front for easy removal.

Potential problems with plenums?

Yes, I too have had a persistent algae problem while running a natural nitrate reduction plenum system. This problem occurred in approximately one year to fourteen months. I "unscientifically" attributed the problem to detritus buildup and high nutrient levels. I took the system down, re-setup with a bare bottom; raised rock system and the algae disappeared. I find this discussion very interesting regarding the "success" of this type of system. Can all this be a coincidence? I don't think so. This NNR as I understood it, was to eliminate and/or drastically reduce water changes. It is a "too good to be true" system. NNR or natural nitrate reduction is, I think, just what it says. We all know that nitrate will be reduced with the correct amount of "live" rock or sand in relation to the bio-load of the tank. It is my opinion that using the "correct" amount will have a significant role in the long term "success" of the aquarium. I use and recommend 1.5 to 1.75 pounds per gallon. Using too much live sand or rock can trap debris/detritus going unseen and will build up a food source for micro-algae as well as to become unfavorably biologically dense for the enclosed system. In my NNR system (a 55-gallon system), the 1.75 inch approximate sand thickness came out to be 80 pounds or 1.45 pounds per gallon. I added approximately 50 pounds of live rock bringing it to over 2.36 pounds per gallon. This leads me to believe that excessive biological medium, i.e., live sand or rock becomes "unmanageable" in regard to nutrient build-up over extended periods of time.

PUMPS

The little giants seem to come in 2 models flow or pressure. I used your formula (125galx6=750+20% =900gph) correct?
Yes, for the skimmer you would want the pressure pump and tank spray bar use a flow, although they could be interchangeable (not to confuse you but they will work in both applications) if you used a flow for the skimmer it then should be of a slightly higher rate.

The way I have been reading about the pumps is that they are rated at 6ft. Would I still need to add 20% to be safe for enough flow?
I would, most likely the pump will be on the floor and your EST (Environmental Tower Scrubber) and tank will be anywhere from 4 to 6 ft above the floor so it would be a good idea.

Their is not much difference in price between models MD3QX-SC-(freeflow) 875gph and model 4 at 1080gph.Next in your book you say to use the same pressure or little less. The pressure models are MD4Q-SC at 765gph or MD5-SC 920gph.
Ideally I would use the freeflow 875 for the tank and the pressure 920 for the skimmer. What size are you planning the ETS to be? Height wise? A regular 5ft? That would be good I think that's the model 1000.

Iwaki's come in 2 versions American a little more expensive than little giant and the Japanese a lot more costly, what is the difference?
From what I understand the Japanese is the highest quality American slightly less. An important consideration here is pump noise... Are you sensitive to pump noise? Some are and the Japanese Iwaki is almost silent the American is very quiet the LG pumps IMO aren't loud but to some they are Some folks like to have everything silent. Keep in mind the ETS is fairly loud, not un reasonable *but* you definitely know its running. So that's pretty much the differences.

Iwaki Japanese = Highest quality silent
Iwaki American = Superb quality
Little Giant = Good quality affordable

Reef Creatures

I saw one larval looking critter cruising on the rock. It is difficult to describe and didn't actually look like the Isopods in your book. Could it be something else?
Does it look like a small shrimp? It possibly could be a mystis shrimp, its is hard to say of course, without actually seeing it. The only undesirable creatures are the large Bristle Worms, Mantis Shrimp and an occasional Isopod—although the Isopods are fairly rare. I find this is the most fascinating aspect of the hobby; we don't know what many of these creatures that live in and on the live rock are! Most are beneficial and harmless. Be observant of everything, and take notes.

What about cleaner shrimp?
Definitely, get several of them at least three or four depending on the size of your tank, usually a 55-gallon would easily support 3 or 4. They are beautiful and extremely hardy. Scarlet cleaner shrimp are practically mandatory for a reef aquarium because they are the natural solution to resolving problems with ich. If your fish ever contract ich they take care of it, pronto, (with no side effects). Cleaners are highly recommended!

Decorator Crabs?
They are neat. You see this creature that looks dressed up, walking around, this week some sponge and Coraline; next week a bit of Gorgonian and sprig of algae. They are never out of style!

Do Astera snails reproduce in your tank?
I have hundreds of what seem to be, baby snails. They are oval, about 3/8 inch long, 1/4 inch wide, (flat on the bottom), about 1/8 inch tall, grayish white in color with a few dark bands traversing the shorter distance (the 1/4 inch width), and some are bright purple. They only come out when the lights are off and have a somewhat hard shell. I have observed some of them growing to a full snail (cone type) algae eater.

What do you feed a Mandarin fish?
Mandarins primarily eat Copepods and macro organisms that live on the live rock. They are attractive fish, but don't survive long because once the food is gone...so are they. I've kept them for about a year and then they vanished. Usually they won't accept dry food or even fresh food. They are not a good choice for a tank, although I recognize that they are beautiful. If you have a Mandarin, the best suggestion is to feed it live Brine shrimp, try the home made food recipe or the best bet is to have a refugium that can support enough live food for the fish.
It's a good idea to avoid the temptation to buy this very attractive fish there by creating less of a demand for retailers to carry these picky eaters.

Hello. I am hoping that I can get some help on a problem that I have been trying to solve. I have a small brown octopus that is not eating anymore and would rather be inside a hole in a rock than searching for turbo snails. If you have any information I would greatly appreciate it.
I don't keep octopus, but from what I understand they like fresh fish. Small shiners, Kelly's, or the like. However introducing live food from questionable sources can be problematic in a reef tank. Also, they are escape artists and constantly *try to get out or in your filtration*. You may want to try some small fresh fish. Was it eating at one time in captivity by you? If it was then chances are it will eat again. They are very interesting creatures but usually don't do well in captivity because of there escapist instinct and predatory nature.

Could you please tell me what little creatures I have growing in my tank? No one seems to know what they are and I'm afraid they are harmful. The first one looks like a little feather duster, it has a white tube shaped shell and comes out of it like a bright red feather duster. They are very small and quite pretty but they are all over my rock hundreds of them.
Those are fan worms and thrive in good conditions, water flow and calcium levels.
The second problem is not quite so pretty and they also are all over my tank they are almost transparent like a jellyfish, and very small. They cling on to my filter and

powerheads mostly, they have a tube like body and attach like an anemone the head is like miniature tentacles. Their body is almost spongy looking, creepy little thing. Please help if you can.

Those sound like glass anemones or apitasta anemones. They reproduce like wild fire if not taken care of. To the unknowing eye they seem attractive… but are probably the most common pest in the tank. This creature seems to reproduce easily but thrive even better in poor water quality. I.e.: infrequent water changes, expended lighting, non-purified water. If the lighting is quality the more desirable life take over the rock if it diminished the apitasta take over. Noticing too many of them usually indicate water or lighting quality going downhill. To keep these unwanted species in check, see removing crabs bristle worms and mantis shrimp there is a sure-fire way to eliminate them.

With the addition of the Maroon Clown I have ich. I have increased the temp to 80 degrees and am decreasing the specific gravity to 1.18 over a period of 3 days. I'm told that shutting off the lights for a day as well is very beneficial, how do you feel about this?

This is why having scarlet cleaners is so important. I would just let the cleaner shrimp take care of it and not go overboard on "cures". Often the cure is worse than the infection. You don't say how long the fish has been in the tank. If it's relatively new 1 week or less I suspect the cleaners to take care of it. Also clowns are fairly resistant to ich, so I would also venture a guess that the fish was somehow subjected to temperature variations to cause the ich. If you already have the temperature and salinity process underway then proceed, but keep in mind to do all changes gradually. My approach would be to wait and see... if any other fish show signs if they did, then do the temp salinity

I'm very leery of medication, yet hear glowing reports of a product called 'Ecolibrium' for reef tanks.

Could be, but I wouldn't use it. I would just let nature take its course Let me know your results

In your reefkeeping article (April 20, 1997) you stated that chocolate chip starfish are easy to keep. I recently added one to my 110-gal reef tank. The pet shop said it was a filter feeder and I really didn't need to feed it or worry about particulars - but I always like to double check. Do you know where I could find information regarding the requirements for keeping them etc.?

Off hand... No, I do not know specific web sites for information on chocolate chip starfish. Personally I love them! They are very easy to keep, extremely hardy and will eat algae, detritus, and un eaten food. They move around very well in the tank and are not shy at all (compared to other starfish) and. its a very interesting creature.

On the other hand, some hobbyists consider them to be destructive and eat corals However that is not my experience at all. As far as I know they are not filter feeders but opportunistic scavengers and also eat a fair share of algae. One thing you will find being on the intent is... getting different reports on the same creature. I only speak from my own experience. I think you'll like it! Just keep an eye on what it eats and you don't have to worry about feeding it. It will easily find its own food.

Reef Salt

I see from what I have read in your book that you use Coralife Salt. I have no complaints with it, but I notice that when I mix the salt with my deionized water from my tap water purifier,
(I use two of them in series), that all the salt dissolves almost instantly.
That is what you want—ideal.

When I do a pH test on the water it always tests out at least 8.7 or higher and I do not know why.
The Coralife mix is probably highly buffered. That's good! As soon as you put in fish or anything alive (the waste then becomes acidic) and there is the battle of trying to keep a decent pH balance between high pH (additions of Kalkwasser and waterchanges with a good buffered salt) and acidic (waste products from living organisms).
So I need to understand whether you are setting up a new tank without any livestock or are you mixing for a water change? For a water change, 8.7 is great. For a new tank, you should be adding all the live rock first so it will cause the pH to drop to acceptable levels for new, more delicate life forms.

I have checked the deionized water before the salt mix and sure enough, you cannot get a pH reading. So I assume that the D. I. Water that I made is good.
Yes, it sounds very good. Reverse osmosis or deionized water should yield a zero pH.

Can you help on a situation that might be amiss? I have a Fish Only Tank. I think there is reason for concern because there exists high pH with the Coralife. I perform my water changes. This fall I plan to convert the Fish Only Tank to a Reef Tank.
I understand. What kind of salt were you using before Coralife? I don't think it will make a negative difference in the pH in your Fish Only Tank and can possibly cause them to acclimate to the new salt and changes to follow. Do the fish seem stressed? If not, I wouldn't worry about it. Test the tank water (for pH) before and after the water change and see how much of a difference results. Livestock can handle changes as long as they are done gradually.

Removing Bio-balls

You also mentioned to remove the bio-ball media that is in the rear chamber of my 50-gallon SYS-II. This way my nitrates will decrease dramatically. By doing this what about the bioload in the tank. Do I have to worry about stress to the tank or will my live rock take care of this for me. I am going to add a few more lbs. of rock. When I remove the media should I do it all at once or in increments?
You may want to get some more live rock, as I said 1.5 to 1.75 lb. per gal of rock or sand for complete denitrification. One downside to adding a substantial amount of rock will be a significant cycle that *will* stress the fish. High ammonia high nitrite temporarily 2 weeks or so. Consider cycling the new rock in a separate tank or clean garbage can as described in other areas of this book.
As far as removing the media, when your confident that you have enough rock and sand per gal, start removing something like 25% per week, that will make a seamless transition of your biological bacteria.

Removing Crabs, Bristleworms, Mantis shrimp from live rock
How to remove undesirable creatures

- Put the tub (upright) on a counter top, floor or what ever. The tub is to keep any dripping water in place. You can use a *clean* (no soap residue) dish pan, large picnic cooler (recommended) or a Styrofoam packing box etc. or a 5 gal bucket.
- Take the rock out of the tank and place it in the container. Use a 5 gal bucket and siphon some water from the tank, this will be to wet the newspaper.
- Get just enough water to wet the newspaper. A towel will also work dampen the newspaper in the water bucket and cover the rock with it.
- This gives the rock & undesirable creatures a sense of security. (darkness) Some of them will begin to venture out if... you don't make any noise or vibrations.
- Leave it alone for an hour or 2 then....
- Quickly snatch off the newspaper and get ready to separate the suspect creatures from the rock. For crabs & mantis shrimp, I like to use a regular kitchen spatula to either whack them or to quickly flip them away.
- The bristleworms once they are out of the rock don't have a chance!

I have 2 very nice 3" false anemone thriving on this rock.
Those can be removed if necessary but that's smarter not to do for now. Is it the same rock the worm is in?

Would the anemone live for an hour out of the water in the plastic box?
No, I wouldn't want to be limited by worrying about if the anemone would make it of not. This is what I would do

- Get a disposable latex glove, put it on and use your hand to fan water around the anemone so it closes up. Keep doing it until the anemone completely shrivels up very, very small.
- Find a very thin piece of plastic something thin but rigid like a rolodex card protector, name badge cover, thin plastic package wrapping, and cut it into the size of a credit card rounding the corners a bit with scissors.
- Once the anemone is completely closed use this home made plastic spatula to separate it from the rock. Be careful! Of course you don't want to damage the creature! Take your time. If after several tries and it doesn't want to come off, you will have to leave it.
- If it *does* come off use only the latex gloves to handle it some oils from your hand may be harmful be safe to you and the anemone and use the disposable gloves.
- If it does come off I would place it temporarily in a fish bag in the tank (floating attached to the tank wall with a cloths pin) this will keep it safe until you finish.
- Then do the procedure with the rock in the tub, the longer you have the rock out the better chance of undesirables coming out/ or falling out as with bristle worms

If the anemone doesn't come off... and you *really* want to get the crab or worm, the only other way I can think of is to simply split the rock with a hammer & chisel (while carefully leaving the anemone in tact.

I have a few suspicious looking crabs. These crabs have 2 claws, six legs, color dark gray, and body kind of oval. They barricade themselves in the rock holes during the daytime.
Sounds like a predatory rock crab I would do everything possible (within reason) to get rid of it. Rock crabs can be nasty predators.
One type of home made trap is to take a clear straight walled drinking glass and place it in the bottom of the tank up right. Put a piece of fish or similar bait inside. Keep an eye on the glass

and frequently the crab will get in the glass but *cannot get out quickly*. This gives you a chance to place a net or covering over the glass and remove the crab.

I have tried nylon pantyhose to catch bristleworms-no luck.
That will work, but you need the proper method.
- Use the stocking on a piece of fishing line. Make a small bait bundle aprox 1 1/2inches in diameter by putting in some fresh seafood.
- Chopped clam, squid, or fish work well.
- After the lights are out, place in the tank where you suspect he is
- Wait 1/2 hour and check it with a flashlight usually he will be on there
- Then carefully pull out the stocking with the fishing line.
- They are pretty unpleasant to touch; latex gloves are a good idea as is a nearby bucket.

I just read in FAMA magazine today that bristleworms clean up the reef sand and are beneficial.
Yes they are useful to the sand but they can eat zoanthids polyp's etc. Also they can get very large! I have had 12in+ fall out of rock when the tank was taken down and moved I suspect ones of this size are eating more than detritus or in a lesser example taking a larger amount of food away from the smaller more beneficial worms.

Unless they multiply in excess it recommended to leave them alone. What do you think?
You can wait and see. It's strange that some creatures of the same species have different levels of aggressiveness. I would try the nylon on fishing line and see what you come up with

I was wondering what your opinion on the Arrow-crab was. I've heard they may eat bristle worms but I've also heard that they might like feather dusters. Is there any truth in that?
Not in my experience, but others seems to say that! I am always hearing stories about the same creatures with different habits, arrowcrabs, chocolate chip stars, pencil urchins etc. The Arrow crab is very interesting and will probably eat bristleworms and he "might" eat your duster worms also. For that reason I would not get him, because you seem to have so many fan worms it would be a shame to have them disappear

Were there bristle worms in the bottom of the shipping box? One way to have a look to see any is again, after the lights are out for about an hour or so carefully examine the tank with a flashlight and if you see any either use the nylon stocking or trap and this will usually eradicate them. If not a more drastic method is to remove the rock for a few hours till they fall out. I understand it would be easier to have a natural predator, But there always seems to be other possible hazards that go along with that.

How do you rid your tank of glass anemones? A friend of mine purchased a creature that supposedly eats them.

It sounds like your friend has purchased a nudibranch. I have heard from many people that they are so small they disappear in the tank.
What I'm about to tell you may seem unsafe but I assure you it is very safe and works *extremely* well.
Here is what you do
- Go to a grocery store and purchase Red Devil Lye (make sure its Red Devil)

- Get a 3 cc syringe no needle just the plastic syringe larger than 3cc is even better if you can find a 6 or 10cc even better.
- Find these at the pharmacy or from a vet you only need one.
- Get a small container with an airtight lid a used fish food container works well.
- Lets say you have a 2 oz dry weight fish food container rinse it out and fill with 3.4 with water. I use DI water. Then add 3/4 teaspoon of the red devil lye (be careful its nasty chemical) stir with a spoon or other utensil or put the airtight top on and shake (be careful if you shake it and make sure the lid is on tight).
- Then simply fill the syringe with the mix and go to the apitasta and give it a small squirt it doesn't take much <POOF> vaporized! Next...repeat as needed.

Sometimes its helpful to give then a little nudge with the syringe so they retract in the rock where the lethal dose can be more effective. When you do this you'll notice a whitish glob like substance, that's the lye reacting with the salt water. Simply swoosh this away with your hand and of course you do not what any of this landing on your corals. A little practice and common sense and you'll have this method down in no time at all. I have found that this works the best.

Next would be to get one or two *peppermint shrimp* not cleaners or camel backs but peppermint shrimp they are known to do a fair job as well...although some do and some don't. Last and most drastic for a tank that is completely overrun you will have to get a copperband butterfly fish. Most copperband's will eradicate the apitasta however; they may also eat any feather dusters or possibly soft corals. Again some creatures do a great job some don't do as well, you just have to try and see for yourself.

Spaghetti Worms

I'm currently in tank curing my Live Rock. 2 days ago, I noticed a 2 inch tentacle sticking out of a piece of rock and pushing a thinner piece of tentacle into the live sand.

It sounds like spaghetti worms very common in live rock and are beneficial in the tank. Have a look in the tank with a flashlight after the lights have been off for a while; you will probably see more of these worms' fully expanded and other strange creatures.

 On one piece of live rock from Fiji, there is a white substance forming that cannot be removed by vacuum. Do you have any idea what this is? Usually anything white is dead although your are saying "its forming" leads me to believe that is some sort of encrusting octocoral or gorgonian. If its gorgonian... eventually you will see little polyps popping out that will become a mat or shag (light pink in color) like covering on the patch that's growing. Or, it can be some kind of octocoral that will develop, have to wait and see. I take it this growth is hard, relatively thin and smooth?

What should I do about it?

Just observe that's what happens with live rock some things die off and new life forms take over. A very interesting part of keeping a reef tank. It sounds like your tank is doing very well, so what ever your doing... keep doing it!

My leather coral didn't extend today during the light cycle. It's the first time its polyps haven't come out, should I be concerned?

This is typical; they go through a period of "sloughing" from time to time. I have 2 Sarcophyton each at one end of the tank and it seemed that one is always closed. One day one would close the next the other. I believe this is some kind of regenerative process. That's a nice easy to keep animal.

Do your astara snails reproduce in your tank?

To be honest I'm not sure exactly what they are. I haven't purchased *any* livestock in about 3 years what I remember is some were astera and some turbo. Turbo being the larger non coned shaped. I have hundreds of what seem to be baby snails They are oval about 3/8" long 1/4" wide/flat on the bottom/about 1/8"tall/grayish white in color with a few dark bands going the shorter distance the 1/4 " width/some are bright purple. They really only come out when the lights are off and have a somewhat hard shell I have observed some of them growing to a full snail (cone type) algae eater

One thing of special interest to us is the Tridacna Clams
They are very nice and hardy... But they need relatively high light in the range of 5+ watts per gallon, which is expensive to run over extended periods of time.

I also like Sea Horses. Are they hard to keep and do they equal fish inches too?
Yes very, I would forget about the sea horses, as far as fish go in a reef you don't really have that many fish just a few for highlight and algae management.
The algae on the back glass there are multiplying some sort of parasite. It is smaller than the head of a pin and there are hundreds of them. They are white and move in a jerky fashion, plus I can see that they are producing larvae. Are they any cause for alarm and if so
I doubt if they are "parasites" there are millions of life forms on liverock and these are just some of them. Keep an eye on them to see what they turn out to be. Don't do anything now, just observe.

Safe tubing
Is plastic pipe safe in the reef?
 Yes PVC, CPVC and clear vinyl tubing are all acceptable for fish/reef setups. Also, you may find "barbed insert fittings" useful for connecting clear vinyl tubing. This makes for a flexible easy to remove/replace plumbing assembly. The insert fittings are gray plastic and come in most common sizes. Ask for them as insert fittings, you may have to shop around a bit but when you find a good supplier it will be worth it. Also, the difference between PVC a.k.a.: poly vinyl chloride and CPVC a.k.a.: chlorinated poly vinyl chloride is CPVC is used for hot water plumbing systems. I would NOT use ABS a.k.a.: acrylonnitrile butadiene styrene (black plastic pipe) this is only used for waste/vents and is not acceptable for potable water.

Sand
I plan to place my rock over a 2-3 inch layer of sand. This will give the advantages of sand, but not have the sand compressed. I want to have the added biomedia of sand.
You can have some sand in the front, but by using live rock, it is not necessary to have much sand. You can use "some," but 2-3 inches... I wouldn't bother. Unless as mentioned in the book, you "primarily" use sand to make up the pounds per gallon and use less rock, it is OK, but not both. Look at my survey; see the substrate "most" people use.

My other question is that I don't like the look of the tank. I am thinking of starting over with an all live sand substrate. Do I need to change all of the water?
No, not at all. You can easily reuse the water.

I like the look of an all sand bottom. Do I need about 45 pounds of live sand?

I'm not sure of the amount in a 30-gallon, but that sounds about right depending on the actual thickness.

Does live sand help buffer the water?
That depends, if it's live sand from a reef or aragonite, live rock will buffer the water slightly. However, it will not buffer enough that you can depend on it as a sole means of buffering. It is helpful and live sand or aragonite *do* have buffering capabilities. However, you can't totally rely on it for complete buffering.

My problem is the expense and the taking of live rock from the reef. I know that there is probably no real substitute for live rock, but can I compensate with better mechanical filtration and more frequent water changes? Which would be better, the fluidized bed filter or is there a denitrification filter that changes the nitrate to nitrogen gas? Without live rock, what would be best for a substrate?
This is an excellent question, and frankly one I've never had before. I would think having enough sand *may* do the job, you'll have to experiment with it and see if you end up with zero or very low nitrate. Also, you could add the column denitrifier in my book (that works well). The main suggestion I have is to stay away from fluidized beds or other conventional aerobic and semi anaerobic filters as these are sure to *produce* nitrate. I suppose you may have the impression that I'm anti sand so that's why you didn't suggest it, but my feelings on sand have been changing so that may be your best bet. Usually when one thinks of a reef tank it has allot of live rock so it all becomes easy with that. Another point is if you invest in the sand say 3 to 4 inches of it then decide you want to add liverock, will that be a problem? I would try and shoot for 1.75 lbs. per gallon of sand. Whether or not you use a plenum will be up to you. I would suspect a plenum being possibly better though, for what you're trying to do. Another idea is this will be a semi reef tank... meaning you have to be careful (not use) medications if your fish get ich. Cleaner shrimp are the best bet for ich. You may need some snails & hermits also. One other idea is to make your own live rock have you seen the GARF site? They have instructions to make aragacrete (homemade live rock) maybe worth a look http://www.cyberhighway.net/~algae/

Setup
I understand the goals of water treatment equipment, and the function of the live rock filter. I'm planning a high intensity lighting system so I can keep a wide variety of corals; hence the water quality is paramount.
A "wide variety of corals" will have an equally wide variety of demands. As you know I am not a proponent of extreme wattage. For beginners, I recommend the easier-to-keep lower light corals. Usually the higher the light requirements, the more difficult it is to keep corals. For example, a high light SPS tank will consume a great deal of calcium. Consequently, a calcium reactor may be in order depending upon your physical location and the heat from lamps and pumps that usually transfers to the water. If you are in this league, I recommend a chiller. Keep in mind, a wide variety can really be "a wide variety," and long term costs of operation are high.

Why have prefilters at all? Won't the pump impellers chop everything up so that the protein skimmer can remove it, if not on the first pass, then on subsequent passes?
The prefilter is used as a "mechanical" filter to remove small particulate matter. It is definitely not a "must" but it does help.
Why not use that space for an additional skimmer if necessary?

I really don't think it takes up that much space.

Since I'm working with a confined space...
I don't like the sound of a "confined space." As I wrote in my book, I think that is the biggest mistake made by hobbyists. One of the fundamentals of a long-term successful tank is ease of maintenance. A confined space is not going to work well (unless you don't mind getting totally frustrated every time you want to do something under there). Believe me, after a few months, the novelty wears off.

I'm thinking about two (or more) smaller skimmers sitting in a wide and long sump with the bottom of the skimmer at the top of what would be a relatively shallow water line.
"In the sump" skimmers such as the turbofloater are available. I haven't used them, but they seem ok from what I've heard from people who have used them.

What do you think about a passive wavemaker?
Usually anything mechanical is prone to failure at some time. What has worked very well is the surge device, although it takes up space and can be noisy. Aside from that, it works wonderful!

I have thought about putting sections of spray bar all around the base perimeter that could be individually operated as either outflows or intakes.
I had thoughts of doing an angled bottom (sloped downward to the front where waste could accumulate and even possibly a drain in the bottom at the lowest point). Then every so often, you just open the valve and "voosh"—out goes the detritus. With just using one spraybar pushing to the front, this arrangement has most of the detritus collecting in one "dead" area—from where it can be removed easily with a siphon. This part of the piping system would have to be a closed to avoid a siphon during a power outage. A powered canister system like Lifeguard might work.
The idea is to keep all areas of the tank in constant water flow. It is necessary to have all water going out of the top and coming in the bottom. This gives a nice swirling motion, especially when accompanied by the alternating surge device.

I'm thinking that the grate/rock would extend up to the front edge.
To the front edge of the tank? No. That space is of paramount importance with the water flow. That's where the actual swirling takes place and the area where debris is removed.

I do not plan any vacuuming from the top either unless absolutely necessary to clean the rocks.
The rock should be frequently vacuumed of detritus.

What do you do when something gets under/behind the grate and dies? Some removable panels of the eggcrate might work to give access to the back/underside.
No, that does not really happen. If anything dies, I think the scavengers devour it. Once the tank is set up, you just leave it alone and Mother Nature takes over. I'm sorry that I appear dogmatic in response to your ideas. Actually I am not, but I see some "improvements" that could become problems and they can be simplified. The absolute, best arrangement is to have a room behind the tank and use that for all the equipment. Then you can do or have what ever you want without having to get everything to fit inside the tank.

I am estimating about $5,000 spread out over time since I'm building my system slowly. After all, it's to be a 250-gallon pride and joy!

That sounds "very" conservative to me. This is the reason for my suggestion about creating a realistic budget. What usually happens is we figure... well probably 5K and end up with a 10K system—a "slight" difference. If money is no object it is fine; but writing a realistic plan will save you substantial money.

New tank set-up...several follow-up questions.

1. You mentioned using the magnum with no medium. I'm assuming you mean no charcoal -- using the filter only as a filter for big chunks and water movement. Do you ever use charcoal to clean up the water?

No I mean *no media* at all. The live rock does all the biological filtering so you don't need a secondary filter! In fact a separate filter will *increase* your nitrate levels

2. I've ordered my second ice cap -- plus 4 URI 110w bulbs. 2 actinic white and 2 actinic 03. Is there somewhere to get more info on these bulbs. I've read something somewhere but can't find it and remember only enough to know there is more to them that I should know.

That sounds great. Ice cap ballasts and URI lamps are a great combination. The most important thing to know is to replace the bulbs in about 6 to 8 months. Other than that it's just technicalities that are in my opinion unimportant

3. Chemicals - Kalkwasser -- I note that Kent has a powder, I assume that I'll just follow the instructions on the package. Anything else I would find helpful?

Yes that's good I would follow the instructions in my book though, as they are much more detailed. Also an excellent alternative to the high price Kalkwasser is simply balls pickle lime. It's the same thing. Calcium hydroxide price difference is about $1.49 for Ball's brand (pickling lime)... $11.99 for Kalkwasser. You will use allot of this so I would buy a case.

Lugol's iodine - I've found nothing that fits this description -- could you give me a brand name, or some more information.

Go to a pharmacy (not a chain, but a small mom & pop pharmacy) and ask for Lugols solution. It come in 16 ounce bottles this will last you a life time... some states require a prescription, just tell them what your using it for... a trace element for a reef tank

Kent has strontium but I can't find anything about ESV.

ESV is a brand name of a very good company that produces chemicals for the tank. They tell you on the label what the concentration is the strontium is about 12 a pint also and will last at least a year.

What should this novice know that is common knowledge for others?

Off the top of my head I would keep it as simple as possible... you don't have to get all caught up as if it were surgery or something... its very easy. And the tank ends up taking care of its self.

My water chemistry ... pH 8.2 nitrates and nitrites, only a trace. Ammonia less than 1.

Is this after the cycle? Did you have a cycle? Usually when you set up a tank the live rock has some dieoff that takes at least 2 weeks to cycle out, ammonia to nitrite to nitrate. Did you add *everything* liverock, corals, fish all at the same time?

Salt - I 'm running at .024 was told that several find that they have great success at running close to sea water between .024 and .026. So far its too early to see results.
Usually .024 is fine .026 isn't that much different?

My calcium is between 450 and 500. Temperature is 78 to 79 lighting is 440 watts for a 90-gallon tank. Do these sound like good conditions?
All sounds very good. The only thing that concerns me is the lack of a cycle. Usually livestock is added in stages to minimize any adverse cycling problems

I've been wondering about which type of epoxy to use for underwater use.
The only absolutely safe underwater epoxy that I know of is epoxy stick sold by 2 little fishies. I'm sure there is an equivalent but I'm not aware of it at this time. I do know that super glue can be used for coral cuttings but that's not what you're talking about

My filtration ---two magnums are supplying water from each end of the tank, piped down to 3/4" plastic pipe with holes drilled - they run the length of the tank under the eggcrate structure. I don't see a lot of water or sand movement from the pipes under the Eggcrate, but there are interesting bubbles that arise from and through the rocks. It adds interest but at this time I haven't reset my skimmer. I'll wait for things to get a little more established.
Yes that's typical, those bubbles will or should go away. That is air in the water probably from cavitation of the pumps, it should all minimize in time. I would keep an eye on ammonia & nitrite to make sure the tank is cycled. Other than that everything sounds great!

Setting up and plumbing a 230 gallon tank

First of all, my tank is pre drilled. It has one hole at the right rear of the tank. This is fine. I was planning to do as you recommend by placing the return spray bar along the back of the tank. The problem is that there are two other holes drilled near the center of this tank. They were originally used as intakes for an Ocean Clear 325 for mechanical filtration. Since I will be utilizing the Berlin method by relying on the liverock and protein skimmer for principal filtration (as well as regular water changes), I want to omit the use of this Ocean Clear filter.
Yes you don't need the Ocean Clear, unless you plan to use it as a pump only.
No media just as a pump. I see it in your diagram.
I feel that it will create an accumulation of waste that will require regular maintenance and the possibility of unwanted biological processes, not to mention the potential onset of micro algae blooms.
Yes, what it will really do is produce nitrate so you don't want any external biological media.

Since the holes already exist, I was thinking of utilizing them for additional circulation. I am planning to extend these outlets through the eggcrate to about mid point within the tank and attach strainers that will be level with the live rock. They should be virtually invisible. My gut feeling tells me that they may also draw minute particles of available foods towards anemones dwelling on the liverock. An in-line pump would provide the circulation with a return line into the top rear of this tank. What do you think?
Ok bear with me here... first I would keep it as simple as possible. Simple IS better, so use only one pump for the main return, and the main return is to the spraybar. I see in your drawing 3 holes in the bottom of the tank what diameter are they? The one on the right can be

used for the spraybar as you show. The other 2 should rise up to the surface of the water and used for overflows also cover them with plastic gutter guard. If they are one inch they will barely be adequate for an overflow 1.25 or 1.5 are much better sizes but I understand you have to use what you have. Possibly use the questionable upper center holes also for overflows.

My second problem is that the system that I purchased came with a wet/dry filter that you do not recommend.
The wet dry container is fine (for a sump) but media in it shouldn't be used.

I will have a few coral fish (mostly herbivores for algae control), but primarily liverock; therefore, the use of this filtration system will not be justified. Your idea regarding the conversion of the wet/dry into a pre-filter appears to be practical, but I have one question pertaining this method. IMO, dirty water from the tank should be allowed to flow over the pre-filter material to remove initial materials. The protein skimmer would then be utilized for secondary removal of organics and oxygenation. The last step would be the return of clean oxygenated water back to the reef tank. In respect to your methodology, water flows directly into the dirty water portion of the sump and is picked up by the skimmer and then filtered through the pre-filter. Wouldn't you want to remove most materials (via pre filtration) prior to dirty water entering the skimmer? Or, is protein skimmer placement versatile?
It can be versatile. The prefilter really acts as a mechanical filter getting what the protein skimmer misses. There has been allot of controversy regarding prefilters saying that they remove necessary food particulate for corals etc. My opinion is. To remove heavily and feed well remove/add. I think folks get into big debates comparing the ocean (nature) to our tanks. The creatures need to be fed however one cannot depend on *set and forget* mentality. Frankly the debates on the net are endless and more importantly inconclusive, also there is no one way that works for everyone. Much of my new version will be concentrating on this mind set. So getting back to your original question re: prefilter I use it. My prefilter is located after the skimmer. This is so that the prefilter, which is cleaned weekly, will pick up any large particles the skimmer misses.
Give me your opinion of this conversion of a wet dry filter.
Do not use media such as bio-balls or the like that will turn biological.
For a sump its fine as long as it is able to hold all the water from the tank when the power goes off.

My third question is directly related to the placement of liverock. I totally agree with your philosophy about the use of eggcrate to suspend the liverock and allow adequate circulation of water from the spray bar. I want to utilize eggcrate material to support my liverock...but in a different manner. I would like to create island topography rather than the usual reef slope. I want to incorporate caves and peaks as well as provide ample swimming room and alternate niches for my livestock. Have you had any experience with such structures? Is it practical?
Quite a few readers want to do this. I suspect it comes from not using the original method or thinking it's too "wall like" I feel one can make a very interesting setup with my method without needing to reinvent the wheel with speculative ideas. When I began, I tried to do shelf's islands etc. it was too much work and not a stable system. Most people who really want or need to do because the tank is viewed form both sides. Then one simply makes inverted V cuts holes through the eggcrate sets the rock around the holes/caves and uses

plastic dowels protruding from the eggcrate to make a shelf for the corals or that special piece of liverock.

I have attached a diagram of my reef tank setup for you to view. Feel free to doodle on it and make any necessary alterations and/or suggestions.
That's a very nice drawing, a couple of things you will need 2 300 watt heaters preferably in the tank or at least one in the tank I would get rid of the denitrification chamber you don't need that I don't see the location of the protein skimmer NO bio balls note a good covering for water intakes is plastic gutter guard & cable ties.

In regards to the pre drilled holes...They are 1 3/4 inch and fitted with 1-inch bulkheads.
Ok, remember that a one-inch bulkhead won't drain that much water. I would suggest a dry run first with plain tap water to make sure it will do the job.

The one at the right rear of the tank is planned to be used as the return for the spray bar. The center two...I am not sure. You said that I should do away with the denitrification chamber and utilize the two center holes for my overflows. First of all, the denitrification chamber will not be used as that. I have eliminated all bio-balls within it. Its sole purpose is anticipated for use as a surface skimmer/overflow.
Ok, I hope it can handle the water flow… you may need more than that.

Secondly, in my opinion, its position is excellent for surface water flow.
Ok, but you may find that you need more overflow and with a good water flow IN you will need good flow OUT this creates substantial movement of the water surface. This eliminates the need for other circulation… a good water pump (say a minimum of all volume of water 5X per hour to 7 X per hour through the spraybar will give you very good surface overflow.

Providing that I have another return at the upper right rear of the tank. I was planning to use the two center holes for additional circulation (and without the use of the Ocean Clear 325 filter). I do not want the strainers set at or near the base of this tank, because they may interfere with particulate movement to the front of the tank as it is dislodged by the rear spray bar. What I wanted to do is raise them to about mid height or a bit lower. This may remove some of the debris before it settles onto the live rock, but not interfere with the bottom and/or surface water movement.
What about any creatures getting sucked in?

My feeling is that, yes these hole diameters are too small to be used as overflows. Also, surface water circulation may be disrupted. One other thing as that the general aesthetics of the reef tank would suffer by the addition of two overflows within its center. I know that aesthetics are not everything, but IMO they are an important part of planning. What do you think?
Yes its important to plan no doubt. I didn't see an overhead view of the tank.. Are they in the center or toward the back? If they are toward the back then simply run a pipe to the surface and it will be used as a drain. However, unless you have an ABSOLUTE water tight seal they can / may drain the tank, so you have to be careful. If they are in the center I think they would probably be unsightly. Then maybe best to plug them and use a surface skimmer box in their place.

In regards about the wet/dry conversion to a pre-filter & sump...The current wet/dry is about 31 gallons (36"L x 11"W x 18"H). This should be ample volume for containment in the event of a power outage, but it will be tested. Remember that my three holes within the bottom of the tank are drilled 1.75" diameter and were fitted with 1.0" bulkhead fittings that would result in insufficient water flow OUT (without the use of a surface skimmer box or additional drilling). I have found a local glass company in town. The problem is that their largest bit is 2.0" which is not large enough to install 1.5" bulkhead fittings, but they can use a router to enlarge them to 2.5" diameter, thereby allowing the installation of 1.5" bulkheads. What I have figured on doing was to enlarge the one right rear hole (originally to be used as spraybar) to fit a 1.5" bulkhead. Two new holes would then be drilled (one in rear left and one in rear center of the tank). All of these three holes would then be fitted with 1.5" bulkheads with plumbing and strainers to the surface for use as overflows. The two original center holes would be left alone, fitted with elbows and Tees (to the rear of the tank) to allow more even water pressure distribution and flow from the spraybar.

Sounds good to me. I'm surprised that a glass company is able to router holes!

I purchased the Turbofloater 1000 protein skimmer. Its pump is rated at 695 GPH. I don't think that it will keep up with the intake; therefore, some of the dirty water may have to flow into the clean sump compartment for return to the tank.

Looking at your diagram (nice job) the 1200gph looks to be able to pull out more water in the side of the sump coming from the skimmer. You may need a hole in the baffle in the sump to regulate the water height there. If the pumps aren't matched. Some observations... The 3 1.5"overflows going into the sump are probably going to be messy. You would probably be better off connecting the 2 on the left to the one on the right. Also, it would be much better to have the 2 on the left. Instead of being somewhat horizontal on the bottom to be at an angle. This will greatly influence the water flow and minimize air pockets that will hinder draining. And, the tops of the overflow pipes will end up being at the *exact* surface of the water. You need that so as to pull air in to the pipes to facilitate draining. The biggest problem here is to be able to have the pipes be *vented* so positive draining occurs. This will probably take place at the surface of the pipe. The plumbing to the spray bar should be a T instead of Y just to make things simpler and much less bulky. The filter in sump going to the little giant is not needed. If anything just a piece of eggcrate or gutter guard would only be used in the case of a snail wanders ALL through the system and ends up to clog your main pump! I see your pretty much dictated by the existing holes of the tank and that you're trying to make the best of the situation. Just take the above ideas and then test it with tap water. Run the whole thing for a few days and see how it goes. It all looks good on paper but when you introduce water... its a whole other ball game. The only other thing I would say is to keep the amount of fittings to a minimum 90 degrees elbows etc. Use flexible clear vinyl & insert (barbed hose fittings) wherever possible. Also use the rubber Furnco so as to be able to detach the hard pipe wherever needed. Other than that everything looks fine

You are right about the 1200 GPH in-line pump. The Rio 2100 pump (695 GPH) will not be able to keep up to it. The Plexiglas pan box before the 1200 GPH pump returns it to the spraybar. Sound okay?

Ok I see. Ideally you want to have the skimmer & main pump about the same. I would just have the OUTFLOW into the sump dirty area to the skimmer and then simply have the rest (what the skimmer pump doesn't get) just overflow the baffle / hole to the 1200 gph little giant. It doesn't make much practical sense to pump the water up and over the baffle.

It may generate unnecessary heat within the tank.
That would only be a problem in the summer but never the less it could still be a problem.

Secondly, the filter that I show within the clean side of the sump (intake to 1200 GPH in-line pump) is actually a threaded strainer. It will be installed for the same reason you mentioned.
Ok but you have to watch out that it doesn't get clogged or that the grating is large enough

Third...In regards to the WYE. I think that you are referring to the fitting below the tank. Correct? Why would you replace it with a Tee? I thought that it would restrict flow to the spraybar.
I just think all those fittings are unnecessary and a T would do just fine. Its what I use with 1200 gph a T is just fine. But of course do what you like or feel would work best for you.

An Ell used to divide the dirty and clean portions of the sump box will be a bit lower than the pre-filter; therefore, some dirty water would be allowed to flow over and into the clean waterside. In my opinion, this may be bad.
The height of the Plexiglas baffle will dictate basically how much water is held in place. If it's not where you want it you may have to drill a hole through it at the desired height. Might is the key word!

I was thinking of perhaps adding a Mag Drive 500 or similar to help match the output of the 1200 GPH in-line.
Where? Into the skimmer? You will be pumping 1200 gph so water will be coming out of the tank at that rate. How it gets pumped from the dirty side to the skimmer... is the question.

The second pump in the dirty water portion would also be used to pump dirty water into the pre-filter Fourth...Intakes to the dirty chamber of the sump box were simply drawn on my diagram for clarity purposes. Yes, these lines will be angled to help prevent air locks and associated noise. Since the strainers on their tops will not be totally submerged, they should allow for adequate water & air mixture.
Fifth and final...Yes, I want to dry run this system ASAP.
You mean WET RUN <laughing> tap water. I think that about covers it. You will find any problems when it's running with water.

In respect to your comment about the dirty water flowing into the clean water side of the sump. I know that it doesn't make much sense to pump water across to match water volumes, but what I had thought was that if I pumped it over and into the pre-filter box, it would be also be filtered through the Marine land #100 material. Therefore, clean water would always be leaving this portion of the sump box. Dirty water would then not be allowed to mix with the clean water returned to the tank and thereby be allowed to recalculate within the reef tank. Does this make any sense? Or am I pissing in the wind here? I agree that the dirty water would eventually flow over the baffle (or drilled hole), but I just wanted to clean it up a bit before sending it back to the reef. I trust your judgment here, but just wanted an explanation why (in this case) the bypassed water shouldn't be at least filtered.
Yes logically it makes sense. To at least get *some* filtration (the filter floss) but for practical purposes electrical savings, heat generated, more plumbing, etc. I don't think its practical or even that beneficial. The skimmer does the real work and the floss is just for

mechanical particles. The floss has come under extensive debate whether or not to use it. I like to use it but some consider it to remove too much form the water. I'm for simplicity. The less electrical connections, plumbing fittings the better. If the skimmer & main don't match then one has to compromise a bit. I feel the whole system is really rated by the skimmer and the main pump is to keep up with that.

Yes, it currently contains Geo Marine fabric, eggcrate, pre-filter material and bio-balls. You don't need or want any media. The liverock does it all

I did not show placement of the protein skimmer in my diagram. It is a controversial issue at this time. I am trying to find a Venturi skimmer that will be adequate for my reef setup. I would like to place it within my sump, but have another dilemma. Clearance within my stand is restricted to 26" maximum. There is no place for external placement unless I build an extension onto one end of the stand. That's the BEST bet. Keep the skimmer on the side above the sump. Its more work in the beginning and can possibly be unsightly but once its up… I guarantee you'll be happy regarding performance, cleaning etc.

Yes, I have one 300W heater that I will place within the sump. Once the tank is dry run prior to cycling, I will be able to determine if it will even be required. Excess heat will be generated from the use of submersible pumps and the metal halide/fluorescent combination canopy. Temperatures will cool off somewhat in the evenings, but should be able to be controlled by the single 300W submersible heater. Time will tell his story. Ok

I reviewed your images with liverock configurations. I understand the concept. If you have additional info on this subject, I would appreciate you forwarding it. The options seem endless, but I want something more than the usual wall of liverock to accommodate my inhabitants. At the same time, I want a low maintenance tank...One that works for me. Yes of course. I think that unless the tank is going to be viewed from front and back the eggcrate setup in my book will do fantastic! The liverock is setup with irregular pieces that will protrude thus not having a "flat wall look" It works! And it works very well. And of course looks beautiful. There are many, many, types of tank setups including not using eggcrate. I recommend my approach because it works well and looks nice too. The other method (simple) if the tank is to be viewed from both sides is to use eggcrate in an inverted V and use that as a framework. My method really gives a 3 dimensional look of a reef rather than the look of a fish tank with liverock in it. People just look and say WOW! It provides a *full* look. Just read and do exactly as described in the book. It sounds to me that you are very much on track and will do exceptional. The *best* advise I can give is to make it as simple, easy to maintain, for the long run because after its set up for a while the novelty wears off and maintenance comes in… that's *really* where the planning comes in. Once you have the liverock I think you will find proper placement and the "LOOK" will just come. Good water flow, and proper skimming placement really pays off.

I cannot accept your recommendation about plugging these two holes. It seems to be a waste of circulation potential; therefore, I have been toying with several ideas. Each of the two 1" bulkheads in question is situated about 23.5" from the sides and about 9.5" from the rear of the tank. This leaves about 14" clear to the front of the tank. Your

original suggestion was to use these two bulkheads (if situated at the rear of the tank and larger than 1" diameter) as overflows. Since the holes are situated more in the center of the tank and are only 1" diameter, they pose a BIG problem. I am still uncertain of the outcome, but will continue to have plumbing nightmares until it is resolved! One option that I have considered is the use of overflows, but not straight up from their location. My idea was to run them up, angled parallel with the eggcrate and then up to the rear surface of the tank fitted with strainers. The return would be routed back into the rear of the tank and perpendicular to the spray bar water flow. Again, I'm still tinkering in frustration.

Ok I'm sure you can get something to work. Just buy some fittings and dry fit until you get them situated the way you want. The *potential for problems* is if any of the fittings leak, even slightly, if and when the power goes off the tank will drain down to that level So IMO that's the most important consideration. Also from my experience one, one-inch bulkhead is able to drain aprox. 250 GPH

According to my calculations, the upper 4" of water within my tank will completely fill my 30 gallon sump, That is without any contents (i.e. protein skimmer, recirculating pump, eggcrate, etc.) That is allot of room for error; therefore, I will continue my quest for additional circulation via the use of existing...but misplaced bulkheads. In regards to waterflow, You say that with the surface skimmer that I will be using for flow OUT, there may be insufficient water flow IN.

No, I mean for flow IN to the tank (from the pump) you need the same or slightly more capacity OUT (with the overflows) this depends on what size pump you use. Usually in a reef tank its a minimum of 5X the tank volume per hour. I have found most hobbyists use at least 5X per hour while 7X is a bit better and quite a few have 10X! Keep in mind you want the skimmer pump and main pump to be about the same for what its worth... I have a 200 with 2 little giant 1200 gph skimmer & main I have 4 1.5 in bulkheads I could get away with 3 but I wanted to have the benefit of extra potential for water flow. So 3 1.5 inch will do 1200GPH Also consider the overflow box you have is really dictated by the size of the pipe not the size of the box.

This - in part may be handled by the use of additional overflow as mentioned above, but I will be using a submersible pump rated at 1200 GPH. I have a Little Giant 5-MD-SC (but may be replaced due to noise) for additional circulation. If you have any more ideas on this topic, please let me know. I'll keep pacing the floor, staring into my empty tank and drifting into plumbing nightmares until the solution has been rectified.

Ok just remember you can easily pump in with a pump regardless of size of the pipe. But when you're draining via Gravity, and have allot of water in, you will need to have sizable pipe

out. These are just a few things to consider. The worst case is you have to fill the tank one or 2 times with tap water to test the plumbing. I *do* know filling a 230 is a fair amount of work. Testing it, filling and letting it run for a week or so. Doing simulated power outages will be well worth it in the long run, showing you where potential problems may be.

First from your book "Simplified Reef Keeping" on page 59 there is a sump in which we plan on building for our 18x24x48 (90) gallon tank. We have a clear understanding of what all the other bulkheads are for but you have a bulkhead on the clean side going through the top cover, What's this for? Is it for air?

That is for the skimmer drain. Although When I added my downdraft I found it better to install another bulkhead directly under the drain and have a piece of corrugated hose to direct the water from the skimmer to the clean side / drip plate.

Next, for the 90-gallon tank, We have figured a sump box 20x24x16/231 = 33.2 gal. We only need 22.5 gallons but (on the safe side) do you think this is too much sump?
It may be bigger than you need but if you have the space I would go with the larger size. That way it will never be an issue whether you have enough capacity.

On the Plexiglas partition for this size sump would you use a 12" coming up from bottom and a 15" coming down from top?
12 inches is probably more than you need. Keep in mind it shouldn't be higher than needed as it may tend to bow from the height / pressure of the water. I would think 8 to 10 inches max more than adequate. You really only need to be able to separate the clean and dirty side without having it overflow. Because of your tank is rectangular you could go with a lower height, opposed to a square box.

We plan on using an air driven homemade skimmer from Ron's salt-water heaven. It is a six foot stand alone skimmer and how would we go about feeding it from this type of sump.
To feed it… its simple, just have a bulkhead connected to a pump and pump the water in. I would make sure you get the correct size pump. Then have it drain into the clean side / drip plate and pump back into the tank.

We live in a small town in which we can not get our tanks drilled; we will need to use a hang on the back overflow. We are looking at the life reef prefilter/siphon that will handle 700-gph flow (Iwaki 700 gph pump)
I use Brian @ Reefers http://www.acropora.com or there are a few others on my links page http://www.connix.com/~reefkeep/links.htm. Sounds like you have done your homework. I know Ron believes in cc skimming and I'm sure his skimmers do very well. Although I think a 6 ft cc will be costly to run air stones air pump etc. I would use an ETS but… I'm sure it will do fine.

Skimmers
As I was cleaning my skimmer today, some globs of skimmate dropped back down the tube.
You should clean the skimmer more frequently, before you get accumulations of globs. Wipe out the inner neck with a paper towel frequently. A clean skimmer is a productive skimmer.

Should I be worried?
No, you should be more careful.

How do you clean your skimmer without returning the gunk to the system?
Carefully and frequently wipe out the inner neck with a paper towel. You can be less careful in the collection cup. I wipe with a paper towel in an "up" and "out" motion. Disconnect the skimmer at "least" once a month and wash it out with a garden hose or the equivalent. Do this outside in a large sink or in a shower. Be careful about soap contamination.

Is lifting the cup off and wiping out the lift tube all that is needed to clean a skimmer on a regular basis?

Basically, but you want to have it "easily accessible," to take outside and rinse out thoroughly with a hose monthly.

Can two skimmers be run off one pump?

Yes, although one usually ends up shutting the other down or makes the flow of one or the other sporadic and somewhat unpredictable, so it's not really advisable.

I have started a 75 gal. Reef tank. How large and what kind of protein skimmer is the best?

Get a skimmer rated for twice the volume of your tank or for a 150 gallon. I like the downdrafts. Venturi skimmers are a second choice, counter current last due to relatively high maintenance i.e.: changing airblocks, air pumps etc.

You suggest the use of a protein skimmer that is at least twice the tank volume recommended. I have heard great rumors about the Aqua Medic Turbofloater 1000. It is 23" tall and recommended for tanks to 300 gallons which is barely sufficient. The CPR SR6 model has an overall height of 26" and also rated for use on up 300 gallons. The CPR SR9 has an overall height of 34" and is recommended for aquariums up to 600 gallons.

I haven't used either but have heard very good things about them both.

Red Sea Berlin models... The Classic is 23" in overall height and recommended for tanks up to 250 gallons. The Berlin XL is 33" tall and recommended for tanks up to 400 gallons. I am so confused! Dan Cole at Mail order pet of Canada is trying to help me make up my mind, but if you have any suggestions, I would be happy to hear them.

First selection would be an ETS on the side above the sump 2nd Turbofloater 3rd CPR or the Red Sea brand last.

Store bought water

Can I use store bought water such as Ozarka or Aquafina instead of buying filters for my tap water? What is the quality of store bought water and should I buy a specific brand?

I'm not sure exactly which brand is the purist. I know that distilled it probably the best quality of store bought. I have to tell you that initially it may seem like an alternative but in the long run its more trouble than its worth. Your tank should evaporate between 5 - 10% weekly. Evaporation is good! Most hobbyists encourage evaporation so as to boost calcium by adding Kalkwasser. If you figure your evaporation and a regular schedule of water changes say, between 15 - 30% monthly...you probably end up having to haul around quite a bit of water. I know this is not the answer to your question but I feel it worthwhile to mention. Also, from the hobbyists I've spoken with and participated in my survey, I don't think anyone uses purchased store water. A less expensive alternative is Aquarium pharmaceuticals TWP system. That is a common fairly reasonable alternative. Personally I like a one-stage DI unit, I've had a ultralife commercial DI unit that holds one gallon of resin and will produce aprox. 500 gallons of purified water. It may be worth your while to investigate cost per gallon of the unit you consider and base your decision on that. Oh yes one more thing, its good that you are choosing purified tap water, that is the cause of most persistent algae problems and if you get a half way decent system, algae should not be an issue.

Sump

I'm wondering which side (if any) of your sump design might be used as a refugium. The "dirty" side makes sense in terms of feeding small critters nutrients from the tank, but then they get sent through the skimmer.

I don't recommend putting anything in your sump as it will take away water volume. With the recommended turnover rates, refugium won't last or do well there. To have a good refugium, you need a separate area where flow can be controlled.

My sump is filled with millions of bubbles, and they are being returned to my main tank! How can I eliminate these bubbles?

If you have the return from the skimmer flowing onto the drip plate, and then through the prefilter material, that will eliminate bubbles. Usually this is a problem when the return from the skimmer is located in the same area as (the intake) for the return to the tank. This is one of the main reasons for setting up the skimmer/sump/clean/dirty side the way I do. I am aware that no principals are set in stone, and that individual circumstances can dictate straying from a particular method. Using other methods, you will need other modifications such as a block of foam, floss material to trap the bubbles or Plexiglas walls (mini dams) to act as settling chambers for the bubbles. The foam or floss can lead to problems with the trap becoming biologically active and trapping waste, unless you give it the same attention as I recommend to the prefilter.

Temperature

How important is it to maintain exact temperatures in the reef tank?

My tank temperature range has been between 70 and 87 degrees maximum. As long as it is a gradual change the tank will be fine. Naturally occurring temperature swings (seasonal) are to be expected. However, the heater is a good idea to keep it from dropping below 75 degrees. I'm sorry I missed your cooling question, but I would recommend a fan(s) to keep the temperature down and help with evaporation. I am not a proponent of keeping the tank at an "exact" temperature.

How can I calculate heat temperatures/distance of the lighting cover so I can select the right cover the first time?

You are better off with glass or no cover. Again, it's the old "don't try and cram as much as possible in a space."

TANK TEMPERATURE

I am currently running my 125-gallon reef tank at a temperature range between 27.8 – 29.4 degrees centigrade. Is this a bit to hot?

Yes "a bit" is about right. Ideally you want to be around 80 degrees and your temps are 82 - 85. 85 degrees is about maximum before the animals get stressed

I've tried injecting copious amounts of air into the dry column & have also installed a ventilating fan with its louvers directing on the water surface of my sump. In addition, lots of air is also forced on the surface of the aquarium. With all these, I only manage to bring the temp as above.

I wouldn't want to see it without the fans!

I've had a chiller before, but got busted a few times also the noise is irritating. I desperately need some advice on how to keep reef tanks cooler or maybe it will be better if you can suggest on some corals that can thrive in this temperature.

You don't say
- How long has it been like this what took place to notice the increased temp
- How old is the tank
- How does the tank look (creatures)
- Is this due to seasonal temp swings?
- Where in the world you live (ambient temp)
- What the room temp is?
- Type of lighting MH?
- Enclosed hood?
- If your tank is lit with MH how many watts?
- And do your creatures need such high light/wattage

I would recommend looking into
- The light/wattage - is it needed?
- Use a room air conditioner if the ambient temp is constantly 80 degrees or higher. Air conditioners work very well.
- Improve your fan situation make sure the hood is adequately ventilated. 85 degrees is max 80 is desired.

Yes, you were right about me not providing you enough info on my tank. Anyway, I live in a tropical 'island' (is now a city/country) near the tip of west Malaysia. Pretty high temps here, around 25 - 35 degrees centigrade all year round. I think can't do anything much to lower my reef tank. Maybe, be a bit selective on inverts. Anyway, I find that reef temps in the sea are around 27 - 29 degrees you know, but I do not see the point of why inverts in our tanks have to be kept at lower temps.
Actually the best advice is common sense. How do the creatures look? That is the BEST indication regardless of what you read or hear. Animals, fish inverts, coral can adapt to a fairly wide range of conditions. The real problem with high temperature is the metabolism of the creature is increased. So it eats more, produces more waste and IMO accelerates its life span. Although if its a hardy animal it will also reproduce more. I really don't like chillers, as they are expensive and expensive to run. If you could get a room air conditioner that would definitely bring down the tank temp as well as keeping you cool.

That's my preference. Actually your tank temps are not that much different then your observations of the sea in your area.

We live in the desert and while we were gone, we had a hot spell. Our chiller unit couldn't keep up and my neighbor didn't turn on the air conditioner. As a result, we our clam died, and our corals are doing awful. They look like they are not going to make it. Is there anything we can do to help the corals out? We would really appreciate any information you could e-mail us.
I don't think here is a miracle cure to use or a way to reverse heat shock. The main thing to do is to keep the tank stable. You may consider doing some 30% water changes, say every 3 days. When you do the first one see how the corals react... if they seem to improve continue in 3 day increments, if they don't seem to like it...stop the water changes. The main thing is stable temperature. Sometimes water changes will help, other times...not. Your corals may or may not make it; you'll just have to see. I wish I could tell you more than what I have here but I cant. Keep the tank stable and try 30% water changes. Let me know how it goes.

Temperature - The ideal temperature for a reef tank is aprox 80 degrees.
Minimum temperature of 76 degrees
Maximum of 85 degrees

About temperature swings.
My tank has been from say 76 to max. of 87 or so and as long as it is gradual the tank will be fine. Naturally occurring temp swings (seasonal) are to be expected. The heater is a good idea though to keep it from going below 75. I would recommend a fan(s) to keep it down and help with evaporation. I am not a proponent of keeping the tank at an *exact* temp, heater on in the am the chiller kicks on in the PM I prefer to have my tank with a slight 5+ degree temp fluctuation

My tank temperature is at 84 degrees!
That's not *that* bad. Above say 88 I would definitely take some action. You can now; freeze some Tupperware or gallon plastic milk jug filled with water and place it in the sump. Temp fluctuations are Ok as long as they are gradual over time. Temperatures between say 76 and 85 are acceptable as long as they are gradual. The ideal temp is around 76 to 80.

WATER FLOW
I am trying to get good circulation with powerheads in 6 feet long by 2 feet deep tanks.
I never cared for power heads in the tank, as they tend to suck in curious creatures. It can stop working from time to time, making it necessary that you submerge your hand into the tank to tweak it again. I like to use a spraybar on the bottom, rear of the tank with a good size pump and place the rock on eggcrate—as described in my book. An excellent method is to use is a surge device, which works well, but is a bit noisy. My device consists of a ten-gallon container that siphons out in one minute and takes approximately ten minutes to fill. I am contemplating to construct a device with a 1-1/2 inch PVC that would *seriously* discharge some water! In my 200-gallon, I have a few Mag 500 GPH available that I am contemplating to set up from the sump to a small spraybar on one side of the tank. I am pondering if I am willing to pay for extra electricity for another water movement source.

As far as water flow is concerned, I have two Little Giant 1200 GPH, one for the skimmer, one for the main and a ten gallon surge device. For some, the SD (surge device) is too big and loud but I don't mind it. In fact, mine isn't that loud. I have covers and a brace inside that keeps the noise reduced. It works great, although it takes patience to get it to perform just right. I think that feeding the pump from the sump is a better idea than from inside the tank. If you are not using a surge device, it is advisable to use a small Mag drive pump, possibly on a random timer.

NOTES:

Chapter 16

Tips & Techniques

Chapter goal:
To pass on additional useful information conveyed by other hobbyists during the survey period. Covering other items not found in the book.

Refugia

The diagram on the following page illustrates a refugia installed inline to the main tank.

Ideas for refugia

Hobbyists often ask, how can I provide more natural conditions for my tank? The answer is to incorporate a refugia tank into the existing system. By installing a refugia as described, one can have a separate area for a large variety of micro and macro organisms that normally would become predated on by fish, crabs and corals. Having a natural food source can greatly enhance coral growth.

This is done primarily by separating the refugia from the main tank with reduced water flow and the absence of predators. Here are some suggestions for a refugia

- Reduced water flow
- No predators at all
- Thick sand bed 1 to 3 inches
- Live rock 1 to 1.5 lbs. per gallon
- Reef lighting low to medium light 1 to 3 watts per gallon

Location

In most cases the refugia tank will have to be under the main tank in order for the water flow and draining to be efficient and natural. By natural I mean having the tank set up so water simply drains in from the main tanks overflow and then flows out of the refugia into the sump.

For some, under the tank will work well and can be set up as shown. However using this setup one needs to be careful that the sumps size can hold the volume of water in the event of a power outage, as the sumps buffering capacity is dictated by the horizontal overflow drain from the refugia.

If your sump box is already located under the tank and you don't have room there; the refugia can go anywhere above the sump so long as it can be easily drained. This will be more desirable if the hobbyist wants to have the refugia as a display. One disadvantage of locating it above the sump is you will have to pump water into the refugia tank. This will generally require a separate pump in the sump configuration or if your pump is strong enough one can install a T fitting and plastic valve to regulate flow.

One of the most important considerations regarding the setup is to have total control of the water flow both in and out of the refugia tank. This allows you to virtually regulate conditions determining how much the tank is skimmed, how many tiny fauna get flushed into the main system or allowed to flourish separately.

A refugia tank is a very good idea and if careful planned can be done relatively inexpensively as it doesn't need to be stocked at once or needing a separate skimmer, eggcrate, setup etc. The diagrams here are fairly self-explanatory but I will continue on with a few ideas to contemplate.

The benefits of separation

You can incorporate a refugia tank with much less pressure than is required when you set up your main system, it can be set up empty to begin with and then add sand, rock and creatures as your budget allows. One very favorable option is that you can completely cut the tank off from your main by using the water control. This is useful if you want to add sand but let the fine particulate settle as it usually requires, once the dust particles settle you can adjust the waterflow to incorporate it into the main system. It can even be used to cycle liverock in or to hold a new delicate fish until it accumulates to your water and is eating.

The very least the refugia needs in minimally stocked conditions is an acceptable airpump to provide oxygen to the environment, of course if the population of livestock increases so would the level of oxygen and water circulation.

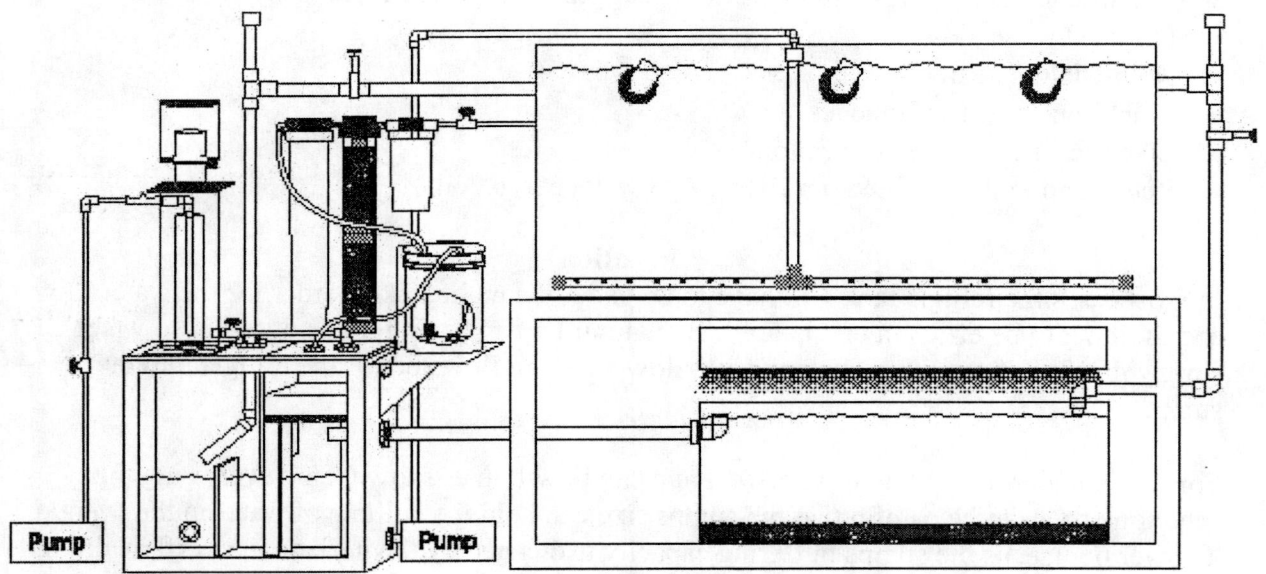

What's involved

The main element of refugia is the substrate. Although my previous opinions of thick substrate where negative, using a relatively thick substrate in a refugia is a very good idea. Sand or similar material will be very useful to cultivate the rich biodevirse conditions desired in this separate tank.

Sand To really be effective you want to use 2 – 4 inches of livesand, aragonite, or silicate free reef specific sand. In most cases a plenum is not used and you simply place the sand on the tank bottom. Although many hobbyists like the look of fine sugar size sand, although its best to use a coarser grade, this makes it much easier for burrowing worms and the like to infiltrate and move around. Also, it makes cleaning (if you ever did it-- to be easier).

Liverock - There are a few ideas of what type of liverock to use; probably the most economical is to use either base rock or homemade aragacrete as described by G.A.R.F. One of the drawbacks of using this approach is that it will take at least six months or longer to have the tank active with the desired organisms. The next preferable approach is to use less desirable rock from your main tank. This is good if you have come across some liverock in a store that you don't want to pass up but may not have the room for it in the main tank. Using rock from your established tank is a very good idea, as it will have suitable life on it that will begin to flourish once its placed in a *non-predatory environment*.
Finally, and of course most ideal is to buy premium liverock as this will have the most diverse life on it. Your budget will dictate which approach you use. They all will work, the difference is how long it takes and using premium liverock is obviously the quickest method.

Creatures – It's important to limit the types of livestock to non-predatory types. This is of course not mandatory… but if you want the full benefits of the refugia do not include predatory animals.

OK	**Possible**	**Do not include.**
Starfish	Very tiny hermit crabs	Fish of any kind
Bristle worms	Urchins	Crabs larger than the size of a dime
Algae eating snails		Long polyp stony corals
Cleaner shrimp		Small polyp stony corals
Mushroom corals, rock polyp's etc.		

By careful choice of livestock you can create the special environment where very few micro and macro fauna get eaten and then thrive to become a very rich environment of live food that will later feed your main tank
Once the refugium is well established, it will become extremely dense with life forms. To truly benefit form this you will need to "flush out" the refugium by increasing the water flow. This will push all the life into your tank where it will be consumed by the corals and other predators. Typically, depending on the population, this function will be performed every 3 to 6 months. When you plan to do the flush:

- Plan to shut down the skimmer for about 2 days.
- Remove any prefilter material.
- Increase the waterflow through the refugia area as much as possible for a period of approximately 4 hours.
- Let your tank ingest the material for one day.
- Reverse the process.

Mangroves and refugia
Mangrove plants have become the hot topic in filtration. Hobbyists are primarily interested in using these plants to take some of the workload off the skimmer, enhance filtration and provide additional habitat for lifeforms in the root system typically a large variety of macro and micro fauna. If you are interested in experimenting with mangroves, a refugia is a perfect environment.

The benefit of using a separate tank is obviously control. Although mangroves are hardy it may not be wise for a hobbyist without previous experience, to depend on them exclusively; at least until they prove their ability over an extended period of time.

So if you were interested in experimenting with mangrove plants to enhance your filtration it would be wise to begin in a smaller tank where you can have more control over the environment.

Also, an important principal to keep in mind is that mangroves are plants and will require substantial lighting. In fact they would probably do better in full spectrum light or direct sunlight, unfortunately that spectrum of lighting will also enhances micro algae and macro algae. This may not be totally undesirable as you are trying to create somewhat underskimmed, nutrient rich, bio diverse area, which may not be as pristine as your main tank but nevertheless becomes rich with micro and macro fauna.

Metal halide would be the lighting of choice for good growth of these plants. Second would be full spectrum or natural sunlight, third florescent actinic reef lighting or power compacts. My advise to the beginner who is interested in mangroves would be to start out small in a separate refugia tank experimenting with different techniques until you get comfortable with the needs and benefits of mangroves.

Affordable Kalkwasser
A low cost replacement for over the counter premium priced Kalkwasser is food grade calcium hydroxide. This is sold as pickling lime and sells for about $1.49 per lb. I have personally used Knerrs brand. Also available is Balls. Some areas of the country this product is more readily available than others. If you cannot find this in your area see the suppliers reference in the back of this book. This is a big money saver.

Affordable Iodine supplement
A low cost replacement for iodine is Lugols solution. This can be purchased at a pharmacy although in some states you may need a prescription. The best approach is to avoid the chain type pharmacy's and deal with a small local business. Tell the pharmacist what you plan to use the product for and chances are good they will get it for you. Caution!! Because the product is so inexpensive it is very easy to overdose

Keeping electronic probes in place
A good idea is to use a piece of Styrofoam in which you make some holes through it   the size of the probe. Several can be inserted and then simply floated in the sump.

Quieting water pumps
Placing a piece of Styrofoam under the pump will reduce noise quite a bit. Computer mouse pads also work well although not recommended in sump (for submersibles).

Estimating sand for the substrate
"To find out how much sand needed, multiply(in inches) the width of the aquarium by it's length, then by the depth of the sand and then multiply by 0.0579 to get pounds needed" - *Bob Goemans, The Reef Scene - TFH, February 1998*

Getting rid of Apitasta anemones

There have been many suggestions on removing these pests such as plugging the hole with chewed bubble gum, injecting the creature with boiling water, calcium hydroxide etc. These approaches may work however the following is guaranteed to get rid of the unwelcome apitasta anemone a.k.a.: glass anemone. What I'm about to tell you may *seem unsafe* but I assure you it is very safe and works extremely well.

Here is what you do…

Go to a grocery store and purchase Red Devil Lye (make sure its Red Devil 100% lye)

Get your self a 3 cc syringe without the needle tip, just the plastic syringe. Ask for at least a 3cc even better if you can find a 6 or 10cc this will save you less trips refilling. Get these at the pharmacy or from a vet you only need one.

Find a small container with an airtight lid a fish food container works well.

Lets say you have a 2 oz dry weight fish food container rinse it out and fill with 3/4 with water. I use DI water.

Then add 3/4 teaspoon of the red devil lye (be careful this is very caustic stuff!) stir with a spoon or other utensil or put the air-tight lid and shake (be careful when you shake and that the lid is on tight).

Then simply fill the syringe with the mix and go to the apitasta and give it a small squirt it doesn't take much something like ¼ of a cc will do the job <POOF> it vaporizes!!!

next...repeat as needed. Sometimes its helpful to give then a little nudge with the syringe so they retract in the rock where the lethal dose can be more effective. Using this approach, as a preventive a maintenance you should easily be able to control apitasta anemones. If your tank is over run with them it may take a week or so to totally get them under control. One you have eliminated them then it simply becomes a maintenance to keep them gone.

When you do this you'll notice a whitish glob like substance, that's the lye reacting with the salt water. simply swoosh this away with your hand and of course you do not what any of this landing on your corals. A little practice and common sense and you'll have this method down pat in no time at all. This method works the best.

Next would be to get one or two peppermint shrimp not cleaners or camel backs but peppermint shrimp.

It's also worth noting that an apitasta anemone in an established tank is usually a sign of poor water quality. You may well consider a series of water changes to improve conditions.

They are known to do a fair job eating apitasta ...although some do and some don't or I should say some do better than others.

Last and most drastic for a tank that is completely overrun you will have to get a Copperband butterfly fish. Most copperbands will eat apitasta however they may also eat feather dusters or possibly soft corals. Again some Creatures do a great job some don't you just have to try and see for yourself. There are specialized apitasta eating nudibranch but from what I have heard they are so small they disappear in the tank.

Moving

I moved last year in Sept. here are some tips and questions. Get someone to help you as a gofer and helper mix up plenty of new SW a few days in advance for the new water change spillage and oversights devote the day to the tank move only unless you have a bunch of friends moving other stuff. Just you & a helper for the tank. Save 2/3 of tank water in clean plastic jugs. or use a new clean trash can. Place the fish in individual bags and into standard Styrofoam shipping box. Place them the same as fish & inverts body up. Try not to use an oversize bag. Once you are ready to move the tank place it on a 3/4 in piece of plywood say 6 in larger then the tank. The plywood is used as a carrying platform to give you something to hold on to and a nice flat base for the tank.

This is an opportunity to clean your rock a bit. As you take out the rock have a 5 gal bucket of water from the tank and vigorously swish dunk the rock. You will be *amazed* at the gunk that comes off, detritus in the nooks & crannies. As the water in the 5 gal gets disgusting looking after about 5 pieces. dump it and siphon again from the tank. That way you are using the 1/3 water you plan to change the rock on the bottom will be the worst. When you do this you will see what I mean.

When you remove the rock, take it out & place it in the box good side up. The most difficult part is to get the tank to look as it did before the move. Also label the boxes - base rock -good rock and the premium top decorative. It's very helpful to have a tape gun handy to seal the boxes. Have your new place prepared for the tank placement, power supplies, drop cloths, towels hoses for siphons a small pump to pump in the natural salt water.

I have a 200 with 375 lbs. of rock set up with a custom eggcrate frame and spraybar 45 gallon sump 6 fish 6 or 8 corals and a bunch of inverts. It took 2 men working all day 10+ hours to take down move and re-setup I only moved about 1/2 hour away My biggest mistake was when I mixed up my natural salt water the resin in my DI was expended and I didn't know it. I did about a 50% WC with bad water, hair algae followed and so did more water changes with fresh DI water. Double check the resin before making up a large batch of new salt water!

Different types of reef tanks.

When considering a reef aquarium, most people will think that all reef tanks are closely the same, meaning they have the same requirements. This is not true! *The selection of animal will have the largest impact on the remainder of your decisions and will dictate the substantial different requirements as you proceed.* Trying to get the best of all worlds in a tank can cause an imbalance due to lighting requirements, incompatibility of corals, nutrient content of the water. *Therefore it is important to choose carefully the inhabitants and plan from the beginning what type of creatures you can have.*

Here is a brief overview of some different types of tanks.

1. **A tank with SPS, clams and fish** – This tank will cost the most because of a high light requirement. SPS and Clams are the most light demanding creatures of the reef they insist on near perfect lighting. One cannot afford to allow bulbs to go over their lifespan, calcium levels to drop or nutrients to accumulate in the tank. Also, fish produce the most waste and can make nutrient levels a nuisance. The general range of lighting is approximately a minimum of 5 up to 10 + watts per gallon. This intense lighting will usually be done with Metal Halide lighting. Most definitely you would need a top quality water purifier via RO/DI water and very powerful skimming usually something along the lines of an ETS to maintain very low nutrient levels. The set-up will need to be carefully planned regarding water circulation, as most SPS thrive in a high water flow. This tank will have an extremely high calcium demand meaning you would have to monitor calcium levels very closely and make adjustments more frequently as these animals use up calcium quickly. *This type of tank is the most expensive tank to set-up and maintain.*

Every thing about this tank is costly. This type of tank is by no means impossible to keep although it is probably best left for the advanced aquarist who has a firm background on managing a reef tank. Lighting in the range of 5 to 10 WPG done with metal halides and a tank turnover of 10 times per hour. Difficulty level 8-10

2. **A tank with LPS:** This is the ideal tank for the beginner. Select lower light corals such as elegance the mushrooms, polyps and other LPS. Be sure all creatures are lower light. This tank should be between 3 – 5 watts per gallon and because you are not inhabiting high calcium creatures such as Tridachna of SPS the calcium demand will be easily manageable via adding Kalkwasser for all makeup water. Stock the tank with beautiful cleaner shrimps flowerpot (anthraplura) anemones. Complete it with premium live rock and this tank will be more affordable to run and easier to keep. Difficulty level 4 - 7

Tips, Tricks & Techniques: From *Gary V. Deutschmann, Sr.*

Noisy Air Pump? If the noise from your airpump is simply from vibration associated with what ifs sitting on, try setting it on a sponge or suspend it in mid-air by hanging it from elastic straps or bungee cords.

Poly Filter Usage: Poly-filters work best when stacked, usually 4 to 6 deep, or 12 deep for molecular absorption (described later). One 4x8 pad can be cut in half, or a 12x12 pad can be cut into 4 inch squares. A Tupperware container can be drilled and used to hold the stack. A molecular absorption reactor can be made from a spent Aquarium Pharmaceuticals TWP (Tap Water Purifier) DI cylinder, Poly-disks fit them perfectly.

Water Pump Seems Weak? In North America, by adjusting your input water jets to allow the water in your aquarium to flow counterclockwise (with the earth's rotation rather than against it) it will in many cases, increase the circulation in your tank dramatically.

Food Heading Directly To Overflow? You can suspend or float a feeding ring in the aquarium to hold the food in a single place till it sinks. Also, forming a two or three ring unit of various lengths allows the food of choice to drop to the level of the desired animal before entering the tanks circulation. Here again, a spent AP TWP cartridge can be cut down to the depth of feeding forming your feeding ring.

I Actinic's won't Start, Regular Lamps Do? Try opening the silver starter can by prying up the little clamps and removing only the capacitor (if any) enclosed inside, leaving the starting bulb wires alone. On rapid start ballast's, you can try increasing the size of the wire that runs from the ballast to the lamps and grounding the ballast case.

End Caps! Why pay big bucks for keystone end caps? Prewire your lamps using simple push-on connectors (leaving enough wire for your point of connection) and then dip the ends in a product called "Plasti-Dip-Your-Grip" available from most hardware centers. After dipping, straighten the wires! You can prewire your starter driven lamps with the starter bulb encased in the plastic dip on the end, running the wire across the top of the bulb. Or, in lieu of wire, stained glass shops sell adhesive copper tape that looks like the aluminum burglar alarm tape, about 1/4 inch wide, works great in place of that starter wire!

Airwoods Why pay $3.99 each for airwoods? Woodcraft sells Basswood (same thing as European Lime) for $2.99 for a 3 inch x 3/4 inch x 24 inch piece. This will render approx. 32 airwoods for less than 1/2 hours labor. Basswood is soft and very easy to cut, drill & tap if you use screw in nipples.

Venturi Inlet Noisy? Take a pillbottle, install a free barb (see free barb in this document) in the bottom, fill with Dacron, leave the cap off or drill a hole in it. The free barb tube should slip over your venturi intake, use size of tube according to this usage.

Free Barbs - Free Nipples! Save money on those little barbs used to connect airlines, etc. to devices! Drill a hole in the device exactly the size of the OD of your airline tube, preferably a little on the snug side. Slip your tube into this hole and pull through where you can easily reach the tube that passes through the inside. Install a short 1/4 inch long rigid tube that fits the ID of your selected tubing into your tubing so that the end is flush with the end of the tubing. Pull the tube back through the hole until it is firmly wedged so that only 1/8 inch of the tubing is still inside the device. This will handle the pressures generated by most airpumps, dosers, powerheads, etc.

Carboy Valves: Do you use 3 gallon or up carboys? Most stores carry the output replacement valve for hot water heaters, they last forever, made of heatproof PVC (naturally) and fit most carboy caps. You can also drill a hole in the bottom side of an empty 5 gallon white bucket and install the valve by placing 3/4 inch screw on flanges on each side of the bucket, using either rubber or silicone sealant for the gaskets. -

Noisy Overflow? Normally, the noise generated by overflow boxes is actually from the length of tubing connected to the overflow, echoing it's way down to your protein skimmer or sump. A simple vented P-Trap cures this problem instantly. A P-Trap can be formed by simply routing your flexible tube from under the overflow in an S-shape, forming a trap that will hold water. However, to keep this water from siphoning from the trap, a vent usually needs to be installed. To make the vent, simply drill a hole in the flexible hose on the downhill side toward your protein skimmer or sump and install a piece of 3/8 inch hose (or larger for large overflows) by sticking it firmly into the drilled hole, do not let it extend into the drain tube more than 1/8 inch. Run the free end of this tube above aquarium height, usually connecting it to the back of the overflow, or to the secondary overflow ahead of the pre-filter if your overflow is so equipped. In any case, keep this tube above the height of the water in your outside overflow box. If siphoning still seems to be a problem, use a T-Fitting in the drain line and a vent the same size as your drain.

Tired of Lugging Buckets of Water? Or stretching hoses across the house. Ifs a very simple task to install a self-piercing valve in your cold water line and running a flexible hose from the cold water source (usually in the basement) up to your aquarium area. Rather than drilling holes in your hardwood floors, I recommend drilling the hole between the walls. By placing a 12 inch extension adapter on your power drill, along with a bit sized at or larger than the extension fitting. You can easily drill a hole just above the baseboards in the drywall, then holding your drill as vertical as you can, drill downward through the 2x4 rooter plate and 1/2 inch flooring below into the basement. Patching drywall is much cheaper and simpler than any other method, should you decide to move your aquarium elsewhere. Icemaker installation kits are perfect for this project! In addition to the icemaker installation kit, you will need a shut-off valve up near your aquarium. Depending on the size of hose you ran, the valve should be designed for compression type fittings, if your tube is vinyl, don't forget the insert for the tube to hold it in the compression fitting. Another tube can be placed at the output of this valve and ran through a carbon filter for freshwater or into your RO, DI or RO/DI unit. Waste can be handled in much the same manner, by installing a drain in similar fashion, through the wall into the basement or to outside. However, on drains, it is required by law to have a P-Trap as anaerobic bacteria will grow in your drain hose. Don't let this stop you, use two 5 gallon buckets, one upside down becomes the base and hides the P-Trap inside and the bucket above becomes your waste sink. Drain outlets are readily available at most hardware stores. Make sure no holes in your drain screen are larger than 1/4 inch and then you can route 1/2 inch tubing to your waste outlet.

Tap Water purification

There are many levels or stages that can be associated with tap water purification. Starting with simple sediment filtration, carbon filtration, molecular absorption and ending with Reverse Osmosis, Cold Sterilization, deionization and Triple Distillation.

What do each of these filters do and what importance do they yield to the aquarist and his cherished livestock. Depending upon the source of your water supply, one or many of the filtration components may be necessary to render the water more suitable for your particular aquatic usage.

Sediment Filters: As the name implies, this filter is designed solely to trap larger suspended particles (above 5 microns) that could possibly clog or damage the following stages of multi-stage filtration systems. It does not change the water quality nor remove any small or microscopic contaminants.

Carbon Filters: The primary purpose of carbon filtration in the tap water line is to remove chlorine, which could be damaging to both TFC (Thin Film Composite) membranes in Reverse Osmosis systems and to the color change (indicator) dyes used on visual type deionization columns. Carbon also removes many other contaminants, the bulk of these being organic or oil based. Oil based contaminants include many pesticides, lubricating oils, gasoline and polychlorinated biphenyl's.

Molecular Absorption: Currently, this type of filtration is the proprietary filtration of Poly-Bio-Marine, Inc. Utilized correctly, molecular absorption filtration outperforms carbon filtration and many organic based resins available to the aquarist. I have not found molecular absorption to suffice for tap water pretreatment as a one pass system, although, when used in the aquaria, on a recirculating system, it can be most beneficial.

Reverse Osmosis: Many aquarists rely solely on Reverse Osmosis systems to pretreat the tap water that goes into their aquariums. I have nothing against reverse osmosis systems, I just don't feel that they perform adequately enough for their high price tags. Even the manufacturers realize that reverse osmosis is not complete and now offer add-on deionization to further reduce the contaminants that reverse osmosis cannot remove. Utilizing reverse osmosis ahead of your Deionization column greatly extends the life of the Deionization column by removing many of the contaminants that rapidly exhaust Deionization systems when run independently. There are currently two types of reverse osmosis systems, those that utilize chlorine, negating the need for a carbon prefilter, usually termed CTA, which refers to the Cellulose Triacetate membrane, and the TFC model, which utilizes carbon filtration to protect the Thin Film Composite membrane, which would be destroyed by chlorine. Both systems use a sediment type prefilter. Assuming your tap water contains nitrates, the CTA type membrane only removes about 50 percent of the nitrates from your water supply, while the TFC type membrane normally removes a little more than 75 percent of the nitrates. Either type reverse osmosis system removes less than 90 percent of the normal contaminants found in most municipal water supplies. The output of reverse osmosis systems falls between 10 and 15 microsiemens.

Cold Sterilization: The use of increasingly smaller micron filters in series can render water quite pure, depending on how fine the filters become. It is possible to literally cold sterilize your tap water by getting down to .10 microns. Using sub-micronic filtration ahead of reverse osmosis systems can greatly extend the useful life of the membrane. Needless to say, the use of sub-micronic filtration is best achieved in several stages, this prolongs the useful life of each sub-micronic filter or cartridge. Most users of sub-micronic filtration systems use disposable 1 micron filter bags, which trap particles that would rapidly clog the smaller pore size filters. Many do not find the necessity to go as far as cold sterilization, as the water is either feeding a reverse osmosis system or deionization column. A quick overview of a cold sterilization filtration system; the tap water passes first through a 5 micron sediment filter, then through a disposable 1 micron filter bag, which usually fits over a .65 micron filter cartridge, the water then passes through a .20 micron filter cartridge and finally g passes through a .10 micron filter cartridge. Again, the .10 micron filter cartridge is usually omitted if the water is going to be further pretreated.

Deionization: Many of you are familiar with the ever popular Kati&Ani system or the newer mixed bed Tap Water Purifier system sold by Aquarium Pharmaceuticals. Kent marine also offers excellent quality Cationic and Anionic resins for sale in bulk quantities for refilling spent deionization columns or for the do-it-yourselfer who has designed his/her own dei6nization system. What makes deionization so popular? The output of Deionization column is .05 to .06 microsiemens, regardless of the quality of the water fed to the deionization system. The only benefits of pretreating the water before it enters any deionization system is the length of time between recharges. Contrary to popular belief, deionization resins last indefinitely, thus can be recharged over and over again. Some low-cost indicator dyes may not last very long, some are not reversible and yet others are of the fade type and not replenished. This is easily overcome by placing a small amount of fresh resin in the top of the cylinder each time you recharge. Mixed bed systems can also be separated quite easily using a base formula of a specific gravity heavy enough to cause the anionic resin to float. Cationic deionization resins are recharged using Hydrochloric Acid (Muriatic Acid) at 14 to 15 degrees Baume, that's a 50150 cut of water and acid for 28 degree to 31 degree Baume hydrochloric acid. Mixed bed systems can be separated utilizing the Anionic recharge fluid if mixed (normally) to this ratio. One 12 ounce can of Lewis Red Devil Lye to 36 ounce's pure water. Be careful, this mixture produces a lot of heat when the ingredients are mixed. If your system is separated, mix the 12 ounces of Lye with 48 ounces of pure water. Rinse each resin thoroughly before using the water in the aquarium. The Cationic can be rinsed with carbon filtered water alone, the Anionic must be filtered utilizing the output from the Cationic cylinder. Yes its that simple!

Triple Distillation: Although not recommended for aquatic use, unless adjusted to proper pH and some of the electrolytes returned to the water. A Barnstead still produces a very high quality lab water, 2 meg ohms, useful for diluting samples for water testing, mixing Kalkwasser and other additives for dosing, etc. Usually out of the price range of the average aquarist. An unnecessary item around the aquarium for most hobbyists. How cheap can you get perfect water? Well, if you don't like recharging those DI columns every couple of weeks, this simple little setup should suffice nicely. Purchase a Bare Bones CTA type RO unit, a I micron filter bag to pre-filter the output of the sediment filter component of the CTA RO, this extends the life of the CTA considerably, then run the output of the RO unit through an Aquarium Pharmaceuticals Mixed Bed DI column, the Tap Water Purifier. You should get roughly 200 gallons of water before finding it necessary to replace the little I micron filter bag and recharging the DI column.

Respectfully Submitted *Gary V. Deutschmann, Sr.*

Survey results

Here are the averages of 95 tanks. 11/28/1999

Average tank size is:
84 gallons.
With a sump of 16 gallons. The is a sump to tank ratio of 5.3%
Containing 97 lbs. of live rock, or 1.25 lbs. per gallon.

Tank costs:
This "averaged" 84 gallon tank would cost aprox $2885 or $30 per gallon.
The averaged wattage is 5.2 watts per gallon, photo period of 10.5 hours per day.
The largest tank is a 300 gallon smallest a 10 gallon.
The most expensive tank was a 220 gallon and had a value of $15,000
3 tanks were above $7000 a 300 and 2 –180 gallons
8 tanks where in the $5000 range
15 between $4000 - $5000
19 between $3000 - $4000
18 between $1000 - $2000
20 in the $500 range
3 below $500
8 had an undisclosed value
The preferred salt mix is Instant Ocean 53 / Coralife 12 / Kent 6 / Reef Crystals 6 /Red Sea 3 / Tropic Marin 5 / Red Sea 3 / Local seawater 2

Lighting

photo period 10.5 hours per day
5.2 watts per gallon

10 use MH&FLO
12 use MH&NO ???
8 use MH&VHO
9 use NO
16 use Power compacts

8 use power compact & some additional lighting
13 use MH
8 use VHO
2 use MH&PC&NO
1 uses VHO&HO
1 uses HO
7 are unknown

Skimmers vary, most being venturi followed by CPR and ETS.

14 hobbyists out of 95 do not use tap water purification. Spectrapure being the most popular

These are the results regarding water changes. I find it extremely interesting that despite all the controversy regarding water changes that hobbyists employ what seems to work best for them. As you can se they vary tremendously!	Here is what you said were the biggest challenges in keeping a reef tank. The diverse answers indicate to me a well rounded, informed reef community.
20% every 3 months ~ 5% twice a month ~ 20% every few months/changing to 5 gal. a week ~ 35gallons every other month 20% every 3-4months ~ 15%monthly ~ 10% every 2 months ~ 15 gallons once a month ~ 5% every 2 weeks ~ 30% every 2months ~ 10 gallons every 2-3 months ~ 10 - 20% per month ~15% once per month ~ 10% every 2 weeks ~ 5% every month ~ 1gal per week ~ 10 - 15% once per month ~ 10% weekly ~ 5% bi weekly ~ 20% a month ~ 10% every 1 - 2 months ~ 10% every 1- 2 months ~ 10% every 1 - 2 months ~ every 4 - 6 months ~ 10% every 2 months ~ 10% weekly ~ 8 gallons every 6 weeks ~ 15 gallons every 2 weeks ~ 10% per month ~ 10% every 2 weeks ~ 10% every 3-4 Months ~10% monthly ~ 20% monthly ~ 15% every 2 weeks ~ none ~ 25% weekly ~ 20 gallons every 3 weeks ~ 7 gal per week ~ 1-2 gal per day ~ 30% 3-4 months ~ 20% monthly ~ 15 - 20%monthly ~ 15 gallons 1 x per Mon. ~ Every 2-3 weeks. 75 or 100litres ~ 2 years since last ~ 2 gal 1 X per Mon. ~ 20% a month ~ 15% bi-weekly ~ 5 gal every other month ~ 10 - 15% every 8 weeks 8 - 16 gall per wk.	Spending hundreds of hours doing research Keeping overflow clear maintaining water conditions finding time to enjoy the tank Getting corals to grow fast & consistently long term costs Maintaining proper water quality & chemical balance Setting up equipment to work properly Nothing its pretty easy vacuuming detritus weekly Setting up & keeping everything healthy Mimicking Natural salt water Maintaining constant conditions, cause & effect Keeping the temp down Algae Aquascaping Understanding concepts planning Understanding water chemistry Planning maintenance, evaporation Understanding the chemistry for a stable tank Properly placing corals Maintaining low nutrient levels Algae wife Sexual reproduction of corals Finding healthy animals cleaning coraline from acrylic keeping temp down Maintaining the fine balance of water
Substrate: Average thickness is 1.4"	

with 14 tanks having less than 1"	chemistry
11 do not use substrate	Getting up to date information
10 use .25"	keeping my shrimp alive
4 use .5"	money
1 uses .75"	Getting un-bias information
15 use 1"	duplicating a natural environment
19 use between 1.5" – 2"	Patience
13 use 2"	having livestock flourish
8 use 2" – 3"	water quality
5 use 3"	learning everything I can
2 use 3.5"	Unknown
4 use 4"	Not looking at it as a challenge
2 use 5"	Control of fish diseases
	Dealing with the LFS
6 hobbyists use an actual plenum system.	keeping water conditions stable
	Getting the tank balanced
21 use aragonite	algae blooms
7 use CaribSea	understanding the requirements &
12 crushed coral	compatibility
18 livesand	Common names
18 some type of reef sand	Patience
17 unknown	Ignoring bad advise
	Finding quality corals
	keeping corals alive & growing
	keeping stable water parameters

Preferred Salt
Survey of 95 Reef Aquariums

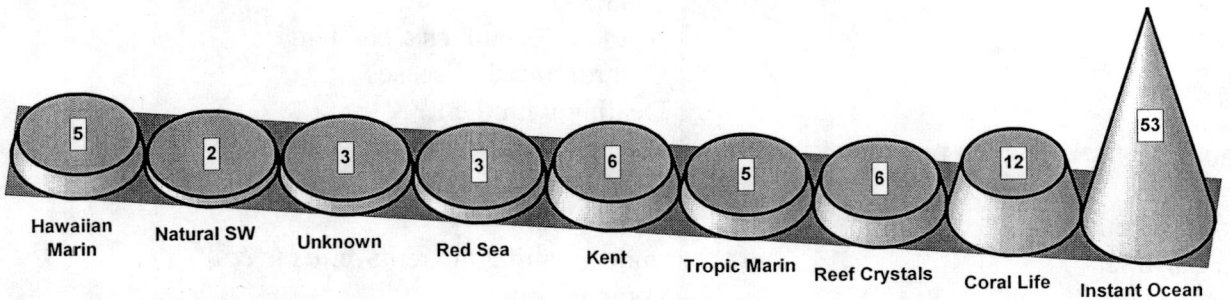

Hawaiian Marin	Natural SW	Unknown	Red Sea	Kent	Tropic Marin	Reef Crystals	Coral Life	Instant Ocean
5	2	3	3	6	5	6	12	53

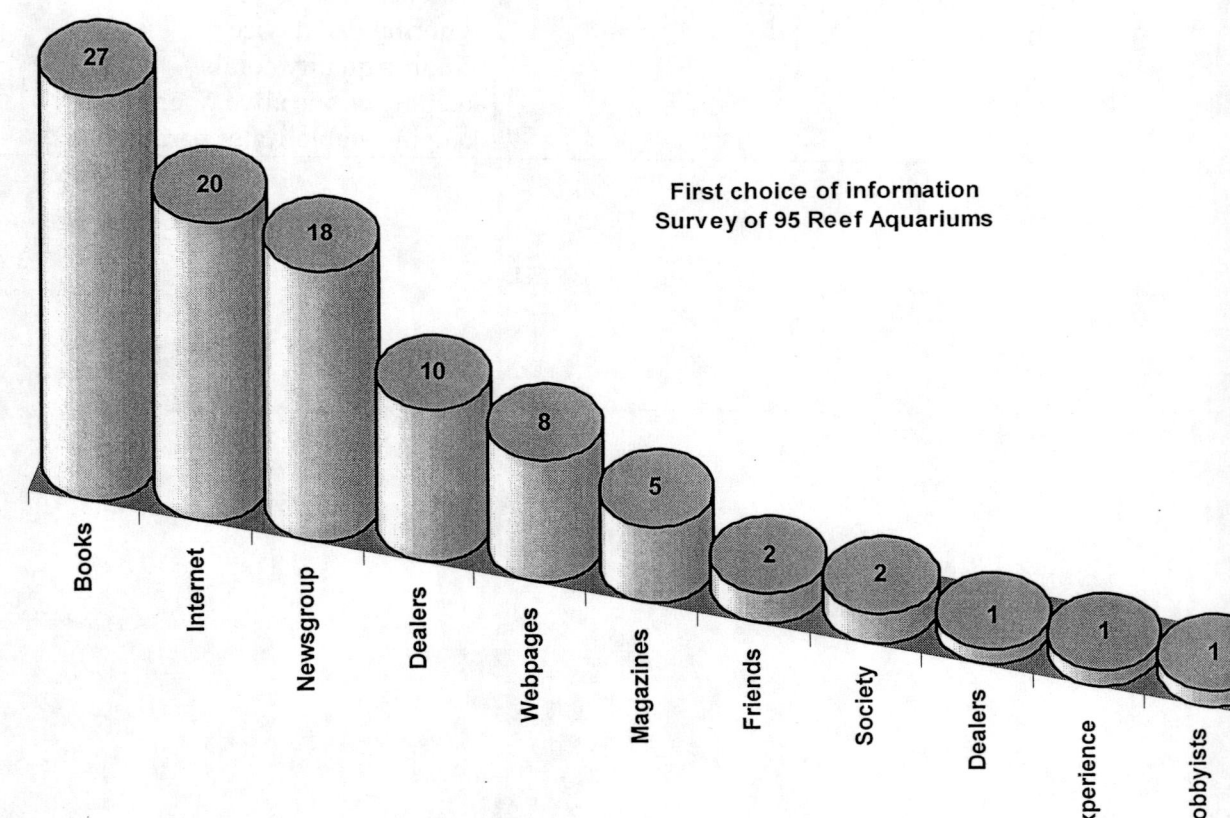

First choice of information
Survey of 95 Reef Aquariums

Books	Internet	Newsgroup	Dealers	Webpages	Magazines	Friends	Society	Dealers	Experience	Hobbyists
27	20	18	10	8	5	2	2	1	1	1

Suppliers Reference Section

A.E. Tech Inc.   (E.T.S. protein skimmer)   (800) ETS-6066
Box 127
Poughquag, NY 12570

American Granby, Inc.   (plumbing supplies)
New York

Aquarium Systems   ("Fastest" test kits)   (216) 255-1997
8141 Tyler Blvd.   Fax: (216) 255-8994
Mentor, OH 44060   Toll Free: (800) 822-1100

CaribSea, Inc.   ("CaribSea" aragonite   (305) 251-2473
P.O. Box 570269   substrate)   Fax: (305) 233-0067
Miami, FL 33257-0269

Energy Savers Unlimited, Inc.   ("Coralife" Salt Mix)   (310) 784-2770
24045 Frampton Ave.   Fax: (310) 784-2767
Harbor City, CA 90710

Mail Order Pet Shop   (supplies)   Customer Service: (800) 326-6677
1338 North Market Blvd.   Order Desk: (800) 366-7387
Sacramento, CA 95834   Fax: (800) 877-3834

Marine Land

Ocean Garden Aquarium   (203) 287-1047
Hamden, CT   (203) 230-2222

Reef Life, Inc.   Phone and Fax: (305) 983-2663
5925 Angler's Ave.   (800) 903-3474
Ft. Lauderdale, FL 33312

Thermoplastic Processes, Inc.   (plastics wholesaler)
Valley Road
Stirling, NJ 07980

Travaro Laboratories, Inc.   (Epoxy sealant, Marine
345 Eastern Ave.   Tex)
Chelsea, MA 02150

Kerrs	Calcium hydroxide	Kerr Group, Inc. P.O. Box 1179 Jackson TN 38302-1179
Ball Anachemia Chemicals	Calcium hydroxide Laboratory Chemicals	Distributed by Rose & Company 640 Hilliard St. Manchester CT 06040 860-645-6400 fax 860- 645-6431
Modern Plastics	All plastics, adhesive Black eggcrate	Contact Raul Flores 678 Howard Ave Bridgeport CT. 06605 800-243-9696 fax 333-4625
E.S.V. Company	Misc. Reef Additives Lugols Solution (iodine)	Brooklyn New York
The Espoma Company	Garden Lime	6 Espoma Road Millville New Jersey 08332
Spectrapure RO/DI	RO/DI Tap water purification	Charles Arizona 602-894-5437 800-685-2783

Glossary

Sources cited:

[AHDS] *The American Heritage Dictionary of Science*. Robert K. Barnhart, with Sol Steinmetz, Managing Editor. Boston, New York: Houghton Mifflin, 1986.

[MI] *Microbiology: An Introduction*. Gerard J. Tortora. Menlo Park, CA: The Benjamin/Cummings Publ. Co., 1982.

actinic

[AHDS] *Chemistry.* of, having to do with, or exhibiting actinism.

actinism

[AHDS] *Chemistry.* the action or property in radiant energy that produces chemical changes, for example in photography, where certain wavelengths of electromagnetic radiation create strong effects on photographic plates or film.

air blocks

Limewood blocks used in counter-current protein skimming driven by strong air pump. Air blocks are made from limewood and have a connection for airline.

airline

A thin (approximately 1/8" diameter), clear flexible vinyl tubing used to connect air pumps to air stones.

ammonia

[AHDS] *Chemistry.* a colorless soluble gas, consisting of nitrogen and hydrogen, that has a pungent smell and a strong alkaline reaction. Ammonia can be condensed to a colorless liquid under pressure and cold. Ammonia is an intermediate in the metabolism of nitrogen. *Formula:* NH_3

ammonification

[AHDS] *Chemistry.* **1** the process of ammonifying or being ammonified. **2** the production of ammonia in the decomposition of organic matter, especially through the action of bacteria. In the nitrogen cycle, by which nitrogen is made available to green plants, ammonification plays an essential role.

ammonium ions (symbol NH_4^+)

aragonite

[AHDS] *Mineralogy.* one of the three crystalline forms of calcium carbonate, the others being calcite and vaterite. Aragonite crystallizes in orthorhombic prisms. *Formula:* $CaCO_3$

baking soda
See "sodium bicarbonate."

ballast, high output (HO)
48" lamp produces 60 watts.

ballast, standard
48" lamp produces 40 watts.

ballast, very high output (VHO)
48" lamp produces 115 watts.

bicarbonate of soda
See "sodium bicarbonate."

CRI
See "Color Rendering Index."

cable ties (also "tie wraps")
Used by electricians to wrap several wires into bundles. Has many uses in this hobby. All plastic, nontoxic.

carbon cycle
[AHDS] *Biology.* the circulation of carbon in nature. Plants take in carbon dioxide from the atmosphere and convert it to carbohydrates by photosynthesis; animals eat the plants and return the carbon to the atmosphere by respiration and decay.

carbon dioxide
[AHDS] *Chemistry.* a heavy, colorless, odorless gas. It is exhaled from an animal's lungs during respiration, and is used by plants in photosynthesis. *Microorganisms bring about the decay of organic materials everywhere, releasing most of the carbon of their organic compounds in the form of carbon dioxide* (Emerson, *Basic Botany*). Formula: CO_2

Color Rendering Index (CRI)
A scale from 0 to 100, which expresses how "natural" an object will appear. The higher the number the better the object will appear.

Color temperature
Measured in Kelvins. 3100K, 3500K, 4100K, describing the whiteness of the lamp. The higher the number, the better.

cycling
Processing ammonia to nitrite to nitrate, allowing bacteria to multiply to waste-level encountered.

deionize
[AHDS] *Chemistry.* to remove ions from, especially to purify (water) by changing ions into acids and using an absorbing agent to remove them.

deionizer
Water purification device using a chemical resin that removes impurities; see also "deionize."

denitrify

[AHDS] *Chemistry.* **1** to remove nitrogen or its compounds (from). **2** to change (nitrates or nitrites) by reduction into a gas such as nitrogen (N_2) or ammonia: *In many soils there are denitrifying bacteria . . . the denitrifying bacteria thrive in situations where oxygen is deficient, and so are likely to be abundant and active in poorly drained soils* (Greulach and Adams, *Plants*).

denitrification

The process by which nitrate is converted to nitrogen gas by anaerobic bacteria and photosynthesis. See also "denitrify."

eggcrate

Light-diffuser material. Grid-like plastic used in suspended ceilings to cover light fixtures.

flow pump

Water pump designed to move water unrestricted.

gallons, calculation

See "volume, calculation in gallons."

GPH

Gallons per hour.

GPI

Gallons per inch.

insert fitting

Plastic plumbing fitting where vinyl tubing is inserted onto the fitting making the connection fasten with stainless steel hose clamp external or cable ties.

invertebrate

[AHDS] *Biology.* —*adj.* **1** lacking a backbone or spinal column. Sponges, worms, clams, and insects are invertebrate animals. **2** of or having to do with invertebrates: *invertebrate zoology.*
—*n.* an animal without a backbone or vertebrae. Worms and insects are invertebrates, in contrast to such vertebrates as fishes, amphibians, and reptiles.

Kalkwasser

Limewater, calcium hydroxide, $Ca(OH)_2$. Used to add and maintain calcium and elevate pH in an enclosed reef.

live rock

Usually porous limestone rock taken directly from a wild reef, with many life forms attached. Sold by the pound.

live sand

Wild live sand is taken directly from the reef and is usually composed of live rock and coral that has been naturally crushed by storms. It contains micro- and macro-organisms, including beneficial bacteria.

lumens

Total lamp light output. The higher the number the higher the output.

Marine Tex

A 2-part thick epoxy used to bond dissimilar products.

media
> Material used for bacteria to colonize.

metal halide lighting
> Socket type light fixture. High intensity. Exceptional color rendering index. High heat generation. Compact. Available in 100, 125, 250, 400, 1000, 1500 watt sizes. Special ballasts required.

mini reef
> A small, usually 10 to 30 gallon reef tank.

nitrate
> [AHDS] *Chemistry.* a salt or ester of nitric acid, important in the nitrogen cycle.

nitrification
> [AHDS] *Chemistry.* **1** a process of nitrifying or being nitrified; the conversion of the nitrogen in ammonia into nitrites or nitrates by the oxidizing action of nitrobacteria. **2** the act or process of combining or treating a substance with nitrogen.

nitrite
> [AHDS] *Chemistry.* a salt or ester of nitrous acid, important in the nitrogen cycle.

nitrobacteria
> [AHDS] *Biology.* any of various bacteria living in soil that take part in the nitrogen cycle, oxidizing ammonium compounds into nitrites, or nitrites into nitrates.

nitrogen
> [AHDS] *Chemistry.* a colorless, odorless, tasteless gaseous element that forms about four fifths of the atmosphere by volume and is a necessary part of all animal and plant tissues.

nitrogen cycle
> [AHDS] *Biology.* the circulation of nitrogen and its compounds by living organisms in nature. Nitrogen in the air passes into the soil, where it is changed into nitrates by bacteria and used by green plants and then by animals. Decaying plants and animals, and animal waste products, are in turn acted on by bacteria and the nitrogen in them is again made available for circulation. *The nitrogen cycle is an example of a material cycle involving decomposers and other soil bacteria which, in part, break down and convert nitrogenous wastes and the remains of dead organisms into materials usable by autotrophs* (Biology Regents Syllabus).

nitrogen cycle
> [MI, p. 687]

1. Microorganisms decompose proteins from dead cells and release amino acids.
2. Ammonia is liberated by microbial ammonification of the amino acids.
3. Ammonia is oxidized to nitrates by nitrifying bacteria.
4. Denitrifying bacteria reduce nitrates to molecular nitrogen (N_2).
5. N_2 is converted into ammonia by nitrogen-fixing bacteria.
6. Nitrogen-fixing bacteria include free-living genera such as *Azotobacter*; cyanobacteria; and the symbiotic bacteria *Rhizobium* and *Frankia*.
7. Ammonium and nitrate are used by bacteria and plants to synthesize amino acids.

nitrogen cycle

[MI, p. 668]

Nitrogen is needed by all organisms for the synthesis of protein, nucleic acid, and other nitrogen-containing compounds. Molecular nitrogen (N_2) comprises almost 80% of the earth's atmosphere; the atmosphere over every acre of fertile soil contains more than 30,000 tons of nitrogen. Despite its abundance, however, no eucaryote is able to make direct use of nitrogen, a molecular gas. Instead, the nitrogen must be fixed (combined) with other elements such as oxygen and hydrogen. The resulting compounds, which include nitrate ion (NO_3^-) and ammonium ion (NH_4^+), are then used by other organisms. The chemical and physical forces operating in the soil, water, and air, together with the activities of specific microorganisms, are important factors in converting nitrogen to usable forms.

   Practically all of the nitrogen in the soil exists in organic molecules, primarily as proteins. When an organism dies, the process of decomposition results in the hydrolytic breakdown of proteins into amino acids. The amino groups of amino acids are removed in a process called **ammonification**, so called because ammonia (NH_3) is formed. . . . Ammonification is brought about by aerobic and anaerobic bacteria and fungi and may be represented as follows:

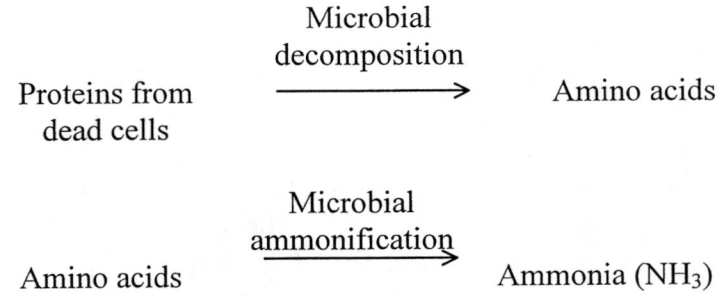

Microbial growth releases extracellular proteolytic enzymes that accomplish this simplification of chemicals. The fate of the ammonia thus produced depends on soil conditions. Since ammonia is a gas, it may rapidly disappear from dry soil. But in moist soil, it becomes solubilized in water, and ammonium ions (NH_4^+) are formed.

$$NH_3 + H_2O \rightleftharpoons NH_4OH \rightleftharpoons NH_4^+ + OH^-$$

Ammonium ions are used by bacteria and plants for amino acid synthesis.

The next sequence of reactions in the nitrogen cycle involves the oxidation of the ammonium ion to nitrate, a process called **nitrification**. Living in the soil are two genera of bacteria, *Nitrosomonas* and *Nitrobacter*, that are capable of oxidizing ammonia to nitrate in two successive stages. In the first stage, *Nitrosomonas* oxidizes ammonia to nitrites:

$$NH_4^+ \xrightarrow{\text{\textit{Nitrosomonas}}} NO_2^-$$

Ammonium ion   Nitrites

In the second stage, *Nitrobacter* oxidizes nitrites to nitrates:

$$NO_2^- \xrightarrow{\text{\textit{Nitrobacter}}} NO_3^-$$

Nitrites   Nitrates

Nitrate is the form of nitrogen most commonly used by plants, which use it primarily for protein synthesis.

At various points in the cycle, atmospheric nitrogen is either added or removed. The loss of nitrogen from the cycle involves a process called **denitrification**, the conversion of nitrates to nitrogen gas, and may be represented as follows:

NO_3^-	Æ	NO_2^-	Æ	N_2O	Æ	N_2
Nitrat es		Nitrite s		Nitrous oxide		Atmospher ic nitrogen gas

pH

[AHDS] *symbol.* a measure of the acidity or alkalinity of a solution in terms of the relative concentration of hydrogen ions in the solution. The pH scale commonly used ranges from 0 to 14, pH7 (the hydrogen-ion concentration in pure water) being taken as neutral, 6 to 0 increasingly acid, and 8 to 14 increasingly alkaline. Most soils are in the range between pH3 and pH10. Technically, pH is defined as the negative logarithm to the base 10 of the hydrogen-ion concentration of a solution. Thus, if the hydrogen-ion concentration of a solution is 10^{-6} (one millionth) of a mole of hydrogen ions per liter, the pH is 6; if it is 10^{-8} molar, the pH is 8; and so on. *The pH is very important in cell metabolism. Big changes in the acidity of the cells of an organism can greatly affect metabolism. The pH of blood in mammals, for example, is kept very close to 7.35. A shift as small as 0.2 can result in death.*

Organisms have evolved chemical systems called buffers, which tend to keep the pH relatively constant (McElroy, *Biology and Man*). [from *p(otential for)H(ydrogen)*]

phosphate

[AHDS] *Chemistry.* a salt or ester of phosphoric acid. It is present in rocks and in the remains of organisms. Phosphates are necessary to the growth of organisms and have extensive use as fertilizers.

photosynthesis

[AHDS] *Biology.* the process by which plant cells make carbohydrates by combining carbon dioxide and water in the presence of chlorophyll and light, and release oxygen as a by-product. Photosynthesis is the source of most of the oxygen in the air. *Photosynthesis thus occupies a primary place in the economy of life. It is the process by which the energy of the Sun is captured and converted to the uses of the living cell. It is, in addition, the beginning process in the transfer of atoms from the inorganic world to the organic* (Harper's). *The primary process in photosynthesis . . . is the absorption of light quanta by the chlorophyll molecule. Since chlorophyll absorbs in the red region of the spectrum . . . we should suspect that the red quanta are the effective ones in photosynthesis* (McElroy, *Biology and Man*). *Amino acids are the main products of bacterial photosynthesis* (D. I. Arnon).

photosynthesize

[AHDS] **1** to carry on photosynthesis: *A red alga is best adapted to photosynthesize in the bluish-green light of deep water* (G. E. Fogg). **2** to produce by photosynthesis: *Plants photosynthesize protein as well as carbohydrates directly under light* (Time).

photosynthetic

[AHDS] **1** of or having to do with photosynthesis: *When the illumination was intense the photosynthetic rate approximately doubled for every 10°C. rise in temperature* (H. Lees). **2** carrying on photosynthesis: *In any large body of water microscopic floating algae, or phytoplankton, are the primary producers of organic matter. Like flowering plants these organisms are photosynthetic and able to use inorganic substances—water, carbon dioxide, and mineral ions—and light energy for the synthesis of organic substances* (New Biology).

polyvinyl chloride (PVC)

A material used in plumbing parts. Safe, nontoxic.

powerhead

A small pump in various sizes used to move water. Submersible, convenient. Magnetic drive impeller.

PPM

Parts per million.

prefilter

Floss or sometimes foam sponge material that traps waste particles from the water flow of the tank.

pressure pump

Water pump designed to force water through some form of barrier or restriction.

protein skimmer

Also called "foam fractioning." A columnar device where fine air bubbles are mixed with flowing water. The protein (waste) adheres to the bubbles, which rise, burst, and collect as foam to be removed from the water system.

PVC

See "polyvinyl chloride."

reagent

[AHDS] *Chemistry.* a substance involved in a reaction, especially a substance used to detect the presence of other substances by the chemical reactions it causes.

reverse osmosis

A more complex water purification usually 3 stage resin with a membrane material the water must go through. Has a waste bypass.

saltwater, natural

Weight 8.5 lbs. per gallon; specific gravity 1.023; pH 8 to 8.2.

salt mix, synthetic

A specially prepared mix used to duplicate natural sea water.

s.g.

See "specific gravity."

sodium bicarbonate

[AHDS] *Chemistry.* a powdery, white crystalline salt with a somewhat alkaline taste, used in cooking, medicine, manufacturing, etc. Sodium bicarbonate is a source of carbon dioxide. *Formula:* $NaHCO_3$ Also called **baking soda** and **bicarbonate of soda**.

sodium chloride

[AHDS] *Chemistry.* a white, crystalline substance, the chloride of sodium, that is the ordinary table salt. *Formula:* $NaCl$

specific gravity

[AHDS] *Physics.* the ratio of the weight or mass of a given volume of any substance to that of an equal volume of some other substance taken as a standard (usually water at four degrees Celsius for solids and liquids, and hydrogen or air for gases). *Abbreviation:* s.g., sp. gr.

strontium

[AHDS] *Chemistry.* a soft, silver-white metallic element which occurs only in combination with other elements, used in making alloys and in fireworks, signal flares, etc. Strontium is one of the alkaline-earth metals and resembles calcium. *Symbol:* Sr

substrate

[AHDS] **2** *Chemistry.* any surface on which a layer of a different material can be deposited.
3 *Biology.* a layer of material on which an organism can grow and multiply.

sump

An external container used to hold, control, divert water from the tank. A drip plate with prefilter is frequently used. Similar to conventional trickle filter, without media to encourage bacterial growth.

surge bucket

A 5-10-15-gallon container that fills gradually from the main pump and empties quickly providing alternating water flow.

test kits

Used to detect elements in an aquarium. Uses reagent that is compared to a color card or chip. Most common are pH, ammonia, nitrite, nitrate, calcium, and carbonate hardness.

trace element

[AHDS] *Chemistry.* an element present in small amounts, especially one used by an organism and considered necessary to its proper functioning.

volume, calculation in gallons

To find gallon amount of a square or rectangular container, multiply its length by its height by its width in inches; then divide by 231. There are 231 cubic inches to a gallon of water.

NOTES:

Index

Order Form

Orders can be placed via mail using this printable form. Simply fill out the information and mail to

Enclose $39.95 + $4 Shipping and handling for a total of $43.95 made payable to:

Shoreline Resources POB 954 Farmington CT 06034

Your book will be shipped within 7 – 10 days upon receiving the check. It will then be mailed and should arrive within 3 days via Priority mail. A typical mail in turnaround time is 14 days.

When your order is processed you will receive confirmation email letting you know the order is on its way.

If you have any questions regarding your order please send an email to order@simplifiedreefkeeping.com

Thanks for your support and I hope you enjoy the book.

Name:_____

Address: _____

City:_____

State:_____

Zip Code:_____

Day Phone (Area Code + Number):_____

Evening Phone:_____

Best Time to call (if necessary):_____

Email Address: _____

Method of Payment:_____

Credit Card (If payment is by CC):_____

Credit Card Expiration Date:_____

Complete customer satisfaction is the goal of both the author and Shoreline Resources. If, within 14 days of receiving this book, the purchaser decides that it does not fulfill his or her needs or expectations, or desires to return this publication for any other reason, the purchaser may return this book, postage paid, in its original condition, for a complete re fund, less the original shipping charge.